UNDERSTANDING INTERCULTURAL COMMUNICATION

JANE SUDERMAN
Georgian College

THOMSON

NELSON

Australia   Canada   Mexico   Singapore   Spain   United Kingdom   United States

THOMSON
★
NELSON

Understanding Intercultural Communication

by Jane Suderman

**Associate Vice President,
Editorial Director:**
Evelyn Veitch

Executive Editor:
Anne Williams

Marketing Manager:
Wayne Morden

Developmental Editor:
Natalie Barrington

Permissions Coordinator:
Terri Rothman

Production Editor:
Wendy Yano

Copy Editor/Proofreader:
Gail Marsden

Indexer:
Dennis Mills

Production Coordinator:
Ferial Suleman

Design Director:
Ken Phipps

Interior Design:
Peter Papayanakis

Cover Design:
Johanna Liburd

Cover Image:
Hans Neleman/Photonica/
Getty Images

Compositor:
Interactive Composition
Corporation

Printer:
Webcom

**Library and Archives Canada
Cataloguing in Publication Data**

Suderman, Jane, 1952–
Understanding intercultural
communication / Jane Suderman.

Includes bibliographical references
and index.
ISBN 0-17-640809-6

1. Intercultural communication—
Textbooks. I. Title.

GN345.6.S92 2006   303.48'2
C2005-907160-5

Contents

Chapter 6:   Understanding Worldview   153

PART III: UNDERSTANDING COMMUNICATION   183

Chapter 7:   Understanding Communication   184

Chapter 8:   Cultures at Cross Purposes   213

Chapter 9:   Exploring Language   240

Preface

This text was written to address what seemed to be a need in the field—that is, a text that looked at intercultural communication from a Canadian perspective. It is designed to be used for a one-semester course, although with the addition of activities and film, could also accommodate two semesters. A suggested filmography is included at the end of the text, and excellent volumes of activities are available to complement a general text of this nature.

Its style mirrors my own teaching style, which is a kind of dialogue with students, a point-counterpoint that aims to make the class lively and engage participants in thinking about the topics under discussion and the relevance of these topics to their own lives. It is the sharing of their reactions, feelings, and experiences that brings a class to life and makes it meaningful, sometimes memorable, for all.

The text is divided into four parts. The first chapter in *Part I* sets the stage for the study of intercultural communication by attempting to answer the questions "What is intercultural communication" and "Why study it?" It goes on, in Chapter 2, to attempt to inspire the appropriate mindset for the study of other cultures, the appropriate mindset being a spirit of openness, respect, honesty, and genuine curiosity. *Part II* focuses on culture itself, on the comparison of American and Canadian culture, on generally acknowledged frameworks (taxonomies) for the comparison of cultures, and on worldview. *Part III* is devoted to communication, its non-verbal and verbal aspects, and on practical illustrations of how differing communication styles can cause misunderstanding between members of different cultures. *Part IV* consists of one chapter devoted to the challenges of intercultural adaptation.

All chapters conclude with *Topics for Critical Thinking and Reflection*, which include activities, discussion topics, and/or case studies.

The *exercise boxes* are a unique feature of the text. They indicate where I would stop and engage students. It is not necessary to use all of them in class. Some may serve simply as breaks for students as they read the text on their own and take a moment to reflect about a point after reading about it. Others may serve as points of departure for a class discussion as a whole, others for group discussions within the class, and others as writing or short research assignments. It is up to individual instructors to decide if, when, and how best to use them.

The text also includes the unique feature of five *Time Outs*. These are four short portraits of regions or countries in focus in the world today: China, Latin America, the Arab World, and India; and the fifth Time Out is an activity to be done after students have completed Chapter 5, and has been placed there in the text for that reason. Otherwise, the Time Outs can be used at any time during the course for a change of pace and practical application of concepts and theories explored in the chapters.

Instructors are free to choose according to the interests and makeup of their classes. See the *Instructor's Manual* for more tips on using the Time Outs effectively in your course.

The organization of the text is flexible. Some instructors may follow it as is; others may choose to make various changes. Chapter 1 should be the starting point for everyone, but could be followed by Chapter 3 on culture, leaving Chapter 2 to precede and accompany Chapter 10. Alternatively, some instructors might prefer to follow Chapters 1 and 2 with Chapter 10, and then proceed with Chapter 3.

FEATURES OF THIS TEXT

- Key chapter objectives at chapter start
- Boxed exercises to encourage class dialogue and enliven presentation
- Boxed inserts on points of interest
- Four Time Outs for up-to-date portraits of key world regions and countries
- One Time Out for thought-provoking in-class activity
- Flexible organization
- Balanced mix of theory and application
- End-of-chapter exercises and critical thinking activities
- Summary and key terms
- Glossary
- List of suggested films, reading, and websites
- Up-to-date research
- Easy readability

FOR THE INSTRUCTOR

Instructor's Manual (0-17-625166-9) with supplementary and complementary material; teaching suggestions; additional Time Outs (Cross-cultural Negotiation, First Nation Spirituality, Issues in Education); activity, project, and test suggestions.

ACKNOWLEDGEMENTS

I would like to thank the many people who contributed to this text by sharing their tales of intercultural communication, experience, and adventure. They include these friends, students, and colleagues:

Esther Albornoz, Irene Albornoz, Tamara Benoît, Dimitra Bilosos, Nancy Blain, John Bobbette, Hans-Christian Bues, Mike Burton, Manya Chadwick, Brian Charles, Charles Craig, Geoff Dalton, Livia DeGennaro, Marlo Desjardins, Carlos Raul Diaz, Kaira Diaz, Oscar Diaz, Iraj Filsoofi, Tamara Fisher-Cullen, Asami Fukumoto, Mac Greaves, Ragheida Hamade, Brian Hobson, Eben Inkumsah, Doris Junger, Janet

Kidon, Kwangee Kim, Zdenek Kutac, Irene Lacharité, Noreen Lerch, Steve Lichty, Bruce MacMillan, Pat MacMillan, Genevieve Marian, Nisha Mathson, Tito Mathson, Yumi Matsushita, Cindy McClusky, Pierre Mineau, Aldo Palma, Dan Phillips, Rajesh Rajan Singh, Lyndsay Taibossigai, Chris Tesseris, Thân Thị Phường Thoa, Diya Thapa, Cathy Volpé, Nigel Ward-Paige and Heather White, to name but a few. If I have forgotten anyone, my apologies.

Special thanks goes to dear friends Mandy Franklin for her constant encouragement, to Lauro Palomba for his editing of critical parts of the text and clarification of many issues, and to Linda Doyle for her generosity of time, academic counsel, and all-around support. It was Linda I could call and to whom I could say, "Do you know what I mean?" and get the answer, "I think what you are trying to say is...." I am also grateful to my parents for their encouragement, and to my son for putting up with an often preoccupied mother.

I would also like to thank Georgian College for sabbatical support, as well as the reviewers whose excellent suggestions were incorporated into the final version to the extent possible:

Ruth Anaya, Trinity Western University

Maria José Erruuza, Concordia University

Judy Grant, Red River College

Rorri McBlane, Capilano College

Don Miskiman, Malaspina University-College

Ahava Newman, Seneca College

Ken Rintoul, College of the Rockies

Barbara Thistle, George Brown College

Dr. Randal G. Tonks, Camosun College

Dr. Barry Whatley, Rocky Mountain College

Finally, my thanks to the editorial team at Thomson Nelson for their patient and professional guidance and assistance—Natalie Barrington, Terri Rothman, Mike Thompson, Rod Banister, Anne Williams, Wendy Yano, and Gail Marsden.

Jane Suderman
Georgian College

Part I
Setting the Stage for the Study of Intercultural Communication

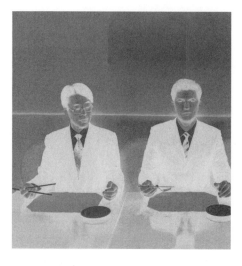

Chapter 1

Understanding Intercultural Communication

In this chapter we will explore:

- The meaning and importance of intercultural communication
- The concept of intercultural competence
- The cultural diversity of Canadian society
- Canada and globalization
- Culture and world future

There has never been a time when civilization stood more in need of individuals who are genuinely culture conscious, who can see objectively the social behaviour of other peoples without fear and recrimination.

Ruth Benedict, 1935[1]

WHAT IS INTERCULTURAL COMMUNICATION?

Intercultural communication, also known as cross-cultural communication,[2] is a multi-disciplinary field that draws on cultural anthropology, cross-cultural psychology, cultural geography, sociology, linguistics, history, communications, and international business management. It borrows research methods and concepts from each of these disciplines and combines them into a framework and context that focus specifically on the interaction between people from different cultural groups and how differences in culture affect that interaction.

At the core of intercultural communication is the premise that culture and communication are not only interrelated, but inseparable. The world's diversity of culture is enormous, and the members of all cultures have their own unique ways of communicating and interacting with each other. These differing ways of communicating are a large part of what distinguishes them from other peoples, and are often at the root of misunderstandings between cultures. The American anthropologist and pioneer in the field of cross-cultural communication, Edward T. Hall,[3] claims that the essence of culture is, in fact, communication, and that the essence of communication is culture. He believes that understanding how a people communicate is the key to understanding them, and by extension, their culture.

Research in intercultural communication uses cultural information provided by experts in its contributing disciplines to analyze interactions between individuals. It proposes hypotheses, or what you might call educated guesses, about how members of different cultures are likely to interact in given situations.[4] It then tests its predictions and collects data by means of interviews with individuals, questionnaires, surveys, and transcripts of conversations. Cross-cultural research also encompasses participant observation, a practice pioneered by anthropologists like Margaret Mead and Ruth Benedict who lived among, interacted with, and observed the peoples they studied in order to understand their cultures.

Why Study Intercultural Communication?

The relatively complacent lives of North Americans have been profoundly changed since the terrorist attack on New York's World Trade Center in 2001. Benedict's comment (above) resonates as much today if not more than it did in 1935. In the post-9/11 world, we don't have the luxury of innocence, of assuming the world is a safe place and people everywhere have their arms open to us. And we can't plead ignorance, because with all the information and intercultural experience available to us, ignorance is no excuse.

We have a choice: we can close in, foster fear of others and other ways of seeing the world, or we can increase our knowledge and promote understanding and cooperation. Canadians, with our cultural diversity and the relatively peaceful evolution of our society, are uniquely equipped to choose the latter. Our internal cultural makeup and the international contexts of the twenty-first century make it natural and necessary for us to learn how to communicate with people of other cultures, and the success of our society can serve as an international role model of a **pluralistic** nation that doesn't so much tolerate, but rather respects, benefits from, and celebrates its diversity.

> A pluralistic society is one in which a variety of cultural, religious, ethnic, and linguistic groups co-exist.[5]

Canada today is a microcosm of the wider world, a cultural environment of change, flux, and fusion. People with different behaviours, languages, religions, values, beliefs, and ways of communicating intermingle and come together in families, schools, places of work, and communities. We interact in business, social, athletic, educational, and political organizations across the country.

Our society is full of the opportunities and challenges diversity implies and our cultural lives are often complex and sometimes confusing. We all have neighbours, colleagues, friends, and often family from different cultural traditions in different stages of adaptation to Canadian life (see Chapter 10). How do we bridge the differences and form bonds that strengthen and enrich us all? For many of us, there is a dichotomy in the way we live: at work and at school, we pursue personal, academic, and professional goals in environments of diversity, while our homes and families may embody a set of cultural realities different from those of the larger society in which we make our way. We may speak English or French at work or at school, and another language at home. We may behave one way at work or at school, another way at home with our parents, another way with our neighbours, and yet another way with our friends. We need to understand our behaviours, our attitudes, and our reactions as well as those of the people with whom we interact in order to make the most of the richness of culture in which we live.

Do you participate in groups that include people from cultural backgrounds different from your own? Do you interact as easily with them as with people more similar to you? If not, why not? If so, how have you bridged differences?

Intercultural Competence

Intercultural competence is an ideal towards which all Canadians should strive. It refers to the ability to communicate effectively with people belonging to cultural groups different from our own when culture, not age or gender or social class, is the main variable in the interaction.[6] LeBaron uses the term *cultural fluency* to describe the combination of knowledge, understanding, skill, and attitude that is the basis of the ability to communicate effectively across cultures.[7]

Have you ever been in a situation where a misunderstanding occurred because you didn't understand a cultural behaviour on the part of someone with whom you were interacting? How did you deal with it?

CANADA AND CULTURAL DIVERSITY

Ethnic Diversity

The enormous cultural diversity of Canada underlies the need for intercultural competence. In the census of 2001, Canadians reported more than 200 different ethnic origins (see Table 1.1). Where once the national dynamic centred principally on the relationship between French- and English-speaking Canadians, it has broadened today to acknowledge the contributions of First Nations and immigrants from around the world. No longer does the national debate play out exclusively between two languages (French and English), two so-called founding peoples (French and English), and two so-called founding religions (Roman Catholic and Protestant).

In 1969, the first Official Languages Act was passed giving French and English equal status. Shortly after, in 1971, Canada adopted an official policy of multiculturalism within the framework of bilingualism. Parliament wanted to ensure cultural freedom for Canadians, guided by the belief that an official identity could not be mandated and that Canadians often maintain a sense of belonging to various cultural groups. An essential part of "Canadianness," in other words, is cultural diversity. In his speech to Parliament, Prime Minister Trudeau recognized that adherence to an ethnic group is influenced not so much by an individual's origin or mother

Table 1.1

Population by selected ethnic origins in Canada, 2001 census, top 15 origins

ETHNIC ORIGIN	NUMBER OF RESPONSES	ETHNIC ORIGIN	NUMBER OF RESPONSES
Canadian	11 682 680	Ukrainian	1 071 060
English	5 978 875	North American Indian	1 000 890
French	4 668 410	Dutch (Netherlands)	923 310
Scottish	4 157 210	Polish	817 085
Irish	3 822 660	East Indian	713 330
German	2 742 765	Norwegian	363 760
Italian	1 270 370	Portuguese	357 690
Chinese	1 094 700		
		Total Population	**29 639 035**

Notes: Total responses are given here, including single and multiple responses. As of January 2005, the total population of Canada was 32 078 819; 2005 ethnic origin updates were not available.

Source: Adapted from the Statistics Canada website http://www.statcan.ca/english/Pgdb/demo26a.htm, date extracted May 9, 2005.

tongue as by a sense of belonging, and by what the Royal Commission on Bilingualism and Biculturalism of the time called a group's "collective will to exist."[8]

In 1977, The Royal Commission on Aboriginal Peoples outlined the principles by which Canada's First Nations and Canadian governments and institutions would restructure their relationship into a fairer and more equal partnership. Finally, the Charter of Rights and Freedoms, entrenched in the Constitution in 1982, further reinforced the value of the multicultural nature of Canadian society by ensuring that Canadians of all ethnicities, races, and religions be guaranteed equal civil liberties and freedoms.

The 2001 census asked Canadians to identify the ethnic or cultural origin of their ancestors (defined as someone more distant than a grandparent). Four write-in spaces were provided, and multiple responses encouraged in recognition of the intermixing of Canadians over generations. "Canadian" was given as a sample choice among the 25 provided. Respondents were encouraged by the examples not to pick racial or

RACE, ETHNICITY, AND VISIBLE MINORITY

Race is a designation for grouping human beings that encompasses genetic factors related to physical features like skin and eye colour, hair characteristics, and stature.

Abuse of the concept in the name of science has led anthropologists to now prefer the multidimensional term **ethnicity**. It describes the historical origins and cultural, religious, linguistic, and geographical environment from which a person or a person's ancestors have come. In Canada, it encompasses all ethnicities including British, French, and First Nation.[9] Although from an official and scientific point of view the term *race* is increasingly avoided, concepts of race still play a role in an individual's sense of identity, and in the labelling of individuals and groups by others.

In Canada, the term **visible minority** describes non-white Canadians and acknowledges the role of race in the social construction of identity.[10] (For more on race, identity, and visible minority status in Canada see Chapters 2 and 10.)

An **ethnic group** is a collectivity within a larger society united by emotional and cultural ties. In pluralistic societies like Canada's, people may self-identify principally with a particular ethnic group for a sense of belonging and identity (Italian, for example), or they may identify principally or only with the larger collectivity (Canadian), or they may identify with both (Italian Canadian). Generational stay in Canada among immigrants—that is everyone except First Nation Canadians—determines to some extent an individual's self-identification.[11]

linguistic categories, but rather to select specific groups such as German, Somali, Jamaican, Lebanese, or Cree.[12]

How would you answer the census question "To which ethnic or cultural group did your ancestors belong?"? Write up to four choices on a piece of paper, and table the diversity of your class.

Canada's Religious Diversity

Canadians show contradictory tendencies when it comes to faith. Many participate actively in religious groups and feel a strong sense of belonging to a community of

Table 1.2

Religious affiliation in Canada

Catholic	12 936 905	Jewish	329 995
Protestant	8 654 850	Buddhist	300 345
Christian Orthodox	479 620	Hindu	297 200
Christian not included elsewhere	780 450	Sikh	278 410
		No religious affiliation	4 900 090
Muslim	579 640		
		Total Population	**29 639 035**

Note: Total population in October 2004 was 32 140 292.

Source: Adapted from the Statistics Canada website http://www.statcan.ca/english/Pgdb/demo30a.htm, date extracted May 9, 2005.

faith. For some cultural groups, such as Sikhs, faith and ethnicity are often interrelated, while other religious communities exhibit greater cultural diversity. Table 1.2 gives the religious affiliations of Canadians according to the 2001 census. (See Chapter 6 for an overview of major religious traditions.) Many Canadians do not actively or regularly practise an organized faith, but nonetheless identify with the faith in which they were raised when it comes to ticking a box on a census form, says pollster Michael Adams.[13]

Nevertheless, Canadians also appear to be becoming increasingly **secular,** that is to say, increasingly free from traditional religious beliefs. Almost five million Canadians, or 16 percent of the population, chose "no religious affiliation" in 2001, a jump from 12 percent in 1991 and about 1 percent in 1971. And in the past 10 years, overall church attendance has decreased by 19 percent, although 78 percent of Christians still claimed to believe in God and 66 percent self-identify as Christian.[14]

Contradictorily, despite the decline in overall church attendance, fundamentalist and evangelical branches of Christianity are growing. "Born-again" evangelism has increased by 13 percent in the past 10 years.

In addition, Islam, Buddhism, and Hinduism have begun to figure in the mosaic of Canadian religious diversity.[15]

First Nations

First Nations are the first threads of the multicultural tapestry of Canadian society, yet they have struggled for recognition, equality, and respect since the period of **colonial** domination by European Canadian institutions and policies began. The creation of

Nunavut in 1999, the historic land claim settlement of the Nisga'a Nation in British Columbia in 2001, and ongoing legal action to compensate victims of abuse in residential schools are examples of slow progress toward cultural revival and a place of honour in Canadian society for First Nations.

First Nation population numbered 976 305 in the 2001 census.[16] Of those, 62 percent identified themselves as North American Indian, about 30 percent as Métis (people of mixed European and Aboriginal heritage), and about 5 percent as Inuit. Aboriginals showed the highest increase in population from the 1996 census, with almost one-third under the age of 15.

Non-Native Canadians interact most with Native Canadians in urban centres and in the western and northern areas of the country. The majority of First Nation peoples do not live in First Nation communities, the preferred term for "reserve,"[17] but rather in urban centres and other rural areas. It is predicted that in a few decades, the Aboriginal population of Saskatchewan will form its majority.[18] At present, 85 percent of Nunavut's population is Inuit, and the largest Métis population lives in Alberta.[19] Winnipeg is home to the largest North American Indian population, followed by Vancouver and Edmonton.[20]

Immigration

Canada accepts about 220 000 immigrants a year, giving it the highest per capita immigration rate in the world.[21] More than one million immigrants came to Canada between 1996 and 2001. Canada is second only to Australia for its proportion of foreign-born citizens: 18.4 percent of the population is foreign born, while in Australia that percentage is 22 percent. With the birthrate in Canada at an all-time low in 2002, immigrants are supplying most of the labour in an expanding job market. In 2001, immigrants accounted for almost 20 percent of Canada's workforce.[22]

Changes to Canada's immigration policies in the 1960s have resulted in an unprecedented growth of diversity that has literally changed the face of the nation. Visible minorities now account for 13.4 percent of Canada's population.[23] Before 1961, the top five sources of immigrants were Britain, Italy, Germany, the Netherlands, and Poland. In the 1990s, they were mainly China, India, the Philippines, Hong Kong, and Sri Lanka. Fifty percent of immigrants now come from the Asia Pacific region, 20 percent from Africa and the Middle East, and 17 percent from Britain and Europe. The black population growth has been dramatic, climbing to 662 200 in 2001 from 34 400 in 1971, although black leaders say the current official number is too low by about 400 000.[24] Until 1971, most black Canadians were descendants of slaves and lived in well-established communities such as Halifax and Montreal. The greatest number since the opening of doors to immigration now lives in Toronto and Montreal.

Demographic Divide: Urban versus Rural

In addition to a change in place of origin of immigrants, there has been a change of destination. Prior to 1960, many immigrants headed to rural areas to farm.[25] For the last ten years, the majority has settled in urban centres.

Seventy-three percent of all new arrivals between 1991 and 2001 made their homes in Toronto, Montreal, or Vancouver, with the remainder settling in Ottawa–Gatineau, Calgary, Edmonton, Hamilton, Kitchener, Winnipeg, Windsor, or London.[26]

A United Nations survey recently revealed that Canadian cities are among the top four worldwide with regard to the proportion of foreign-born residents, beating cities like New York, London, and Sydney. Toronto placed second, after Miami, with 44 percent of Torontonians born outside Canada, while Vancouver, at 37 percent, placed fourth after Los Angeles. These percentages, however, do not reveal the whole story. Miami's foreign-born come mainly from Cuba and Central America, while Los Angeles' foreign-born are also mainly Hispanic in origin.[27]

The largest groups of immigrants to Toronto in the five years before the 2001 census came from China, India, and Pakistan, while more than 90 different cultural groups are represented in the city. The predominant cultural groups in Vancouver are Chinese Canadians and Indo Canadians, although many other groups are also represented.[28]

A recent Stats Canada study indicated that two distinct societies are emerging in Canada. They are the "increasingly polyglot and diverse cities embedded in a national fabric that hasn't changed, demographically speaking, in 50 years."[29] Toronto, Vancouver, and to some degree Montreal, are closer to South Asia, Asia, or the Caribbean, than to the mythological Canadian (Anglo-Celtic or French) homelands. Rural Canada and provinces with less immigration such as Nova Scotia, do not in general reflect the diversity of the major urban centres.

Atlantic Canada has tended to receive few immigrants, but an ambitious program in the Maritimes has been launched to lure entrepreneurs and skilled workers to the East Coast.[30] Why did the region not attract immigrants, and why is it seeking to increase its share?

Demographic Divide: Neighbourhoods

Canada's multicultural cities are divided in their own way. Immigrants often congregate in certain neighbourhoods or suburban areas where they feel at home, and where they have community support groups that can help with integration into Canadian society.

In 1981, Canada had six neighbourhoods where 30 percent of the population came from a single visible minority. By 2001, that number had jumped to over 250, nearly all of the neighbourhoods in Toronto and Vancouver, followed at a distance by Montreal.[31] Canada's once "two solitudes," divided essentially on the basis of language, appear to be morphing into a number of "new solitudes."

A potential negative, in the long run, is the ghettoization of particular cultural groups if satisfactory integration does not occur.

Canadian Attitudes to Diversity

Most Canadians, whether immigrant or Canadian-born, urban or rural, share an accepting attitude towards ethnic diversity. A *Globe and Mail* 2003 poll carried out by Ipsos-Reid revealed that 57 percent of respondents in the country's major cities (Halifax, Montreal, Ottawa, Toronto, Calgary, Edmonton, and Vancouver) say that multiculturalism makes them very proud to be Canadian. Among rural respondents, the figure was 52 percent.[32] A 2004 poll indicated that 73 percent of Canadians think that immigrants are a good or somewhat good influence.[33]

Canadians under the age of 30 are more comfortable with diversity than their elders. In the 2003 poll, only 13 percent agreed that "Canadian children growing up surrounded by people of different ethnic and cultural groups will be left without a solid cultural base."[34] Eighty-four percent of Francophones and 82 percent of Anglophones said they felt comfortable when they hear languages other than English or French being spoken in Canada.[35] Twelve percent of Canadians thought that relations between different ethnic groups are a very big problem, compared with 30–50 percent in the U.S., the U.K., France, and Italy. In Britain, 60 percent of respondents recently claimed to think that immigrants were a problem.[36]

Do you feel proud of Canada's cultural diversity as outlined above, or are you ambivalent about it? Why?

Intercultural Marriage in Canada

Canadians of diverse origins come together in families as members of different cultural groups intermarry, have children, and generally mix and match in society.

Rui Umezawa, a Canadian of Japanese descent, is married to a Canadian whose parents came from Newfoundland and Italy. Not only did the fact that he was of Japanese descent and she wasn't not enter his mind, he says their very Canadian mixing of cultures has enriched the lives of their children. "I add a little Japan in the mix, and my kids have relatives on three continents," he says.[37]

Cultural combinations in marriage are a recurring story in Canada. In 2001, more than 3 percent of all existing marriages and common-law unions self-identified as mixed, mostly between European Canadians and members of a visible minority. Japanese Canadians, although a small percentage of Canadians, are Canada's best mixers, with 70 percent in a mixed union. Latin Americans are next, at 45 percent, followed by blacks (cultural origins not supplied) at 43 percent.[38] Only 10 percent of Canadians agreed "that it is a bad idea for people of different races to marry one another" in the 2003 Ipsos-Reid survey.[39] In contrast, interracial marriage is opposed by 30 percent of non-black Americans.[40]

In Vancouver, Canada's gateway to the Pacific, cultural fusion is the order of the day. There, mixed race couples form 7.2 percent of the married population, and one in eight couples aged 20–29 is part of a mixed race couple. One young woman in Vancouver of Japanese descent about to marry a Canadian of European background said, "I forget I'm Asian—I just feel Canadian from Vancouver."[41]

Fulfillment of Personal and Professional Goals

To say that Canadians are in general comfortable with diversity does not suggest that differing ways of viewing the world and communicating do not cause misunderstandings in Canadian society. However, most of us are united in at least one important aspect of life: we seek the same thing, that is, lives of personal and professional fulfillment for ourselves and our families.

Intercultural competence promotes the achievement of that common goal in a diverse society. People working together with the same aim but different ways of expressing and attaining it will better succeed with knowledge of and respect for each other's ways. Diversity, when valued and understood, enhances the debate and encourages creative problem-solving that strengthens the foundations of the country and its institutions.[42]

Trompenaars and Hampden-Turner's research supports the premise that while cultural groups differ, they face similar dilemmas and seek to achieve similar goals in life and in the workplace.[43] Managers who recognize the common denominators beneath the apparent diversity of their teams and who learn to reconcile conflicting values and ways of communicating are able to foster a positive synergy to bring about the common desired goals. (See Chapter 5 for Trompenaars and Hampden-Turner's research and conclusions).

The same is true in making Canadian society as a whole function creatively and for the common good: effective communication aimed at resolving and reconciling differences will result in the fulfillment of all Canadians' personal and professional aspirations.

Canada's diversity: Canadians from many different cultural backgrounds enrich the cultural fabric of Canadian society.

Source: © David R. Frazier, Photolibrary Inc./Alamy

Canadian organizations are learning to use diversity to their benefit. Banks and businesses have instituted diversity hiring projects and built teams of people whose styles of negotiation and management are vastly different. They have recognized that teams where everyone has the same ideas are unlikely to be innovative, and that managers who utilize the cultural diversity of their teams and markets will achieve better results than managers who are insensitive to culture-based styles of communication, problem-solving, and negotiation.[44]

Intercultural competence also contributes to increased profits. In the tourism industry, for example, hotel managers in Whistler who know how to make Japanese guests feel comfortable will ensure that word of mouth will bring them more Japanese tourists. Procter & Gamble, the world's largest consumer goods company, believes the recruitment of employees of varied backgrounds assists the company to better understand its customers and "sell more soap and toothpaste."[45] Alan Middleton of the Schulich School of Business regards a diverse workforce as "an essential way of doing business in Canada today."[46]

Procter & Gamble also sees increased productivity among employees working in an environment that respects their diversity. It organized a "diversity summit" to celebrate the 40 different countries and 30 different languages represented by the 800 employees at its Toronto headquarters.[47] Nonetheless, many companies still have a way to go: while diversity is increasingly on the minds of major Canadian employers, white males still predominate in the executive ranks.[48]

YOU AND YOUR WORK EXPERIENCE

Have you worked in an ethnically diverse environment and, if so, what were some of the benefits and drawbacks of it that you experienced or observed? How was diversity harnessed, or how could it have been harnessed, to enhance the workplace environment?

CANADA AND THE WORLD

The Global Village

Marshall McLuhan predicted in the 1960s that the world would one day become a **global village.**[49] His predictions were based on his early insight into the implications of emerging electronic technology. He foresaw that technology would enable human beings to transcend both space and time to experience faraway events on their television screens at the very moment they were happening. The world would become a community, a global community in which everyone is connected and everyone an actor on the same stage.

The transformation of parts of the world into McLuhan's vision began to occur after World War II; until then, most human beings had never strayed far from the villages in which they were born.

In the hilltop southern Italian town of Castropignano, for example, for hundreds of years, the village's 5000 people rarely ventured further than the sound of their church bell. Their sense of space, distance, and time, and their relationships, were all determined by that bell. Villagers were closely connected, for better or worse, through family, fields, flocks of sheep or goats, church, commerce, community, and local dialect. Now, the 2000 or so who still live there have Internet access and commute to work and shop in larger centres. They speak Standard Italian (see Chapter 9 for language variants), learned in schools now available to all, and only the old men gather for coffee and gossip in dialect in the town square in the cool of the evening. Emigrants like Canadian Aldo Palma, now an internationally known chief engineer, return to find the ancient stone houses where they were born, or to renovate them as a way of maintaining contact with their past. But their horizons, like those of the villagers who remain, stretch far beyond the sound of a church bell or any other such symbol of safety and community. Their story is the story of millions of people around the world.

Now, much of humanity is closely connected through technology the way village dwellers once were. People round the world shared, for example, the tragedy of the 2004 Indian Ocean tsunami as it unfolded, and seeing the devastation led to unprecedented generosity as people realized that such disasters could happen anywhere to anyone.

Technological connectivity binds us by means of mass transportation; cell, satellite, and telephones; the Internet; and mass media. We can go almost anywhere, if not in reality, then virtually. We have access to information about other people in other places—what they have, what they think, what they do. It gives us ideas about what we might have and think and do. And this information can translate into power and bring about social, political, and economic change.

According to Gwynne Dyer, modern communication technology was largely responsible for the overthrow of communist regimes in Eastern Europe. Disenchantment with the old regimes increased as awareness of the West's freedoms and consumer advantages grew thanks to media access. The defeat of Mexico's long-ruling Institutionalized Revolutionary Party (PRI) came about peacefully through the ballot box in 2000 as information about government corruption and the policies of opposition political parties was made available thanks to international networks that arrived to cover the Chiapas Revolution of 1994. Until then, Mexican television stations, controlled by the government, did not report news unfavourable to the ruling party, but when international news media arrived and did, Mexican voters got valuable information that helped them make more informed election choices.[50] The international focus on Ukraine's election in 2004 also broadcast and strengthened its people's will for democracy and change.

Was McLuhan's vision utopian? While many of us can communicate, travel, and cross boundaries with ease, economic, social, political, cultural, geographic, and technical barriers to such mobility and connectivity exist for masses of human beings. Are we really a global village?

Can the efforts of rock stars like Bob Geldof and U2 in harnessing modern communication technology to unite the world to end global poverty at such events as the 2005 Live 8 concert really influence governments and turn the world into a caring community—the "single global tribe"[51] envisioned by McLuhan?

Human beings are not only increasingly virtually connected by means of modern communication technology, they are also physically on the move. Vast numbers of people flow from place to place as economic migrants, immigrants, and refugees. Fifteen million refugees alone need a homeland[52] and millions more people are displaced within the borders of their own countries.

In addition, representatives and employees of multinational corporations crisscross the globe in ever-growing numbers. As destinations become commonplace, the entrepreneurial adventuresome seek out isolated corners of the world. Few places remain untouched by the forces of modern technology and the flow of people, rendering the need for intercultural understanding and competence all the more compelling.

Geert Hofstede listed the common forms of intercultural encounters with which the globalizing world is familiar.[53] They include encounters in:

- Tourism
- Education
- International development cooperation

CARIBBEAN/MEXICAN SEASONAL WORKERS PROGRAM

Canada has a program that facilitates the hiring of seasonal workers from the Caribbean and Mexico. In effect since 1966, and starting originally with Jamaica and then extended to Mexico, it allows for eight-month work visas for agricultural workers. In 2003, 19 000 came to Canada to work picking tomatoes, corn, and pumpkins. They are paid about $7.25 an hour and are not eligible for benefits, although deductions for them are made. Other foreign workers may also be granted temporary visas. In 2003, over 82 000 temporary visas were granted in more than 40 different labour categories.[54]

- Migrants and host countries
- International diplomatic and political negotiations
- Multinational corporations: negotiations, branch plants, management

Economic Globalization

Economic globalization describes the international mobility of goods, services, labour, technology, and capital, and the increasing connectivity and interdependence of the world's markets and businesses.[55] Wal-Mart, IBM, Shell, Disney, Noranda, McCains, McDonald's, and Magna International are well-known examples of giant multinational corporations with headquarters in one country and branches in others.

Supporters of globalization claim that it brings increased opportunities for employment around the world and will ultimately result in global prosperity.[56] The World Trade Organization, of which Canada is a member, is composed at present of 144 members and is at the forefront of the promotion of globalization. Its mandate is to set rules to govern global trade and capital flows, and to ensure that the rules are followed in the drive to make the world a global marketplace.

ANTI-GLOBALIZATION

Not everyone has jumped on the globalization bandwagon. Grassroots organizations in many countries, international aid organizations, environmental organizations, and the leaders of some developing countries like Brazil are not in agreement with the way it is unfolding. What are their arguments against it?

Canada and Economic Globalization

Canada is a trading nation and international service provider. Canadian architects and engineers work with their counterparts in Asia, Europe, and Latin America to build state-of-the-art skyscrapers. Canadian entrepreneurs seek markets and invest in multinational operations. Canada is a member of NAFTA, the North American Free Trade Agreement linking it with Mexico and the United States, and of APEC, the Asia–Pacific Economic Cooperation agreement. It has bilateral free trade agreements with Costa Rica and Chile. Canada supports negotiations for the FTAA (Free Trade Area of the Americas), and has sent trade missions to Brazil, Russia, China, and other countries in a bid to expand trade with emerging markets.

Canada is also an attractive place in which to invest for multinational companies based elsewhere. Wal-Mart and McDonald's are successful in Canada, and China has sought to take over Noranda mines while other government-owned Chinese enterprises are looking at investment in Alberta energy development projects. China, the new power on the block, needs natural resources to fuel its phenomenal rate of development, and Canada can provide them.

Canadian multinational giants are found in the insurance, mining, energy, telecommunications, rail, utilities, broadcasting and cable, and communication equipment sectors. Names like Magna International, Bombardier, Alcon, Nortel, Onex Corp., Thomson Corp., Quebecor, Royal Bank of Canada, McCains, Finning, and many others are well known.

Nonetheless, for some industries in Canada, there is a downside to economic globalization. Huntingdon, Quebec, for example, is a 180-year-old mill town whose textile plants are closing down as China and other low-cost producers such as India and Pakistan can now market to Western markets with the ending of import quotas set by the World Trade Organization in 2005.[57]

Cultural Globalization

Cultural globalization refers to the global spread of ideas and trends. It can introduce new elements into traditional cultures and modify existing elements.[58] It is the most visible form of globalization and is fuelled in part by economic globalization and modern communication technology.

The Simpsons is now available in the Arab world, translated into Arabic and edited for cultural content. And Barbie dolls are available in cross-cultural versions. Fula, for example, is the popular Islamic Barbie, modestly dressed and reflective of conservative Muslim values. There is also an Inuit Barbie designed in Canada.

Extensive media coverage, whether about natural disasters, fashion trends, consumer products, or political and humanitarian movements, shows to what extent media have the power to create and channel our priorities as well as influence our choices.

Access to mass media can be a double-edged sword, however. Information does not automatically provide meaning. A news clip from Afghanistan contains information for North American viewers, but it is filtered first through a reporter's and then a network's biases, then through our own as we watch (see Chapter 2 on perception). Its meaning for different individuals varies accordingly.

Watching a sitcom like *Friends* if you live in rural India may not equip you to separate what is real from what is Hollywood, let alone to understand what forces have shaped the lives and beliefs of the culture that produced *Friends*. That visual window transmits a slice of life, conversations, and appearances, but not necessarily meaning. We need tools to interpret what we see and hear. North Americans may watch a movie made in Mumbai, but what does that teach about life, aspirations, and communication on the sub-continent? In Canada, First Nations and visible minorities have complained about negative images of their communities predominating in the media to the detriment of the public's perception of them. Mass media and their corporate sponsors manipulate us—both intentionally and unintentionally—and genuine knowledge about global issues and other cultures onto which we have a window may be the victim (see box below).

Many Cubans spend Sunday afternoon watching American movies broadcast throughout the island. A Cuban immigrant had this comment after visiting an upper-middle-class Canadian home. It was situated on an acre of land overlooking a ravine, had a swimming pool in the backyard, a yacht on its trailer outside, and gold-rimmed crystal and china. The wife did not work outside the home, and the couple took annual first-class cruise vacations:

"I thought you said they were rich."
"Well, let's say they're well off."
"No they aren't. They would have butlers if they were. That's how it is in movies."

Mass media have the power to inform and the power to distort. We need intercultural competence to delve beneath the surface of news, movies, and television for the meaning in what we see and hear.

Canada: The Global Village Within

Canadians have access to 657 television stations, according to a CRTC report. They include 156 conventional stations, 394 community, specialty, and pay stations, and 107 non-Canadian services.[59] Satellite radio stations will increase our access to even more.

Canada and Other Areas of Global Cooperation

Canadians in many fields require training in intercultural communication to meet the needs of a connected world.

Education

Canadian educational institutions are setting up campuses from India to China to Saudi Arabia, and fostering exchanges of faculty and students with partnering institutions. Many international students choose Canada for post-secondary educations.

In 2001, there were 154 000 international students at Canadian post-secondary institutions; by 2003, that number had grown to 172 000.[60] This number is expected to rise as the United States increasingly closes its doors to international students.[61] The international middle class is growing and looking for a competitive edge to their children's educations; China sends the largest number of international students to Canada, followed by India.

Diplomacy and International Politics

Canada supports multilateral action and diplomacy. It has initiated and promoted the concept of the "responsibility to protect" through the United Nations, arguing that international forces must be ready to protect civilians in instances where their governments are unable or unwilling to do so, or are perpetrating human rights abuses themselves. Canada promotes the official formation of the more inclusive G20, an expansion of the G8 industrialized countries whose leaders regularly meet. Meanwhile, Canada quietly sends missions to assist in the building of democratic institutions in countries without long traditions of democracy, and participates in international monitoring of elections.[62]

International Development

Canadian aid agencies work with partners throughout the developing world to assist in projects for sustainable development and increased participation in the world economy. Canadian international development agencies like CIDA and numerous non-governmental organizations (NGOs) provide training and support in developing countries.

Peacekeeping

Canadian military personnel are engaged in peacekeeping and assisting in building democratic institutions in places such as Afghanistan, Bosnia, and Haiti.

Science

Scientists from Canada share information and collaborate on projects with other scientists from around the world. They form part of the Arctic Council made up of scientists from eight countries with Arctic territory whose influential report on global warming was released in November, 2004.

The Arts

Musicians travel the globe and fuse homegrown rhythms with other cultural traditions. Canadian jazz artist Jane Bunnett, for example, is an expert on Cuban music and collects instruments for musicians in Cuba. Musicologist Catherine Potter of McGill

University specializes in North Indian sitar music. Artists in all fields benefit from the varied cultural traditions flourishing in Canada.

CULTURE AND WORLD FUTURE

There are conflicting views about which way the world is headed. Here are five scenarios. Which one—or combination—do you think most likely to come to pass?

Cultural Convergence

Francis Fukuyama predicted ultimate worldwide cultural homogenization in a controversial work entitled *The End of History and the Last Man*.[63] He foresaw the world converging under the values of liberal democracy and free markets amid a general cultural homogenization that would be Western, and predominantly American.

Superficial evidence might support the view of a general Westernization: people everywhere wear blue jeans, drink Pepsi or Coke,[64] and watch television programs and movies produced in North America. Markets are globalizing, world trade has grown, and many formerly non-democratic countries have embraced democracy.

Other Western cultural patterns and values are also being absorbed.[65] For example, one study monitored the mothers of school children in Beijing. In the 1980s, the mothers were concerned about group harmony and the ability of their children to relate well with others. Ten years later, the mothers were concerned with the things Western mothers are: having the skills and independence to get ahead in the world.[66] As capitalism flourishes in China, Western brand names are the rage, and plastic surgery to create "Western" eyelid folds and sand down the jaw to make the face less round is popular.[67] Will liberal democracy be next?

Cultural convergence suggests the eventual possibility of one world culture. What would be the benefits of such an outcome? What would be the drawbacks? Is an analogy drawn from natural science relevant: when species stay differentiated, most survive, while if they become too similar and compete for the same resources, the chances of survival are reduced?

Other evidence indicates, however, that Westernization at other deep cultural levels is not happening. Brazilian soap operas and Indian movies are vastly popular around the world. Chinese films like *Crouching Tiger, Hidden Dragon* and *The House of Flying Daggers* were popular in the West, and China has influenced camera work, directing styles, and action sequences in such films as *Kill Bill, The Matrix,* and *Charlie's Angels*.[68] American movies are popular, but American music is not edging out other cultural forms of music, and American literature is not more popular than home-grown literature in other parts of the world.[69]

And cultural empires come and go. Every great power from Spain to France to Britain to ancient Greece and Rome to the United States has exported its culture. Who is to say that China won't be the next dominant culture?[70] Or India? It too is emerging on the world stage, and has a cultural industry that exports widely (see box on Bollywood).

BOLLYWOOD

India has the world's largest film industry, producing more than 1000 films a year in all the nation's many languages. It also has the world's biggest box office. Bollywood is nicknamed after its production base of Bombay (now called Mumbai). Indian movies are widely available in Canada. Suketu Mehtu, an Indian-American writer and avid watcher of Bollywood's Hindi movies, says they are unlikely to lose their international popularity any time soon because they are happy, have singing, show respect to mothers . . . and do not show a "lone American singlehandedly taking on armies of brown people."[71]

Cultural Fragmentation

While economic globalization seeks to connect nation states through trade and the harmonization of trade policies, and while Fukuyama predicts a new liberal order and Americanization of cultures, other scholars argue that people will continue to identify with discrete cultural groups.[72]

Cultural homogeneity within modern nation states is a rarity. They are seldom unified in terms of culture and, although a dominant culture or group generally controls the political, social, and economic institutions, many modern nation states, like Canada, are pluralistic societies. France has five million Muslims, many from North Africa; Germany is home to millions of Turkish workers and German citizens of Turkish descent; Belgium is home to many Poles.

Conflict over immigration and cultural pluralism has begun to unsettle countries like The Netherlands since the murder of film maker Theo Van Gogh by a Dutch Islamic fundamentalist in 2004. Britain, too—after the subway bombings of 2005 revealed that the perpetrators were British-born members of minority communities—has begun to question the limits to which multiculturalism can be accommodated. Also in 2005, French youth of Islamic and North African descent protested their marginalization in French society. Elsewhere, Iraq and Afghanistan are uneasy collections of cultures and traditions, African nation states are usually multi-ethnic, and so on.

DOMINANT CULTURE

A dominant culture is the culture of power or influence in a nation state. It is often the majority or founding culture. It usually provides a dominant national language and dominates a common mass media, a national education system, a national political system, the army, and representation in sports events with strong symbolic and emotional appeal.[73] When we talk of a national culture, we are referring to the dominant culture of a nation state. Canada's dominant culture is European Canadian, but there are significant divisions. Quebec's dominant culture is of French origin while the rest of Canada's dominant culture is of Anglo-Celtic descent.

SUB-CULTURE

A sub-culture is a minority culture in a society. Canada's ethnic and religious groups are sub-cultures. They share cultural traits and customs with the dominant culture, but maintain others that set them apart.[74] Other sub-cultures are based on such variables as age and social class.

Nation states are weakening in many parts of the world as cultural groups make demands in the name of **cultural nationalism.** In some regions, they seek autonomy within larger states; in others, they seek outright independence in order to form nation states on the basis of their culture. The Basques of Spain, the Kurds and Palestinians in the Middle East, the Chechens in Russia, the Indépendentistes of Quebec, and many other groups seek nation-state status. When the Soviet Union broke apart, independent states emerged largely on the basis of ethnicity and cultural affiliation.

Some cultural nationalists do not seek nation-state status, but rather autonomy or equality within a nation state. First Nations in Canada, Australia and New Zealand, Bolivia and Peru, to name just a few, seek equal status with the dominant cultures of colonizing nations whose cultures, laws, and institutions were imposed upon them during the period of European cultural imperialism.

John Ralston Saul believes the world is in the throes of the collapse of economic globalization, what he calls "looking at civilization through the prism of business."[75] He believes rather that a resurgence of cultural nationalism is taking place.

CULTURAL NATIONALISM

Cultural nationalism is also referred to as *ethnonationalism*. It can mean two things: loyalty to a nation or ethnic group that does not have its own state, or loyalty to an ethnic group within a specific state or country.[76]

Canada, despite its treatment of First Nations and its French–English tensions, serves as a model to some multi-ethnic or multi-linguistic countries. The President of Latvia, Vaira Vike-Freiberga, for example, is a Canadian citizen who returned to Latvia to serve the country of her birth. She looks to Canada and Quebec for ways to preserve the Latvian language and culture amidst the powerful influence of Russian and Russian immigrants who settled in Latvia when it was dominated by Russia.

Nation States: A Refresher

Nation states are political units into which the world is currently divided and to which all human beings supposedly belong from a passport point of view. They are a relatively recent invention in human history, dating from the 19th century and coalescing strongly in Europe. Many modern nation states stem from the colonial system. Borders were often arbitrarily drawn by colonial powers and based on colonial divisions not related to ethnic or cultural groupings. Nation states, therefore, are not really societies, which developed social forms of organization organically. Africa, divided up by European powers in many areas, gives numerous examples of nation states whose borders are not based on ethnic groupings. Nevertheless, in the **postcolonial** world of today, people in them often have developed a sense of national identity and a loyalty to the concept of their nation state; in other instances, conflict arises amongst the different ethnic groups thrown together into these artificially constructed political entities.

CULTURAL GENOCIDE

Cultural genocide is the attempt to suppress or annihilate another ethnic group through outright murder, as in Rwanda in 1994, or by other means. History is full of attempts at cultural genocide. What are other twentieth and twenty-first century examples?

ETHNIC CLEANSING
Ethnic cleansing is a euphemism for the removal of an ethnic group from an area claimed by another. Like cultural genocide, it can involve outright murder.

Cultural Clash

Samuel Huntington has predicted an Armageddon-like global cultural clash between the strongly different cultures from the East and West which he calls the "clash of civilizations."[77] The most volatile region at present is the Middle East where Western political, economic, and military influence and intervention in predominantly Muslim regions have resulted in various forms of protest. Iran underwent an Islamic revolution in 1979, and Middle Eastern countries are struggling with the rise of Islamist fundamentalists who categorically reject Western ideas and culture.[78] According to Huntington, the clash will continue to be predominantly cultural, not economic or political: the region is struggling to adapt to the sudden onslaught of the modern technological world and the spread of Western culture in a short period of time.

Critics like Edward Said consider this view an example of Western arrogance. Said called Huntington's view "The Clash of Ignorance."[79] The West, according to Said, has constructed fictionalized views of the East as irrational, childlike, passive, and uniform, based on clichés and centuries of assumptions of European superiority. Eastern scholars and experts were not consulted in the imaginative construction of "the East" by the West, and Western views were premised on "the silence of the native."[80] The "natives," viewed as underdeveloped and uncivilized, loomed as dangerous in the Western mind: violent and antimodernist—China, for example, was once called the Yellow Peril. Western views on Muslims and the East do not reflect reality but have led to dangerous conflicts. Said named the West's philosophy of misconceptions about the East **Orientalism.**

Meanwhile, China's population of 1.3 billion and its growing economic power and participation in the World Trade Organization have placed it in a position to challenge the economic and cultural preeminence of the West. China's potential superpower status and economic rise may "lift all boats" or its authoritarian political system could cause an ideological clash with the West.[81] India, vastly different from China and with millions of well-educated, entrepreneurial, and middle-class citizens of its own, is on a comparable course of rapid economic development.[82]

Peaceful Resolution: Acceptance and Celebration

The world today is tense with opposing movements. Co-existing but contradictory forces of cultural convergence, fragmentation, and clash are easy to pick out.

Peaceful resolution is also a possible scenario, an optimistic one perhaps, and certainly one that requires education, interest, and will.

To achieve it, we must give up traditional models of thinking, such as the view that the East is inevitably westernizing, or that we are involved in unavoidable culture clashes.[83] Both models assume that secular Western forms of society are the only reasonable options, but such an assumption is not acceptable to many Eastern cultures with different cultural frameworks. The West and East have much to teach and learn from each other.[84] (See Chapter 5 for an East/West cultural comparison.) African and Aboriginal cultures also have much to offer. Fostering human rights, economic development, and global security must be done in ways that respect the religions, political structures, ideas about public good, and ways of resolving conflict in all cultures. China has a long and unbroken history; it is unlikely to be taken over by the West or want to be. Nonetheless, many Chinese are fascinated with the West, and many Westerners are fascinated with China.

Peaceful resolution implies cultural globalization in terms of the cross-fertilization of cultures and personal freedoms it offers, if mostly, at present, to citizens of the developed world. For the first time in history, we can cross borders and mix and match beliefs to construct global and virtual communities of like-minded people. This was McLuhan's vision: a global tribe in a global village. This kind of globalization "... can free people from the tyranny of geography. Just because someone was born in France, does not mean they can only aspire to speak French, eat French food, read French books ... Globalization not only increases individual freedom, but also revitalizes cultures through foreign influences, technologies, and markets. Thriving cultures are not set in stone. They are forever changing from within and without...."[85]

Vancouver is a Canadian city evolving naturally into this vision of the future where people, cuisines, visual art, music, dance, and ideas blend into a multiplicity of combinations where fewer and fewer people can really claim only one or two ethnic and cultural origins, and many would not want to.[86]

The celebration and fusion of difference is one facet of postmodernism, the scenario which follows.

Postmodernism

Postmodernism is a nebulous but popular term among mainly European and North American academics. It describes certain recent changes in Western culture. One aspect of it is the postcolonial acceptance and celebration of difference,[87] a direct challenge to colonial concepts of European cultural superiority. Beyond that, its meaning varies.

One interpretation is that Westerners are freeing themselves from assumptions about reality imposed by established authorities in the form of the institutions, religions, and ideologies that have guided them since the Enlightenment. Underlying the master- or meta-narratives[88] of these authorities, tales told to make us believe and conform, are ideas about the nature of Truth (it is knowable, objective, and absolute), about the importance of science (it can explain the workings of the universe), about the nature of experience (it can be understood rationally), about the nature of society (it is a unified whole), about the nature of time (it moves forward), about the nature of technology (it is responsible for progress), and about the nature of the "story" itself (it has a beginning, middle, and end).

Lyotard maintains that meta-narratives legitimized what was accepted as knowledge and contained the principles on which society was founded. Those principles are changing. The elites of the postmodern, cybernetic world are those who control information and have turned knowledge into a commodity.[89] Knowledge itself gains legitimacy not by means of grand principles but by means of how well it performs—its "performativity." If it achieves the results we want, it is legitimate.

Postmodernism challenges modernism's truths. It tolerates contradiction. We can both be one thing *and* the other, not one thing *or* the other. It negates the concept of the whole and embraces the concept of "deconstruction"—of nation states, ideas, identity, and words. There are no answers: modern theories and movements and religions are false and have nothing to do with the daily life of an individual. Science has done little to end poverty or the threat of war. It is no more truth than magic. There are no "master narratives," only local stories. There is no capital-T Truth. Truth is personal and individual (experience is subjective—your truth is yours and mine is mine; emotions and mysticism are more important than reason), unity and order are illusions (society is fragmented), and there are no absolutes (truth, values, and morality are relative; "good" and "bad" are relative—see Chapter 2). In other words, we are in the process of deconstructing the structures and foundations of thought upon which Western society rests.[90]

Even words have lost their meaning. Too often used to dominate and disenfranchise the masses by elites in power, they are, in the end, unstable in their meanings and not to be trusted.

Postmodernism in its negative expression reflects malaise, societal chaos, disintegration and violence, and resistance to established ideologies. Rap music is an African-American musical expression of postmodernism: rhythm and beat take precedence over words to express individual subjective experience and emotion.[91] Words are deconstructed into sounds, patterns, and repetitions to express anger and discontent about the marginalization that stems from the hierarchical society constructed by white Europeans. Rapper Kanye West has used rap to inform his fans about diamonds linked to violence in Sierra Leone.[92]

Postmodernism in its positive expression represents personal freedom,[93] if primarily only to privileged members of society, who, as suggested above, are free to construct their own identities by picking and choosing from the myriad options now available. It goes beyond the choice suggested above, however, in that it rejects modern nation states as states of mind—passé, artificial constructions causing more harm, in the form of conflict and war, than good. Human beings can, have, and will unshackle themselves from their constraints as well as other outdated ideas.

Richard Gwyn has argued that Canada is the world's first postmodern state, in other words, a state without any national identity.[94] Canadians are interested in personal fulfillment, not in submitting as citizens or soldiers to the authority of a nation state.[95] Do you agree? (For more on the concept of a Canadian national identity, see Chapter 4.)

Postmodernism may, in the end, be a Western academic conceit: all around the world there is evidence that human beings cling to the concept of national identities and nation states, as evidenced, for example, in the Dutch and French voters' rejection of the European Constitution, and to enduring ideas about universal Truths and the benefits of science for humankind.[96]

May you live in interesting times is an ancient Chinese curse. How would you explain it in light of today's world?

SUMMARY

This chapter introduced a number of terms and their definitions to set up a context for the study of intercultural communication. It also detailed elements of the cultural diversity of Canada and touched on issues of cultural conflict and cooperation around the world. What we have seen is that culture counts. It is part of what defines individuals, communities, and nation states, and part of what defines relationships between individuals, communities, regions, and nation states. We have also seen that communication counts: we are all part of a global village whose members interact, for better or worse, on many fronts. One of the challenges of the twenty-first century is to communicate effectively interculturally in order to accommodate the needs of differing cultural groups while at the same time managing the forces of globalization for the peace, well-being, health, and prosperity of all.

KEY TERMS

colonial 8	ethnic group 7	postcolonial 24
cultural convergence 21	ethnicity 7	postmodernism 26
cultural genocide 24	global village 14	race 7
cultural nationalism 23	nation state 24	secularism 8
dominant culture 23	Orientalism 25	sub-culture 23
ethnic cleansing 25	pluralism 4	visible minority 7

TOPICS FOR CRITICAL THINKING AND REFLECTION

1. *The Globe and Mail* with Ipsos-Reid undertook a national survey on The New Canada in late April and May, 2003.[97] One of the questions involved choosing a spouse: *Is it important to choose a spouse of a similar ethnic background?* Answer yes or no.

   Take a poll in your classroom and compare your results with the national results in Appendix I. Indicate your answer on a slip of paper. Indicate also "F" if you are female and "M" if you are male.

   What are your reasons for making the choice you did?
2. In groups, discuss and compare the importance of the following to your personal identity: passport nationality, ethnicity, religious affiliation, regional attachment, local attachment, and membership in other sub-cultures to which you belong. Alternatively, write a paper on the topic.
3. Using the Statistics Canada website, research the cultural diversity of your neighbourhood, town, city, province, or territory.
4. George W. Bush's comments after the terrorist attack of September 11, 2001 about a crusade and the "axis of evil" formed by Iran, Iraq, and North Korea were controversial. What view of the world's future does he appear to share from these comments and the actions of his administration?
5. Why are temporary visas issued to seasonal workers in Canada rather than resident permits leading to citizenship?

Chapter 2

Understanding How We View Ourselves and Others

In this chapter we will explore:

- Perception and its relationship to intercultural competence
- Perceptual barriers to intercultural competence
- Attitudes and skills that foster intercultural competence

PERCEPTUAL FILTERS

You have probably had your eyes tested. What happens when the optometrist drops lenses of different strengths in front of your eyes? How do you ultimately reach 20/20 vision?

Our ability to look at and understand the behaviour of other cultural groups is like the ability to see. It too can be affected by lenses, in this case, perceptual lenses. Perceptual lenses act like filters. They alter what we see and are what this chapter is about, because no one naturally "sees the world with pristine eyes."[1]

Perceptual filters can be affective or cognitive, positive or negative. Affective filters refer to our emotions and how they affect our ability to see, and cognitive filters to our thought processes and their influence on our thinking.[2] Negative filters encourage us to interpret the behaviour of others negatively, and positive filters to seek to understand it before passing judgment. We are often unaware of the perceptual filters that affect our vision.

Before examining them, we need to say a few words about the nature of perception itself.

PERCEPTION

Human beings absorb information by means of their senses. But as we saw in Chapter 1, information itself is without intrinsic meaning: human beings create meaning from information. Perception is the process by which we select and organize the barrage of sensory stimuli that bombard us every moment of every day. It functions to interpret and construct our reality. It gives meaning to our environment. It makes us feel secure by creating an ordered universe from the potential chaos of uninterpreted sensory stimuli.

Perception is most often based on what we *see*, but it also relies on hearing, touching, smelling, and tasting. Arguments often arise between people about what is true, or what really happened, or what conclusions should be drawn from an incident. Who has not said or been told, "Well, that's your perception!" Our perception of events and incidents is what we believe about them according to how we've processed information, not necessarily according to what is "objectively" true. Perception is like freeze-frame photography, the ongoing process of an individual's construction of reality, and every individual's construction is a little bit different from everybody else's because each person sees things just a bit differently from everybody else at any given moment.

Can you think of an occasion when your perception of an event or person was completely different from someone else's? Why do you think your perceptions varied so greatly?

The well-worn optical illusions such as those in Figure 2.1 can teach us a few things about perception.[3] First, things are not always as they initially appear: perception may play tricks on us. Second, we perceive selectively, often only what is important to us, or what we are programmed or want to see. Research has shown, for example, that young people usually see the young woman first in the illustration above, and older people, the old woman. Third, we often find it hard to perceive something in the same way other people do.

A number of factors inform perception:

- who we are—our own unique combination of attitudes, motives, experience, knowledge, and expectations;

Figure 2.1 Optical Illusions

Do you see an old lady or a young lady? A duck or a rabbit?

Source: Mary Evans Picture Library

- what we are perceiving—the object or event we are interpreting; and the context within which we see events or objects.[4] Eyewitness testimony of crime scenes and identification of suspects in police lineups is unreliable partly for reasons related to perception. We all see and remember different details, and the accuracy rate for identification is only about 60 percent.[5]
- our culture. Culture is perhaps the most important element of mental programming that informs our perception of reality.[6] One of the reasons we are confused when immersed in unfamiliar cultural environments is that we are unable to see its reality the same way as the people who live there do. A classic study, for instance, involved rural Mexican children and children from the American dominant culture. When shown split-second images in which one eye was exposed to a baseball game and the other to a bullfight, in general, the Mexican children reported seeing the bullfight, and American children, the baseball game.[7]

Movies often play on the theme of perception and reality. In Kurosawa's iconic *Rashomon,*[8] a woman is raped and her husband killed. The woodland crime scene is described and replayed through the eyes of each of four defendants in the case, each account and recreation of events adding a little more to the whole. In the end, it is unclear to the viewer what really happened. The point of the movie is to illustrate that there is no absolute reality, rather each person's individual perception of it.

Control Room[9] is a documentary about the 2003 invasion of Iraq as perceived by the producers and journalists of the Arab network Al Jazeera and by various Americans from President Bush to the young lieutenant in charge of military media headquarters. Their perceptions are explored and compared: their perceptions about the war—its rationale, its progress, its consequences—and their perceptions about Arab and American culture, and about Arab and American leaders. The stories told by Al Jazeera and the images transmitted on their network are very different from the stories told and images transmitted by American journalists on American networks, yet both sides claim to be attempting to present the war's reality to their audiences.

Perceptions about Canada and the United States, whose national cultures are perceived to be one and the same to many foreigners, are often heavily influenced by mass media. Sitcoms and movies are a key source of information about North American culture and newcomers are often surprised to find that their social experience is not exactly that of a TV program they have seen—North Americans are not all wealthy, and not all the girls are available to sleep with. German writer Hans-Christian Bues described his family's surprise on travelling through the United States for the first time and seeing so many obese people. "Our perceptions came from movies—we thought everyone would be slim and beautiful."

> ### CANADA THROUGH THE EYES OF VISITORS
>
> Chief engineer Palma (see Chapter 1) was showing a group of Dutch executives around Toronto on a cold January day in 2004. After the tour, he asked them what they thought.
>
> "It's a wonderful city," they said, "but there is an amazing amount of prostitution here—prostitutes in the doorways of major buildings even in broad daylight, and in this kind of weather! It's incredible."
>
> Palma was mystified until the Dutch explained that they thought all the women and men smoking in doorways on coffee and lunch breaks were prostitutes and potential clients. In the Netherlands, you can smoke inside.
>
> A Japanese magazine, *Canada Japan Journal*, chose St. Catharines, Ontario as the "tourism destination of the year" in 2002. It claimed the Japanese are tiring of the Rockies and Prince Edward Island, and want to see the "real Canada": white people, rolling hills, and people who play hockey. St. Catharines was both surprised and flattered. A previous winner was Yellowknife, for the alleged aphrodisiac powers of the Northern Lights.[10]
>
> What's your perception of "the real Canada"? Of "the real Japan"?

PERCEPTION AND INTERCULTURAL COMPETENCE

Our perceptions of others and our ability to interact effectively with them are coloured by filters. Negative filters include ethnocentrism, Eurocentrism, stereotyping, assumption of similarities, prejudice, racism, and bigotry. Positive filters include cultural knowledge, an understanding of cultural relativism, and mindfulness.

Our perceptions can also be influenced by something as simple as a bad experience: if we travel to a destination expecting the best, two weeks of rain may affect our perceptions of both the place and the people. If we meet one person who treats us rudely, we may come away feeling that this person represents the nation, even if we know intellectually that this is not the case.

Unfortunate experiences cannot always be avoided, but we can teach ourselves to be aware of and control negative filters that we have learned as well as to develop positive ones.

BARRIERS TO INTERCULTURAL COMPETENCE: NEGATIVE PERCEPTUAL FILTERS

Ethnocentrism

Ethnocentrism is the two-part assumption, often unconscious, that our own culture is better than other cultures, and that people from other cultures really want to be like us. It derives from the Greek word *ethnos* meaning *people* or *nation* (*ethnos* is also related to *ethos,* meaning *character*) and the Latin word *centrum,* meaning centre.[11]

Anthropologists generally agree that all human beings are by nature ethnocentric. We label as "good" what we know and "bad" what we don't know. Ethnocentrism derives from a competitive impulse: it is based on group membership and the standing of our own group relative to the standing of other groups.[12] In evolutionary terms, "otherness" represented a possible threat to survival. As a result, human beings simplified their concepts of others to protect and identify themselves as groups and elevate their opinions of themselves. "We" have generally come out better and more interesting than "they," and "they" have come out as simpler and less complex than "we."

Ethnocentrism has been associated with positive social outcomes such as strong social identity, group loyalty, and group survival. However, negative outcomes can include increased competition, fear, anger, hate, and conflict.[13]

HISTORY AND ETHNOCENTRISM

The Chinese once considered everyone outside their borders "barbarians." The characters for China, first written 4000 years ago, meant "centre of the universe." Emigration from China was once considered a capital crime because it was believed that only enemies of the empire would voluntarily leave the greatest civilization on earth. In 1712, the Emperor decreed that anyone who had settled overseas and came back should be beheaded.[14]

During Greece's Golden Age, people who spoke Greek were "cultured," while those who didn't were *barbarikos* (barbarians) because of the *barbar* babbling noises they made.[15]

When Europeans "discovered" America, they viewed Amerindian cultural groups and civilizations as primitive. Pre-Columbian peoples, on the other hand, considered Europeans uncivilized. The Aztecs of Mexico not only feared the Spanish conquistadors, but were shocked by their lack of personal hygiene. Aztecs were instructed to hold handkerchiefs in front of their noses when speaking to the Spaniards.[16]

Expressions of Ethnocentrism

There are degrees of ethnocentrism. It can be subtle, brutal, and just about anything in between. Because it is often a subconscious filter, it frequently reveals an element of naïveté. Individuals, institutions, or nations may perceive themselves to be well meaning and respectful of others, but their actions and words may indicate a deeply embedded, implicit ethnocentrism. In other instances, ethnocentrism is deliberate and explicit: individuals choose to communicate a sense of superiority.

Naïve, unconscious expressions of ethnocentrism include happily pointing out when we are not asked how "we" do things. More offensively, it can be a lack of grace when invited to participate in the customs of others—refusing a glass of water when arriving at someone's home (a common offering in hot climates), for example, or not trying an unfamiliar food item.

More insidious forms include the assumption that our peers are less competent or qualified than we are because they come from elsewhere and their qualifications are from other countries. Deliberate ethnocentrism also includes using pejorative words for other cultural groups, dismissing their traditions as strange or weird, making faces when someone from a different cultural group proposes an idea, and looking down on how people live without taking the effort to find out why. At the extreme end of the continuum is the stereotypical "Ugly American,"[17] an expression that has entered the lexicon and evolved as a metaphor describing anyone who is well-meaning but self-righteous, arrogant, overbearing, politically naïve, lacking in cultural awareness,[18] and for these reasons, potentially dangerous.

People on the receiving end of intended or unintended slights usually notice them. The damage may not be grave, but a thoughtless statement or act, or series of them, can lead to miscommunication, mistrust, or dislike.

How We See Ourselves

Here are some attitudes commonly held by Canadians about themselves and their country. The exercise assumes that Canada has a national culture, something most Canadians tend to agree on. A recent poll indicated that 85 percent of those polled rated 'nation' as the element most important to their personal sense of identity.[19] Which of these statements do you believe to be true?[20]

1. Canadians are nicer than most other people.
2. Canadians are more honest than other people.
3. Canadians treat everybody equally.
4. Canada has a clean record internationally: it has not been involved in "dirty deals" that exploit other countries or people either militarily or economically.

5. Canada's environmental record is one of the world's best.

6. Much of the world population remains poor because, unlike Canadians, people haven't taken the initiative to develop themselves and improve their economies.

7. Canadians are compassionate and contribute heavily to foreign aid.

8. Canadians are the world's foremost peacekeepers.

9. Canada is consistently ranked in the annual United Nations Human Development Report as the best country in which to live.

What theme runs through all of the above statements? Can any of them be verified factually? Some Canadians might object to some of them. Who and why?

REALITY CHECK: CANADA AND FOREIGN AID

The *Reality of Aid* is a report produced by a consortium of aid agencies and development groups in 2004. It ranks G7 countries among others on their contributions to foreign aid as a percentage of gross national income based on 2002 statistics. Canada contributed 0.28 percent, well below Denmark's 0.96 percent, Norway's 0.89 percent, and Sweden's 0.83 percent. France contributed 0.38 percent, the United Kingdom 0.31 percent. G7 countries with marginally lower annual contributions than Canada include Germany, Japan, Italy, and the United States in that order. These countries share the bottom of the list of donors with Greece and Portugal.[21]

REALITY CHECK: CANADA AND THE ENVIRONMENT

According to the Conference Board of Canada, in a study comparing 24 leading industrial countries, Canada came 16th in environmental rankings in 2003. Canada made the top 12 in only five categories. This study is based on 100 economic, social, and environmental indicators, unlike the United Nations Human Development Index which uses four indicators.[22] You might want to look up these studies to see how Canada fares in other areas of comparison.

Eurocentrism

"The best history is like, like real history, like the best history is like European history, because it's like real. . . ."

"I know."

(College student exchange)

Why do you think these students see history this way?

The above conversation is an example of **Eurocentrism,** the belief that European (usually Western European) cultures are superior to non-European cultures. Eurocentrism is a product of the colonial era and at the heart of Western misperceptions about the East (see Chapter 1), and about other cultures colonized by European powers.

It was the prevailing attitude in the Canadian government's relationship with First Nations in the nineteenth and twentieth centuries. Residential schools and the Indian Act are products of this mentality. Residential schools were created to assimilate First Nation children into European Canadian culture while the Indian Act reflected the view of First Nations as 'children' in need of the paternal control of the Canadian government and the Indian Agent, often a European Canadian. Eurocentrism in Canada's attitude towards First Nations continues despite the efforts of both First Nations and other Canadians to dispel it. "Aboriginal peoples have yet to be recognized for their rightful place in Canada," says Harry Laforme, Canada's first Aboriginal appellate judge.[23] He is open about the sense of inferiority with which he still struggles despite his success in the larger Canadian society.

Nineteenth and twentieth century European colonial expansion into Africa, Asia, and Latin America also carried with it Eurocentric views. The term *white man's burden* was coined to refer to the self-imposed obligation European cultures assumed to implant their institutions into the cultural groups they colonized in the belief that European ways were superior and more "civilized." Social Darwinism was another popular 19th and early 20th century European concept based on Darwin's theory of evolution. Social Darwinists believed that the social world mirrored the biological world in terms of "the survival of the fittest"; consequently, technologically advanced European cultures saw themselves as superior to other cultures, and took for granted and considered it "a law of nature" that less technologically advanced cultures would succumb to the more advanced or "fittest." They defined progress largely in terms of the technological sophistication that allowed them to dominate less technologically advanced peoples. They failed to understand, however, that the main conquerors of the New World were, in fact, Old World germs and viruses, not technological superiority.[24]

Can you think of any examples of Eurocentric policies of individuals, institutions, or nations evident in the world today?

The Rejection of Cultural Identity

Sometimes people reject their ethnic or cultural identity. When Tunisia was a French protectorate in the early part of the twentieth century, its population consisted of mainly Muslim Tunisians with a few French and Italian colonials and a small Jewish community. In *Portrait du colonisé (Portrait of the Colonized)*,[25] Albert Memmi described the attempts of the Jewish population to transform themselves into Europeans. They thought the West was the height of civilization and culture and, unlike the Muslim community, adopted French language, Italian clothes, and European ways in rejection of all that was Eastern. Memmi considered this an example of "identifying with the aggressor," a psychological defence mechanism whereby people try to transform themselves into "the other" when under assault or perceived assault. Individuals may do so after a trauma, or out of fear, and cultural groups also may do so when they are in a colonial or colonial-like relationship.

Can you think of instances where cultural groups modify or have modified their personalities or physical characteristics to be more like a cultural group perceived to be more successful or powerful?

Are there instances where cultural groups, particularly young people within them, modify their behaviour and physical characteristics just for fun—to try out a new identity? For example, Japanese girls may bleach their hair blond. Is there always underlying psychological trauma, or is "just for fun" sometimes "just for fun"?

Appropriation of Cultural Identity

The postcolonial era is witnessing the rebirth of cultural pride among groups formerly colonized. It has also brought into focus the postmodern preoccupation with **cultural appropriation,** the taking over of aspects of another group's cultural identity as if they are one's own. At heart is the question: does anyone have the right to take on the voice (through music or literature, for example) of an ethnic or cultural group to which they do not belong? Does a white person like Madonna, much as she may admire black culture, have the right to cast herself as black by inclination? Could she understand the experience of being black? Or is her appropriation an example of misuse of power, lack of respect, and exploitation of the inequity between blacks and whites in American culture? She chooses blondeness despite her appropriation of stereotypes of black sexuality, because blonde, white, and innocent represent the American female ideal. In so doing, she perpetuates white supremacy, and, in her videos and performances, dominates, exploits, and humiliates blacks even as she appropriates their moves.[26] "Like a Prayer," sung at the Live 8 Concert in London, used blacks as cultural backdrop, with Ethiopian famine survivor Birhan Weldu, voiceless and passive, led around by the hand by a powerful blonde successful Madonna, dressed in white.

Can a novel written from the point of view of a man by a woman, or vice versa, have an authentic voice?

Stereotyping

Stereotype (from the Greek *stereos* meaning hard and *typos* meaning model)[27] has several meanings. In printing, it is a metal plate taken from a mold of a page of set type, a fixed printing surface from which to make copies.

In human relations, it is a fixed and overgeneralized notion of a person or group of people held by an individual or group of other people. Stereotyping dismisses the uniqueness and complexity of individuals and brushes off critical, objective, and analytical thinking about them. In the end, it is a misrepresentation, putdown, and form of labelling. Stereotypes can be positive or negative, but either way, they are simplistic assessments. "Chinese people are good at math," "Maritimers are friendly," and "Cubans are good dancers" may be attempts at compliments, but do not account for the feelings of Chinese people who aren't good at math, or Cubans who account for the feelings of Chinese people who aren't good at math, or Cubans who can't dance, or Maritimers who find the stereotype condescending. Statements like "Argentines are arrogant" or "Albertans are rednecks," on the other hand, are negative stereotypes.

In contrast to ethnocentrism, which is grounded in competition and a desire to feel superior, stereotyping is grounded in an effort to understand.[28] People stereotype because it helps them categorize large amounts of information about others into manageable bits.[29] Because human beings are inherently anxiety-prone, we create stereotypes to reduce the threat of the unknown by making it predictable.[30] In the context of culture, if we can assign a few labels to Mexicans, or Italians, or South Asians, our sense of security is increased because we feel we know something about them.

The tendency to stereotype is not limited to any particular culture: as a species, we do it, and within the same culture, we judge and stereotype other individuals or groups. We might think all old people are cranky, or all religious fundamentalists are terrorists-in-waiting, or all conservatives are unfettered capitalists, or all rich people are penny pinchers. The power of our organizational filters is hard to overcome and we don't easily give up our stereotypes.[31] "Others" are always a mystery to us until we take the trouble to learn about them as individuals.

Popular wisdom has it that travel broadens the mind, but travellers who lack cultural knowledge run the risk of confirming preconceived notions they may have, thereby supporting stereotyping because of the human tendency to perceive selectively pieces of new information that correspond to images they already have.[32] And so stereotypes can perpetuate and reinforce themselves among the well-travelled and supposedly knowledgeable.

Groups may **autostereotype** themselves by taking on others' images of them.[33] What stereotype of Canadians does this joke play on?

> *How do you get 10 Canadians out of your swimming pool?*
> *Say to them, "Please get out of my swimming pool."*[34]

Often buried deep within a stereotype is a grain of truth related to what may be a common practice or custom of a cultural group. Nonetheless, to assume that everyone of that culture blindly is, believes, or practises something is to stereotype them.

Generalizing and "Mindful Stereotyping"[35]

While stereotyping inhibits our ability to appreciate individuals, generalizing about cultural groups is sometimes necessary as a starting point in our attempts to understand them. It is difficult to talk about cultures without some generalization.[36] Generalizations may be relatively accurate about groups, but are never wholly true of individuals.[37] There is always a broad range of behaviour in any group, but certain traits or preferences may predominate. Many Canadians like donuts, beer, and hockey, but that doesn't mean we all do.

Ting-Toomey differentiates between "mindless stereotyping" and "mindful stereotyping."[38] Mindless stereotyping shows a closed mind-set while mindful stereotyping (generalizing) implies a willingness to change stereotypes we may hold upon closer inspection, firsthand contact, and increased knowledge.

Geri-Ann Galanti is a California nurse who worked with patients whose beliefs and practices deviated from those of the American health care system. Her experience taught her that "A stereotype is an ending point. No attempt is made to learn whether the individual in question fits the statement. . . . A generalization, on the other hand, is a beginning point. It indicates common trends, but further information is needed to ascertain whether the statement is appropriate to a particular individual."[39]

For example, she might start with an assumption such as "Mexicans traditionally have large families" when she meets Rosa, a Mexican. If she says to herself, "Rosa is Mexican—she must have a large family" she is stereotyping. But if she thinks Mexicans often have large families and wonders if Rosa does, she is generalizing.

When caring for Hispanic or Asian or Middle Eastern patients, having studied and observed their medical cultures, she was able to make generalizations about their health beliefs and practices with the aim of caring for them more sensitively and effectively.

HOW OTHERS SEE US

What stereotypes about Canadians have you heard of? Think of four or five common stereotypes held by others about Canadians. Is there a kernel of truth buried in the stereotype? If so, what might it stem from?

Assumption of Similarities

Underlying ethnocentrism is the belief that all human beings are the same at heart. This assumption of similarity is dangerous because it does not recognize and accept that other people operate successfully according to "different principles of reality."[40] The "They are just like the folks back home" syndrome[41] and the "people are people everywhere"[42] happy thought are among the most persistent and widely held misperceptions about others.[43]

We assume this because the thought that deep down everyone is the same, feels the same, wants the same, is comforting.[44] It leads directly, however, to ethnocentrism, part of which holds that everyone would really like to be like us. This "myth of similarity" is particularly dangerous as elements of Western culture spread across the globe and increase the illusion of similarity while negating genuine differences in behaviours, values, and feelings among different cultural groups.

To overcome ethnocentrism, we need to shift from a belief in one reality (ours) to a respect for multiple realities.[45] Ethnocentrism prevents us from seeing things in other cultures that we admire or share. Tamara Benoît spent a summer in Egypt as the artist on an archaeological dig. Before leaving home, she automatically assumed that Egyptians would envy Canadians for their freedoms and material wealth. But once there, she found herself envying the Egyptian sense of family and community, and was disappointed that some people did indeed express admiration for microwaves and Western life. Her tender portrait of an Egyptian woman in *hijab* trying to keep her face veil in place by holding it between her teeth while simultaneously buying vegetables in the market, carrying one child, and holding the hand of another shows Tamara's appreciation for the new reality in which she was immersed. It is also a portrait of motherhood, something which she could share with many of the Egyptian women she observed despite genuine cultural differences (see illustration, page 44).

Tamara was able to shift from her original ethnocentric belief in the superiority of the Canadian reality to an appreciation of aspects of Egyptian culture. Her experience was an object lesson in the recognition of multiple realities.

The function and frequency of smiling across cultures can be used as a typical example of misperceptions caused by the assumption of similarities.[46] Japanese students in the United States may not know what to make of the smiles received from complete strangers. "If someone smiles at a complete stranger in Japan, especially at a girl, she can assume he is either a sexual maniac or an impolite person."[47] Americans in France tend to perceive the French as cold because they do not smile as frequently as do Americans, while the French tend to be mystified by the frequent smiles of Americans.

Hijab is a headscarf covering the face and hair of Muslim women.

Source: Reprinted with permission of Tamara Benoît, School of Design and Visual Arts, Georgian College.

Prejudice and Racism

Stereotyping and ethnocentrism can be stepping stones to prejudice and racism.

Prejudice, or *pre-judging,* is a negative perception of others without regard for facts or information. It implies intolerance and irrational generalizations about groups or individuals on the basis of such things as race, social class, sexual orientation, gender, language, age, religion, and sexuality. Prejudice is an emotional reaction to others based on strong beliefs about morality and behaviour.[48] Prejudices are learned, and acted out in many ways.

Blatant prejudice is open, and includes negative actions and statements about the targeted group: "they should go back where they came from"; "they are lazy," or "dirty," or "uncivilized." Other forms of prejudice are subtler but equally insidious. They can be practised by individuals or institutionalized in society. Here are a few examples:

1. People express concern that disadvantaged groups have an advantage over dominant groups in some way. A comment such as "First Nations get free education and don't pay taxes—that's not fair" is an example. How would you counter this?

2. People preface remarks with, "I'm not prejudiced but . . ." Students sometimes begin this way, and at the same time glance over at an international student or Canadian from a minority group. They may be trying to show sensitivity, although it can embarrass the student it is intended to reassure. Why do you think people preface comments this way?

One student began with "I'm not prejudiced but . . .," and then asked why students from India always seemed to hang out together. Her remark may be a sign of prejudice, or it may imply a lack of international or minority experience. Either way, how would you answer the question?

3. Prejudice can also be reinforced or transmitted by the media. News media may regularly present a negative portrayal of certain cultural groups without adequately balancing bad news with positive. Sitcoms and movies often stereotype cultural groups. Can you think of groups that suffer from a media bias? Why do you think media stereotype in this way?

4. Educational institutions have practised prejudice by automatically favouring certain groups over others, for example, in administering "intelligence" tests based on information more readily available to some than to others and by celebrating or acknowledging only Christian holidays.[49]

    Teachers sometimes call on members of minorities when the topic of discussion relates to that minority, as if that person is automatically an expert or speaks for the group.

5. Political parties in Canada occasionally foster prejudice and division by "appealing to the ethnic vote" rather than campaigning to show how all issues are important to all Canadians. Jacques Parizeau, former leader of the Parti Québécois, blamed in part the ethnic vote for the defeat of the Quebec sovereignty vote in 1995 to the dismay of both his followers and opponents. Conservative leader Stephen Harper appealed to conservative religious minority groups to oppose same-sex marriage.[50] And in 1999, the Ontario Progressive Conservatives conducted a poll to find out if Canadians would be "comfortable voting for a 'member' of the Canadian Jewish Congress."[51] A public outcry resulted in an apology.

Racism is based on the belief, unsubstantiated by science, that some "races" are superior to others in terms of intelligence or inherent moral character. A variety of aggression with the aim of devaluing others,[52] racism is at the heart of Eurocentrism and movements like Nazism and neo-Nazism, and the Ku Klux Klan organization. Ironically, the "racial purity" espoused by these movements is virtually nonexistent: human beings have been to-ing and fro-ing and interbreeding across continents for thousands of years. Norse traders, for example, co-existed with Mongols and Slavs on the steppes of the Ukraine, and mingled with Celts in Ireland and Anglo-Saxons elsewhere over a thousand years ago.

Eban Inkumsah, a Ghanaian-born Canadian, reported that when he gets into an elevator, women have clutched their purses and said things like "I don't have any cash on me." He is angry and hurt enough by such incidents to have come to the conclusion that "multiculturalism is a joke" in Canada.

Racism is not limited to Europeans.[53] Arabs, for example, have historically felt superior to black Africans and traded them as slaves. African migrant workers in Libya and Filipino and South Asian workers in the Gulf States also typically suffer human rights violations.[54]

However, the very concept of race is becoming clearer as geneticists discover more about the evolution of human beings.[55] Varying regional characteristics like eye, skin, and hair colour have evolved due to factors related to geography and the wandering of groups of people from a common origin in Africa to different parts of the world over time.

In African latitudes where human beings are exposed to much direct sunlight, skin, eye, and hair colours remained dark because they contain more melanin than light-coloured skin or hair. Melanin is a dark pigment that protects the body from harmful ultraviolet rays. Over time, groups who migrated to European regions needed less melanin for protection. Paler skin facilitated the absorption of more light, which in turn led to the ability to synthesize Vitamin D in shorter periods of time. In addition, because of colder temperatures, European migrants wore more clothes thus exposing less skin and requiring the body to do more work to synthesize Vitamin D.

Migratory groups who settled in cold regions like Siberia, such as the Chuchki of Eastern Siberia, adapted to the environment by reducing the area of body surface to keep heat from escaping. They have relatively short legs, arms, and fingers. Before the end of the last Ice Age, an offshoot of this group crossed to North America and evolved into the Inuit of the Arctic.

According to geneticist Spencer Wells,[56] we are all African under the skin, and only 2000 generations separate us from our African origins.

RACE AND CULTURAL IDENTITY

Race less and less accurately defines cultural identity in societies where generations of miscegenation have occurred. Tiger Woods refuses to be pigeon-holed into orthodox racial classifications. He calls himself "Cablinasian" to reflect his Caucasian, black, Indian, and Asian ancestry.[57]

Cablinasian is Woods' avowed cultural identity, the image he has of himself; **ascribed** cultural **identity** is the one other people assign us. Ascribed and **avowed identities** do not always correspond. Why not?

Both Canadian and American census takers have devised new terms to incorporate changing definitions of ethnic, cultural, and racial identity (see Chapter 1).

Discrimination

Discrimination is negative treatment of individuals or groups based on prejudice or racism. It can be personal and it can be systemic. Canada's Charter of Rights and Freedoms was expressly designed to protect individuals and groups from policies and practices that discriminate on the basis of race, ethnicity, language, sexual orientation, and religion. The Charter is increasingly used by groups to challenge laws perceived to be discriminatory.

Growing intolerance towards racism and prejudice in Canada gradually led to changes in immigration policy. In 1896, immigration minister Clifford Sifton crafted a policy to populate the West based on newcomers' ability to assimilate to the perceived superior Anglo-Celtic dominant culture. This is how immigrants in Winnipeg were ranked by author J.S. Woodsworth in 1909 (see Figure 2.2).

A head tax on all Chinese immigrants between 1885 and 1903 was imposed to reduce immigration from China. Other actions barred South Asians and Asians. Between 1923 and 1947, all Chinese were excluded on the basis of race. After World War II, the Canadian government favoured certain ethnic groups over others (Dutch and Germans over Jews and Italians, for example), but the combination of decreasing tolerance for racism and the need for labour expanded the list of "acceptables." In 1951, Canada signed an agreement with the newly independent governments of India and Pakistan to accept

Figure 2.2 Woodsworth's "Ethnic Pecking Order"[58]

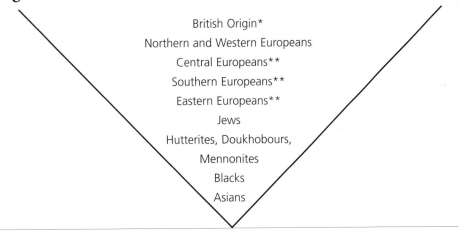

British Origin*
Northern and Western Europeans
Central Europeans**
Southern Europeans**
Eastern Europeans**
Jews
Hutterites, Doukhobours,
Mennonites
Blacks
Asians

*United Kingdom, Ontario, the United States
**poor, diseased, illiterate, morally lax, politically corrupt—possibly acceptable for farming
Source: Adapted from "The Peopling of Canada, 1891–1921, 1946–1976," from *A Province of Immigrants: The Face of Prejudice,* © 1997, The Applied History of Research Group, The University of Calgary. http://www.ucalgary.ca/applied_history/tutor/calgary/pecking.html, accessed May 9, 2005.

a limited number of immigrants from these now sister Commonwealth countries. The list has gradually grown to make Canada the multicultural mosaic, or pluralistic society, it is today. We have, in short, come a long way.[59]

That said, the reality of discrimination has not disappeared. An "ethnic pecking order" persists in society. Members of ethnic or linguistic minorities in Canada who have been socialized and self-identify as Canadian may have their Canadianness, intelligence, or integrity questioned by members of the dominant culture. There also exists a regional cultural bias—Newfoundlanders, for example, are the target of "Newfie" jokes.

The Centre for Research and Information on Canada reports that 74 percent of respondents believe there is still a lot of racism left in Canada, with women (80 percent) more likely to believe so than men (24 percent). However, 65 percent said that "at work or at school, just about everyone succeeds or fails on the basis of how well they do their work." Visible minorities were more likely to say that prejudice is a factor for many people at school or work, with 42 percent agreeing.[60] A question on police and their dealings with minorities revealed that a majority of visible minority respondents believe that black and Aboriginal people are treated unfairly by police, compared to 40 percent of other respondents.

Racial profiling is a form of discrimination based on race where law enforcement officers, potential employers, "people in elevators," and others take race into account in reacting to or dealing with visible minorities. First Nations continue to be over represented in the criminal justice system, and Canada's attention has been brought to the tragic deaths by freezing of Aboriginals like 17-year-old Neil Stonechild, abandoned in sub-zero temperatures outside Saskatoon by police in 1990.[61] A 2002 series of articles in the *Toronto Star* revealed incidences of racial profiling against blacks in Toronto. Minor offences resulted in arrests more often than not in the case of blacks, contrary to the experience of other Canadians, and they were stopped or detained simply on the basis of colour in many instances.[62]

GLOBAL RACISM

In 1994, Rwanda experienced cultural genocide when the majority Hutus massacred 800 000 Tutsis as the international community watched and did little despite the pleas of Canada's General Roméo Dallaire who was in charge of the small United Nations force there. He has since said that he believes the world did not respond in part because the victims and perpetrators were Africans.[63] What do you think? Is this an example of racism at the international level? Is the international delay in dealing with what appears, at this writing, to be cultural genocide in the Darfur region of Sudan also an example of racism on the part of the world community? What other reasons might there be for the world's hesitation?

Bigotry

Bigotry is a general term that describes ignorance, intolerance, and prejudice regarding the opinions, practices, and beliefs of others.[64] A person who holds such views is called a bigot.

Bigotry and Prejudice in Canada

Statistics Canada released a report in 2004 that compiled information regarding hate crime in Canada. Twelve major police forces provided information for the report that, while incomplete, provides a glimpse into prejudice in Canada.

According to the report, 57 percent of 928 reported hate crimes were motivated by race or ethnicity, 43 percent by religion, and 10 percent by sexual orientation. "Other" accounted for 8 percent. The largest target group was Jewish people, followed by black, followed by Muslim, then South Asian.[65]

AIDS TO INTERCULTURAL COMPETENCE: POSITIVE PERCEPTUAL FILTERS

Knowledge

The foundation of intercultural competence is knowledge about our own and others' **cultural patterns** (patterns of thought and behaviour). The behaviours of others are not the problem; rather, it is our expectations about behaviours that cause misunderstanding or frustration.[66] The ways to prevent it are to stop assuming other people are like us or want to be like us, to become aware of our own cultural patterns, and to observe the cultural patterns of others with whom we interact. (Chapters 3 to 8 explore cultural patterns in depth.)

Cultural Relativism

Cultural relativism (or ethnorelativism) is a lens that counterbalances the instinct towards ethnocentrism,[67] which dominated European colonial attitudes and justified itself with pseudo-scientific theory. Cultural relativism fits into the larger context of postmodernism's assertions that truth is multifaceted and morality is relative, making terms like "good" and "bad" and "right" and "wrong" meaningless. Cultural relativism is premised on the belief that cultures are "different but equal" and on the idea that we can understand another cultural group's behaviour by entering *its* frame of reference rather than evaluating it from the perspective of our own and how we do things.

Ethnorelativism acknowledges that cultural patterns are not universal, or even comparable, having emerged from different traditions and moral responses to issues of survival. Ethnorelativism respects multiple realities and differing moralities.

Internalizing the concept of multiple realities of equal value takes time, experience, and openness. Until after World War II, most human beings didn't have to understand their own or anyone else's behaviour, since the behaviour of the people they were likely to encounter was largely predictable and didn't require cultural insight.[68] But decolonization, mass migration, and globalization have made the world less insular.

The "Airport Incident" below is an example of a moment where two responses are possible: an ethnocentric and an ethnorelative one.

AIRPORT INCIDENT

This incident occurred in a Canadian airport in 2003. A Canadian woman noticed a family waiting for a flight. The woman was dressed in *hijab* and the man in a *dish-dasha* (the full-length cotton robe worn in the Gulf and Saudi Arabia). Two children, a boy of about six, and a girl of about eight, were waiting with them. The little girl was playing and dropped her purse, and the father, with a gesture, instructed the boy to beat the girl. The girl did not resist. The Canadian was horrified and approached the family. "This is Canada," she said, "and we don't allow this here." The father stopped the little boy but was angry.

Analysis

Did the Canadian do the right thing? Was her response ethnocentric or ethnorelative? What was the Arab father* trying to teach the children? How were the representatives of the two cultural groups left feeling about each other? To help you in your discussion, it's important to know that in Arab families, the father is absolutely responsible for the home and family. It is his duty to ensure that his daughters are marriageable. Should something happen to him, the son assumes that responsibility.

Also, beating, like spanking in Canadian families, is not a form of discipline in all Arab families.

*The family was Arab in origin, but may have been Canadian in terms of nationality.

Cultural Relativism and Ethics

Sometimes people think that being interculturally sensitive might require them to give up ethical or moral principles about what is right and what is wrong. This is a misconception. For example, the statement "It is good to have three wives" is substantially different from the statement "It is good to know that forms of marriage are evaluated differently in different cultures."[69] In other words, we may not agree, but we need to be aware that there are other sets of ethical or moral guidelines.

Some people hold the universalist position that ethics go beyond culture—that deep down, all humans have the same ideas about what is right and wrong and that postmodernism's concept of moral relativity is unfounded. The universalist view is close to ethnocentrism ("my views are the right ones") or the assumption of similarities ("we all think the same at heart") and can contribute to cultural conflict.

Extreme cultural and moral relativism is also difficult to justify. An extreme cultural relativist would logically have to accept the views of Nazis and pro-apartheid South Africans, both of whom perpetuated policies and social systems based on racism, on the basis that their views were valid within the context of their cultures at the time.

There is a middle road. Ethics can be a combination of universalism and moral relativism in recognition that "all ethics involve a tension between what is universal and what is relative."[70] Together, they are flexible, strong, and able to deal with the complexities of human behaviours; separate, both are rigid and unworkable.

How do you react to these cultural practices: female genital mutilation, polygamy, child labour, spanking of children, preference for male children, wearing of *hijab*, wearing Sikh daggers in Canadian schools, capital punishment?

Mindful Awareness

Mindfulness is a term associated with Buddhism (see Chapter 6). It implies empathy, reflection, and compassion, and mirrors a First Nation belief that sees the foundation of communication as interaction with others in a spirit of kindness, from an internal "place of kindness."[71] We can practise mindful awareness and communicating with cultural kindness in a few simple ways.

Word Usage

There is a danger in using such words as "primitive" and "civilized."[72] Eurocentric Western belief tends to equate technological progress, technical sophistication in the arts and sciences, and even Judeo-Christian religion with "civilization."

Often forgotten is that other cultures value other qualities and achievements that elevate their culture from their point of view. The Dogon of Mali live in a remote valley beneath the Cliffs of Bandiagara. By Western technological standards, they live a basic, agricultural, pre-industrial existence—a primitive existence, some would say. And yet, they have developed a society very sophisticated in terms of social respect. A Dogon doesn't greet another person with something as simple as "Hi, how are you?" A Dogon ritually asks not only about the individual, but also about each relative. Greetings and their responses take some time—in short, they are, from the Dogon point of view, "civilized."

Most of us no longer use terms such as "underdeveloped" to describe other countries. Even the terms "developing" and "developed" carry an ethnocentric, Western twist.[73] Attempts to come up with appropriate terms have included LDC (less developed country) and LEDC (less economically developed country); MDC (more developed country) and MEDC (more economically developed country); NIC (newly industrialized country); NIE (newly industrialized economy); and preliterate and preindustrial societies. To some degree, all of these terms evoked the image of a pyramid with developed countries at the top and a descending hierarchy of others beneath.

"Third World" is another term that is based on an attempt to avoid implicit superiority in terminology. It originally represented countries that fell neither into the First (democratic, capitalist) World nor the Second (communist) World. Since the fall of the Soviet Union in 1991, "**First World**" has come to refer to all developed countries, and Second is no longer used. "**Third World**" now refers to less economically developed countries in general. (Fourth World is a term seldom used, and refers to indigenous communities within wealthier nation states and regions that are excluded from participating in the global economy.)

"**North**" and "**South**" involve another set of assumptions but also represent an attempt to avoid ethnocentrism. The point is to be aware of the meaning of terms and to train ourselves to move away from assumptions of superiority and inferiority in the words we use.[74]

DEVELOPED AND DEVELOPING

What are the criteria used to establish development? Do some research and list some indices of development:

1.
2.
3.
4.
5.

Poverty

Why are people poor? Why do so many people go hungry? What are "the politics of food" in the modern world?

It is important to remember that so-called developed countries have regions and minorities living in developing or Third World conditions, and so-called developing or Third World countries have minorities living in developed or First World conditions. First Nation peoples living in some First Nation communities in Canada live in what can be described as Third World conditions. Popular movies like *Y tu mamá también*,[75] set in Mexico, and *Monsoon Wedding*,[76] set in India, depict the First World, middle- and upper-middle-class lives of people in these otherwise developing countries. India and Thailand, supposedly developing countries, both rejected aid after the tsunami crisis on the basis of their own ability to provide for their citizens.

Certain terms are unacceptable. They include such expressions as "getting gypped," "Indian giver," "Jew down," and pejorative names for ethnic groups. Such speech increases the psychological distance between the speaker and members of other groups.[77]

Finally, a warning about the word "tolerant." Canadians often pride themselves on their "tolerance." Linguist Max Figueroa Esteva, a fluent speaker of nine languages and worldwide acknowledged expert on Cuban Spanish, suggested that Canadians rethink their use of this word. "Tolerance" implies superiority: the "tolerant" person feels superior, but lets the inferior be what he or she is. Max suggested Canadians learn to replace the word "tolerant" with "respectful," and the word "tolerance" with "respect" to better reflect Canada's commitment to pluralism and to phase out an example of ethnocentrism in our thinking and language use.

Sometimes when students discuss discrimination, white students hesitate to use or apologize for using the word "black." Black students often respond by saying, "That's okay. You can use the word!" Why do you think some people are afraid of the word "black"? Students have also asked if it is okay to use the word "Jew." Why do you think they are afraid of this word?

Mindful Observation

Mindful observation is "being aware of our own and others' behaviour in the [a] situation, and paying focused attention to the process of communication taking place between us and dissimilar others."[78] We need to observe and listen carefully, as well as ask questions when clarification is required and actively participate in cross-cultural dialogue while recognizing that our style of communication may be quite different from that of others (see Chapters 7 and 8).

Describing Before Judging

If we focus on description rather than on interpretation or evaluation when observing people and events we can train ourselves to delay judgment. Perception is based largely on the observer's cultural programming and background and evaluating should be postponed until we can interpret from an ethnorelative point of view.[79] An extension of this guideline is to treat our interpretations as working hypotheses.[80] We may alter them as we learn more about a situation and the people involved.

Embracing Paradox

Within each of us and within the various cultural groups to which we belong, there are contradictions, inconsistencies, and paradoxes.[81] "All men are created equal" is a central tenet of American thought, but who got to be equal took several hundred years to work out, and Canadians only slowly opened the doors to diversity. We need to acknowledge our own inconsistencies and accept their existence in others if we are to harmonize our differences and work constructively together. Rather than responding negatively to contradictions as they arise, it is more useful to embrace and use them to work towards inclusive and positive outcomes.

Practising Empathy

Empathy is the ability to put ourselves into someone else's shoes. In intercultural situations and environments, we need to keep in mind the frames of reference and experience of others in order to acquire insight into differing human behaviours.[82]

SUMMARY

This chapter focused on perception and the factors that influence it, and on perceptual filters that help shape our perceptions of truth, reality, ourselves, and others. It discussed both barriers to intercultural competence and the positive foundations upon which intercultural competence and fluency are based.

KEY TERMS

ascribed identity 46	cultural appropriation 40	North/South 52
assumption of similarities 43	cultural patterns 49	perception 31
	cultural relativism 49	perceptual filters 31
autostereotyping 41	discrimination 47	prejudice 44
avowed identity 46	ethnocentrism 35	racial profiling 48
bigotry 49	Eurocentrism 38	racism 45
Cablinasian 46	First/Third World 52	stereotyping 40

TOPICS FOR CRITICAL THINKING AND REFLECTION

1. Are there instances where you have behaved in an ethnocentric way without intending to? Have you ever been on the receiving end of ethnocentric behaviour? Do you think it was deliberate or inadvertent?

2. What is your avowed identity? Does it match, in your experience, your ascribed identity?

3. Policy-makers in pluralistic societies face controversial issues. The Toronto School Board is at this writing considering gathering race-based statistics on school achievement. Those against see it as a form of discrimination[83]; those for claim programs can be developed to improve performance of students in particular groups.[84] Is race an appropriate way to identify and assist academic underachievers in your opinion? How would you resolve the issue of cultural groups and scholastic achievement? Or would you link the two at all?

Another decision involves Muslim students and discussions of same-sex marriage in class. Some Muslim parents asked that their children be excluded from such discussions on the basis of their beliefs. The school board refused arguing that excluding them would violate the rights of children of same-sex parents. "Religious beliefs do not trump human rights" argued a human rights expert on the board.[85] Do you agree?

Quebec does not allow public schools to prohibit Muslim students from wearing head-scarves; however, it does not at this writing have legislation regarding private schools, some of which have banned the wearing of head-scarves. Thirty percent of Quebec students are enrolled in private schools.[86] How do you think the Quebec government should deal with this issue?

4. Locate a copy of your own institution's list of employees—the institution's telephone directory will serve. Are the majority of top administrative and faculty positions held by white males and females with Anglo-Celtic names? Does the hierarchy reflect the cultural diversity of your city or region?

5. Maher Arar is a Syrian-born Canadian who was detained by American officials in New York in 2002 and deported to Syria, despite carrying a Canadian passport, on suspicion of links to al-Qaeda. He spent a year in a Syrian jail. Do you think the treatment of him by Canadian and American officials represents an example of Orientalist thinking or racism?

6. **Case Studies**

Lana

Lana taught English for a company in Japan. Because of the heat, she wore sun dresses to class, and sandals without stockings. Eventually, she decided to ride her bike to class, and changed from shorts and running shoes to her dress and sandals in the company washroom.

Lana upset the other Japanese women teachers there. They dropped hints, but never explicitly told her the dress rules, hoping she would figure them out from their hints and their example. Lana didn't, and they complained to a supervisor that she was embarrassing them. The head of the company spoke to Lana but not forcefully. Lana persisted in wearing what she wanted. ("It was hot.") Ultimately Lana was given a letter outlining appropriate dress code for professionals in Japan: suit, knee-length skirt, stockings, and close-toed shoes. She never knew the full story of the upset she had caused and complained about being passed over for advancement despite her self-described excellent qualifications.

What do you think was the problem? What would you have done in Lana's place?

The French, the English, and the Canadian

This story illustrates not only ethnocentrism, but also the historic rivalry between the English and the French. A Canadian, Cathy, was tramping through Iceland with a group of hikers from England and France. At the end of a long, cold day, they arrived at their destination eager to get at the rudimentary shower on site. The Icelandic guide stipulated that signup for showers was to be individual, and that people were to sign up later at a designated time. Hot water was limited. When Cathy went to sign up, everyone was already there, and much name-calling between the French and the English was taking place (phrases to the effect of "bloody French" and "maudits Anglais" and so forth). As it turned out, one French person had gone early and signed up all the French members of the expedition, and when the Brits went to sign up all the first and best times, because they were guaranteed hot water, were taken. Cathy, a supposedly neutral observer, was asked to solve the stand-off. She successfully did so: what do you think her solution was? (See Appendix I for Cathy's solution.)

Time Out for China: Land of the Dragon[1]

Live long and prosper. (Chinese proverb)
In the new China, you are what you have.[2]

The world is witnessing the transformation of an ancient empire into a twenty-first century superpower. The rise is rapid as China's 1.3 billion people are on the move, hungry for success and international recognition in all spheres of human endeavour: economic, cultural, political, military, artistic, and athletic. China is anxious to put its best face forward to the world for the 2008 Olympics, and the modernization and cleanup of Beijing proceed apace. Meanwhile, spectacular architecture continues to enhance this and other cities whose skylines are etched with cranes and high rises.

Canada is now attracting Chinese investment in addition to large numbers of immigrants, particularly in mining and energy as the demand for the latter is enormous in China's rapid modernization. China is slowly becoming a market for Canadian investors and multinationals, and Canadian entrepreneurs of Chinese descent often set up businesses or serve as advisors and intermediaries; they are invaluable in navigating the cultural, linguistic, and bureaucratic challenges of doing business in China as "the Dragon" awakes from its long slumber and is reborn, for now, into the world's factory.

Keys to Understanding Modern China

Economic Change

1. Communist political rule remains unchallenged in China, but the economic changes instituted in the early 1980s have catapulted it into capitalism, consumerism, and competition. Cars, golf, and European clothing labels are the new status symbols. Consumerism is the new ideology, money the new religion. Unfettered capitalism is giving rise to extreme exploitation of workers by many Chinese entrepreneurs whose wealth is staggering. Wealth, however, is largely an urban phenomenon: there are still 800 million peasants in China.[3]

   Deprivation rules in the rural areas from which workers flock and in the urban sweatshops where they toil. Hospitals are supposedly free, but urgent surgery in Shanghai requires substantial bribes to poorly paid surgeons. "There's more genuine socialism in Alberta," writes Ian Brown.[4]

Social Change

1. Economic change has bred social change, although thus far the social revolution is urban. In large cities like Shanghai and Beijing, Chinese citizens interact daily with foreigners and absorb new ideas. Work is valued, but exploited workers live in desperate poverty and work in environmentally questionable and unsafe conditions[5]: "decades of cradle-to-grave collectivism [had] left everyone convinced it was better to receive than to give . . . The Cultural Revolution followed by two decades of me-first capitalism [had] wiped out the last vestiges of empathy."[6]

2. China's deepest values and traditions have endured for thousands of years; its traditional worldview and value system are based on balance and harmony, obedience to authority, and obligation. The importance of the family and collective was established early, and reinforced by over half a century of communist rule.

    The value placed on family endures, but will the shape of family change? The concept of the collective stops there for many in the new China. Otherwise, individualism is on the rise. Urban one-child families have showered all their resources, affection, and ambition on a new "Me Generation"[7] on whom Western movies, Western fashions, and Western values are making their mark. In Shanghai, fitness classes are the rage, and plastic surgery to create "Western" eyelid folds, or squarer jaws is popular.[8] Restaurants have greeters, Wal-Mart style,[9] and wealth, power, and status are the new China's values, at least in the glamour of Chinese cities.[10]

    Are conspicuous consumption and the pursuit of wealth changes in historic values, however? Perhaps not. . . . Confucius praised prosperity,[11] and Chinese New Year's wishes focus on long life and prosperity. The Chinese approach to materialism is not associated with Calvinistic guilt: it is culturally acceptable, in fact, overtly encouraged, to get rich.[12]

Nationalism Reborn

1. Pride in its long history, the world's oldest continuous civilization, marks much of China's worldview. The vast nation of majority Han Chinese saw others as barbarians, including the ethnic minorities that still inhabit the fringes of the empire. Minorities are disadvantaged and subject to racism and repression of their religions and languages, although increasing tourism to the western reaches of the empire may stem the suppression of non-Han culture. Nationalism along with consumerism is replacing communism. Past injustices are remembered—on the part of Japan, in particular—and China seeks reunion with Taiwan, which it claims. Extreme Chinese nationalists see globalization as a U.S. plot to imprison China, and young urban Chinese are anxious for international respect of their culture.[13]

Cultural Tips

1. Relationships and connections (*guanxi*—see Chapter 8) are still the basis of doing business in China. Rules are flexible. "The rule is no rule, only relationships count."[14] Officials must like you if you are to get through government bureaucracy, and it helps to pick a lawyer on good terms with relevant judges.

2. Facts and figures are not the only bases of doing business: intuition counts, favours are remembered, and the Chinese like to do business with people they like.

3. It is important to understand the concept of face. All players should be seen to be winners in contract negotiations and consensus should be reached without conflict. Intermediaries may be useful.

4. Dinners imply large amounts of food. Men may drink heavily, although women don't. No one should leave feeling hungry or the host will lose face. Dinners start on time and end quickly: "nothing ends faster than a Chinese meal."[15]

5. Indirect communication is the norm (see Chapter 8). Westerners have to get used to reading between the lines in a culture where a direct *no* is considered impolite.

Critical Thinking

1. Should Canada link curbing human rights abuses in China to its increasing desire to do business with the Chinese?

Part II
Understanding Culture

Chapter 3
Exploring Culture

In this chapter we will explore:

- Culture and its components
- Theoretical perspectives on culture
- The purpose of culture
- Cultural universals
- Culture and change
- Culture and individual identity
- Culture realms

All around the world, human beings fight to defend their culture, struggle to preserve it, and parade to celebrate it. Yet vital as we instinctively know our culture to be, it is often a mystery to us, an environment we take for granted and in which we thrive or do not. We may not know what forces have molded it or what it stands for and why. It is like water to a fish, a universe which sustains us and in which we live and breathe, but of which we take little notice. We realize our dependence on it only when we are no longer in it[1] or when it is under siege. Just what, then, is this vital element of our lives?

CULTURE

> ## CULTURE: A WORKING DEFINITION
>
> Culture is a set of learned patterns of thought and behaviour shared and passed down by a group of people. It consists of traditions, beliefs, values, norms, and symbols, the meanings and importance of which are shared in varying degrees by members of the community. Culture includes material and artistic objects (artifacts) created and used by the group.[2]
>
> Culture is dynamic and ever changing. When we speak of "a" culture, we are referring to a particular group of people in a particular place at a particular time.[3]

Every word in the basic definition of culture above is significant. The nouns naming its components probably jump out first, but the six characteristics embedded in the definition are equally significant, namely that culture is *created, shared, passed down* from generation to generation, *dynamic, changing,* and *learned.*

We learn our culture through experience; imitation; informal instruction from our parents, peers, and family; formal instruction in schools and other institutions; and through mass media. The process of learning our culture is called enculturation. Culture is neither genetically determined nor biologically inherited. Children who are adopted by Canadians, whether born to Chinese, Salvadoran, Romanian, or other parents, grow up enculturated into Canadian culture unless their adoptive parents make an effort to teach them their birth culture.

Hofstede calls culture "the collective programming of the mind that distinguishes the members of one group or category from another."[4] He refers to cultural patterns as "mental programs" and the "software of the mind,"[5] patterns of thinking, feeling, and potentially acting that are developed in the family and in childhood and reinforced in schools and organizations.

Nancy Bonvillain uses the term **cultural models** to expand the definition of culture.

A cultural model is a construction of reality that is created, shared and transmitted by members of a group. It may not be explicitly stated by participants but it is, nevertheless, used to guide and evaluate behavior. For example, people in all cultures construct models expressing their views of the dimensions of the physical universe, the structure and functioning of their society, and proper ways for people to live and treat each other. Because cultural models are shared and accepted, they are assumed by members to be natural, logical, necessary, and legitimate. As they become a background for behavior, they are not recognized as culturally constructed but, rather, are considered the natural order of life.[6]

These implicit constructions are the *natural order of life* until we come face to face with another set of assumptions about *the natural order of life*—the water in which someone else swims. The cultural patterns we take for granted—concepts of relationships, of social behaviour, of how to communicate, of when to speak and when to stay silent, of how to request, of how to refuse, of *when* to request and *when* to refuse (the list is endless)—are not universal, but behaviours and ideas created by our culture and absorbed and assumed by us to be right.

There is no aspect of life untouched by culture. Food, sports, dress, art, architecture, music, literature, health and healing, education, religion, language, agricultural practices, attitudes towards animals, concepts of beauty . . . everything is assembled under the all-encompassing umbrella of culture. Yet while all cultures contain the same components, every culture is unique. Every culture has developed its own particular responses to the challenge of survival.

According to a theoretical sociological perspective on culture called *functionalism* (the first of four we'll mention in passing in this chapter), all elements of culture have developed to serve the biological and psychological needs of a group. Its customs and social, economic, and political institutions and relations must be read in terms of how they benefit the group and maintain its stability and cohesion.[7]

CULTURE'S COMPONENTS

Traditions, symbols, and behaviours are the external, observable components of culture, while beliefs and values are the invisible core from which emerge the visible components. Culture has variously been compared to an iceberg,[8] and to an onion.[9] Such metaphors evoke the complexity, mystery, and depth of culture. Material culture is a term used to describe the visible, audible, and tangible elements of culture: it forms the surface layers of the onion and the part of an iceberg above water. Ideal culture is the term used to describe what is invisible and intangible: the assumptions about existence, and the values and meanings represented by observable symbols and behavioural norms.

Traditions

Traditions are a cultural group's customs and rituals. They communicate much of what holds meaning for the group. Traditions form part of every cultural group's patterns of behaviour, from food choice to greeting to naming customs, from birth to marriage to funeral rituals. Sometimes they are so ancient we can only speculate as to their origins, so beyond the bounds of recorded history did they originate.

Customs

What is the custom for greeting? For taking leave? For serving food to guests? For eating? Do people eat on the floor and serve themselves from communal serving dishes, or do they sit at a table and pass food around? What is the custom for presenting a business card? For smoking? Do people prefer clay or water pipes?

Our days are structured by custom. Greek men go off to the local coffeehouse after supper; Italian women in small villages sit in the doorways of their homes in the evening and chitchat. The Spanish take a siesta after lunch, and go back to work from mid-afternoon to eight or nine in the evening (although globalization is phasing out that luxury for many). Uruguayans and Argentines eat the last meal of the day after ten o'clock, often close to midnight.

In this section, we'll look at more examples of customs around the world.

Food Customs: Traditional cuisines have often evolved in relationship to climate and geography. Northern China is cool and conducive to the cultivation of wheat. Noodles made from wheat flour are a basic ingredient of its cuisine. Southern China, where it is warm, is rice based. Wheat was the staple grain of Europe, corn of the Americas. Northern French and Belgian cuisines are famous for butter and cream-based sauces because cows thrive in this part of Europe. Southern France, like Italy and Greece, has a Mediterranean climate and bases its cuisine on olive oil. The land is too dry for cows, but ideal for olives (and goats, hence goat cheeses).

What a culture defines as food derives from the plants and animals with which it has come into contact and what it has collectively decided to call food.[10] Guinea pigs are food in the Andes, pets in Canada; grasshoppers are food in parts of Africa but pests on the prairies; seals are food in the Arctic; horses are food in France. Potatoes are a staple in the Andes, introduced to Europe after 1492. Europeans also brought back squash and tomatoes, without which much Italian cuisine would have evolved differently. Europeans brought pigs to America, introducing that staple here. Coffee originated in Arabia, tea in China.

Food customs die hard. Even McDonald's bowed to changes in local menus in recognition of dietary preferences in many of the 121 countries where it operates. In Eastern Canada, it features McLobster Burgers; in France, wine is available; in India, Maharaja Macs are made of lamb; and in South Korea, *kimchi* burgers contain the fermented cabbage that is a staple there. In Uruguay, burgers are bigger than in North America, recognition of the big role beef plays in Uruguayan culture. Marketers call these cultural adaptations "glocalization." In France, many people are up in arms over the appropriation of French cartoon heroes such as Astérix the Gaul now used to promote McDonald's. The McAlexandrie contains eggplant and olive sauce, and the McLutèce contains emmenthal cheese to commemorate the adventures of the comic-book hero, Astérix the Gaul, in his fight against the Romans.[11]

CLIMATE, GEOGRAPHY, AND CULTURE

Climate and geography play a role in many aspects of the development of cultural traditions, not just in food, but also in clothing materials and styles, for example. Why do the Bedouin and other nomadic peoples of the Sahara cover up?

Environment has also played a role in herbs used for healing; in games and sports (Inuit games, for example, focus on the endurance, agility, and patience needed to hunt in the Arctic); and in farming and agricultural practices. How are fields organized in mountainous regions? What does a culture use for fuel? In Andes villages above the tree line, llama dung is used. Climate and geography also play a role in architecture and building materials. What building materials were traditionally used in Egypt? In the Arctic? In the American Southwest? How has climate influenced the construction of homes in Canada?

Cultural materialism is an anthropological theory and is relevant here. It sees the development of cultural elements as adaptations to physical environment. The Inuit and the Bedouin are examples of cultures that have adapted to extreme conditions.[12]

Nowadays, modern technology allows many peoples to transcend physical environment in a way that earlier ages did not. For example, thanks to refrigerated modern transport, Canadians eat tropical fruits year round. Bananas were not known to most North Americans until the 1800s when an enterprising businessman imported a shipment from the Caribbean to New York.[13] And in Dubai, indoor ski resorts now allow vacationers to ski in the desert.

Naming Customs: Names help reveal what is important to a culture. In Arab culture, a boy is often given three names: his own, his father's, and his grandfather's. A little boy in Egypt once announced proudly but uncertainly to me, "My name is Mohammad Mohammad . . . . . Mohammad." Sometimes the names are linked by *bin* or *ibn* (son of) or *bint* in the case of a girl (daughter of). Osama bin Laden is Osama, son of Laden. The name may be given a prefix like *abdul* ("servant of") followed by an attribute of God (*Abdul-Rahmaan* means "servant of the merciful"). *Abu* is common, meaning "father of." *Umm* means "*mother of.*" *Al/El* indicates royalty: Sheik Al-Nahayan, for instance, is part of the Abu Dhabi royal family.[14]

In Chinese culture, the last name is given first as in Mao Zedong.

In Latin America (excluding Brazil) and Spain, a child is given two last names: first the father's, then the mother's. For example, baby Carlos Raul's name is completed by Diaz, his father's last name, followed by Albornoz, his mother's. His full name is Carlos Raul Diaz Albornoz although he may later introduce himself as just Carlos Raul Diaz.

In Iceland, names are patronymic. A girl's last name is her father's first name with the addition of *dóttir*. A boy's last name is his father's with the addition of *son*. So, if baby Margrét is born to Bára and Ólafur, her name is Margrét Ólafur*dóttir*. If a brother, Jóhann, is born, his name is Jóhann Ólafur*son*. Phone books in Iceland use first names.

In Quebec, women do not customarily take their husband's name when they marry.

What do these naming practices suggest about what is important to the cultures above?

Rituals

The word "ritual" has a spiritual connotation not associated with "custom." Rituals are a universal form of communication, visible expressions of deeply held beliefs and group belonging.[15] Many rituals encompass ceremonies and rites revolving around birth, marriage, death, and other meaningful passages of life. They may also involve food preparation, animal slaughter, and dietary laws, such as Jewish *kosher* laws and Muslim *halal* rules. We'll explore just a few rituals in this section.

Birth and Childhood Rituals: The *bris* is a 4000-year-old circumcision ritual performed on Jewish boys eight days after birth. It symbolizes the bond between God and Abraham that is the foundation of the Hebrew nation. Another example of an ancient ritual involves the naming of newborns among the Blood Indians of the Blackfoot tradition. An elder, purified by burning sweetgrass, marks the palm of his hand with red ochre dye and then paints the baby's face with the sign of the tribe. The baby is held up and shown to the sun so that its radiance will follow the child through the circle of his or her life. At this moment, the baby receives a name, identifying the child both as an individual and member of the tribe.[16]

A ritual haircut for boys often signals a passage of life for groups as diverse as Balinese Hindus, Masai warriors of Kenya, orthodox Jews, recruits into armies, and Burmese schoolboys entering a monastery.[17]

What do water and the baptism of babies signify in the Christian tradition?

Initiation Rituals: The rite of passage from childhood to full-fledged membership in society as a responsible adult involves a ritual ceremony for many cultures. Circumcision at puberty is a ritual for both boys and girls in many Muslim and sub-Saharan African cultures. In Egypt, evidence of clitoridectomy has been found on mummies,[18] although internal forces within Egypt and African cultures have led to a reduction in this practice nowadays.

In some Native American cultures, young men were traditionally sent on vision quests from which their name emerged. In Ojibwe culture, every person has a Spirit name dreamed by a respected elder chosen by the young individual. The name is revealed and bestowed in a Naming Ceremony.[19] First Communion for Catholics signifies conscious acceptance of Christ and entrance into the religious community.

Wedding Rituals: Marriage celebrations are as varied as culture itself. In places like Pakistan, Northern India, and Morocco, a bride's hands are elaborately hennaed before

Mehndi (henna) for a bride[20]

Source: © Steven S. Miric/SuperStock

the ceremony. In Vietnam, a bride is accompanied by her family to her new family's home. Chinese and Indian brides wear red for good luck.

Why do brides in Canada, the United States, and Australia traditionally wear veils? What does the new husband's lifting of the veil symbolize? In Europe, throwing rice dates back to the Middle Ages when the new couple was showered with grains and seeds. What do you think this ritual symbolizes? Why do brides carry flowers? The carrying of the bride over the threshold is common across cultures. What does it mean?[21]

Mourning and Funerals: Among Hindus, the dead are cremated as part of the process of returning the body to Earth. Vietnamese Buddhists do not have funeral homes because it is bad luck to touch a dead body—tradition leaves it to the family to prepare and bury the dead. When Peter Le opened a funeral home in Canada, he was shunned by some friends because of potential bad luck.[22] In China's Buddhist tradition, death is a gateway to rebirth, and therefore a time of joy, but wailing and crying are encouraged as signs of love and respect for the deceased.[23] In Cuba, when insufficient mourners were present to cry during the procession to interment, women were traditionally hired to wail along behind. This ritual gave rise to a humorous saying reserved for any event that has not been adequately celebrated: *esta muerte no está bien llorada* ("this death hasn't been well mourned"). In Ireland, wakes are held to celebrate the life of the deceased, and in Canada, funerals are changing to become celebrations of life rather than rituals of sorrow. In Muslim regions, men and women are separated at funeral ceremonies; women raise their voices in a high-pitched trilling cry called ululation, also used at times of joy.

Cemeteries also differ around the world. In Latin America, they are like little cities, with avenues and mausoleums above ground. Cairo's City of the Dead is a series of cemeteries in which people have taken refuge inside and among the mausoleums because of the shortage of housing.

What are some rituals and customs you and your family cherish? Why? Do they relate to religion, to Canadian culture, to your ethnic heritage, or just your family?

Cultural Narratives

Myths, legends, and folktales are the traditional narratives of culture, the stories passed down to explain the origins and evolution of a people. According to Mexican Toltec myth, chocolate was a gift of the Gods to humans; according to Mayan myth, humans emerged from corn. Myths and legends also elevate and recount important moments of a cultural group's journey through time. The Icelandic Sagas, stories once passed down orally to keep alive the myths that sustained the culture, are broadcast now on radio and learned in school. A tsunami in 1700 off the coast of B.C. had such an impact on native cultures there that the event was transformed into a myth about a giant thunderbird fighting a massive whale, which then became an artistic motif in Northwest totem poles, masks, and paintings.[24]

Creation myths are central to a cultural group's mythology. The Bible's account of creation is an article of faith to many Christians, while others read it as a creation myth. How does Genesis explain creation? What are some other accounts of creation you know of?

Folktales are tales that usually contain legendary or mythological elements that are handed down orally. The Irish have their leprechauns, the Icelanders their mean-spirited *hulderfolk,* and the Ashanti of Ghana have the trickster, Anansi the spider. According to structural anthropologists, all folk narratives follow the same basic form, which goes something like this: a hero sets out on a quest, must overcome obstacles in that quest (implying a villain), generally encounters a helper, and ultimately succeeds in the quest.[25] The hero may be human or animal, the helper may have magical qualities, and there are consequences and lessons to be learned from the quest.

Cultural narratives are teaching tools for enculturation that explain:

- How the world works, in general principle and in particular context.
- Our place in the world, in terms of our personal and social identities
- How to act in the world.
- How to evaluate what goes on in the world: what is good or bad, what is safe or dangerous.[26]

Search the web for a folktale from the culture of your choice and be prepared to tell it to the class. What does it teach about the world?

Festivals and Celebrations

Human beings celebrate everything from life to harvests to full moons to death. In Mexico, death gives rise to one of the most important celebrations of the year, the Day of the Dead. On the night of November 1–2, families spend the night in cemeteries honouring departed family members. They place altars to them in their homes, and for weeks ahead celebrate with candy skulls and other mementos both mocking and celebrating death as a fact of life. Chinese New Year is a 15-day festival based on ancient agrarian customs celebrating family and traditions. Diwali, the joyful Hindu Festival of Lights, is celebrated throughout India with the giving out of sweets and the burning of lamps and lights to symbolize goodness and knowledge. In Latin America, families hold a party when a daughter turns 15 in a celebration called the *Fiesta de Quince*. The Scots have Robbie Burns Day to celebrate all things Scottish.

Some festivals have their origins in ancient religious rites. Harvest and spring festivals once part of ancient pagan rituals celebrating nature's bounty have been absorbed and transformed into today's celebrations. Hallowe'en derives from a Celtic harvest festival and celebration of the dead masked by a Christian name designed to absorb it into "all hallows eve" and Christian tradition.

Artistic Traditions

Cultural artistic traditions reflect the human need to create. The development of the arts is often related to religion: Islamic visual art is renowned for its decorative qualities, mainly because Islam forbids the representation of living beings. Western and South Asian art had no such prohibition. Cultural globalization of music has led to the growth of World Music labels and international appeal of artists across cultures. Meanwhile, modern architects often try to design buildings that communicate something of the land where they are built or the culture that they represent.

Search the web for a photo of the Burj Al Arab Hotel in Dubai. What feature of Arab culture does it mirror? Now search for a photo of the First Nations University of Canada in Saskatchewan. Who is the architect and how did he communicate elements of Native culture through its design?

Symbols

A symbol is a representation of something, often of a mystery beyond human comprehension or of a wish or desire or belief. Human beings have used all of nature to represent the mysteries of existence: trees, flowers, gems and stones, the moon and stars, the sun, insects, animals, and colours have all been called into play in our need to visualize our ideas and yearnings. We have further assigned meaning to numbers, designs, and objects of our own creation.

Love, the divine, nature, creation, fertility, mother, hope, mourning, grief, immortality, victory, strength, courage, humility, masculinity, femininity, luck . . . almost every imaginable aspect of life and culture has been symbolized in some way.[27]

Clifford Geertz defines culture in terms of symbols: ". . . man is an animal suspended in webs of significance he himself has spun, I take culture to be those webs, and the analysis of it to be therefore not an experimental science in search of law but an interpretive one in search of meaning."[28]

Universal Symbols

Some symbols transcend cultures. The Tree of Life, for example, is an ancient symbol the world over for "the Great Mother in her nourishing, sheltering form."[29] A tree is rooted deep in the earth yet reaches to the heavens and eternity. It promises rebirth and fertility. The sun is often a symbol of creativity, light, life, and masculine strength, while the moon with its pull on the tides and its cycles often represents woman. The moon also symbolizes water and pregnancy, the dark, and, because of its waxing and waning, the cycle of birth, death, and rebirth. Flowers are a universal symbol of fertility (see Wedding Rituals, pages 68–69).

Jung developed the theory of the "collective unconscious" to explain the recurrence of symbols and rituals across cultures. The collective unconscious is a sort of memory bank of our ancestors' shared and forgotten experiences.[30] Dreams of being pursued by monsters, of running for safety, or of dangers lurking in the dark are universal. Heroes, God figures, mothers recur. Jung termed these universal images "**archetypes.**" We continue to recognize them and connect to them. In movies, plays, and novels we respond to the flash of a message or symbol suggesting the idea of mother, fertility, goodness, harvest, evil. Stephen King is a master in evoking the collective unconscious. He shows us things we are afraid of—being isolated in the snow, losing our minds—and we react like cave dwellers afraid of the dark.

ARCHETYPES AND YOU

Do you believe in the Sasquatch? Bigfoot? What Jungian archetype might they represent?

What does "evil" look like to you? Compare your mental images with those of your classmates! What feelings do they evoke?

What does "the hero" look like to you?

The female principle, which Jung called the "anima," appears in various forms such as mother, goddess, temptress, princess, witch. The masculine principle, or "animus," appears as a god, a king, a prince, a wizard, or a demon. These images in dreams can represent an aspect of ourselves, or a parent or loved one.[31]

The gods, goddesses, and superheroes of today are rock stars and film and sports stars who embody archetypes of powerful and heroic men and admirable women. Like heroes of old, they embody superhuman qualities: Lance Armstrong is a modern hero for conquering cancer and winning the Tour de France; Shania Twain is a modern goddess for her beauty, for overcoming poverty and loss, and for mothering her siblings. Bob Geldof and Bono mobilize the Western world for poverty relief in Africa.

A rock concert can be a spiritual experience. "Instinctual urges can be seen at rock concerts when members of the audience strike matches, light lighters, and hold up candles to express their devotion to their idols. The resultant sea of flames harks back to the symbolism of fire in religions and cultures throughout history."[32]

Another Jungian archetype is the shadow, the dark side of our subconscious, our minds at their most elemental level full of terror or guilt about unspoken fears and desires. In dreams, it can be represented by a forest, a wilderness, or a fearful place such as the woods through which Little Red Riding Hood must walk to meet her grandmother.

Fairy tales often contain elements of magic and archetypal symbols. They both enchant and teach children. What is your favourite one? Psychologists say that your favourite fairy tale contains your own life script!

National Symbols

Nations create symbols to inspire their citizens with patriotism. Flags, images of heroes, historical figures on coins, and animal symbols are chosen to represent the nation and its ideals. Companies, schools, and institutions also create symbols to inspire their workers with loyalty.

Symbols often emerge naturally as a nation develops. When Air Canada accidentally bumped the Stanley Cup off a flight to Fort St. John, B.C. where it was to be viewed, there were cries of outrage. "The Stanley Cup is the holy grail," cried one astonished citizen, according to the *Alaska Highway News*. "The Stanley Cup is the most important non-religious artifact in Canada," claimed the editorial.[33]

Cultural heroes personify the human ideals of a group. They are often associated with noble qualities such as strength, sacrifice, and risk to the point of death to save the nation. Stories and myths grow around a culture's heroes: "Evita" of Argentina, Joan of Arc of France, Ernesto "Che" Guevara of leftist revolutionaries, and many others fall into this category.

Religious figures predominate among some peoples: Italians revere Padre Pio, a humble priest famous for his stigmata. The French revere writers and artists. Modern Dutch heroes, on the other hand, are often bungling, uncompetitive, unachieving characters—anti-heroes who reflect the Dutch unwillingness to create and revere super humans.[34] A popular cartoon character is Ollie B. Bommel (Mr. Bumble), a clumsy and naïve character that even Dutch intellectuals enjoy.

Who are some Canadian heroes? What ideals do they represent?

Religious and Ideological Symbols

Religions are laden with symbols. A *mezuzah,* a little case containing religious texts, is often posted by the door of a Jewish home as a symbol of faith. Christianity has the cross. Islam has the crescent moon and star, often part of an Islamic nation's flag. Judaism has the Star of David. First Nations have the circle, a spiritual symbol of the cyclical journey of life and the unity of nature. In Hinduism and Buddhism, the lotus symbolizes creation: all life emerged from water like the lotus. In Buddhism, it also symbolizes purity and enlightenment. The rose is a universal, therefore archetypal, symbol of love and beauty; in Christian symbolism it is believed to have sprung from a drop of Christ's blood.[35]

The *swastika* is a revolving cross with bent beams. The symbol existed in North American native cultures, and has been a symbol of longevity and good luck throughout eastern Asia for thousands of years, adopted by both Hinduism and Buddhism. In Chinese sculpture, the symbol often appears on the Buddha's chest as an eternal reminder of his teachings and his virtue. It became known in Europe where it was ultimately appropriated, modified, and given a new, horrific ideological meaning by the Nazis.[36]

Smoke has symbolic value in many spiritual traditions. A ceremonial pipe was smoked by First Nations to send smoke to the Creator for a blessing to seal an agreement. Once the Creator sealed a covenant, humans could never go back on their word. Before feasts, sage smoke is wafted over the food and a prayer of thanks offered to the Creator. In Mayan cultures, shamans use smoke to purify people and places, and smoke is symbolic of purification in West African religions and their Afro-Cuban and Brazilian derivatives. In Cuba, when a person lights a cigar, he or she may waft the first puffs of smoke into the corners of the room.

Language

Language is a system of symbols, oral and often written. It is a culture's most important symbolic system the loss of which often signals the death of a culture.

Language is so essential to culture that imposing one is a way of forcing a conquered people to integrate into a dominant culture. In France, this was done systematically through the schools by making "Standard" French the language of instruction in regions where French was not spoken (see Chapter 9). The aim was to encourage nationalism and create a sense of Frenchness among the various linguistic and cultural groups in what we know today as France. In the 1970s, I met an old woman in southwestern France who did not speak French. She had had little schooling and spoke only a dialect of Provençal, the historic language of that region. Today, it would be hard to find a person born in France who did not speak and feel French, although attempts are being made to revive Provençal regional dialects by people who do not want to forget that language.

Spain too is a patchwork of diverse cultures and languages woven into a country, yet there is still dissent from Basques and Catalans. The Catalans have struggled to maintain their language and culture, and have made Barcelona their capital. The Basques continue to speak Euskara and many agitate for an independent state.

The former U.S.S.R. imposed Russian on its various non-Russian Republics. China imposed Mandarin on Tibet after its invasion in 1949. Canada imposed English or French in the now infamous residential schools, where native children were beaten for communicating in their own languages.

In Canada, the language issue has always been central to the fabrication of a national culture out of the two founding European nations, French and English. If anywhere the relationship between culture and language is clear, it is in Quebec, where a language battle is ongoing to maintain its French character. Immigration policy, signage, and language of education laws are designed to promote this end.

Colour Symbolism

Colours are light waves of different lengths. They have no intrinsic meaning. Nonetheless, culture attaches symbolic meaning to colour. In the West, white is the colour of purity. In India and Asia, white evokes sadness: it is worn at funerals and by widows. Among Muslims, white may be worn by people who have made the pilgrimage to Mecca. A white dove is a symbol of peace. Doorways of Tibetan homes often display red, white, blue, and yellow cloths, symbols of fire, cloud, sky, water, and earth. Green is the holy colour of Islam and often appears on the flags of Muslim nations. Red symbolizes good luck and prosperity in Asia.

Number Symbolism

The number 4 in China and Japan is considered unlucky because it is a homonym in Mandarin and Cantonese for death. Conversely, the number 8 is lucky, because it rhymes with getting rich. Many Chinese are willing to pay extra for a licence plate with the number 8, or to live on the 8th floor.[37] In First Nation cultures, the number 4 is good because it relates to the four cardinal points: east, west, north, and south. The number 13 is unlucky in Western culture, because there were 13 people at the Last Supper (Christ and his 12 apostles).

Artifactual Symbolism

Cultures often wear good luck charms or amulets as symbols of protection. The scarab beetle is a good luck charm in Egypt, and a popular souvenir choice for tourists. Totems are animal or plant symbols that represent clans and family lineages among certain Canadian and Australian Aboriginal groups. The Maori twist, often carved from jade, is a symbol of life and the continuity of relationships.

> *Symbolic interactionism* is the second major sociological perspective on culture. Symbolic interactionists believe that human beings are actors who act and interact according to their interpretation of the symbolic meanings of daily events, routines, and actions.[38] We are thus active participants in the maintenance and evolution of our culture, not mere passive vessels of enculturation.

Beliefs, Values, and Norms

Our first impressions of a new cultural environment usually revolve around material culture, which initially enchants us or fails to. We respond to sights, sounds, and tastes, unlikely to be exclaiming as we roam around, "What a nice set of shared values these people have," or "Don't they have an interesting shared system of meaning!"[39] Nonetheless, it is the deeper levels of a culture that define its essence and that we need to understand to be interculturally competent.

Beliefs

Beliefs are fundamental assumptions about what is true. They respond to a need to know about the origins of man, the purpose of life, the existence of God, the meaning of death. Answers are often found in belief systems provided by religions, philosophies, and ideologies such as Marxism and capitalism (see Chapter 6).

> *Conflict theory* is the third major theoretical perspective on culture. Conflict theorists believe that ideologies and religions serve the interests of dominant groups in society who use them to exert power over and exploit groups or classes with less power.[40] Marx, for example, taught that capitalism exploited workers and that religion was "the opiate of the masses."

Cultural traditions that predate modern religions and ideologies are also a source of beliefs. In Asia, Africa, the Middle East, the Mediterranean, and Central America, belief in the evil eye, for example, is widespread.[41] In India, a *bindi,* or black dot is painted between the eyes on the forehead to provide protection from it; this spot is believed to be the place of union between body and spirit and vulnerable to the evil eye. In Arab culture, the colour blue can ward off the evil eye, or conversely, people with blue eyes are believed to have the power to use the evil eye. In Bangladesh, various fungi and bacteria may attack pumpkin crops. Local indigenous people attribute this to the evil eye and hang up inverted earthenware pots painted black with white circles to protect them. In Peru, bull's horns are hung outside the doors of Aymara and Quechua Indians as protection from it.

Values

Our sense of cultural identity is strongly related to the values we hold as a group. Values are beliefs about what is important, what is good, what is fair, and what is right.[42] In many ways, they are the soul of a culture and of its individual members, guidelines for action and behaviour. (Chapter 4 explores Canadian and American cultural values.) Values exist on a continuum of very important to less important, with a core value of all cultures being survival,[43] the premise of the popular *Survivor* reality television series.

Hofstede[44] defines values as fundamental attitudes about life and about people, with a good and a bad dichotomy built in. Dirty contrasts with clean, evil with good, irrational with rational (in Western cultural tradition—see Chapter 5), and so on. Extreme situations may clarify values: we may strongly value life, but if, to save our child, we had to deny another child food, what would we do? Your answer will tell you something about your own deepest values and about the dilemmas faced by people in desperate economic or environmental situations.

Values differ between cultures and between generations of the same culture.

YOUR VALUES

What is important to you? Family? Work? Freedom? Religious faith? Romantic love? Friendship? Appearance? Wealth? Status? Youth? Having fun? Keeping fit? Financial security? Children? Material possessions? "Success"? World peace? Good health? Country? Cleanliness? Marriage? Personal independence? Adventure? Career? The environment? Virginity until marriage? Wisdom? Equality? Other?

Make a list of the five values most important to you. Which five are least important to you? Now place all ten on a continuum from most to least important. Give examples of how your values guide your actions.

Family: The value placed on family is often a major point of comparison across cultures. Cultures that place a high value on family tend to fall into the broad category of collective cultures. They emphasize the value of behaviour that benefits the group rather than behaviour that fulfills the needs of one individual member alone (see Chapters 5 and 6).

Chinese, South Asian, Asian, Latin American, Mediterranean European, and African cultures are examples of cultures in which the bonds that link family members are very deep: everything an individual does is for the maintenance of family survival, family harmony, and family honour. In such cultures, several generations and extended family members may live in the same home, parents are highly involved in children's schooling and career choices, and children feel obliged to follow parental guidance. Elders are highly respected, and children cherished and parented by many people. Marriages may be arranged and divorce is uncommon. Family members pitch in to help other members in need.

The extended family serves both an economic and sociocultural role. In Latin America, for example, if cousins or distant relatives come to seek work in a city where other family members live, they will live with the established family until able to establish their own base. Sometimes, any person from the same town will be considered a family member and be treated the same way. Rajesh Rajan, a student from India, was surprised to meet Canadian students living at home and paying rent—happy about it because they were getting a good deal! This would be unheard of in India, he said.[45] Families, of course, fight and quarrel, but the family in the end almost always holds together.

BUSINESS AND CULTURAL VALUES

If you were doing business in a culture that places a high value on family, what kind of business organization and practices might you expect?

At the root of the value placed on family is the ancient and enduring concept of blood and bloodlines. As a consequence, virginity and chastity for women before marriage have historically ensured the continuation of the legitimate bloodline. Medieval European chastity belts ensured compliance. In strict Muslim cultures, so important is virginity among unmarried women that it is the basis of family honour, and women may be killed by male relatives for breaking the rule.

Blood has value at family, tribal, and sometimes national levels. For example, despite the high costs of reunification and challenges associated with differing values between the former East and West Germany, Germany has repatriated hundreds of thousands of ethnic Germans from former Russian republics over the last fifteen years. They may return if they can prove German ethnicity even if their families have inter-married with others and even if they have lived in Russia for generations.[46]

Absolute and Statistical Norms: A fundamental hypocrisy can exist when people make statements about their values.[47] What they want for the world may not be exactly what they want for themselves. Someone riding around in an SUV with a bumper sticker urging respect for the environment would fall into this category. What is desirable (a clean environment) reflects an absolute norm; a statistical norm reflects reality—what people actually do. All cultures embody contradictions because it is difficult for human beings to live up to their ideals.

Moral relativity is the idea that every society has its own morality and other societies do not have the right to impose theirs on others, there being no verifiable absolute truth about right and wrong. How does this cartoon suggest the dilemma of cultural and moral relativity (see postmodernism, Chapter 1, and ethnorelativism, Chapter 2)?

Source: Reprinted with permission of *The Globe and Mail*.

Values and International Marketing: International marketers try to identify values to better sell their products and adjust marketing campaigns to suit values. Campbell's Soup undertook research with the idea of marketing to Italy, where homemakers spend about 4.5 hours a day making meals in contrast to the 60 minutes spent by North American homemakers. A random poll of Italian homemakers asked this question: "Would you want your son to marry a canned-soup user?" The answer was a resounding no by 99.6 percent.[48] Campbell's did not market its soup in Italy.

Imagine you want to market a line of cosmetics for both men and women in Mexico. What research questions would you ask to learn what products (soaps, perfume, makeup) might sell?

Proverbs and Maxims: Proverbs and maxims mirror a culture's beliefs and values. What do the following proverbs suggest about the values of the cultures from which they have sprung?

I against my brother, my brother and I against our cousin, my brother, cousin and I against our neighbour, and all of us against the foreigner. Bedouin
God helps those who help themselves. American
Life will break your heart. Irish
The heart has reasons the mind cannot know. French
War does not determine who is right, only who is remaining. Finnish
You can't wake up a man who's pretending to be asleep. Uruguayan
God tightens but He never strangles. Cuban
Better to be a fool with the crowd than wise by oneself. Mexican
A family is like a forest. When you are outside, it is dense, but when you are inside, each tree has its place. Ghanaian
A closed mind is like a closed book. A block of wood. Chinese
The speaker is a fool; the listener is wise. Japanese
A rolling stone gathers no moss. English
There are mountains beyond mountains. Haitian
He who is afraid of doing too much always does too little. German
He that wishes to eat the nut does not mind cracking the shell. Polish
If you have soup, why put it in someone else's bowl? (It should go in the family bowl.) Kuwaiti

Norms

Norms are rules about behaviour, guidelines for how individuals should or should not behave. They are often based on values and morality.[49]

Theoretically, each culture reflects in its members the total variation of behaviours. Take, for example, behaviour related to formality and informality: in all cultures, some people will be more formal and others less formal in a given situation, but a norm will emerge for each culture. This may cause misunderstanding between cultures. Americans tend to view the French as arrogant (the norm of behaviour is more reserved in France than in the U.S.) or hierarchical (French culture is more formal than American), while the French tend to view Americans as naïve or aggressive, because American culture tends towards openness and informality.[50]

Sociologists distinguish between *mores*—norms whose violations produce strong moral aversion such as murder or rape, and *folkways*, norms that do not provoke such moral outrage.[51] Few people in Canada, for example, are highly morally outraged by littering, but they may disapprove of it.

Taboos are prohibitions of behaviour. They can reflect deeply held views about life or simple daily activities. Sex and sexuality are at the root of many taboos. Homosexuality is forbidden in Islam. Buddhist monks may not be touched by women. Another taboo in most cultures relates to cannibalism, but is it an absolute taboo? The movie *Alive*,[52] based on the true story of a Uruguayan soccer team whose plane crashed in the Andes leaving them stranded for 45 days, would suggest not.

Some religions have food and eating taboos. Judaism and Islam forbid the eating of pork while Hinduism forbids the slaughter of cows. Muslims may not eat with the left hand—the left hand is reserved for personal hygiene.

Scientists believe they've uncovered practical reasons underlying certain taboos. Why do you think incest is a common prohibition? What would be a danger in eating pork, for example, in very hot climates? How could cows better serve a large and hungry population if they are left to roam rather than be raised, fattened, and slaughtered?

CULTURAL UNIVERSALS

Early anthropologists were interested in finding cultural universals or patterns of behaviour common to all cultures. In the twentieth century, they began to look more for value variations in different cultures' responses to universal problems (see Chapter 5 for classification systems based on values) and concluded that all societies face the same essential problems of existence and that only their answers vary. Their answers—beliefs, ecological choices, social organizational strategies—are what make them unique.[53]

George Murdoch identified some 70 features as universal in human societies.[54] They include structural universals such as division of labour, status differences, and age grading, and cultural features like body adornment, music and dance, greetings and joking, and sexual taboos. However, while cultures have developed practices in each of these areas, they have not addressed them in the same way. Incest seems to be a universal taboo, but different cultures define incest differently. Inca emperors married their sisters, so sacred was the blood line believed to be, and marriage between cousins is common in the Arab and Muslim world.

The need for spirituality is a cultural universal. Geneticist Dean Hamer claims to have discovered a gene or genes for spirituality, raising questions about whether there is a biological basis for faith. Humans are the only animals, as far as we know, that hunger for God or a force outside themselves. Humans may also be the only animals that have self-consciousness—the mind's awareness of being conscious.[55]

Human nature itself is a cultural universal: "The human ability to feel fear, anger, love, joy, sadness, the need to associate with others, to play and exercise oneself, the facility to observe the environment and to talk about it with other humans all belong to this level of mental programming. However, what one does with these feelings, how one expresses fear, joy, observations, and so on, is modified by culture."[56]

Gender and Status

One of the most important universals regards the relative status between men and women in society.[57] In many societies men have more political power and social prestige than women. Such societies are called **patriarchies.** In other societies, men dominate in some areas, but women have corresponding power in other domains, somewhat balancing the inequity. They may be, for example, the "power behind the throne," or have special status in their role as mothers, or they may have economic power. However, there is no evidence of a true **matriarchy,** that is, a society where women have had more political power and social prestige than men. While patriarchy may not be a cultural universal, matriarchy appears to be a negative universal— something that does *not* exist universally.[58]

Since women's and men's cultures within cultural systems exist, it is difficult to challenge traditional gender roles. Many women and men within patriarchal cultures are working for change within the context of their cultural frameworks.

Which cultures do you know of that are strongly patriarchal? What aspects of their lives do women control in such cultures? Consider sexuality, reproduction, education, choice of marriage partner, profession, freedom to circulate in society, vote, drive. What various means are used to enforce patriarchal control?

In which cultures do women have a strong if not overtly dominant role? Do they behave differently with husbands in public than in private?

The *feminist* theoretical perspective on culture (the fourth major sociological perspective) sought reasons for the subordination of women throughout the world and concluded that reasons vary according to specific economic and social conditions. Feminists also emphasize the female experience in the study of culture, something history has largely ignored.[59]

CULTURE'S PURPOSE

The word culture comes from the Latin verb "to cultivate the soil" (*colere*; past participle, *cultus*).[60] Human beings cultivated social structures, agricultural traditions, scientific knowledge, and belief systems to solve problems of existence. Culture provides a framework that:

- directs our actions by supplying appropriate behaviours for social and environmental stimuli. In Japan, people learn to bow in greeting; in Canada, to shake hands.
- answers questions about "the meaning of life" that have come to the human spirit throughout the ages.
- binds us into groups and gives us the sense of belonging and social membership essential to most individuals.
- provides security in predictability and continuity through heritage.[61]

CULTURE AND CHANGE

Cultures change. Some cultures change slowly and others change quickly. Some cultures have change thrust upon them. Change can be stimulated in a number of ways. Innovation, economic change, and diffusion are three sources of change.

Innovation is a term that refers to advances in technology, a major stimulus for cultural change.

What changes in technology have made your lives very different from those of your grandparents? Have they contributed to a change in values between the generations?

Economic changes, such as those underway in modern China, cause cultural change (see *Time Out for China*). In developing countries and in prospering immigrant communities, as a family's economic situation improves, women have fewer children because they feel less dependent on their children to look after them in old age. Such is the case in Mexico, among Hispanic women in the United States, and among immigrant women in general in Canada.[62]

Change is also caused by contact between cultures, a catalyst for change called *diffusion*. Where two cultures live side by side, there is often a cross-fertilization enriching and changing both. In other instances, a stronger culture may penetrate a weaker one with its material and ideal cultures. Diffusion is at the heart of cultural globalization and of Fukuyama's theory of cultural convergence discussed in Chapter 1.

All aspects of culture are subject to change. And because culture is like a machine with all parts moving and interconnected, a change in one area has a domino effect on others. A change in women's roles in society, for example, such as inclusion in the world of work requires adaptations in men's roles, family practices, and workplace environments. Taliban rule in Afghanistan forbade education to women, resulting in their exclusion from professional and economic life and in the imposition of *purdah*, or seclusion in the home. Now, Afghan society is working to reintegrate women into political and professional life.

WHY DO CANADIANS DRIVE ON THE RIGHT?

Travelling on the left side of the road made sense in times past when robbers roamed the roads of Europe. Since most people are right-handed, they used to put their weapons and right arm between them and oncoming assailants. During the French Revolution, however, driving on the right was made mandatory, something Napoleon (who was left-handed) later imposed on countries he conquered. Most countries in the British sphere of influence continued to drive on the left, and in the French sphere, on the right. The United States went right partly to override colonial influences, and then exported millions of right-hand-drive vehicles in the twentieth century. Today, about a third of the world's population still drives on the left.[63]

Religious practices and doctrine may be reinterpreted in light of social change. Women are now ordained in various Protestant and Anabaptist Christian churches, and some Protestant churches now support gay marriage. The Roman Catholic Church, however, despite calls for change by some, holds firm on the validity of marriage between only a man and woman, and on other controversial issues such as abortion and the celibacy of priests.

CULTURE AND THE INDIVIDUAL

Of all the variables that shape an individual, culture has the most profound impact on the formation of our identity. Our genetic potential, our environmental influences, and our personality are guided by the patterns and standards of our culture[64] and by the meta-narratives (or lack of them) that dominate it.[65] In a sense, we negotiate our identities and perform, to greater or lesser extent, the roles made available to us by our culture in our time.[66]

We absorb and observe cultural family patterns, dating rules, familiar rituals, festivals, what and when to celebrate, what to believe. If we identify with Chinese culture, we learn to look forward to Chinese New Year, to Caribana if we live in Toronto and are of Caribbean origin, to a Bar or Bat Mitzvah if we are Jewish. Patterns communicated intergenerationally make our lives meaningful and provide a large share of our individual identity.

In Canada, many families are in cultural transition. Immigrants who hold strongly to their culture of origin often experience conflict with their children whose values and behaviours are changing to meet dominant Canadian cultural norms, in areas such as dating, for example. In other instances, transition is relatively seamless, as individuals and the ethnic groups with which they identify evolve in tandem. Chapter 10 deals in depth with the process of cultural adaptation and identity change.

We may also, like actors, play different facets of ourselves depending on where, when, and with whom we are interacting. We may behave differently with peers in our age and gender groups from the way we behave with family. The behaviour and belief choices available to us are multiple because we belong to multiple groups each of which has established its own symbols, traditions, and patterns. National, regional, ethnic, linguistic, religious or non-religious, age, gender, sexual orientation, social class, and many other groups to which we belong often have different, at times conflicting, values.

Identity is fluid and changing. Our values and beliefs often change over time, moving with or against the currents of our era. Sometimes we experiment and go outside the norms of our cultural and social identities to find ourselves. Identity is also mysterious: we may spend the better part of a lifetime trying to figure out and "perform" who we really are and to establish a core set of values and beliefs.

Identity is ultimately "a construction of the mind,"[67] an interplay between us as individuals and the definitions of ethnicity, race, gender, and culture created by society at a given time.[68] We assemble it as we go along the way we assemble a puzzle, although we may not always know exactly where we are going. At the heart of our identity choices, however, are options proposed by our culture in its time.

THE VIEW OF SELF IN THE GREEK CULTURE

According to Dorothy Lee, the most important element of a Greek's view of self is self-esteem. Anyone not understanding this is unlikely to have a good relationship with a Greek. It is called in Greek, *philotimo*. "Everyone has his *philotimo*, as an individual, as a member of a family, and, most of all as a Greek. On this rests Greek individualism, and Greek democracy and equality, as everyone, both as a person and as a Greek is equal in his *philotimo* to everyone else, neither superior nor inferior. A shoe shiner is equal to a king; inferiority comes only by giving up the *philotimo*. Greek nationalism rests on *philotimo*, the concept of a glorious past, and Greeks, despite the odds, were fierce in their resistance to the Nazi occupation in World War II. *Philotimo* is not pride. The essence of it is inviolability and freedom. Greeks tend to be touchy if their Greekness (*philotimo*) is offended."[69]

CULTURE REALMS

Cultural geography explores human cultures in relationship to space. It has given us the idea of culture realms.[70] These are regions where different cultural groups share a number of cultural patterns. Culture realms can be defined using different criteria: there are language realms, ethnic realms, agricultural realms, political realms, religious realms, health and healing realms, and so on. Culture realms often overlap. As you would expect, maps are particularly useful in looking at culture realms.[71] Chapters 5 and 6 identify and explore essential differences in the world's major culture realms.

Sub-Saharan Africa, the Middle East, East Asia, and North American Native are also examples of broad culture realms. Latin America is typically a major culture realm, yet closer inspection reveals great diversity within it.[72] *Time Out for Latin America* (following Chapter 4) explores this region.

Europe is a broad culture realm (see Table 3.1, page 88) which can be subdivided and mapped according to various culture-related criteria. Its regions are roughly defined on the basis of geographical, linguistic, religious, and family life patterns, work relations, and political affinities.[73] Overlap exists among them—France, for example, has cultural affinities with Italy.

Table 3.1

Regions of Europe[74]

NORTHERN EUROPE	SOUTHERN EUROPE	WESTERN EUROPE	EASTERN EUROPE
Scandinavia or Nordic: Denmark, Finland, Iceland, Norway, Sweden Anglo-Celtic: Ireland, United Kingdom	Greece, Italy, Portugal, Spain, Albania, Yugoslavia, Bosnia-Herzegovina	Austria, Belgium, France, Germany, Luxembourg, Netherlands, Switzerland	Bulgaria, Czech Republic, Hungary, Poland, Romania, Slovakia, Croatia

Source: Adapted from *World Regional Geography* by Robert E. Norris. © 1990. Reprinted with permission of West Publishing, a Division of Thomson Learning www.thomsonrights.com. Fax 800-730-2215.

SUMMARY

In this chapter, we have looked at culture to show the diversity of expression in traditions, symbols, beliefs, values, and norms. We have seen that there are similarities among cultures in the form of symbols and narratives that spring from the shared dawn of human existence. We have also seen that cultures change over time, influenced by other cultures, changes in technology, and economic opportunities. Finally, we have explored the purposes of culture, and seen that cultures may be grouped into regions or realms that share broad cultural traits but contain diversity within. Embedded throughout the chapter are brief descriptions of the four major sociological theoretical perspectives on culture, and one anthropological perspective.

KEY TERMS

archetype 73

cultural model 64

cultural narrative 70

cultural universal 82

culture 63

culture realm 87

matriarchy 83

norm 82

patriarchy 83

symbol 72

taboo 82

universal symbol 72

TOPICS FOR CRITICAL THINKING AND REFLECTION

1. Humans mold landscape. If you were to fly over Quebec, Peru, or the Canadian prairies, you would see this graphically. How were farms in Quebec laid out? On the prairies? In Peru?

2. Look at these two city layouts on the following page.[75] Both are large cities set on elongated, hilly sites surrounded on three sides by water (rivers, ocean, bay), and connected to the mainland by bridges. One is San Francisco, the other Chongqing, China. Compare the street patterns and notice how different they are. In Chongqing, the streets adapt to the hilly terrain, while in San Francisco, a grid system was applied to the degree possible. San Francisco has a smaller population, but takes up more land. What do these differences suggest about the two cultures' relationship to nature?

3. Words have different meanings across cultures. In this exercise,[76] we'll see what two words mean to you. After you have done the exercise, look at the results of responses in the United States, Japan, France, and Korea in Appendix I, and compare them to your class results.

   → What does the word *marriage* imply? Check off the five most important meanings for you.

___ mutual encouragement	___ respect
___ family	___ problem sharing
___ compromise	___ sex
___ interpersonal sensitivity	___ maturity
___ passion	___ understanding
___ united	___ love
___ helping each other	___ accepting mutual freedom
___ children	___ mutual fulfillment
___ trust	___ responsibilities

   → What does the word *family* mean? Choose the three most important meanings for you, then tally the responses of the class to see which choices predominate.

___ family size, sex	___ togetherness, cooperation
___ children, brother, sister	___ mother, father
___ love, friendship	___ family support, livelihood
___ home	___ relatives
___ happiness, fun	___ activities, life
___ miscellaneous	

Figure 3.1 Chongqing, China, and San Francisco, California city layouts

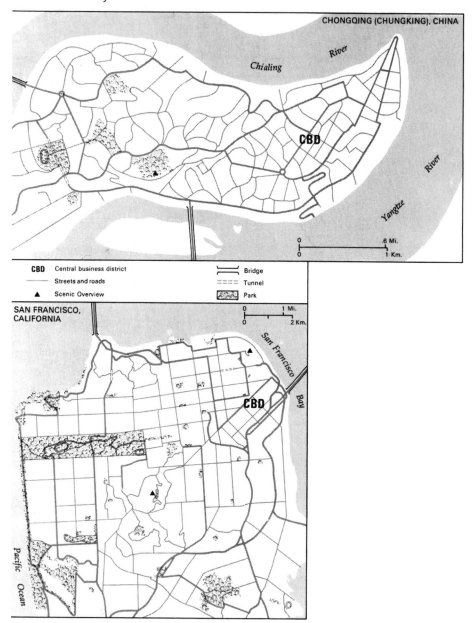

Source: From *The Human Mosaic: A Thematic Introduction to Cultural Geography* by Terry G. Jordan-Bychkov and Mona Domosh. © 1986 by W.H. Freeman and Company. Used with permission.

4. **Case Study**

   A Buddhist funeral ceremony held in Kitchener included a ceremony in the parking lot after midnight in which the mourners, dressed in white, burned paper in bowls with wishes on them for the deceased. The police and fire department arrived, having received a report that the Ku Klux Klan was burning crosses.[77] What caused the cross-cultural mix-up?

5. Which Canadian city does this architectural style represent? Does your city or region have a distinctive style?

Source: © Corel

Chapter 4

Exploring North American Values and Beliefs: Canada and the United States

In this chapter we will explore:

- A shared cultural legacy
- American cultural patterns
- Canadian cultural patterns
- The diversity of values within Canada
- Theories about values divergence and convergence between the United States and Canada

T his chapter will examine commonalities and differences in values and beliefs between the United States and Canada. (Mexico is part of the Latin American culture realm explored in *Time Out for Latin America*.) Both Canada and the United States have strong regional and minority cultures, but most historians, sociologists, and political scientists agree that, so far, both nations have national identities even though the ties that bind may be tenuous and the divisions deep.

THE CANADIAN IDENTITY: A BRAINSTORMING EXERCISE

Let's try some brainstorming about Canadian identity and national culture. Once you have run through the exercise, you can try it with regard to American identity and national culture, or to Québécois identity and culture, an acknowledged distinct society within Canada.

1. A nation is a people who share the same myths and illusions about themselves.[1] They grow to share a cultural memory and cultural imagination, and to enjoy telling and hearing the stories that support their illusions. Pierre Berton became a Canadian cultural icon because of his ability to bring to life Canada's narratives. Berton once quipped that "A Canadian is someone who knows how to make love in a canoe."[2] The canoe certainly is a symbol of Canada: an object created by First Nations and shared with the French and English voyageurs who travelled the rivers flowing north when the fur trade was the impetus for European exploration and imperialism. Former Prime Minister Pierre Elliott Trudeau, a committed nationalist of Anglo-French descent, liked to be photographed in a canoe while wearing a buckskin jacket, thereby bringing together Canada's three founding cultural legacies.

    Think of other symbols, stories, heroes, illusions, and traditions that are part of the cultural imagination and national identity of Canadians.
2. Now brainstorm for values and beliefs you think Canadians share as a nation. Do you as an individual share the values you have identified? (According to Hofstede,[3] each of our "individual mental programs" contains a component of national culture.)

CANADA AND THE UNITED STATES: A COMMON LEGACY

Canadians and Americans are linked by both geography and a common cultural heritage.

Source: CP Photo/*Winnipeg Free Press*/Ken Gigliotti

The British colonial heritage provided the essential values, beliefs, and cultural patterns common to both nations. The dominant cultures of both were originally white, Anglo-Saxon, Protestant (WASP) elites that defined and controlled their political, social, linguistic, and commercial development of the British North American colonies both before and after their independence. Legislative institutions established by the early settlers were similar to those of the mother country and voting rights, for example, as in England, were first restricted to loyal British subjects and men of property, only gradually evolving to include other sectors of society. In Canada, the British were destined to be administrators and commercial leaders, the Scots to be the managerial class, and the Irish to provide labour, resulting in a majority Anglo-Celtic population outside Quebec.[4]

Despite political, social, and economic shifts, the fundamental bases of power of both countries remain WASP according to Peter C. Newman,[5] and core value systems remain the same. Early values common to English Canada and the American north included liberty, legal equality, democratic sovereignty, equality of opportunity, and pluralism.[6] (The American south, founded on slavery, has a dissimilar regional culture.[7])

Both cultures were influenced by the Protestant Reformation, which emphasized the value of the individual (with racial and religious exclusions), the **rule of law,** and the value of work. The Puritan founders of the Thirteen Colonies additionally emphasized morality and righteousness, a spiritual legacy of moral certitude still evident in American culture today. The Canadian Establishment remained loyal to England after the American Revolution in the 18th century, and after Confederation in 1867 balanced the push and pull of attachment to England with the push and pull of continentalism—attraction to the United States—while attempting to maintain sovereignty and a sense of Canadian national purpose. Economic, political, and cultural linkages to our North American neighbour seemed logical to continentalists, while imperialists looked to England for economic, political, and cultural ties in the formative years of Canada's history.

Quebec evolved separately. After French Canada came under British control, the Quebec Act of 1774 allowed for religious and linguistic freedom. The inhabitants of French Canada maintained the right to speak French and practise Roman Catholicism, as well as to elect a legislative assembly. Nonetheless, commercial and political power was consolidated among British colonials, and Québécois culture slumbered in the moral grip of Roman Catholicism and the economic grip of Anglo Canadians until the Quiet Revolution of the 1960s when Quebecers rejected both the Church and the economic and linguistic dominance of Anglo-Celtic Canada. The power imbalance between English- and French-speaking Canadians was lessened through a series of political measures both federal and provincial, although a strong sense of nationalism still drives the wish of many Québécois to separate from Canada and form a sovereign nation state.

In a 2004 Ipsos-Reid poll,[8] 80 percent of Canadians agreed that Canadians were fundamentally different in values and outlook from Americans, while 50 percent of Americans said the same.

Why do you think the perceptions of the two peoples are so different?
What differences in values do you think exist between Americans and Canadians?

UNDERSTANDING THE UNITED STATES: AMERICAN CULTURAL PATTERNS

Much has been written and said about American culture and the dynamic, innovative, and powerful nation it has produced. The United States achieved independence from England by means of revolution, and like other nations where revolutions have overturned an established order, the revolution was a profound and defining moment in the nation's history. American mythology often sees its revolution in the context of the European Enlightenment, a period during which new ideas such as the value of freedom from tyranny in all its forms—freedom from the tyranny of the Church and of the aristocracy, for example—caught fire. However, the American Revolution's roots were in part also material; the upheaval was a middle-class tax revolt as much as a revolution about freedom. Its rallying cry was "No Taxation without Representation," not the grand "Liberty, Equality, Fraternity" of the French Revolution a few years later.[9] Nonetheless, the American Revolution also embodied enlightenment values about individual freedom, and spawned a democracy that evolved by stages and a nation with a strong sense of itself and its mission.

Here are some of the values and beliefs at the heart of American cultural patterns.

Manifest Destiny

Nineteenth century American political leaders believed that the United States had a God-given destiny to govern from the Atlantic to the Pacific and from the Arctic to the Gulf of Mexico and Caribbean; some believed that American rule should extend even to Asia.[10] The concept rested on the early Puritan conviction that they were a chosen people destined to found God's New Israel, the biblical City on a Hill. America saw itself a redeemer nation with a "manifest destiny" to set an example of freedom and morality for the world.[11] Twentieth-century presidents including Ronald Reagan, George H.W. Bush, and Bill Clinton responded to the call to provide moral guidance[12] and, most recently, President George W. Bush has reflected and reinforced the moralistic strain in the American psyche. In a speech given to the United Nations on September 21, 2004, he said, "Our wider goal is to promote hope and progress as the alternatives to hatred and violence. Our great purpose is to build a better world. . . ."[13] In his inaugural address in 2005, he vowed to spread freedom "to the darkest corners of the world."[14]

Judeo-Christian Morality

God has been a major player in America's belief systems since the Puritans landed on Plymouth Rock. He figures in major speeches delivered by American presidents—no annual State of the Union Address is complete without a reference to God. Presidential candidates since John F. Kennedy (whose Catholicism was an issue) have been obliged to state their religious affiliation. The U.S. House of Representatives passed a law on September 24, 2004 preventing the Supreme Court from taking out the phrase "under God" from the Pledge of Allegiance.[15] It has been part of the pledge since 1954 and still reads: *I pledge allegiance to the flag of the United States of America and to the Republic for which it stands, one Nation under God, indivisible, with liberty and justice for all.*

A recent Gallup poll revealed that 90 percent of Americans said they believed in God, compared to 71 percent of Canadians and 52 percent of Britons; while 70 percent believed in the devil compared to 37 percent of Canadians and 29 percent of Britons surveyed.[16] Forty-two percent of Americans consider themselves born again, and over 40 percent believe that God created heaven and earth in seven days, while 35 percent accept Darwin's theory of evolution.[17]

Evangelical Christianity is playing an increasing role in the workplace, with many institutions and businesses holding prayer and faith sessions. (**Evangelical** means "to spread the gospel," or evangelize.) Muslim and Jewish groups do not evangelize on the job, or rarely, and religious-discrimination complaints to the Equal Employment Opportunity Commission have increased 84 percent since 1992 and 30 percent since 2000.[18] Evangelical Christianity is also rejecting public and school Christmas festivities "that have taken 'Christ' out of the holiday" and made it a non-religious celebration that is in line with pluralistic religious beliefs but means nothing, they claim, to anyone.[19]

Individualism and Individual Freedom

John Locke was a 17th century philosopher whose ideas regarding the supreme value of individual freedom are often said to be the basis of American values. He was opposed to authoritarianism and the blind acceptance of institutions such as church and government.[20] Freedom of religion and separation of church and state were guaranteed early in the United States. Over time, however, the Puritan religious ideal melded to the Enlightenment political ideal of freedom from the tyranny of church and state. In a sense, America has two sets of founding fathers: the Puritans of Massachusetts, and Enlightenment thinkers like Thomas Jefferson.[21] They have been in conflict and yet merged with time into a political culture imbued with fundamentalist Christianity. This peculiar blending created a secular yet at the same time extremely religious society, opposed not to religion as such, but rather to the authority of established religions like the Church of England and Roman Catholicism affiliated with governments.

Religion has mixed with the national political life "until it is difficult to distinguish between the two, and usually leads to a blurring of religion and patriotism and of religious values and national values" writes historian Robert Linder.[22] The election of George W. Bush in 2004 revolved around this uniquely American mix of values summarized neatly into three words: faith, family, and freedom.[23] The President did not relent in his vision that America must spread freedom and serve as a model to the world. He did not falter in his fundamentalist Christian beliefs regarding marriage, the family, abortion, and medical practices such as some stem cell research that might interfere too deeply in a universe created by God. Just over half of Americans voted for him and his political mix of City on a Hill, Lockian freedom, and fundamentalist Christianity; those who voted against Bush remained more in tune with Enlightenment values stressing freedom from religion in politics.

The 2004 presidential elections, however, revealed a nation divided geographically between Enlightenment values embracing individual freedoms (centred in the Northeast), and fundamentalist Americans (centred in the South) becoming increasingly intolerant of freedoms seen as immoral such as gay marriage and the right to abortion. French philosopher Alexis de Tocqueville said 200 years ago, that "while the law permits Americans to do everything, there are things which religion prevents them from imagining and forbids them to do."[24]

Whether Enlightenment- or fundamentalist-oriented, the American value system across the board holds strongly that individuals are responsible for their lives and that a society that fosters individual freedom will prosper as a whole. In its isolationism from Europe after the American Revolution and later during the Industrial Revolution, the United States did not subscribe to collective movements that tempered Western and Northern Europe's attraction to such strong individualism. Union movements, socialist ideas, and intervention by governments to assist society's needy were and still are viewed by many Americans with suspicion and seen as fetters to individual freedom at best, and communism at worst.

The American absolute faith in its form of democracy and free market capitalism are reflections of the American emphasis on individualism and its religious zeal to reform the world (see Chapter 2, *The Ugly American*, page 36) in its image. The two ideologies are often equated and while mutually compatible, are not one and the same: one is a political ideology, the other an economic ideology. In the American understanding of them, however, they are often equated with freedom per se. The preference for small over large government rests on the belief that a government must not interfere with the freedom of its citizens to control all aspects of their lives, including their economic lives.

Americans are generally credited with valuing individualism, but a contradictory view is that they are actually highly conformist.[25] How would you debate this?

Materialism

A marriage between individualism and materialism also underlies American value patterns. Rags-to-riches stories are part of the mythology: anyone who works hard enough can succeed, and success is often evaluated in terms of material wealth. Poverty is somehow the fault of an individual. The wealthy, self-made man or woman is admired. Such stories have been proven often to be true and sustained the myth in America, a land of opportunity for countless immigrants and their families.

Equality

In 1776, the Declaration of Independence established the founding principle of equality: "We hold these truths to be self-evident: that all men are created equal, that they are endowed by their Creator with certain unalienable Rights, that among these are Life, Liberty, and the pursuit of Happiness." Americans hold firmly to their belief in equality and to its sidekick, the **American Dream,** an elusive concept related to freedom and equality of opportunity.[26] The reality may not exactly fit the dream, as it is impossible for a society to be free and equal at the same time, according to Linder.[27] Michael Moore, in *Fahrenheit 9/11*,[28] illustrates the gap between the ideal and the real in showing how the army recruits from amongst the unemployed and underprivileged in greater proportions than from among the middle classes who have better chances of living the American Dream and, consequently, more to lose in going to war. The brutal aftermath of hurricane Katrina in 2005 also tragically revealed the inequities of wealth and race in American society.

Do you agree with Linder when he says it is impossible for a society to be both free and equal at the same time?

A classic metaphor for the American Dream is a house with a white picket fence. Why is it an apt symbol?

What is the meaning of "happiness" in Jefferson's Declaration? Can it be pursued?

Competition

Winning, excelling, and being number one are highly valued in American culture, a logical extension of the cult of the individual. Heroes are cherished, their ambitions supported, their achievements cheered. If you drive through the United States, you will become aware that almost every town or hamlet is number one for some reason: it has produced the largest pumpkin, has the biggest this, the smallest that, the tallest something, and so on. The gospel of success has helped promote the United States to its position as the world's superpower and leader in many fields. Michael Adams contends that in the United States, church life provides community and a refuge from Darwinism and the competitive life.[29]

Science and Technology

American culture has been strongly imbued with the Western concept of progress, a belief that science and technology can solve all the problems of life and lead human beings towards an ideal existence. The belief is based on the Western faith in rational, **empirical,** scientific thought as superior to intuition and emotion.[30] From the Greeks to the Age of Reason to modern times, the Western need to take apart, understand, and analyze the workings of the universe has led to major discoveries in all scientific fields including those related to warfare, and enabled imperialistic Western civilizations to dominate cultures based on other values. (For more on the foundations of Western thought, see Chapter 5.)The United States passionately embraced a belief in science and technology as the key to survival and to controlling reality, and has been at the forefront of major advancements in medicine, engineering, space exploration, and all other areas of scientific investigation. Societal improvement is mirrored by a need for individual improvement in American culture, and self-improvement books abound while plastic surgeons perfect those who see themselves as physically inadequate.

Change

Change goes hand in hand with belief in progress. Change connotes improvement and, in the context of ever moving forward, is positive for the individual, the nation, the world. Americans do not fear change, are risk takers in business, and focused on the future. The proverb "the best is yet to come" reflects this optimistic outlook.[31]

Work and Leisure

Americans are products of the **Protestant work ethic.** They value hard work and its perceived material and moral rewards. "God helps those who help themselves" is a proverb that embodies belief in God, work, and the individual. People often ask upon meeting each other what they do for a living, a common opener that helps illustrate the importance ascribed to work. A recent Gallup poll indicated that Americans live up to their workaholic reputations: on average, they work 42 hours a week and 38 percent say they work more than 45 hours a week. (Canadians work 41 hours a week, the

British, 39 hours, while 30 percent of Canadians and 28 percent of Britons say they work more than 45 hours a week.) Interestingly, the poll also revealed that although they work more hours, they not only enjoy work more than Canadians, but also rely less on work for a sense of fulfillment. Forty percent said they were completely satisfied with their opportunities for promotion, compared to 29 percent of Canadians, and 25 percent of Brits. The survey was based on 7000 American, British, and Canadian workers.[32]

Another reward of work is leisure, although American culture tends to value leisure time filled with productive activity and self-improvement pastimes over activity-free, "wasted" spare time. Leisure thus becomes a form of work.

America: The Melting Pot

The United States has believed strongly in "Americanizing" its immigrants and assimilating them into American dominant culture.[33] It does so willfully in an effort to support a strong national culture of uniform values. Opposition to official bilingualism is strong even in regions where Hispanics are a significant minority, although in reality, in cities like Miami and San Diego, even street signs are often in two languages. America publicly stands for one language, one value system, one nation. To go against dominant cultural patterns and the national purpose can be seen to be "un-American." In reality, however, the United States is a pluralistic society with many ethnic, linguistic, and religious groups who come together as patriots. Hispanics, now the largest ethnic minority, number over 41 million, followed by African Americans at 36 million.[34]

Twenty-First Century Challenges to American Identity?

Samuel Huntington fears that the American national identity is being challenged. In his latest book *Who Are We? Challenges to America's National Identity,* he argues that the globalization of America's elites and the rise of the Hispanic minority may result in a bilingual, bicultural nation with a weakened sense of identity.[35] Huntington is a believer in nationalism, and admits that his preference is for a United States with an Anglo-Protestant-dominated national identity that stands for a strong work ethic, individualism, and morality.[36] According to Huntington, these are the values that created America.

Huntington has his critics. Fukuyama, for example, asserts that the "the real Protestants" today are not America's Anglo-Saxons, but rather the Korean corner-store owners, Taiwanese engineers, and Russian cab drivers and Mexican migrants working long hours to achieve the American Dream.[37]

CANADIAN CULTURAL PATTERNS

Canada has engaged in and continues to engage in soul-searching in an effort to define its most cherished values and beliefs. As a nation that evolved and continues to evolve through negotiation and compromise, not revolution, our defining convictions are less spectacularly evident than in nations like the United States and France where revolutions forced the early identification and declaration of deeply held beliefs. Canada's long affiliation with Europe influenced its development, and collective values that emerged from the Industrial Revolution in Europe and from the rigours of pioneer life here, where going it alone tempted fate, tempered its individualism.

Australian writer David Malouf sees similarities between Australia and Canada. "Both countries decided early on to be moderate. I have called it decency. There is an essential civility in Canada vis-à-vis immigration and others."[38] While his contention is disputable (see Chapter 2 for racism towards First Nations and discriminatory immigration policies), both Canada and Australia maintained ties to the British Empire and later to the Commonwealth, a connection that influenced their developments.

According to a comprehensive Angus Reid survey,[39] about 78 percent of polled Canadians believed that Canadians hold many values in common, and 91 percent felt that these values are important in binding people as a nation. Also, almost three-quarters of Canadians believed that the multiculturalism policy ensured that people from different backgrounds had a sense of belonging to Canada. It is also noteworthy that 89 percent of people interviewed identified themselves as Canadians and only 6 percent used another form of identification. The Ethnic Diversity Survey was undertaken by Statistics Canada and the Department of Canadian Heritage in 2002 and supports the earlier survey. Its results indicate that, despite a variety of ethnic origins and substantial immigration, Canadians quickly establish a sense of belonging to Canada: by the third generation after a family's immigration, 63 percent identify only British, French, and/or Canadian origins.[40]

Canadians, in other words, do seem to have a sense of shared values and identity. In the section that follows, we'll look at some of the Canadian beliefs and values that underlie Canadian cultural patterns. (Others, such as *materialism* and *belief in progress and technology* are shared with Americans, although Canadians are generally less enthusiastic about *change* and *risk taking* than Americans.)

Compromise and Mistrust of Revolutionary Upheaval

Both historians and sociologists have claimed that the most significant difference between Canada and the United States is our anti-revolutionary character.[41] According to Ramsay Cook, we have an anti-revolutionary character both in Quebec and in Anglo-Canada, although for different reasons.[42] Loyalists who left the American colonies at the time of the American Revolution in the 1770s brought with them conservative, Establishment values and reinforced the conservatism of the British colonists in Upper and Lower Canada. Quebec was already quite distant from France at the time of the French Revolution in 1789, and the Quiet Revolution of the 1960s was largely non-violent. Quebec nationalists came to power democratically in 1976, and democratically accepted the close results of the 1980 and 1995 referenda on sovereignty. The story is not over, but negotiation, compromise, and democracy have thus far prevailed over violent revolution.

ARE CANADIANS REVOLUTIONARY?

Michael Adams claims that Canadians are becoming the true revolutionaries of North America. We are in the process of creating a new social order based on multiple, flexible roles and individual exploration in spiritual, sexual, and family relationships. Like Tocqueville, he sees religion as placing constraints on American individual freedoms, and claims that Americans now defer more to authority in greater numbers than do Canadians.[43]

What do you think?

"Peace, Order, and Good Government"

These are the key words of the British North America Act of 1867, an Act of the British Parliament that created the Dominion of Canada out of four British colonies. It was Canada's Constitution until 1982 when it was patriated by Prime Minister Pierre Elliott Trudeau and renamed the Canada Act. Little was changed, except for the addition of the Charter of Rights and Freedoms to enshrine **civil liberties** in the Constitution.

A prime example of Canada's commitment to peace is Canadian Prime Minister Lester B. Pearson's initiative in creating international peacekeeping, for which he won the Nobel Prize for Peace in 1957. According to Adams, Canada's history has been peaceful and dominated by three themes: building a nation and holding it together, providing ever more services to the Canadian people, and managing our relations with the United States.[44]

The Sponsorship Scandal with its taint of unethical and illegal maneuverings brought to light during the 2004–5 Gomery Inquiry shook many Canadians' faith in good government, although it could be argued that the very existence of the inquiry is testament to a commitment to good government.

Individualism Tempered by Collectivism

Canadians tend to be less ideological than Americans in their belief in unfettered capitalism and strong individualism.[45] In terms of political culture, Canada's leading federal parties (Liberal, Conservative, NDP, and Bloc Québécois) have traditionally been farther left—that is to say, oriented more towards policies focused on the collective rather than the individual—than either the Republicans or the Democrats.

European industrial age movements were carried over to Canada and Canada, thanks also in part to Tommy Douglas, former leader of the New Democratic Party, evolved as a social democracy. A poll by *Maclean's* indicated that 38 percent of Canadians believed that a major difference between Canadians and Americans is our support for social programs.[46] A universal health care system is supported by the vast majority of Canadians and all major federal parties, despite its costs. Adams claims that Canadians are becoming less deferential to authority in general, but still expect government assistance.[47]

The Charter of Rights and Freedoms is an example of Canada's commitment to individual freedoms within the context of the collective good. It has become a cornerstone of Canadian values by ensuring rule of law and civil liberties for all Canadians without distinctions based on race, religion, language, ethnicity, sexual orientation, or gender. Its emphasis on protecting the freedoms of individuals only to the extent that they do not jeopardize the collective good (Section 1) distinguishes it from other such documents around the world including the American Bill of Rights.[48]

Internationally, Canada strongly supports multilateral institutions like the United Nations, which aims for international standards of human rights and laws, and its judicial body, the International Court of Justice (ICJ), whose mandate is to settle disputes between nations and whose rulings have been ignored by the United States on a number of occasions. Canada is also signatory to the Kyoto Protocol on the reduction of greenhouse gas emissions, and the International Criminal Court (ICC), a tribunal set up to prosecute individuals for genocide, crimes against humanity, and war crimes. The United States, in contrast, signed neither.

Margaret Atwood views Canadians as less oriented towards individualism than Americans from another perspective. She considers the American dynamic to be based on winning (see *Competition,* page 99), and the Canadian on survival. Nature is such a powerful force in Canada that winning, an individual pursuit, is less important than survival, which forces people to work together.[49]

Respect for Authority

Canadians tend to respect institutions, follow rules, and value order (see above). Pierre Berton considered Canadians to be more respectful of institutions than of the people who run them, with the reverse being true of Americans: "We're good at institutions—banks ("it's our Scottish heritage"), insurance companies, churches."[50] Seymour Lipset alleged that Canadians maintained allegiance to established, hierarchical churches such as the Church of England and the Roman Catholic Church in Quebec that had long histories of cooperating with governments.[51] Canadians were thus historically more inclined to place faith in institutions than Americans whose founding church (Puritan) was a breakaway sect unaligned with and opposed to government. According to Adams, the very fact that Canadians remained with established churches has also meant that we feel free to question them, as we have done other institutions.[52] In the 1950s, more Canadians than Americans went to church regularly; now, fewer do, however, suggesting perhaps a loosening of the power of established religious authority among Canadians.[53]

Related to our historic respect for institutions is our historic respect for rules.[54] The Hudson Bay Company once ruled one-eleventh of the planet, all in Canada, and rule of law was established by the RCMP in the expansion west to counteract the Wild West lawlessness to the south.[55] Peter Newman notes that we were "a company town, with an ethic of deference to authority": as Canada expanded west, towns founded by "the HBC, the Mounties, the CPR, the banks, and the clergy arrived in that order." On a main corner of western towns, he claims, you'll find three out of four of those institutions represented.[56]

Do you think Canadians' deference to authority might help account for the stereotypes of the apologetic Canadian (Canadians who apologize for everything) and the modest Canadian (Wayne Gretzky is often named as the quintessential modest Canadian)? What other factors might help explain these stereotypes?

Respect for Cultural Diversity

As we saw in Chapter 1, Canada's 1969 official Languages Act gave French and English equal status throughout the country to recognize the two founding [European] nations and languages. In 1971, Canada's policy of multiculturalism acknowledged that Canada is made up of numerous ethnicities and religions, "a mosaic" of stones of equal value. The drive to "Canadianize" all citizens into adopting one language and one national culture of identical values is not strong.

Respect for cultural diversity has been slow to include respect for Aboriginal peoples as Canada's original inhabitants and caretakers of the land, however, something the Royal Commission on Aboriginal Peoples acknowledged.[57] The Report proposed a new relationship between Aboriginal and non-Aboriginal Canadians based on respect, mutual recognition, and equality; fulfillment of this aim is ongoing.

OTHER OBSERVATIONS ABOUT CANADA

Do you agree with the following observations? Do some of them help explain why Canada is often considered an amalgam of British and American culture?

- Canadians are not publicly emotional ("our stiff upper lip heritage," said Berton). The late ABC news anchor Peter Jennings said that his training in Canada taught him to keep his own emotions out of his journalism. "In America, there is just more passion about everything," he added.[58]
- Canadians are less violent than Americans. "How can you have a gun fight," asked Pierre Berton, "at high noon in Moose Jaw in January, decked out in mittens, parka, and toque . . .?"[59] He claimed our climate may have mitigated the kinds of passionate outbursts that have occurred in the U.S. "We are a cold climate. Have you ever noticed that race riots always happen in summer?" Sociologists also note that Canada is less violent. Violent crime is higher in the United States although there are fewer police officers per capita in Canada. Adams relates this to higher poverty and illness rates in the U.S. than in other industrialized states, and to the extreme competitiveness of the culture.[60]
- "If some countries have too much history, Canada has too much geography." Prime Minister Mackenzie King.[61]
- "Canada is like a mouse that sleeps next to an elephant, and every time the elephant twitches or turns, the mouse wakes up."[62]
- "Canadians," says writer Lauro Palomba, "unlike Americans, are not in the pursuit of anything."

CANADIAN SOCIAL VALUES: DIVERSITY WITHIN

Michael Adams' extensive research on Canadian values has led him to break down Canadian society into four age-related groups, each with three or four typical sets of values that place them into a *Value Tribe* within the context of their group.[63] Eighty percent of the *Elders* (those over 60 in 1997) believe strongly in rules, order, the Judeo-Christian moral code. The *Boomers* were born between the mid-1940s and the mid-1960s, and fall into four Value Tribes, although across tribes they share a strong concern for the environment and mistrust of big business and authority. The *Generation Xers* were born between the mid-1960s and early 1980s, and are fragmented into five Value Tribes despite such common values as experience-seeking and concern with personal image among their peers. A new post-Generation X born between 1977 and 1997 has been labelled the *Net Generation* and is currently being studied. They show characteristics of creativity, curiosity, flexibility, and high self-esteem.[64]

Table 4.1

Proud to be Canadian

A national poll asked Canadians what made them proud of being Canadian. Compare your answers to the national results in Appendix I.

	VERY PROUD (8, 9, 10)	NEUTRAL (3–7)	NOT AT ALL PROUD (0–2)
The vastness and beauty of the land			
When the UN ranks Canada as the best country in the world in which to live			
When Canadian airports took in American planes that were diverted on Sept. 11, 2001			
The fact that people from different cultural groups in Canada get along and live in peace			
Canada's participation in peacekeeping activities around the world			
Canada's politeness and civility			
Canada's scientific inventions, like the Canadarm			
Canadian Olympic hockey team victories			
The Charter of Rights and Freedoms			
Canada's participation in key battles of World Wars I and II			
Multiculturalism			
The success of Canadian musicians or actors or artists			
When Canada decided not to participate in the war on Iraq			
Canada's health care system			

(Continued)

Table 4.1

Proud to be Canadian (*Continued*)

	VERY PROUD (8, 9, 10)	NEUTRAL (3–7)	NOT AT ALL PROUD (0–2)
Having two official languages, English and French			
The CBC			
Pierre Trudeau			
The Queen			

Source: From "A New Canada: An Identity Shaped by Diversity," Andrew Parkin and Matthew Mendelsohn, The CRIC Papers (Canadian Opinion Research Archive). Montreal: Centre for Research and Information on Canada, Oct. 2003, p. 11. Reprinted with permission of The Centre for Research and Information on Canada (CRIC).

VALUE TRIBES

Into which Value Tribe do you fall? Are you a Thrill-Seeking Materialist? A New Aquarian? An Autonomous Post-Materialist? A Social Hedonist? Or something else?

Check out the Environics website and see http://erg.environics.net/tribe/default.asp.

To what Value Tribe do you think your parents belong? Your grandparents?

Quebecers' value patterns diverge from the Canadian norm, as can be expected from the difference in cultural traditions. Francophones tend to be more group oriented than the more individualistic Anglo Canadians.[65] They have convincingly moved away from the Church since the Quiet Revolution, are more likely to live in common-law relationships than other Canadians, and have a slightly lower birth rate than Canada's average.[66]

Quebecers have a strong sense of cultural cohesion: they support their pop stars (singers, actors, directors), their media, their traditions. The top ten TV shows in

Quebec are produced there, while the top ten in the rest of Canada are produced in the United States. There are seven magazines in Quebec devoted to homegrown "stars" and Quebec movies regularly outdraw American movies, while Quebecers love and see themselves reflected in their soaps and sitcoms.[67]

Research shows that Quebecers are also distinct in childrearing practices: they are less likely than other Canadians to try to increase the intelligence of their babies by using such aids as flashcards, and are less likely to spank as a disciplinary measure. In fact, only 22 percent of Quebecers versus 62 percent of Albertans support spanking.[68] Quebecers are also more relaxed about sexual matters than Anglo Canadians.[69]

Quebecers older than 30 are less likely to have friends of different cultural backgrounds from themselves than are the rest of Canadians, although this difference disappears with Quebecers under the age of 30.[70]

CANADA AND THE UNITED STATES: VALUES DIVERGENCE OR CONVERGENCE?

Historians and sociologists have long been interested in the similarities and differences between the values and belief systems in the United States and Canada and how they change over time. Canadians, in an effort to distinguish themselves from Americans, have had a tendency to define ourselves in terms of what we are *not* in relation to whatever Americans define themselves as being. This attempt at self-definition has often resulted in anti-Americanism and given us a kind of negative sense of identity. It may also have been an example of what Freud called "the narcissism of small differences"—"the natural tendency for . . . similar groups of people to exaggerate otherwise superficially minor differences. The more alike the groups, the more they will seek ways to differentiate from each other. . . ."[71]

Either way, Jack Granatstein says we can't use anti-Americanism as a bulwark forever.[72] How long could such a view last anyway in light of economic realities? Eighty-five percent of trade goes to the United States, and we trade more south of the border than amongst ourselves. One-third of Canadian dollars is spent at American chains. NAFTA has led to the harmonization of certain trade policies. We were once seen as a branch plant of Britain, and some Canadians fear we will become a branch plant of the U.S. through the Americanization of our trade and its effect on changing our laws and political culture.[73]

Values Divergence

There is evidence, nonetheless, that Canada is developing a sense of identity based on confidence about "the unique experiment" we have built north of the 49th parallel.[74] Jennifer Welsh is a British historian who argues that Canadians no longer have to be

What's in a label? To what degree are your consumer choices influenced by feelings of nationalism?

Source: CP Photo/Jonathan Hayward

anti-American to be Canadian, even though we share basic and historic Enlightenment values with our neighbours. In her book, *At Home in the World,* she argues that we need to understand and admire the United States for some things in order to develop foreign and domestic policies that further Canadians' security and prosperity.

Despite concerns about the Americanization of Canada, evidence exists that at the social level, Canada is not moving closer to the value patterns of Americans, but rather away. Very different in 1867, Canadian values converged with American after World War II, but have been diverging since 1982, when Canada passed the Charter of Rights and Freedoms and the United States, under Ronald Reagan, let the Equal Rights Amendment lapse in the same year.[75] In other words, Canadians look to government to solve problems, while in the United States, government is the "declared enemy."

Pollster Allan Gregg also notes that Canadians question whether unbridled materialism is a worthwhile quest, and he believes there is renewed interest in the government's role to serve as a vehicle to advance our collective interests albeit not on a full-scale interventionist model.[76]

Adams has identified a number of differences in values between Canada and the United States. In *Sex in the Snow,* he sees Americans as having more faith in the family, the country itself, religion, and the marketplace.[77] Americans are more comfortable with big business, although that faith has been shaken in recent scandals involving Enron and other corporations. Canadians, he claims, are less ideological, and less comfortable with success.

According to Adams, Canadian and American social values have diverged in a number of ways in the past twenty years.[78] For example, in 1983 he and his colleagues asked Canadians if they strongly or somewhat agreed or disagreed that "The father of the family must be the head of the house." (About 100 other such questions were included in the poll.) This question measures a traditional, patriarchal attitude to authority in society's most important institution, the family, and has been used to track values in Canada and the United States ever since.

In 1983, 42 percent of Canadians agreed that the father should be master, 15 percent strongly and 27 percent somewhat. Almost 58 percent disagreed, 26 percent strongly, and 31 percent somewhat (numbers are rounded). Zero percent had no opinion. Every year after, smaller proportions of Canadians agreed. In 1992, when Kim Campbell became our first female prime minister, only 26 percent of Canadians believed father should rule. (In France, the same sort of decline appeared.) In 1992, when Environics began tracking American responses, 42 percent believed father should be the head of the house; 57 percent disagreed and 1 percent had no opinion.

By 1996, only 20 percent of Canadians agreed, but 44 percent of Americans agreed. (In France, the percentage agreeing had dropped to 30 percent in 2000.) Even among men, only 23 percent of Canadian men still agreed; Canadian support continued to drop in all age groups.

In 2000, 48 percent of Americans believed father knows best. Most surprisingly, 43 percent of American women agreed, up 9 percent from 1992. Large percentages of African and Hispanic Americans could statistically skew results by only one or two percent, but Adams does not believe the "ethnic" factor was significant. If so, in Canada, where 17 percent of the nation is foreign born, it would have been expected that agreement here would be higher. All categories of respondents showed higher percentages of agreement in the United States, from religious fundamentalists to atheists to women to men in all age ranges.[79]

Despite the porous border between Canada and the United States, Canadians seem to be remaining, or becoming even more, Canadian. Social values are less conservative in general in Canada. Not only has Canada had a female prime minister, but the wife of Prime Minister Joe Clark, Maureen McTeer, kept her own name. Even Hilary Clinton did not dare go that far.

Our social values may be bringing us closer together as a nation. At the end of 2003, 58 percent of Canadians approved of Canada's decisions to allow same-sex marriage and decriminalize marijuana and 75 percent approved of Ottawa's decision not to invade Iraq. The results cut across regional boundaries, and although support for Ottawa was less in Alberta on the decision not to join the Iraq war, the majority was in agreement. Quebec was most likely to commend Ottawa for both the decision not to go to war *and* the decision to allow same-sex marriage.[80] (Quebec's responses may indicate only Quebecers' stand on the issues, and not necessarily a stronger commitment to federalism. For example, a resurgence in the popularity of Quebec sovereignty, not a priority after the 1995 referendum, occurred as a result of the Sponsorship Scandal.)

In 2004, an Ispos-Reid poll confirmed further divergences in social values: 60 percent of Americans agreed their religious life was important to them in daily life, while 33 percent of Canadians said the same. Seventy-one percent of Americans continued to support the death penalty, while only 42 percent of Canadians polled did.[81] According to Peter Newman, "for the first time we can differentiate our social policies from the Americans."[82]

The American presidential election of 2004 saw Canadians sharply divergent from Americans in their views of whether John Kerry, the Democratic candidate, or George W. Bush, the Republican candidate, should lead the United States. Seventy percent of Canadians would have voted for John Kerry who received about 48 percent of the American popular vote.[83]

What values do you think made the majority of Canadians prefer Kerry?

The Narcissism of Small Differences

The opposing view is that our pride in differences of opinion with the U.S. on these matters is exaggerated: we like to look cool and see the U.S. as religious and stodgy.[84] We like to make fun of Americans on programs like Rick Mercer's "Talking to Americans."

Our common heritage and long-standing close economic and cultural relationship give us too much in common to diverge greatly. A survey done for the Washington-based Woodrow Wilson International Centre for Scholars and the Canada Institute on North American Issues shows that certain deep social values are similar in the two countries.[85] Solid majorities in both countries agree that the government has a responsibility to take care of the poor and the elderly, that they don't want economic growth to take priority over the environment, and that they have the personal freedom to say what they wish about the government. There was a marked difference in response to this statement, however, "If a family member was [sic] hospitalized, I would be worried about how to pay for it," with 63 percent of Canadians disagreeing, and 62 percent of Americans agreeing, an indication of the current gap between the countries in national health care programs.

The Effect of 9/11

A 2005 Ipsos-Reid poll suggests that the events of and after 9/11, such as the invasion of Iraq, have led to a cooling of sentiment between Americans and Canadians at present. Only 53 percent of Canadians now see the U.S. as our closest ally, down from 60 percent in 2002; and only 14 percent of Americans cite Canada as their closest ally, down from 18 percent.[86]

Gregg believes the same events have been significant in that they have served to define the essential character of our culture and led us to confirm that Canadians and Americans see the world through different eyes. Our sense of being different has contributed to "a new, more outward, more confident nationalism."[87] He says that since 9/11, the majority of Canadians have wanted to upgrade the military, not so much for the sake of military might, but from the realization that if we are to exert ourselves and our views in the world, we must participate actively in it. His conclusions contradict the idea that Canada is a postmodern state, or a state without a national identity (see Chapter 1). We may simply have a national identity that is a paradox: Canadians are postmodern within the context of a sense of national sovereignty and attachment to the nation state of Canada and what it represents.

SUMMARY

This chapter looks at the similarities and differences in Canadian and American belief and value systems. Both nations share a British Protestant colonial heritage and language (with the exception of Quebec) with value placed on work, the individual, and the rule of law. However, they diverge in some respects that are considered superficial by some and profound by others. It does appear that Canada has begun to confirm a strong national identity, particularly in the wake of 9/11, although there are significant divisions in social values within the nation as there are within the United States.

KEY TERMS

American Dream 99

civil liberties 103

collectivism 104

empirical 100

evangelical 97

individualism 97

Manifest Destiny 96

Protestant work ethic 100

rule of law 95

TOPICS FOR CRITICAL THINKING AND REFLECTION

1. Do you know the story of your family's immigration to Canada? (This question does not apply to First Nation students whose immigration generally precedes recorded memory.) When, from where, and why did they come here?

2. How strongly do you identify with being Canadian? Check one and discuss your choice:
   (a) It is important to me.   ___
   (b) I rarely or never think about it.   ___
   (c) I have a positive view of it.   ___
   (d) I have a negative view of it.   ___
       If you were to be born again, what nationality would you choose if different from your own? Why?
       Does your sense of being Canadian and your pride in it depend on circumstance? For example, are you blasé about being Canadian at home, but proud when you are in another country? Why or why not?

3. The University of Calgary launched a course in 2003 called "The Culture of the Calgary Stampede." "It's a statement about contemporary values, contemporary issues, and contemporary belief systems," says the professor who is teaching it.[88] Students will study cowboy life past and present; Western identity; the relationship between the stampede, the city, and Native people; even the meaning of Calgary's nickname, Cowtown. The Stampede itself is about agriculture, ranching, art, politics, volunteerism, economic and urban development, and Western icons—it is a cultural phenomenon that defines Calgary and its region.
       Devise a course that reflects your particular region in the same way that "The Culture of the Calgary Stampede" reflects Calgary and that part of Alberta. Create a curriculum and a rationale for it, and research appropriate teaching and learning materials.

4. Here is a list of topics. Discuss the degree to which laws, behaviours, and attitudes reflect American and Canadian cultural patterns as identified in this chapter:
   (a) Gun control
   (b) Ballistic missile defence
   (c) Decriminalization of marijuana
   (d) Canada's sovereignty over the Northwest Passage
   (e) Cost and public funding of post-secondary education
   (f) Publicly funded health care

5. The CRTC has approved satellite radio services in Canada that will greatly expand the number of available channels. Canadian content standards apply, but what effect, if any, will this expansion have on Canadian artists and their music?

6. In the United States, controversy exists over the teaching of the theory of evolution in science classes versus the teaching of "intelligent design," which accepts the biblical account of creation. The majority of Americans (65 percent) favour teaching both as theories, while almost 40 percent favour intelligent design only. What are the arguments put forward by supporters of intelligent design? How do evolutionists view their theory? How do the proponents of intelligent design view evolution?[89]

Time Out for Latin America:
Diversity of Land and People

Latin America is a culture realm that, despite immense cultural, ethnic, and geographical diversity, is unified by a common Iberian colonial heritage. Spain and Portugal imposed their languages, their religion (Roman Catholicism), and the educational, social, judicial, political, and economic institutions that still dominate the region. The dominant culture throughout Latin America is of European descent; indigenous cultural groups, Latin Americans of African descent brought to parts of Latin America as slaves, and cultural groups of mixed heritage struggle for socioeconomic and political equality everywhere. Even the term *Latin* America reveals the European sources of its dominant elite.

However, despite the Iberian overlay, Latin America is culturally diverse.

- *Mexico*, although largely Spanish speaking, has important indigenous cultural influences. Ninety percent of Mexicans have some indigenous blood.[1]
- *Brazil* is Portuguese speaking with major African cultural influences.
- *Caribbean Latin America* includes Dominican Republic, Cuba, and other islands as well as Panama, coastal Venezuela, and Colombia. The region is largely Spanish speaking, but reflects African cultural influences and societies affected by plantation agricultural practices and economic dependence.
- *European Latin America* includes Argentina, Uruguay, and Chile. It is Spanish speaking and predominantly European (Spanish, Italian, British, and German) in flavour, culture, and character. Southern Brazil and the Colombian interior also reflect European norms.
- *Indian Latin America* includes Guatemala in Central America, and the Andean countries of Bolivia, Peru, and Ecuador in South America. The majority of people in these regions is indigenous, may speak only indigenous languages, and still follows indigenous cultural patterns. Paraguay is a blend of indigenous and European, with two official languages, Spanish and Guaraní.

Canadians are linked to Latin America through immigration and migrant worker agreements, trade agreements such as NAFTA, tourism, and increasingly through diplomatic and cultural exchanges. Brazil, with a population of almost 180 million and increasing exposure on the world economic scene, has been identified as an emerging power with which Canada should especially seek closer ties.

Keys to Understanding the Latin American World

Change

1. Inequity is at the root of the revolutions and dictatorial regimes that shook Latin America during the twentieth century. Democracy has taken hold, however, and the early part of this century is seeing a new phenomenon: grassroots organizations taking charge of the process of change. Indigenous groups in Bolivia, landless peasants in Brazil, and unemployed factory workers in Argentina are seeing some success in improving their lives and challenging long-established elites through mass, non-governmental popular movements.

2. Political change is occurring through the ballot box also. After half a century of brutal repression of socialist and left-wing political movements by military and right-wing forces, many countries have elected "leftist lite" governments— pragmatic leaders interested in development and globalization that brings with it social justice. President Luiz Inacio Lula da Silva of Brazil is one such leader.

3. Corruption has been another stumbling block to positive change in Latin America. Latin American society and governments are attempting to reign in corruption in political, economic, and judicial spheres.

Essential Values

1. Latin Americans respect power and status. When doing business, it is necessary to find the top person in the hierarchy because others, however friendly, are unlikely to have the authority to make decisions. Titles are respected as is intellectual achievement. "People like to do business with people who are somebody," said one commercial attaché, meaning somebody who has written a book, published poetry, or demonstrated the intellect in some way in addition to doing business.[2]

2. Latin Americans are not ruled by the clock. Punctuality is not essential, although Westerners are expected to be on time for meetings.

3. Men are expected to be dominant and women submissive. Ideally, men are *macho*: strong, caring, generous. The darker side of macho tends towards womanizing and empty bravado. Women are respected as mothers and nurturers, the guardians of family and spiritual values. Women have been able to achieve some success in the business sphere, particularly in Brazil, but have not made great inroads in politics.[3] Foreign women are treated with respect although flirtation often remains an undercurrent when they work with men, with the exception of Chile where a woman (Michelle Bachelet) has been elected president for the first time.

4. Family is highly valued as are relationships in general. Business is conducted on the basis of trust and close relationships. (See *personalismo*, Chapter 8.)

5. Passion and intuition about a project are more likely to determine a business deal than facts and figures alone.

6. Latin Americans like to celebrate life; they are generous hosts and convivial social companions. They can be, however, sensitive to perceived insult.

Cultural Tips

1. Take time to establish a relationship before trying to do a business deal. Many visits, lunches, and dinners are required for trust to be established. It is important for Latin Americans to *like* you when doing business. An introductory letter or introduction from a connection is the best way to get a foot in the door.

2. Latin Americans are high contact. A hand on your arm or back and other friendly gestures are frequent. Greeting between friends, women and women and men and women is often a kiss on the cheek (*un beso*). Men shake hands. If you are unsure as to whether to kiss or shake hands with people as you move from acquaintance to friend, take your cue from your host. Women initiate a *beso* with men, however.

3. Professional dress and appearance are important. Women doing business should dress conservatively to send the right message.

4. Do not expect Latin Americans to be punctual in business or for social events. "Latin American time" prevails. Pot-sweeteners often accompany deals. They are known as *mordidas* (bites) in Mexico.

5. Latin Americans eat late. In Uruguay, dinner may be at ten or eleven at night. Lunches may be followed by a siesta as in Spain.

Common Expressions in Spanish (Portuguese equivalent)

Buenos dias/Buenas tardes (Bom dia)/ Buenas noches (Bom tarde)	Good morning/Good afternoon/ Good evening
Hola (Olá)	Hi
Ciao (Até a vista)	Bye
Por favor (Por favor)	Please
Gracias/muchas gracias (Obrigado/muito obrigado)	Thank you/thank you very much.
Gracias a usted	Thank *you*
De nada/por nada/no hay de que (De nada)	You are welcome
Permiso (Disculpe)	Excuse me (when you are trying to get by someone)
Disculpe (Disculpe)	Sorry (when you have bumped into someone)

Chapter 5
Cultures in Comparison

In this chapter we will explore:

- Underlying cultural patterns and value systems of East and West
- A classification system for comparing cultures based on communication norms
- Three classification systems for comparing cultures based on values
- International business cultures as they relate to values

CULTURE REALMS: EAST AND WEST

Oh, East is East, and West is West, and never the twain shall meet,
Till Earth and Sky stand presently at God's great Judgment Seat;
But there is neither East nor West, Border, nor Breed, nor Birth,
When two strong men stand face to face, tho' they come from the ends of the earth!

From *The Ballad of East and West*[1]

Rudyard Kipling's famous ode to East and West suggests that the East and West are worlds apart, but we know that the two culture realms have met often and influenced each other throughout history. Nonetheless, major differences in values and cultural patterns have existed between them for thousands of years.

East and West are the broadest and perhaps most historically influential of the world's culture realms. As we saw in Chapter 3, culture realms can be broken down into smaller regions, which in turn can be broken down into yet smaller cultural groupings much like a Russian *marushka* nesting doll houses smaller and smaller dolls. Think of the East as one *marushka* doll, and the West as another, an apt metaphor since Russia is a place where East and West meet and merge (other examples are Turkey and Lebanon). The East, for the purposes of this discussion, primarily includes China, Japan, and Korea, the latter two countries heavily influenced by China, and the West includes Europe, predominantly Northern and Western Europe, and colonies established in Canada, Australia, New Zealand, and the United States.

Other major culture realms include the Middle East, a Eurocentric term coined in Europe along with "Near" and "Far East", a region heavily influenced by Islam (see Chapter 6). Sub-Saharan Africa also embodies distinctive cultural patterns and values, as do South Asia (see *Time Out for India*) and Latin America, another Eurocentric term coined in France.[2] (See *Time Out for Latin America.*)

There is overlapping of culture realms, and their characteristics and borders mutate over time. Nonetheless, to lay the groundwork for an examination of cultural classification systems, we'll look at the major underlying differences in philosophical traditions that have underpinned East and West for thousands of years and served as the foundation for their value systems and cultural patterns.

East

The Chinese orientation toward life was shaped by the blending of three different philosophies: Taoism, the most ancient, closely followed by Confucianism and Buddhism (see Chapter 6). All three philosophical traditions placed an emphasis on social harmony and moral living. Confucianism provided practical guidelines for ethical living, Taoism taught a way of life in harmony with nature, while Buddhism stressed compassion, moderation, and non-violence.[3]

Early Chinese civilization was technologically advanced, but practicality was the source of its inventive genius, not an abstract interest in scientific theory and investigation.[4] The Chinese, for example, invented the seismoscope, to detect earthquakes, and the magnetic compass over 2000 years ago, as well as papermaking, printmaking, fireworks, and gunpowder.

Gods were believed to exist, but more significant were family and the ancestors. In ancient China, every Chinese was first and foremost a member of various collectives: the clan, the village, and most importantly, the family. Collective harmony and obedience to elders and social superiors were the chief moral obligations of early Chinese society.

Taoism was founded by Lao Tzu, a philosopher who lived about 600 B.C.E. The word itself comes from *Tao* meaning "Way." Taoism is a guide to a harmonious existence in and with nature, and among human beings. Two principles underlie Taoism.

First, paradoxically, change is the one unchanging factor in the universe.[5] Cycles, oppositions, and contradictions form a moving whole: to accept one state of affairs is to acknowledge the existence of the opposite. The **yin** and the **yang** are ancient Taoist symbols that express this interconnection of opposites (see Figure 5.1).

Second, the way to exist in nature and in society is not to strive, but to "go with the flow" of nature to harness it to good use without aggressive intervention:

The highest good is like water. Water benefits all things generously and is without strife. It dwells in the lowly place that men disdain. Thus it comes near to the Tao.

Figure 5.1 Sign of the Tao

The *yin* is the feminine, dark, passive principle of the universe. It alternates with *yang*, the masculine, light, and active principle. *Yang* exists only because *yin* exists, and vice versa. Male and female are symbols for all opposites and work together for harmony, good, and wholeness. Happiness implies sadness, good implies bad, negative implies positive. This basic universal duality is reflected even in "sweet and sour" Chinese recipes.

The highest good loves the [lowly] earth for its dwelling. It loves the profound in its heart, it loves humanity in friendship, sincerity in speech, order in government, effectiveness in deeds, timeliness in action. Since it is without strife, it is without reproach.

Lao Tzu, *Tao Te Ching*[6]

Taoism is mystical and intuitive. In combination with pragmatic, non-religious, relationship-oriented **Confucianism,** it was the foundation of Chinese society for centuries. Confucius (the Latin name for Kǒng/Qiū, 551–479 B.C.E.) codified China's early sense of moral obligations into an organized, hierarchical system. He was concerned with Virtue,[7] the moral life, and the maintenance of a stable society. He accepted traditional deities without believing that they intervened in human lives, a concept very different from that of Western religions.

Confucius stressed five fundamental and reciprocal obligations necessary for living an honourable life: obligations between emperor and subject, between parent and child, between husband and wife, between older brother and younger brother, and between friends. Confrontation and debate were discouraged and loyalty and self-control encouraged.[8]

Confucianism (and Buddhism) took up the Taoist dynamic of **holism.** The traditional healing arts in China are based on the yin-yang principle and the essential elements of earth, fire, water, metal, and wood. Unlike Western healers, the Chinese were reluctant surgeons; to operate would be to disturb the harmony of elements. Many Chinese still dislike giving blood, and nowadays may be offered incentives at work to do so.[9]

The early Chinese conviction about the fundamental relatedness of all things led to the perception that objects are altered by context, that objects in and of themselves, like people, have little intrinsic meaning outside their context. Relationships exist among all things and relationships between people are the basis of society more than are institutionalized laws.[10] There is no word for "individualism" in Chinese,[11] and Japanese has many different words for each of "you" and "I." The appropriate ones are chosen in conversation according to the social context of the situation and the relative status of the speakers.[12]

Eastern logic derives from the yin and yang principle: if A is true, B might also be true, and result in knowledge more complete than either A or B, although it is always partial rather than absolute.[13] "Truth," then, depends on context; it is not absolute.

Cornerstones of Eastern culture stemming from Taoism, Confucianism, and Buddhism can be summed up to include collectivism, change as a constant, holism, truth derived from context, and knowledge derived from intuition.[14]

Communism did not erase thousands of years of cultural thought, and the ancient value systems remain a profound influence on Chinese and other Asian cultural patterns. Cultural change does occur, however, and as *Time Out for China* suggests, ancient Chinese values may be in the process of change.

West

Definitions of the West vary considerably, but wherever the borders are drawn, it is agreed that Western European culture and its offshoot cultures in North America and Oceania trace their origins to Greek and Judeo-Christian thought. Fundamental to both were the search for Truth,[15] and an early belief in the value of the individual and **personal agency.**

It is debatable as to whether the Greeks or the Hebrews invented individualism.[16] Both cultural groups viewed human beings as unique individuals with their own personal attributes, thoughts, and goals.

The sense of personal agency among the Greeks led to a tradition of competition in debate (not to mention sport), discussion, and personal opinion, and by the 5th century B.C.E. to democracy. The Greeks valued the skillful debate of ideas based on fixed organizational patterns, or rhetoric, which developed into the Western concepts of logic still used today.

In Canada, for example, we learn to write essays and make presentations that begin with an introduction, state a thesis, develop material "logically" by following various rules for the development of ideas, and end with a conclusion.

The Greeks were also curious about the fundamental nature of the world, and documented their observations looking for underlying rules that explained natural physical phenomena. They were empirical in orientation, that is, they attempted to build theories through observation and experience. They sought Truth, not Virtue.[17] Truth could be reached by means of a theorem such as if A is true, then B must be false, unlike the more fluid and intuitive Eastern concept of truth in context.

The Greeks believed in an essentially unchanging world governed by laws. Individual objects had observable attributes, and could be put into categories and subcategories on the basis of similar or different characteristics. Aristotle believed that the heavenly bodies moved, but were unchanging in their nature and the order of their movements,[18] and that the laws governing their movements could be discovered.

Greek logic developed alongside physics, and evolved into a linear and abstract kind of logic based on patterned reasoning, deductive and inductive, and on empirical fact, not **intuition.** The Greek emphasis on logic and rational, objective thought underlies Western notions about nature and truth. Logic was the road to "reality,"[19] and nature a big puzzle of laws that could be uncovered. Western science derives from Greek concepts of logic and nature,[20] and has been concerned with understanding the laws and rules of the universe—of reality—ever since Greece's Golden Age (with the exception of the "Dark Ages," a period of religious fervour and intellectual decline during which Greek logic and philosophy were preserved by the Arabs until the European Renaissance).

Both the Greeks and the Hebrews established the Western tradition of rule of law. The laws of the Jews came directly from God to Moses, and are the early basis of much of Western law and ethics today.

Northern and Western Europeans show most clearly the Western heritage of analysis, logic, and **rationality**.[21] Euro-Latin (Southern European) cultures are more person oriented, and more accepting of intuitive knowledge. Trompenaars and Hampden-Turner claim there is a clear-cut cultural border between the Northwest and Euro-Latin cultures; they claim a parallel line can also be drawn in Belgium between the Protestant Dutch northwest and the Catholic French Belgians southeast.[22]

In summary, cornerstones of Western thought and cultural patterns deriving from Greek and Judeo-Christian thought can be summed up to include individualism, knowledge derived from objective, rational thought, truth derived from unchanging principles, monotheism, and rule of law.

Hall believes that Westerners have become alienated from nature and suffer from a number of delusions, one of which is that life should "make sense."[23] Freud and Jung offered another reality of dreams and mental processes that do not follow the ordered patterns and **linearity** imposed by Western reason, but many Westerners remain skeptical of realities that cannot be empirically proven.[24] Meanwhile, the search for Truth continues: the 2004 Nobel Prize for physics was won by three Americans for revealing how forces in the atomic nucleus keep it from exploding, a discovery that moves us one step closer "to a 'grand theory' of how the universe operates."[25]

The broad brushstrokes of cultural differences between East and West will come up again as we elaborate on them in chapters to come. In the meantime, how do you approach the world? When it comes to making important decisions, do you value your intuition over objective, rational thought (do you make lists of advantages and disadvantages, for example), or do you go with your "gut feeling"?

COMPARING AND CLASSIFYING CULTURES

It will probably strike you right about now that to compare and classify cultures is a uniquely Western kind of activity! Nonetheless, we will take a look at the classification systems of twentieth-century anthropologists, sociologists, and international management consultants who have studied ethnic and national cultures.

EDWARD T. HALL: HIGH- AND LOW-CONTEXT CULTURES

Edward T. Hall is considered by many to be the father of intercultural communication, so much did his theories about culture derive from his observations of how people communicate. He grew up in the American Southwest, home to a variety of cultural communities such as Native, Spanish, and Anglo-American, and served with African-American troops in World War II in the Philippines and in Europe, then later as the Director of the Foreign Service Institute.

Hall recognized that information and meaning are two different things: all human beings receive and process data by means of the same senses, but the meaning we derive from that information comes largely from cultural assumptions we have absorbed (see Chapter 2). According to Hall, culture in its many forms dictates what we pay attention to and what we ignore.[26] This helps spare us from "information overload."

Hall divided cultures into two categories, high- and low-context, according to the sources of information from which they primarily derive meaning: either words, or a more holistic framework of communicative signs and symbols. He ranked cultures on a continuum of high to low, acknowledging that no culture is completely one or the other.

High-Context Cultures

In high-context communication, most of the information is either in the physical context or internalized in the person. Very little is in the verbal transmission of a message.[27] Meaning is implicitly transmitted. Explicit—written or verbal—information is not greatly required because people already share a lot of knowledge about each other. High-context cultures are usually culturally homogeneous, with a long history of traditions that bind members and make their thoughts and reactions predictable.

Contextual clues from which meaning is drawn come from data provided by the environment, the situation, and from the players: their age, sex, family and social background, and professional status. Body language, facial expression, use of space, and use of silence also transmit meaning. So much information can be gathered from contextual clues that little needs to be verbally defined. In Japan, for example, the smallest gesture or movement "speaks volumes." It is the unspoken that is understood.

In high-context cultures, conflict is often dealt with discreetly in order to maintain an environment of harmony. Direct confrontation is rare. In business, mediators and go-betweens are used in negotiations behind the scenes.[28] The assumption is that a relationship must be formed, and that the relationship will be long. Consequently, overt disagreement is best avoided. Contracts are often verbal, and may change as circumstances change.

Formality is often a feature of high-context cultures. Rules help keep members from straying into unpredictable communicative waters. Prescribed, ritualized responses are safe, and an effort is made to divulge as little as possible either verbally or through gestures and facial expressions. This cultural pattern has given rise to the Western stereotype of the "impassive" Asian.

High-context cultures include Japanese, Chinese, South Korean, African, Native American, and Arab, identified in that order by Hall.[29]

Low-Context Cultures

In low-context cultures, words carry much of the information required to communicate meaning. Low-context cultures are often culturally diverse and words are necessary because much less cultural knowledge can be assumed about people.

In such cultures, contracts are written out, signed, and binding. Details are explicit, "spelled out." Expressions like "lay your cards on the table," and "say what you mean" reveal the directness valued in negotiations. Negotiations proceed quickly with this no-nonsense approach, and competitive bidding is common. Facts take precedence over relationships and intuition; informality is accepted.

In low-context cultures, disagreement tends to be dealt with openly. Opposing parties state their positions to reach a resolution verbally clarified for everyone. It is acceptable to say "no" in low-context cultures (see Chapter 8) and "no" is not usually taken personally.[30]

Low-context cultures in the order identified by Hall include German-Swiss, German, Scandinavian, American, French, and English.[31] Cultures falling in the middle of the continuum include Greek, Latin, and Italian.

In communication between members of high- and low-context cultures, a high-context culture tends to try to create a communicative comfort zone. The Japanese, for example, like predictability and, in business, attempt to get to know their counterparts over time and through bonding over socializing after hours. Americans, in contrast, for example, do not feel the need to "know" their businesses partners, and are content with contracts and factual data.[32] They are often interchangeable cogs in an organization; negotiating a deal for them is an objective, not a subjective exercise.[33]

KLUCKHOHN, KLUCKHOHN, AND STRODTBECK'S VALUE ORIENTATIONS

Clyde and Florence Kluckhohn and Fred Strodtbeck proposed that all human societies must answer a limited number of universal problems regarding the meaning of life, and that their solutions are also limited in number and based on values. Different cultures have different preferred value-based responses (orientations) to these universal problems. Their theory has been tested in many cultures, used to help negotiating ethnic groups understand one another and to examine intergenerational value changes caused by migration.[34]

Clyde Kluckhohn began research in the 1930s. His wife, Florence, and student, Fred Strodtbeck, wrote *Variations in Value Orientations* based on their combined research. It was published in 1961 after Clyde's death. It is a warm account of people and life in the villages in which they lived, and includes transcripts of their conversations and interviews with villagers.

They studied five communities in the U.S. Southwest over a period of about twenty years: an off-reservation settlement of Navaho, a Zuni (Pueblo Indian) community, a Spanish-American village, a Mormon village, and an English-speaking farming village of Texan and Oklahoman homesteaders. While the cultural distinctions of each of these communities were marked, their physical environments were similar, with only water supply a key variant. This stunning region of mountains, canyons, valleys, and *arroyos* (streams or gulches) was famously photographed by Ansel Adams during the 1930s when much of this research was carried out (see photo, page 128).

Despite their concerns about the complexities of cross-cultural research methods and analysis based on the imperfect medium of language and translation,[35] the Kluckhohns and Strodtbeck proposed that, even though cultures change over time, all cultures must respond to the following five problems, and that there are three possible universal responses to each problem. (Chapter 9 discusses the relationship between culture, language, and thought.)

What Is a Culture's Time Orientation?

Do members primarily focus on the past, on the present, or on the future?

Past-oriented cultures look to the past as a guide to the present. When Mao Zedong, Chairman of the Communist Party of China until 1976 and leader of the Chinese Revolution in 1949, was asked what he thought of the French Revolution of 1789, he famously answered, "It's too early to say."[36]

Past-oriented cultures include China, with its long history of accumulated wisdom and tradition; France, focused on past cultural and conquest-related glories; England with its monarchic tradition, love of ritual, and colonial past; and Japan, with its ancient Shinto values.[37] World maps made in England once showed Britain's colonial possessions in pink or red, and school children gazed in awe at the extent of the Empire and England's influence. "The sun never sets," it was said, "on the British Empire."

Moonrise, Hernandez, New Mexico

Source: © Ansel Adams Publishing Rights Trust/CORBIS

Past-oriented cultures move slowly when making business deals and creating partnerships. They are more likely to create long-term than short-term plans, as time is long and change is slow. In Japan and China (not including Hong Kong with its own fast-paced culture and fast-changing cities like Shanghai), people feel pressured with questions like "How soon can you get back to us?"[38]

How would you explain this Maori saying: *the past is in front of us, there for guidance, and the future behind us*?

Present-oriented cultures include Filipino and Latin American. *Hay que vivir el momento* ("Live for the moment!") is a common popular expression. Tomorrow is uncertain, the past is part of the present, but better not dwelt on due to defeats and disappointments of various kinds, and the future is unknowable. Only "now" is real and to be lived to the fullest. Latin American governments have attempted to curb their peoples' penchant for staying out all night by passing laws that oblige bars and nightclubs to close at 4 or 5 a.m. to encourage workers to get home for a few hours sleep to be productive the next day. They have met with limited success. Getting to work on time is part of the future, and leaving a good party because a person has to get up early for work takes second place to the enjoyment of the moment. North Americans doing business in Latin America can be frustrated by the present orientation; the drive to complete a project and bring it to fruition by a specific date is less urgent.[39] *Mañana*, meaning "tomorrow," has stereotypically become associated with Latin Americans by North Americans partly because the tendency to be vague about the future is perceived to be laziness.

Among Muslims, looking too far into the future is discouraged: only God knows what the future will bring. *Bukra* is a word often heard in the Arab world. It means "tomorrow" literally, but has a vague meaning of sometime possibly in the near future—which is unknown by anyone but God.[40]

Future-oriented cultures include Canada and most strongly, the United States. Individuals save for the future, establish goals and steps to reach them, and engage in all kinds of pursuits aimed at a better, more productive, wealthier future. As nations, they look to the future—planning, controlling, and molding it. They are optimistic nations whose short pasts have justified their optimism.[41] Their business cultures emphasize short- and medium-term goals.

What kinds of frustrations might you predict in business negotiations between a future-oriented Canadian team and contacts in the Middle East or Latin America?

What Is a Culture's Relationship to Nature?

Are human beings masters of nature, submissive to nature, or in a relatively equal relationship with other elements of nature?

Western cultures have taken the view that human beings *dominate* nature. Judeo-Christian beliefs hold that God has dominion over man, and man over nature. This hierarchical concept contributed to the Western will to use science and technology to harness, tame, and exploit nature for the needs of humanity.

Cultures that see human beings as *subject to* the will of outside forces may believe strongly in fate, God, astrology, or genetics.[42] In Hinduism, human beings are often subject to the forces of fate, gods, or magic; in India, for example, astrology is popular as people see their fate related to movements of the stars. Fatalism is a cultural pattern in Latin America where the fusion of Catholic, indigenous, and African traditions resulted in a tendency to believe in destiny and luck and in the forces of magic and spells. Fidel Castro often makes reference to his "destiny" in interviews, and in the streets of Havana he is said to be attended by both Western-trained doctors and a Cuban *babaláo,* a priest from the Cuban-African religion of *santeria,* just in case (*por si acaso*). Islamic cultures are also fatalistic: human beings are absolutely dependent on the will of God, their destinies decided by Him alone.

Cooperative cultures view human beings as a part of nature and see spirituality in all its aspects. They include North American and other indigenous peoples around the world, as well as Asian cultures with Taoist and Buddhist underpinnings.

What Are Social Relationships Based On?

Do people relate in a hierarchical or **"lineal"** way (*lineal* means "in a direct line") in relationships predicated on authority? Do they interact as equals in "collateral" relationships with an emphasis on group consensus? Or do they relate as individuals with each member of the group in control of his or her own destiny?

Arab and Latin American culture is *hierarchical.* Latin American cultures respect power, and authoritarian rule often predominates in political, business, and family spheres. The hierarchical structures of the Roman Catholic Church and Spanish top-down colonial rule married well with indigenous hierarchical systems (Maya, Inca, Aztec) to create cultures respectful of power.

Arab cultures are also highly respectful of power, and people who do not value themselves highly or assert power are not respected.[43] In Abu Dhabi, for example, licence plates indicate a person's level of authority: the lowest numbers are for the most important families. Police may hesitate to stop a car with a low-number licence plate.

Collective cultures stress the good of the group—family foremost, then larger social entities. Collective cultures predominate in the world, and include many African, Asian, South Asian, and Aboriginal cultures around the world.

Western cultures stress the preeminence of the *individual.* They tend to be democratic in political orientation, and democratic in a social sense, with less respect for power than for the equality of individuals. Western cultures exhibit degrees of individuality, with Mediterranean cultures more family- and group-oriented than Northern European cultures.

What Motivates Activity?

Do people have a "being" motivation that validates authentic, internally motivated behaviour and aspirations? Do they have a "being-in-becoming" motivation and seek activity that leads to personal, often spiritual, growth? Or does "doing" motivate action, with stress on achievement and both internal and external validation?

Being cultures value personally satisfying activity. Latin American cultures tend to be being oriented; they stress the moment, the present, spontaneity, pleasure. Leisure time is spent chatting with friends, drinking coffee, extending an enjoyable moment without guilt.[44] Arab cultures also enjoy socializing and extending pleasurable time in talk. Business can wait. In Latin America a common toast is *Salud, amor, y pesetas, y el tempo para gozarlos:* health, love, and wealth, and the time to enjoy them.[45] The pleasure derived from these activities has a humanistic, almost spiritual, value.

Being-in-becoming cultures are motivated by activity focused on personal growth and often the spiritual dimension of life.[46] Buddhism, with its stress on compassion, Taoism with its focus on patience and waiting for revelations of Truth, and Hinduism with its focus on daily devotional acts reflect being-in-becoming cultural patterns. Many North Americans are turning towards these traditions in search of a life of meaning beyond consumerism.

Doing cultures stress achievement, action, productivity, efficiency. Validation for activity is often external, in the form of praise or bonuses or prizes. "Actions speak louder than words", "Done!" and "No sooner said than done" are common expressions reinforcing action. People are in a hurry to get more done in less time. Multi-tasking is good. "Time is money" goes the American saying. The action-oriented vision of life has helped create the dynamic, powerful, and innovative culture of the United States.

What Is the Orientation towards Human Nature?

Do people believe that human beings are born evil, cannot be trusted, and must be controlled? And if so, are they capable of change (mutable), or not (immutable)? Or do they believe human beings are a mixture of good and evil? If so, are they able to improve or regress (mutable), or not (immutable)? Or do they believe that human beings are inherently good and well meaning? If so, are they capable of corrupt actions (mutable), or do they maintain goodness (immutable)?

The authors applied this orientation to American dominant culture. They noted, for example, that the Puritan orientation to human nature would be described by most as basically *evil,* although human nature is perfectible with much effort and control. They also note that there may be a shift in the United States in which more people are "now" (1961) seeing human nature as a mixture of good and evil: control and effort are required to maintain goodness, but on the whole lapses need not be severely condemned. That orientation may be shifting back again at present.

Islam suggests that people naturally veer towards evil and require control. Rules for daily conduct and strict punishments for infractions of forbidden activities and temptations are believed to have been dictated by God to keep people on a path of virtue.

Kluckhohn, Kluckhohn, and Strodtbeck viewed the majority of cultures as tending towards **mixture of good and evil** views of human nature.[47] The Taoist philosophy of balance suggests a vision of human beings forming a natural part of a balanced universe. Europe's tradition of humanistic philosophical thought also tends towards this variation.

Kluckhohn, Kluckhohn, and Strodtbeck propose that a society perceiving human beings to be **inherently good** may not exist, but that it is a variant position within societies. Buddhism is most associated with the belief in the essential goodness of humankind: the Dalai Lama, for example, is an international icon of goodness and kindness. Confucius was said to be a kind, compassionate, and humble person. His teachings are summed up in the word *jen,* which implies love and respect for the dignity of human life.[48] The Anabaptist view of infant baptism as unnecessary also implies that human beings are born pure, but are mutable, and must consciously choose good (baptism) as adults.

GEERT HOFSTEDE AND CULTURE'S VALUE DIMENSIONS

The research of Geert Hofstede from the Netherlands also confirmed that cultures differ most at the level of values. Hofstede's work with national cultures has been useful in theories and practices of cross-cultural management.

Hofstede studied IBM affiliates in 64 countries using a total of over 116 000 questionnaires in a massive research project centred on national cultural differences. It resulted in the publication of *Culture's Consequences* in 1980. Hofstede identified four independent dimensions of culture based on values. He revisited his study ten years later, identifying changes that had occurred around the world affecting cultural values, and adding research based on a fifth value dimension that addressed the Western bias of his first study. A second book resulted, *Cultures and Organizations: Software of the Mind,* published in 1997.

The original IBM studies used a questionnaire conceived by Western minds. Non-Western respondents were obliged to answer the questions in translation, and researchers were concerned about cultural bias: could the results really express their values accurately? Such words as "freedom" and "respect," for example, mean different things in different cultures.[49]

Further research led by Canadian cross-cultural psychologist Michael Bond aimed to address the concern over cultural bias. Bond asked social scientists from China and

Taiwan to prepare a list of 10 basic values for Chinese people. The new survey was called the Chinese Value Survey and was administered to 100 students in 23 countries. The additional research resulted in the identification and validation of a fifth dimension of culture.

Hofstede's Five Value Dimensions

Power Distance refers to the extent to which the members of a culture accept inequality of power and authority whether within institutions such as the family or in wider social, political, and economic spheres. There is a power distance within all societies, but some societies are "more equal than others." Power Distance scores are high for Latin, Asian, and African countries (i.e., relatively greater inequality is accepted) and smaller for Anglo Celtic, Germanic, and Nordic countries. (See Table 5.1, page 134.)

Individualism–Collectivism refers to the preference of a culture to promote the good of the individual over the good of the group, or the good of the group over the good of the individual. Members of individualist cultures are applauded for pursuing personal goals and expressing personal opinions; members of collectivist cultures are shy about expressing their personal feelings or opinions openly. Individualism prevails in Western countries, while collectivism prevails in much of the rest of the world, with Latin American countries dominating in this study. (See Table 5.2, page 135.)

Masculinity–Femininity refers to the roles assigned to men and women within the culture. According to the IBM studies, women's values vary less than men's, and men's values across cultures cover a range from very assertive and competitive to modest and caring, the values Hofstede associates with femininity. The assertive end of the masculine–feminine dimension is labelled masculine, the opposite end of nurturing values, feminine.

The women in feminine countries have the same modest, caring values as the men; in the masculine countries, women can be somewhat assertive and competitive, but not as much so as the men. Their assertiveness may also take different forms. Masculinity is high in Japan (ranked number one) and in European countries Germany, Austria, and Switzerland. It falls mid-range in Anglo countries and ranks low in the Scandinavian countries and the Netherlands. It is quite high in some Latin countries and Italy, while relatively low in France. (See Table 5.3, page 136.)

Uncertainty Avoidance refers to the degree to which members of a society tolerate ambiguity and uncertainty and to the degree to which they feel uncomfortable in unstructured situations without established rules for conduct. Such a situation elicits discomfort and uncertainty for a culture at the high, fearful end of the continuum. Members of these cultures may also be prone to emotional behaviour in public.

Cultures at the opposite end of the continuum are more tolerant of differing opinions and responses and are comfortable without large numbers of rules. People are not expected to express emotions in public.

Table 5.1

Power distance index (PDI) values for 50 countries and 3 regions

RANK	COUNTRY OR REGION	PDI SCORE	RANK	COUNTRY OR REGION	PDI SCORE
1	Malaysia	104	29/30	Iran	58
2/3	Guatemala	95	29/30	Taiwan	58
2/3	Panama	95	31	Spain	57
4	Philippines	94	32	Pakistan	55
5/6	Mexico	81	33	Japan	54
5/6	Venezuela	81	34	Italy	50
7	Arab countries	80	35/36	Argentina	49
8/9	Ecuador	78	35/36	South Africa	49
8/9	Indonesia	78	37	Jamaica	45
10/11	India	77	38	USA	40
10/11	West Africa	77	39	Canada	39
12	Yugoslavia	76	40	Netherlands	38
13	Singapore	74	41	Australia	36
14	Brazil	69	42/44	Costa Rica	35
15/16	France	68	42/44	Germany F.R.	35
15/16	Hong Kong	68	42/44	Great Britain	35
17	Colombia	67	45	Switzerland	34
18/19	El Salvador	66	46	Finland	33
18/19	Turkey	66	47/48	Norway	31
20	Belgium	65	47/48	Sweden	31
21/23	East Africa	64	49	Ireland (Rep. of)	28
21/23	Peru	64	50	New Zealand	22
21/23	Thailand	64	51	Denmark	18
24/25	Chile	63	52	Israel	13
27/28	South Korea	60	53	Austria	11

Source: From Hofstede, Geert. *Cultures and Organizations: Software of the Mind*. New York: McGraw-Hill, 1997, p. 26. © Geert Hofstede BV, reprinted with permission.

Table 5.2

Individualism index (IDV) value for 50 countries and 3 regions

RANK	COUNTRY OR REGION	IDV SCORE	RANK	COUNTRY OR REGION	IDV SCORE
1	USA	91	28	Turkey	37
2	Australia	90	29	Uruguay	36
3	Great Britain	89	30	Greece	35
4/5	Canada	80	31	Philippines	32
4/5	Netherlands	80	32	Mexico	30
6	New Zealand	79	33/35	East Africa	27
7	Italy	76	33/35	Yugoslavia	27
8	Belgium	75	33/35	Portugal	27
9	Denmark	74	36	Malaysia	26
10/11	Sweden	71	37	Hong Kong	25
10/11	France	71	38	Chile	23
12	Ireland (Rep. of)	70	39/41	West Africa	20
13	Norway	69	39/41	Singapore	20
14	Switzerland	68	39/41	Thailand	20
15	Germany F.R.	67	42	El Salvador	19
16	South Africa	65	43	South Korea	18
17	Finland	63	44	Taiwan	17
18	Austria	55	45	Peru	16
19	Israel	54	46	Costa Rica	15
20	Spain	51	47/48	Pakistan	14
21	India	48	47/48	Indonesia	14
22/23	Japan	46	49	Colombia	13
22/23	Argentina	46	50	Venezuela	12
24	Iran	41	51	Panama	11
25	Jamaica	39	52	Ecuador	8
26/27	Brazil	38	53	Guatemala	6
26/27	Arab countries	38			

Source: From Hofstede, Geert. *Cultures and Organizations: Software of the Mind*. New York: McGraw-Hill, 1997, p. 53. © Geert Hofstede BV, reprinted with permission.

Table 5.3

Masculinity index (MAS) values for 50 countries and 3 regions

RANK	COUNTRY OR REGION	MAS SCORE	RANK	COUNTRY OR REGION	MAS SCORE
1	Japan	95	28	Singapore	48
2	Austria	79	29	Israel	47
3	Venezuela	73	30/31	Indonesia	46
4/5	Italy	70	30/31	West Africa	46
4/5	Switzerland	70	32/33	Turkey	45
6	Mexico	69	32/33	Taiwan	45
7/8	Ireland (Rep. of)	68	34	Panama	44
7/8	Jamaica	68	35/36	Iran	43
9/10	Great Britain	66	35/36	France	43
9/10	Germany F.R.	66	37/38	Spain	42
11/12	Philippines	64	37/38	Peru	42
11/12	Colombia	64	39	East Africa	41
13/14	South Africa	63	40	El Salvador	40
13/14	Ecuador	63	41	South Korea	39
15	USA	62	42	Uruguay	38
16	Australia	61	43	Guatemala	37
17	New Zealand	58	44	Thailand	34
18/19	Greece	57	45	Portugal	31
18/19	Hong Kong	57	46	Chile	28
20/21	Argentina	56	47	Finland	26
20/21	India	56	48/49	Yugoslavia	21
22	Belgium	54	48/49	Costa Rica	21
23	Arab cultures	53	50	Denmark	16
24	Canada	52	51	Netherlands	14
25/26	Malaysia	50	52	Norway	8
25/26	Pakistan	50	53	Sweden	5
27	Brazil	49			

Source: From Hofstede, Geert. *Cultures and Organizations: Software of the Mind*. New York: McGraw-Hill, 1997, p. 84. © Geert Hofstede BV, reprinted with permission.

Latin countries, along with Japan, scored high in uncertainty avoidance, and lower scores prevailed in Anglo Celtic, Nordic, and the (non-Communist) Chinese cultures of Singapore and Hong Kong. (Mainland China was not part of the study.) Greece showed the highest score for uncertainty avoidance. (See Table 5.4, page 138.)

On the philosophical and religious level, this dimension also deals with Truth: to what degree do cultures require Absolute Truth(s), and to what degree can they cope with relative truths and "gray" areas of morality and conduct?

Confucian Dynamism* or *Long-term versus Short-term Orientation is the fifth dimension uncovered by Bond in an effort to find values that explained the phenomenal economic success of the "Five Dragons"—Hong Kong, Taiwan, Singapore, Japan, and South Korea.[50] The questionnaire designed by Chinese scholars focused on Virtue and uncovered values related to Confucianism. (See Table 5.5, page 139.)

Long-term orientation (LTO) values are thrift, perseverance, ordering relationships by status, and having a sense of shame[51]; they are oriented towards the future. Values associated with short-term orientation (STO) are respect for tradition, personal stability, reciprocation of gifts, greetings and favours, and protecting one's "face"; they are oriented towards the past and present. While both poles are Confucian, it seems that the LTO pole supports entrepreneurial activity, while the STO pole, if overstressed, discourages it.

Criticism of Hofstede

Hofstede's research has met with criticism regarding methodology and the Western bias of his early work. The Individualism-Collectivism continuum has been questioned, for example; several studies put into question, refute, or nuance the supposed Japanese tendency towards collectivism. Other studies do not support the labelling of the United States as a highly individualistic nation, and rather suggest that Western European nations such as France come closest to the individualistic ideal. Finally, other studies indicate that India incorporates elements of both collectivism and individualism.[52]

Hofstede has also been criticized for assuming that IBM employees accurately reflect national cultures, and that questionnaires can accurately reflect values of groups.[53]

Other researchers felt that shifts in work-related value dimensions had occurred after Hofstede's 1980-based conclusions due to environmental changes since then. They studied nine countries, seven of the forty ranked by Hofstede, and added the People's Republic of China and Russia. Among their results, both Russia and China scored high in uncertainty avoidance and on masculinity–femininity (at the top of the masculinity end), while Germany shifted more towards the feminine side as did the U.S.[54]

Hofstede rejects other criticism directly challenging his choice of terms for the Masculinity–Femininity Dimension. Critics would prefer he use the terms

Table 5.4

Uncertainty avoidance index (UAI) values for 50 countries and 3 regions

RANK	COUNTRY OR REGION	UAI SCORE	RANK	COUNTRY OR REGION	UAI SCORE
1	Greece	112	28	Ecuador	67
2	Portugal	104	29	Germany F.R.	65
3	Guatemala	101	30	Thailand	64
4	Uruguay	100	31/32	Iran	59
5/6	Belgium	94	31/32	Finland	59
5/6	El Salvador	94	33	Switzerland	58
7	Japan	92	34	West Africa	54
8	Yugoslavia	88	35	Netherlands	53
9	Peru	87	36	East Africa	52
10/15	France	86	37	Australia	51
10/15	Chile	86	38	Norway	50
10/15	Spain	86	39/40	South Africa	49
10/15	Costa Rica	86	39/40	New Zealand	49
10/15	Panama	86	41/42	Indonesia	48
10/15	Argentina	86	41/42	Canada	48
16/17	Turkey	85	43	USA	46
16/17	South Korea	85	44	Philippines	44
18	Mexico	82	45	India	40
19	Israel	81	46	Malaysia	36
20	Colombia	80	47/48	Great Britain	35
21/22	Venezuela	76	47/48	Ireland (Rep. of)	35
21/22	Brazil	76	49/50	Hong Kong	29
23	Italy	75	49/50	Sweden	29
24/25	Pakistan	70	51	Denmark	23
24/25	Austria	70	52	Jamaica	13
26	Taiwan	69	53	Singapore	8
27	Arab countries	68			

Source: From Hofstede, Geert. *Cultures and Organizations: Software of the Mind*. New York: McGraw-Hill, 1997, p. 113. © Geert Hofstede BV, reprinted with permission.

Table 5.5

Long-term orientation index (LTO) values for 23 countries

RANK	COUNTRY OR REGION	LTO SCORE	RANK	COUNTRY OR REGION	LTO SCORE
1	China	118	13	Poland	32
2	Hong Kong	96	14	German F.R.	31
3	Taiwan	87	15	Australia	31
4	Japan	80	16	New Zealand	30
5	South Korea	75	17	USA	29
6	Brazil	65	18	Great Britain	25
7	India	61	19	Zimbabwe	25
8	Thailand	56	20	Canada	23
9	Singapore	48	21	Philippines	19
10	Netherlands	44	22	Nigeria	16
11	Bangladesh	40	23	Pakistan	0
12	Sweden	33			

Source: From Hofstede, Geert. *Cultures and Organizations: Software of the Mind.* New York: McGraw-Hill, 1997, p. 166. © Geert Hofstede BV, reprinted with permission.

Achievement–Nurturing, but Hofstede defends his choice arguing that values associated with masculinity and femininity are understood and accepted universally: "I believe these critics hold a shallow view of the roots of human behaviour. Sexes and sex roles are one of the most profound facts of human existence."[55]

TROMPENAARS AND HAMPDEN-TURNER'S FIVE CULTURAL ORIENTATIONS

Fons Trompenaars and Charles Hampden-Turner suggest a Taoist, dynamic and holistic model that, with a business-oriented twist, aims to show how opposing cultural values can be reconciled to facilitate intercultural business management. The ultimate goal of Trompenaars and Hampden-Turner is to harness and reconcile apparently conflicting values implied by diversity in order to create wealth.

Knowing cultural values helps cross-cultural managers understand other ways of seeing, thinking creatively, and providing leadership, which is about solving dilemmas.

When opposing values are harmonized, conflict is replaced by a positive synergy, they claim. Opposing values are not negations of each other, but rather reflections of reverse priorities of the same values.

For example, in China, Japan, and Southeast Asia, a book starts at "the back," people read left to right, and usually in vertical columns, and names are last name, then first. In the West, family names are usually second, and books start at "the front." Such oppositions are not stumbling blocks when they are understood. They reflect choices made long ago that have led to logical patterns that need to be understood for the creative resolution of blendable oppositions.[56]

Trompenaars and Hampden-Turner's model can appear contradictory: cultures may score close to one end of a continuum on a dimension, yet exhibit behaviour that would indicate a score closer to the other end. The pair is aware of this, and explains apparent contradictions by emphasizing the dynamic nature of culture. As they put it, cultures "dance from one end to the other of continuums; they are not stuck in one position."[57]

Their books are highly readable and have a tongue-in-cheek quality. Trompenaars uses personal anecdotes to illustrate points, and often draws on humour that borders on stereotyping. He defends his approach by saying that cultures satirize and stereotype themselves; by laughing, we remind ourselves of superficialities as well as the need to get beyond them.[58]

Trompenaars, who began the research, studied national cultures. He presented the dilemma in the box below to participants in training workshops around the world and to 65 000 managers in his cross-cultural data base of 65 countries. Their answers to this dilemma and others like it reveal culture-based values.

"Dilemmas are universal," writes Trompenaars, "while the answers, it seems, are culturally determined."[59]

DID THE PEDESTRIAN DIE?

You are a passenger in a car driven by a close friend. He hits a pedestrian driving 30 miles an hour in the city where the maximum speed allowed is 20 miles an hour. There are no witnesses. His lawyer says that if you are prepared to testify under oath that he was only driving 20 miles per hour it may save him from serious consequences.

1. What right has your friend to expect you to protect him?
   (a) My friend has a *definite* right, as a friend, to expect me to testify to the lower figure.

(b) He has *some* right, as a friend, to expect me to testify to the lower figure.

(c) He has *no* right, even as a friend, to expect me to testify to the lower figure.

2. Would you help your friend in view of the obligations you feel towards society?

(d) I would testify to the lower figure.

(e) I would not testify to the lower figure.

Source: Trompenaars, Fons. *Did the Pedestrian Die?* Oxford, U.K.: Capstone Publishing Ltd., 2003, pp. 1–2.

The above question illustrates the ***universalist versus particularist*** value dimension. In the universalist cultures of Switzerland and North America, over 93 percent of respondents chose (c) and (e). In particularist cultures like China and Venezuela, less than 35 percent chose that combination.[60]

Why? According to Trompenaars, in countries where Protestantism predominates, core values include law and authority, codified in writing and "checked by God and lawyers"! In Catholic cultures like Venezuela, people are charmed by the exception (the "particular") rather than the rule and are more community than law oriented. Besides, "God wasn't looking" and guilt is often ridiculed in Catholic cultures.[61]

"Is the pedestrian dead?" someone asked at a seminar. "Yes, very dead," replied Trompenaars. A French woman became angry at this response. She said she would not have chosen (b), but rather (a) had she known. Sticking by friends would be more important than the law in such a dilemma.

China and other Asian cultures are classed as being more particularist because of the value placed on relationships and connections in these societies.

Now that you've had a taste of the Trompenaars–Hampden-Turner methodology, we'll look at their taxonomy. Each pair of seeming oppositions reflects the other. In "Building Cross-Cultural Competence" the authors use examples from the political, ethical, scientific, business, and artistic spheres to back up the dimensions as they are ascribed to various countries and regions. For example, they analyze American movies and show how they embody values ascribed to American culture.

Universalism–Particularism

Universalism emphasizes rules that apply to everyone (a "universe" of people), while particularism emphasizes the uniqueness of each situation and exceptions to the rule. Neither approach is superior to the other. American culture stresses the resourcefulness of the individual; Chinese culture stresses the survival of the group. Both cultures made choices that led to survival, not destruction. The diverging values stem from the same dilemma, and looked at from this perspective, can be reconciled.[62]

The U.K. tends towards universalism, as does Canada, although the U.K.'s love for its eccentrics gives it something of the particularist. France, according to Trompenaars and Hampden-Turner, has more particularist characteristics with its emphasis on unique and superlative cuisine and wine.

Japan falls into the particularist fold along with France. Particularism in the form of Zen gardens and flower arrangement celebrates the aesthetic component of particularism.

Universalism is conducive to equal rights and international law, while particularism can be hostile to conforming to it.[63] The United States, while largely universalist, often resists conforming to international law—dancing, in this instance, to the other end of the continuum.

Individualism–Communitarianism

Individualism emphasizes the individual, personal freedom, and human rights, while communitarianism stresses social responsibility, harmonious relations and cooperation within the family, organization, community, and nation in which an individual has membership.

The continuum of these apparently opposing tendencies can be redrawn as a circle. In other words, in individualist cultures, the individual's effort assures community benefit (Adam Smith believed that self-interest led as if by an "invisible hand" to social and public benefit), just as the communitarian culture assures individual benefit through group effort.[64]

Among the most individualist cultures fall Canada, the United States, Czech Republic, Denmark, Switzerland, Netherlands, Finland, and Australia, in that order. Negative sides to the form of individualism adopted in the United States are its fear of cooperative movements, and its high consumption of the world's resources.[65] Canada, while statistically a touch more individualist, does not have the same fear of cooperative movements, falling more along the lines of European expressions of individualism. The norm in Canada is thus both universalist and individualist.

Among the most communitarian cultures are Egypt, Nepal, Mexico, India, Japan, Brazil, the Philippines, France and China, in that order.

Specificity–Diffuseness

Specificity emphasizes precision, reductive analysis, and "getting to the point," while diffuseness looks to wholes, relations of parts, and to the larger context. Numbers and words are specific; patterns, configurations, and images are diffuse—Chinese words often combine apparent opposites to create subtlety of meaning (see Figure 5.2).

Trompenaars and Hampden-Turner put Protestantism at the root of specificity, and Catholicism as the root of diffuseness in Western cultures.[66] Protestantism

Figure 5.2 Chinese Word for *Risk*

The Chinese word for risk combines the character for *opportunity* and the one for *danger*.

conceived of a mechanical universe (Newtonian physics) that contributed directly to the industrial revolutions in Britain and America, while Catholicism stressed a more mysterious reality.

Relatively specific countries include the United States, the U.K., the Netherlands, Canada, Denmark, and Australia, with the addition of Eastern European countries with bad memories of communism such as Bulgaria, Czech Republic, Russia, Poland, and Hungary.[67]

More diffuse countries include South Korea, Japan, Thailand, Malaysia, Singapore, the Philippines, France, Portugal, Brazil, Venezuela, Mexico, and the regions of East Asia, Catholic Europe, and South America.

The authors acknowledge that there are many diffuse thinkers in the West, and differences between the West and other realms are not as marked as under the individualist–communitarian dimension. They speculate that the right-brain, left-brain dichotomy may have something to do with the specificity–diffuseness dimension. The right brain is associated with holistic, synthesizing, intuitive, and visual perception, while the left brain is analytic, reductive, rational, verbal, sequential, and segmented.[68] Individuals across cultures may exhibit right- or left-brain dominance.

Achieved–Ascribed Status

In some cultures, status is achieved by means of a person's record of success and merit; in others, it is ascribed through birth, connections, and "who you are," not "what you have done." The United States followed by Canada, Australia, the U.K., and Sweden ranked highest at the achieved end of the scale, with Yugoslavia, then Korea, Poland, Russia, Japan, China, and Belgium at the ascribed end.[69]

Inner–Outer Direction

Are cultures motivated by internal guilt, convictions, and conscience, or do they modify their behaviour according to external influences, such as the whims of fate or forces of nature? Inner-directed images predominate in Judeo-Christian cultures in which human beings strive to dominate nature, while outer-directed cultures adjust themselves to external forces of nature and events and attempt to harness new or unexpected forces to their own purposes.[70]

Eastern martial arts reflect an other-directed motivation, as did the war philosophy of Sun Tzu who focused on using terrain and natural elements to "naturally" defeat the enemy. Alexander the Greek, in contrast, won wars by his brilliant strategy of organizing troops. Both were winners.

This dimension is also about Virtue, Beauty, and moral direction, which can come from within, or be imposed by society.

Canadians and Americans, followed by Germans, most strongly exemplify the inner-directed approach. They believe in taking charge of a situation and not leaving things to chance or nature, the majority agreeing with the statement "Trusting to fate never turned out well." China and Indonesia were the most strongly outer directed, followed by Japan, Thailand, and Singapore.[71] Their preference was for the statement "Getting a good job depends on being in the right place at the right time," rejected by most Canadians and Americans.

Sequential–Synchronous Time Orientation

Is time linear, like a line of sequential events that pass us by at regular intervals,[72] or is it cyclical and repetitive, encompassing past, present, and future like the seasons and cycles of nature?

The Chinese thought of time as a thread joining the past to the present and stretching into the future. They also thought of time as a winding or circular track, following natural cycles of decay and regeneration. The two conceptions operated in tandem, like *yin* and *yang*.[73]

Trompenaars and Hampden-Turner suggest that individuals in cultures leaning towards a sequential view of time like to do one thing at a time and work in stages towards the completion of a task. In shops in sequential cultures like the Netherlands and Belgium, customers take a number and wait their turn to be served in orderly lineups. Individuals from synchronous cultures are comfortable doing a number of things at once—talking on the phone to a friend while serving a customer, for example, or serving customers at the same time.

It may be argued that the Chinese have a profound future as well as past orientation (see Kluckhohn & Strodtbeck, page 126). North Americans make long-term plans of 10 years; in China, 40, 50, or even 60 years is not uncommon, and concern for future generations goes beyond children and grandchildren, as evidenced by the one-child policy adopted in 1979 to ensure China's ability to feed itself.

How does such a seemingly dual orientation fit Trompenaars' and Hampden-Turner's interpretation of the Chinese orientation to time? How does it tally with Hofstede's Confucian Dynamism?

Hong Kong, Israel, South Korea, and China are synchronous; while Turkey, India, Canada, and the United States appeared to be more sequential in their use of time.

VALUES AND DOING BUSINESS AROUND THE WORLD

The popular *Kiss, Bow, or Shake Hands: How to Do Business in Sixty Countries*[74] presented a way of comparing cultural value systems based on three criteria as they play out in business. The first is the locus of decision making: are decisions made by individuals or are they collective? The second relates to the source of anxiety reduction. All people suffer stress and anxiety and find ways of reducing it. Cultures typically favour one of four sources of stress reduction: interpersonal relationships, religion, technology, law (rules). Finally, inequality exists in all cultures. Who controls the power and economic systems of a culture? Is power based on race? socio-economic status? ethnicity? or a combination of these factors.[75] See Table 5.6 (page 146) for a compilation of their observations.

SUMMARY

In this chapter, we have seen that the world can be divided into very broad culture realms such as East and West. East and West have developed value systems and ways of perceiving reality that differ in significant ways. These ancient value systems have endured, and are reflected in modern classification systems of culture that have attempted to describe differences in national and ethnic cultures based on value systems, ways of communicating, and ways of perceiving and organizing reality. These classification systems have been useful in intercultural conflict management, and in international business management.

KEY TERMS

Confucianism 122	lineal 130	rationality 124
high context 125	linearity 124	Taoism 121
holism 122	low context 126	yin/yang 121
intuition 123	personal agency 123	

Table 5.6

What you need to know to do business in . . .

DOMINANT CULTURE OF . . .	LOCUS OF DECISION-MAKING	SOURCES OF STRESS REDUCTION	POWER INEQUITY
Brazil	Individual, but family counts in decision	Family on both sides (also religion)	Class system based on race and wealth; women have less power
Canada	Individual within context of company policy	Belonging to social organizations; recognition of achievements	Emphasis on ability and merit in promotion; First Nations and some minorities unequal
China	Collective/family but may be changing	Family, group harmony	In theory equal, but economic divisions now
England	Individual	Rules, courtesy	Class system but laws apply to all
France	Individual but strong central authority	Status, rank, formality, allowed to show feelings	Legal equality; superiors are deferred to; status counts more than gender; minorities struggle
Germany	Individual	Rules, order, formality	Hierarchical; bias against some minorities
India	Moderately collectivist (strong caste attachment)	One knows one's place within castes; emotions may be shown	Rigid structure of inequality based on caste; males dominant
Japan	Group	High anxiety, high suicide rate; work ethic gives structure and stability	Age is revered; males dominant; youth and women want change
Mexico	Individual within family interests	System of sponsorship (mentors) and extended family	Extreme rich–poor gap with race element, males dominant
Russia	Formerly party, now strong individualism . . .	Few ways to reduce stress—church resurfacing	Inequity based on income, minority status
Saudi Arabia	Male leaders through consensus	Islam; family, tribe, but considerable stress in kingdom	Equality under Islam, but rich–poor divide between Saudi nationals and foreign workers
United States	Individual, but everyone is a replaceable cog in the company	Time management and efficiency; work ethic, religion	Laws apply to all but disenfranchised exist

Source: Adapted from Morrison, Terri, Wayne A. Conaway, and George A. Borden. *Kiss, Bow, or Shake Hands: How to Do Business in Sixty Countries,* Holbrook, Mass.: Adams Media Corporation, 1994.

TOPICS FOR CRITICAL THINKING AND REFLECTION

1. Look at these three objects. Which two go together in your opinion?

What goes with the cow? A or B?

A   B

Source: Reprinted with permission of The Free Press, a Division of Simon & Schuster Adult Publishing Group, from *The Geography of Thought: How Asians and Westerners Think Differently . . . and Why* by Richard E. Nisbett. © 2003 by Richard Nisbett. All rights reserved.

See Appendix I for an explanation of your choice.

2. Japan ranks as the "most masculine" of the countries researched by Hofstede. Research the roles of women and men in Japan to understand something of Japan's culture in this regard. Do Japan's high suicide rates reflect the stress of the pursuit of achievement common to masculine cultures?

3. Canada is one of the cultures where Trompenaars and Hampden-Turner have carried out research. Compile a portrait of Canadian values and decide whether or not you think Trompenaars' and Hampden-Turner's conclusions are valid. What Canadian movies illustrate the value dimensions ascribed to Canada?

4. According to Trompenaars and Hampden-Turner, American and Western market research companies like opinion sampling and statistical breakdowns, while the Japanese prefer open-ended conversations with customers.[76] How does this support their specificity–diffuseness dimension?

5. Using Hofstede's value dimensions compare and chart British-based cultures such as Canada, U.S., Australia, and Great Britain itself to explore their differences.

   Do the same for Europe (or Asia) to compare and contrast national cultures often perceived to be similar.

Time Out for the Culture Compass: You and Your Value Orientations

Rank the following statements according to their similarity to your own perspective.

3 = most like me · 2 = next most like me · 1 = least like me

1. ___ a. My decisions are primarily guided by what I have learned.
   ___ b. I "go with the flow" and adapt my decisions to quickly changing circumstances.
   ___ c. When I make a decision, I focus on the result I am looking for.

2. ___ a. I tend to take each day as it comes.
   ___ b. I tend to keep lists of tasks that I need to accomplish each day.
   ___ c. Things do tend to work themselves out.

3. ___ a. It is hard for me to stop worrying about upcoming events or deadlines.
   ___ b. Life has its own wisdom. Worrying is a waste of my energy.
   ___ c. Let's focus on all that today brings, and take care of the rest one day at a time.

4. ___ a. We are meant to attend to nature's needs as much as to our own.
   ___ b. Humanity's progress and survival depend on our control of natural resources.
   ___ c. Nature's own power will determine progress and survival; humanity's power can neither match it nor truly control it.

5. ___ a. In truth, we are much better off now that we can make more effective use of our natural resources.
   ___ b. For all our great plans and projects, nature could put humankind in its place in an instant.
   ___ c. "Effective use of natural resources" is the same as saying "exploitation of the natural world."

6. ___ a. No matter where you live, in the country or in the city, there are a variety of forces operating which control your destiny.
   ___ b. In my life, I strive to live simply, which is closer to the natural world.
   ___ c. Modern conveniences actually help us appreciate the natural world.

7. ___ a. Developing my potential and my sense of self is the most important thing I can do with my life.
   ___ b. Being alive and healthy is the most important thing to me; my accomplishments are secondary.
   ___ c. It would be a waste if I did not achieve something important in my life.

8. ___ a. I prefer to relax and enjoy life as it comes.
   ___ b. Peace of mind is possible regardless of external circumstances.
   ___ c. I feel useless if I'm not doing something constructive with my time.

9. ___ a. Taking action is more important than commitment to a belief.
   ___ b. We exist only in relation to other people.
   ___ c. It is essential to be a good person; being a successful person is not the point.

10. ___ a. You have to be guided by what you think is right, even if you can't please everyone.
    ___ b. It works best to have a good leader to make the decisions; everyone should cooperate accordingly.
    ___ c. Decisions affecting the group are more effective if everyone participates in the decision-making.

11. ___ a. It is the individual whom I respect—not his or her position.
    ___ b. Leaders of a group deserve respect because of their position.
    ___ c. First and foremost comes unity; people who think of themselves first live at the expense of others.

12. ___ a. The head of a group has to take responsibility for its success or failure.
    ___ b. If someone in my group is having a problem, I am partly responsible for resolving it.
    ___ c. I am accountable for my own success or failure.

Now score your individual culture compass.

Place the number recorded beside each statement in the appropriate space below and add at the right.

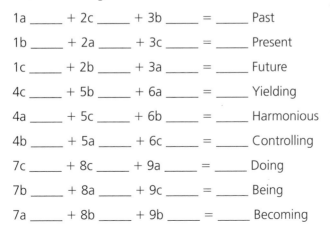

1a _____ + 2c _____ + 3b _____ = _____ Past

1b _____ + 2a _____ + 3c _____ = _____ Present

1c _____ + 2b _____ + 3a _____ = _____ Future

4c _____ + 5b _____ + 6a _____ = _____ Yielding

4a _____ + 5c _____ + 6b _____ = _____ Harmonious

4b _____ + 5a _____ + 6c _____ = _____ Controlling

7c _____ + 8c _____ + 9a _____ = _____ Doing

7b _____ + 8a _____ + 9c _____ = _____ Being

7a _____ + 8b _____ + 9b _____ = _____ Becoming

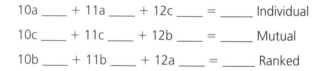

10a _____ + 11a _____ + 12c _____ = _____ Individual

10c _____ + 11c _____ + 12b _____ = _____ Mutual

10b _____ + 11b _____ + 12a _____ = _____ Ranked

Mark the number corresponding to your score for each sub-dimension on the Culture Compass. You may wish to shade in each section to the appropriate level. The highest number for each dimension indicates your preferred approach.

My Culture Compass

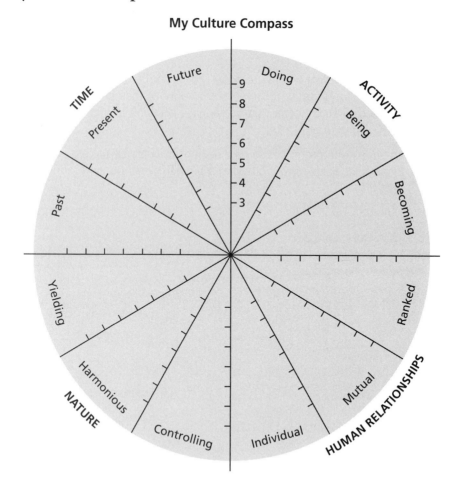

Profile of Cultural Perspectives

Mark an *x* beside your results for each orientation according to the Culture Compass.

Orientation towards Activity

Doing ___ Taking action is the most important activity for you. You find meaning in accomplishments and achievements, and pursue work to define your life. Relationships are secondary, and work and play are separate activities for you, although you may both work and play "hard."

Being ___ Self-expression is the most important activity for you. You find meaning in spontaneous expression, being yourself, and affiliation. Work is not directly attached to your ego, nor is it necessarily considered a separate activity from leisure. Social and work relationships may be closely intertwined. Relationship development at work is time well spent; it builds morale and group identity/feeling.

Becoming ___ Self-development is the most important activity for you. You find meaning in process, purpose, and intention of activity. There is a deep investment in the *type of work* and its process; both aspects add to your personal development.

Orientation towards Time

Past ___ For you, today flows out of the legacy of the past. You find meaning in serenity, surrender, and history as context and teacher. Work for you is a place to establish and nurture relationships and traditions. There is an awareness of, connection to, and obligation toward the legacy of such relationships and traditions.

Present ___ Today is the only reality for you. *Carpe diem* ("seize the day") is your philosophy. Work, like life, is to be enjoyed. Present-oriented individuals often bring to work an energy and vitality not as frequently embodied by the other orientations.

Future ___ Today is a step towards tomorrow's goals. You find meaning in establishing and working towards goals, and a work ethic. You keep your eye on deadlines and goals and evaluate the present in relationship to its utility in moving toward the future. You are rarely satisfied with achievements, rather focusing on the next.

Orientation towards Human Relationships

Individual ___ You believe individuals are responsible for what happens in their lives, and must watch out for their own rights and welfare. You find meaning in personal accountability, and a competitive ethic. Work is a place to be recognized for your achievements. You expect upward mobility and other forms of recognition; group needs, rewards, and achievements are not as satisfying.

Ranked ___ You believe each of us has his or her own place, and respect is due according to one's position. You find meaning in tradition, hierarchy, family, protocol. Work is a place to enhance or strengthen, but not necessarily advance, your social position. Protocol is for maintaining the weave of the social fabric. There is a higher value placed on being respectful than on being frank.

Mutual ___ You believe your purpose is to make a contribution to the larger whole and you find meaning in interdependence, group goals, and affiliation. Work is a place to make a contribution to the group effort. You need to have a sense of belonging to projects and to see the connection to a larger goal or effort. Public praise and competition among or comparison to others may cause embarrassment.

Orientation towards the Environment/Nature

Controlling ___ You believe human welfare is primary; nature serves to meet our needs. You find meaning in taking charge of challenges, putting mind over matter, and using resources effectively. Work is a place to manage and control tasks, resources, employees. Problems are to be solved, knots in the system to be untied, hurdles to be jumped or dismantled.

Yielding ___ You believe nature is in charge of life on earth. Nature rules humankind; we have little control. Work must be done. Within an organization, you may feel dominated by the organization and try to adapt to their roles and assignments rather than influence them.

Harmonious ___ You believe our relationship with nature is symbolic. Care for the physical world will pay off with a balanced and peaceful existence. You find meaning in harmony, doing your share. Work is part of a contract of balance wherein people contribute their share toward a symbiotic relationship with society, nature, and all aspects of life.

Source: This exercise is based on Kluckhohn, Kluckhohn, and Strodtbeck's "Value Orientations." From *The Culture Compass* by Paula Chu in Seelye, H. Ned, editor, *Experiential Activities for Intercultural Learning*, Volume 1, Yarmouth, Maine: 1996, pp. 155–170. Reprinted with permission of Intercultural Press.

Chapter 6
Understanding Worldview

In this chapter we will explore:

- The concept of worldview
- The relationship between worldview and
  - Eastern spiritual traditions
  - Western spiritual traditions
- The relationship between worldview and ideology
- The relationship between worldview and historical experience

HOW DO YOU SEE THE WORLD?

Do you think life is essentially a harsh and difficult experience, or rather a positive and joyous one? Do you think the purpose of life is to prepare for an everlasting spiritual existence, or do you think "this is all there is"? Is there a Creator? What should we try to achieve in life? How should we organize society: should we own resources collectively or privately? Should we sublimate our personal wishes to family or group needs? Should we fight to preserve our way of life, or should we be pacifists? Does God or fate determine our life script, or do we have control over our destiny?

How you have answered the above questions gives you some idea of your **worldview,** a term translated literally from the German word "Weltanschauung." It refers to our personal philosophy of life and the universe[1] and determines how we define reality and how we act. We often share the same worldview, or important aspects of it, with other members of the cultural group(s) with which we identify.

The ancient Maya believed that human beings were the "timekeepers of the universe." Their priests were astronomers who charted the movements of the heavens and whose calculations of time came within a fraction of a second of the accuracy of atomic clocks. They could predict eclipses thousands of years into the future. The Maya, technically a stone-age people, did not develop the wheel and yet were able to develop the concept of zero in their mission to calculate and maintain for the gods the "mathematics of time."[2]

A culture's worldview is composed of what it collectively believes and what it collectively remembers.[3] What it believes and remembers comes from:

- Belief systems—spiritual and philosophical traditions and ideologies from which stem values.
- Historical experience—memories of a collective past, idealized or fraught with challenges or persecution or both.

Worldview in conjunction with territoriality is often at the core of conflict. It is not easily altered, so fundamental is it to an individual's sense of worth and identity. Superficial aspects of culture may be easily changed. To go from washing clothes on the riverbank to using a washing machine, or from eating with forks and knives to eating with chopsticks or vice versa may be easily accomplished. Technology and eating utensils are not necessarily at the core of culture, however useful they may be, nor are they necessarily part of a people's worldview. *Not necessarily* is the operative phrase, however, because if technology or eating utensils are related in some way to worldview, then changing the way one washes clothes or eats will not be easy. The Amish, for example, have thus far resisted much technological change in their belief that to live a simple life is what God wishes.

WORLDVIEW AND SPIRITUAL TRADITIONS

Spiritual traditions are belief systems based on questions about the meaning of life, its origins, its purpose, and its nature.[4] Millions of people around the world sustain themselves morally and spiritually through established belief systems, and, whatever path they follow, such people tend to show concern for moral and ethical values, and ideally, to act according to these values.[5]

Five powerful religious and philosophical traditions have coalesced in the past five thousand years and endured as the bases of belief for much of humanity. These five traditions are Hinduism, Buddhism (often considered more of a philosophy than a religion), Judaism, Christianity, and Islam, each with many offshoots like branches of a large tree. They are examined below.

Equally meaningful, however, are the belief systems of tribal and indigenous cultures throughout the world, and the **secular** worldviews of millions of people in modern and postmodern societies. They too embody moral and ethical values that are a basis for action.

Even if you define yourself as a secularist or postmodernist, you may find that your worldview contains beliefs drawn from one or more of the major world **religions** and philosophical traditions as well as from your own personal experiences and observations.

Knowing something about the worldviews of others makes us think a little bit more about what we believe. The main character in Yann Martel's *Life of Pi* is born a Hindu, but happily and simultaneously practises Hinduism, Christianity, and Islam before philosophically coming to the realization that "The universe makes sense to me through Hindu eyes."[6]

If someone from another country were to ask you how best to prepare herself to visit Canada, would you recommend that she read the Bible or rather that she read a few Canadian novels and watch a few Canadian television programs? Why?

EASTERN SPIRITUAL TRADITIONS

Chapter 5 examined Taoism and Confucianism, which underlie the value systems in much of Asia. Now we'll examine Hinduism and Buddhism, two spiritual traditions originating in India. Hinduism is still largely associated with the sub-continent, where there are over 650 million followers, while Buddhism spread throughout Asia and East Asia and married compatibly with the value systems already established by the older traditions.

Hinduism

The origins of Hinduism, which date back over 5000 years, make it the most ancient of the world's major religions. Its oldest sacred scriptures, the *Vedas,* were written down between 3000 and 4000 years ago and contain teachings and formulas for rituals. Hinduism is not so much a system of ethics in the Western sense of religion as it is a way of life centred around ritual and worship.

It is a kaleidoscope of ritual, deities, festivals, and forms of worship. There is no central organized church or authority, no founder, no saviour, no dogma, and no prescribed ritual or rule of practice. Religion, art, music, drama, and daily life merge inseparably in Hindu life. Temples to millions of gods are visited by millions of people daily. Hindus ring bells to announce their arrival to the god or goddess within, burn incense and bring offerings to summon and celebrate him or her, and perform countless rites of devotion. Hinduism is above all the everyday carrying out of countless symbolic acts of worship (*pujas*). Many homes have an altar room for this purpose, and the final act of many Hindus is to travel to a city on the holy Ganges River to die on its banks because ". . . a few drops on the tongue at the moment of death cleanse the soul of sin."[7]

At the heart of Hinduism is the concept of Brahman, the Supreme Being, the source of universal life, the soul of the world. Brahman is divine essence, "beyond description, beyond approach: with our poor words, we sew a suit for it—One, Truth, Unity, Absolute, Ultimate Reality, Ground of Being."[8] Brahman reveals itself in the form of gods who can be described, understood, represented, and worshipped by human beings on the premise that "Truth is One . . . They call Him by different names."[9]

Atman is the spiritual force within individuals that can be called the soul, "the finite within the infinite."[10] Atman seeks unity with Brahman, and after many lifetimes on earth, reborn in different forms, atman is released from the cycle of reincarnation and liberated, united at last with Brahman. **Nirvana** is the name given to this liberation. Rebirth functions in the form of **karma,** a divine justice that has people reborn higher or lower on the food chain according to the actions of past lives. An individual's *wheel of karma,* cycle of life and rebirth, is stopped only by liberation from the experience of individual consciousness.

Hindu Gods

Hinduism embraces up to 33 million gods kept alive through thousands of years of storytelling. The epic *Bhagavad Gita,* for example, tells the story of Krishna, the eighth incarnation of the God Vishnu (see below) and the embodiment of love and divine joy. The gods represent life and the divine in all its forms and colours.

There is, however, a basic trinity of divinity, three manifestations of Brahman: Brahma, Shiva, and Vishnu.

Brahma, associated with light, is the Creator and source of knowledge. Vishnu is the Preserver. He preserves the harmony and balance of the universe, and perpetuates life. Followers of Vishnu can be recognized by red vertical stripes or a V-shape dabbed on their forehead. Vishnu has had ten incarnations including the popular Krishna, and Buddha, the ninth (theoretically a false incarnation and disavowed by Hindus for several hundred years). Shiva is the Destroyer. Shiva represents the power of destruction in which all existence ends and from which all is born. Shiva is also the embodiment of enlightenment, and has three eyes that symbolize the sun, the moon, and fire. The third eye, fire, is the eye of higher perception, wisdom, and power. It normally looks inward, but if directed outward, burns all in its path. Three white horizontal stripes on the forehead indicate a follower of Shiva.[11]

A red dot (*bindi*) is often worn on the forehead by Indian women to indicate they are married, although it may be worn by both women and men as a symbol of Hindu faith.[12] A black *bindi* dabbed on the forehead is protection against the power of the third eye of Shiva.

This triad of gods represents male energy; each is married to a goddess who embodies the complementary female energy known as *shakti*. Each god has produced numerous other forms of gods. A popular god is Ganesha, the elephant god, remover of obstacles, patron of science and the arts, and symbol of prosperity.[13]

Other Hindu Beliefs

Meditation, deprivation of the senses, and silent prayer help in the attainment of liberation from *maya*, the physical world. Hindus may chant a *mantra*, or devotional sound such as *OM*, the name and symbol for Brahman, to help them focus on their meditation.

Yoga is a form of devotion. It has the same Sanskrit root as the word "yoke" and means "union with the divine." There are different kinds of yoga. *Bhakti* is service to fellow man. *Kama* is knowledge. *Raja* is contemplation. Strict physical exercises accompany these forms of devotion to overcome the body and its functions—obstacles to concentration. *Hatha* yoga involves extreme physical contortions which symbolize obstacles in the path to nirvana and assist in controlling the mind.[14]

All Hindus are born into one of four **castes** or social classes: Brahman (priest), Ksatriya (warrior), Vaisya (merchant), and Sudra (peasant). Each caste is composed of sub-castes that number more than 3000. A Hindu's last name is his sub-caste designation and often refers to a trade or occupation. Mohandas Gandhi's last name, for example, refers to the trade of merchant, specifically "green-grocer" indicating that he was a member of the Vaisya caste.[15] *Mahatma*, meaning "Great Soul," was his title, not his name.

The *Dharma* determines the caste and class into which everyone is born. Hindus are required to accept the dharma and the position in life they have been assigned by karma.

A kind of fifth caste developed and, despite affirmative action programs and laws against discrimination in modern India, its members are highly stigmatized, particularly in rural India. This is the so-called untouchable class that does work considered unfit for caste members such as dealing with human and animal waste and dead carcasses. Branded as impure from birth, one in six Indians belongs to this group. They may not enter temples or drink from the same well as caste members of the same village. They call themselves *Dalit*, a Sanskrit word meaning "broken."[16] Many are kept as bonded labourers, a bondage from which they and their families never escape. Dalit women are frequent victims of sexual abuse.

Buddhism

The sangha (monastic community) is one of the "Three Jewels" in which Buddhists take refuge. The other two are the dharma (religious principles) and the Buddha.

Source: Chris McGrath/Getty Images News

Buddhism is a religious philosophy and reform movement derived from Hinduism. It is more philosophy than religion in its rejection of gods or a god. It outlawed the caste system, priests, and all rituals and devotions to traditional Hindu gods, but retained the concepts of karma and reincarnation.[17] Founded in India, where it died out, Buddhism spread quickly to other countries throughout Asia. It has also become popular in the West. Buddhism is a monastic faith with two major divisions and many minor. Southern or Theravada Buddhism is followed in Burma, Thailand, Laos, Cambodia, and Sri Lanka; the northern division is followed in Japan, Korea, parts of Vietnam, and China and is called Mahayana Buddhism.

Buddhism's founder was Siddhartha Gautama (about 566–480 B.C.E.), an Indian prince possibly born in Nepal. He was not allowed outside his gentle palace world, but one day sneaked out and discovered a different reality of pain and suffering. He saw an old man, a sick man, a dead man, and a wandering beggar. At the age of 29, traumatized by what he had seen, he shaved his head, left his wife and son, and set out alone to search for a new meaning of life. After wandering as a monk, he became enlightened sitting under a fig tree and took on the name *Buddha,* meaning "enlightened one."

Buddhism stresses the impermanence and illusory nature of the material world. Excessive attachment to physical reality—striving for material things and worldly achievements—results in suffering and selfishness. Buddhism teaches a "middle way" of compassion and moderation. Relief from suffering comes from acknowledging the *Four Noble Truths* and living a life of kindness, equality, harmony, and mercy made possible by following *The Eightfold Path.* It is not a doctrinaire philosophy, however, and accepts that there are many paths to spiritual enlightenment.

The Four Noble Truths[18]

1. All life is suffering.
2. Suffering is due to ego, to attachment to the material world, and to desire.
3. Suffering ends when attachment to desire ceases.
4. Freedom from suffering is possible by practising the Eightfold Path.

Explain in your own words how attachment to the material world and ego can be the cause of much human suffering.

The Eightfold Path[19]

Three Qualities	*Eightfold Path*
Wisdom	Right View
	Right Thought
Morality	Right Speech
	Right Action
	Right Livelihood

Meditation	Right Effort
	Right Mindfulness
	Right Contemplation

Nirvana is the ultimate aim. Buddhism defines nirvana as extinction—of karma, of pain, of delusion. The Buddha said nothing about an afterlife as such, and nirvana, according to him, was indescribable.[20] It is possible to become enlightened, or achieve transcendent understanding, as did the Buddha, through meditation. Buddhists offer prayers to the Buddha and to spiritual leaders who may assist them.

Theravada Buddhism teaches that the fastest way to nirvana is to become a monk. Monks shave their heads, wear yellow or saffron robes, and take vows of chastity and humility. They beg for their food, but may not look at a woman who puts food into their bowl. They are vegetarian, having vowed not to take life. In some countries, all young boys spend a period of time as monks, and men may enter a monastery from time to time and then return to civil life. Women don't have a monastic order, but may live communally nearby as nuns.

Buddhists who give to monks or undertake acts of kindness and self-denial may acquire merit, a kind of point system that improves their karma. In Rudyard Kipling's novel *Kim*, the kind red monk allows a rather annoying woman to acquire merit in her acts of kindness towards him, kindnesses that he would have been happier to do without.[21]

Mahayana Buddhism means "the great vehicle" of freedom. Buddhism arrived in China about 2000 years ago and developed as a slightly different version. (It was discouraged in China after the 1949 Communist Revolution but did not die out.) Monks worked and carried on a regular life in China with intervals of contemplation and prayer. The emphasis was on Buddha's life of selfless service to mankind. Mahayana Buddhism stressed an intermediate step on the road to Buddhahood called *Bodhisattva.* A Bodhisattva is someone who has held back from entering nirvana in order to comfort others. Mahayana Buddhists believe there are Buddhas and Bodhisattvas living on many levels of existence who may choose to incarnate on earth when they are needed. Mahayana Buddhism has a monastic order for women.[22]

The Dalai Lama and Tibetan Buddhism

A *lama* is a teacher or *guru* in the Tibetan tradition; *Dalai* means "ocean." The words *Dalai Lama* suggest the vastness of the wisdom of the Dalai Lama, god-king and spiritual leader to Tibetan Buddhists. Some lamas are said to reincarnate earlier leaders, or even a Buddha or a Bodhisattva. The current Dalai Lama is a worldwide icon of compassion and spirituality.[23]

He is the 14th of a series of sacred leaders and was selected in the traditional way involving attention to omens. At the death of the 13th Dalai Lama, a holy lake in the Himalayas seemed to show the reflection of a turquoise-edged roof that was believed would lead to the next Dalai Lama. A turquoise-roofed farmhouse was located nearby where Tenzin Gyatso had been born in 1935.[24] The little boy showed signs of spiritual merit: prominent ears, shoulder marks that might indicate the remains of a deity's extra arms, and the ability to recognize objects from a previous life.[25] After being identified, he was brought to the Potala Palace in Lhasa, the capital of Tibet, where he was raised by monks. He learned the difficult skill of Tibetan chanting, which uses a deep pitch and haunting overtones, and studied philosophy and the scriptures of the Tibetan tradition. Forced into exile in 1959 after the Chinese invaded Tibet in 1949–50, the Dalai Lama now lives in Dharamsala, India, with about 100 000 Tibetans in exile. He represents the cause of the Tibetan people whose culture has been ruthlessly suppressed by the Chinese.

Tibetan Buddhism is distinctive in its use of prayer wheels and prayer flags. Prayer wheels are inscribed with an essential prayer and spun by people passing by to waft the prayer heavenward, and prayer flags whisper messages and prayers to the winds and Buddhas.

Buddhism in Japan: Zen and Pure Land Buddhism

Zen Buddhism requires adherence to a master. Its aim is **satori,** a sudden split second of enlightenment that breaks through the reasoning mind to make contact with intuition and oneness with the universe.[26] It can be achieved by discipline and techniques like sitting still and concentrating on symbols and repetitions of sounds. The popular Japanese game of *pachinko* produces a Zen-like effect in that its repetitions numb the conscious mind. Riddles like "What is the sound made by one hand clapping?" also aim to provoke satori.

Students of Zen may be awakened in the middle of the night and called to training. The master may shock them into a state of "no mind" by zaps with a rod, or sudden laughter, or shouting. Zen stresses courage and oblivion to physical discomfort, which gave it appeal to the warrior class or *samurai*. Their descendants in fearlessness were the *kamikaze* pilots of World War II.[27]

Pure Land Buddhism, also popular in Japan, offers hope of rebirth in a pure land under a Buddha called "Infinite Light" and "Infinite Life."[28]

Japanese culture stems largely from Buddhism. Rituals involving death and dying are often Buddhist. The tea ceremony, now largely folkloric, was a Zen ritual, and flower arrangements are symbols of man caught halfway between earth and paradise.[29] Zen gardens of rocks and sand symbolize the universe, and every rock, plant, or arrangement of sand has symbolic meaning. The number three is often represented in these gardens as symbolic of the sky, earth, and humanity. Zen gardens are serene environments where a person can meditate and practise mindfulness (see photo, page 162).

Shinto is a form of nature worship meaning "way of the Gods" that originated in Japan.[30] Entrances to Shinto shrines are marked by Torii gates, symbols of the

A Zen garden is intended to be viewed in order to inspire meditation and contemplation. What feelings does this garden evoke in you? What do the elements in a Zen garden represent?

Source: Corel

entrance to heaven. Many Japanese are Buddhists, but also practise Shinto rituals, especially for joyous life ceremonies such as weddings.

WESTERN SPIRITUAL TRADITIONS

If God did not exist, it would be necessary to invent him. Voltaire[31]

How would you explain Voltaire's statement?

Western spiritual traditions are religions in the Western understanding of the word, in that they are based on the belief of a supreme God and Creator who requires not only worship and faith in Him, but also obedience.

Judaism, Christianity, and Islam originated in the Middle East and are considered to be the Western religions. The three are closely related. They share a belief in one all powerful, all knowing, omnipresent God, the source of all Truth. Christianity accepted much from Judaism, the first of the major Western faiths; and Islam, the youngest Western faith, honours all of the Judeo-Christian prophets and recounts many of the same Old Testament stories as Judaism and Christianity, but from its own perspective.

The three Western religions are primarily concerned with morals, ethics, and Truth.[32] They share a number of common denominators that differentiate them from Eastern religious traditions. First, they are monotheistic rather than polytheistic. Second, they emphasize *believing* unlike the Eastern emphasis on *doing*. A Hindu doctor was struck by the fact that, while living in Holland, his Dutch hosts always wanted to know what he believed. "Where I come from, what counts is the ritual, in which only the priest and the head of the family participate. The others watch and make their offerings. Over here, so much is mandatory. Hindus will never ask if you believe in God."[33]

Judaism

Judaism is over 3000 years old and the first monotheistic religion. It originated among the Hebrews who, until that point, worshipped idols. A patriarch named Abraham received a revelation from God: He promised to make the Hebrews his "chosen people" and a great nation in return for their absolute faith.[34] Judaism is based on this Covenant, or promise, between God and the Jews. Abraham's first order was to leave his homeland in Mesopotamia (present-day Iraq) and search for the Promised Land (Genesis 12:1–3).[35]

When commanded by God to sacrifice his son, Isaac, as a sign of faith, Abraham was about to comply when God intervened, satisfied that Abraham's devotion was absolute. The Hebrews' wanderings eventually took them to Egypt where they were enslaved for many years before being led out by Moses, an Israelite (another name for Hebrew) raised by an Egyptian princess. Pursued by the Egyptian army, the Hebrews approached the Red Sea and the waters parted just long enough for them to cross and enter the Sinai Desert.

One day, God told Moses to climb Mount Sinai, where He revealed the Ten Commandments, the basis of Jewish law. Moses did not reach the "promised land," but wrote down the Ten Commandments, which were carried in the "Ark of the Covenant." King David took the Ark to Jerusalem, where it was placed in the Temple. Jerusalem was ruled by a number of kings until taken over by the Romans in 63 B.C.E. The Jews revolted, but were defeated, and the Temple was destroyed in 70 B.C.E. All that remains today is the Wailing Wall, a centre of pilgrimage and place of prayer for Jews from around the world.[36] Jews were reunited after almost 2000 years when Israel was founded in 1948.

Beliefs, Scriptures, and Values

Hear, O Israel: the Lord our God, the Lord is One.

The above words are called the *Shema* (Deuteronomy 6:4) and are the words most often recited by devout Jews. They contain the essence of the Jewish creed: first, the idea that the people are a community of faith, and second, the affirmation of the absolute oneness of God.[37]

The first five books of the Old Testament (Genesis, Exodus, Leviticus, Numbers, and Deuteronomy) contain the backbone of Judaism and are called the *Torah*. The Torah is a series of narratives and laws that tell, in chronological order, the history of the world up to the death of Moses, believed by both Christians and Jews to be their author. The Old Testament also contains the books of the prophets that number 34.

THE TEN COMMANDMENTS

Look up Exodus 20:1–17 in a Bible to find out what the Ten Commandments are. Which ones are reflected in Canadian law?

Studying the Torah is an act of worship for Jews. The *Talmud* contains commentary and interpretations of the Torah, and is the source of Jewish law and how to apply it.[38]

Study and knowledge are highly valued in Jewish culture and derive from respect for study of the Torah and Talmud. Justice is also an important value. It is based on the concept of a just God whose commandments and relationship with his "chosen" people are fair. Jews also value a strong commitment to family life and marriage.

Festivals, Rituals, and Customs

Judaism celebrates major and minor festivals. High Holy Days include:

Rosh Hashanah (Day of Remembrance): Jewish New Year, usually in September, is the start of ten days of penitence and self-examination.

Yom Kippur (Day of Atonement): begins ten days after Rosh Hashanah. Jews ask forgiveness of others and repent their own sins.

Pesach (Passover): celebrates deliverance from slavery in Egypt. Jews eat unleavened bread (*matzoh*) in memory of the Israelites fleeing in the desert.[39]

Many other rituals, dietary customs, and symbols make up Jewish practice. Judaism is divided into a number of groups (Orthodox, Conservative, Reform) depending on how the traditional laws are observed in daily life. The Kabbala is a mystical intricate Jewish doctrine currently trendy among global celebrities, although devout followers are often offended by what they perceive to be a superficial attraction. Madonna (a.k.a. Esther), David Beckham, Demi Moore, and Brittney Spears are all current members of "Kabbalah-la Land."[40] They wear the *bendel* (red string bracelet deriving from Yiddish folk tradition) to ward off the evil eye.

THE GOLDEN RULE

"The Golden Rule" is a global ethic shared by all religions and philosophies.[41] Why has so much conflict occurred in the name of religion despite the shared ethic of the Golden Rule?

Confucianism: *One word that can serve as a principle of conduct for life [is] reciprocity. Do not impose on others what you yourself do not desire.*
Christianity: *Whatsoever you would that men should do unto you, do also unto them.*
Hinduism: *Men should always treat others as they themselves would wish to be treated.*
Buddhism: *Practise the truth that thy brother is the same as thou. Whatever is disagreeable to yourself do not do unto others.*
Islam: *No man of you is a believer until he loves for his brother what he loves for himself.*
Judaism: *Do not seek revenge or bear a grudge against one of your people, but love your neighbor as yourself.*[42]

Christianity

For God so loved the world that he gave his only begotten Son, that whosoever believeth in him should not perish, but have everlasting life.

John 3:16

Christianity has the largest number of adherents of all religions. Ironically, a religion based on love has been the source of much conflict within and between cultures around the world. Christianity originated in Palestine during the Roman occupation of the Jewish homeland, and its founder was Jesus of Nazareth, a Jew whose teachings spread throughout the Roman world and beyond after his death about 2000 years ago. Jesus' disciples Peter and Paul are credited with the early spread of the new religion.

At a young age, Jesus showed interest in matters religious. He spent much time in the Temple studying, and became a follower of John the Baptist, a Jewish prophet who baptized, or immersed in water, those who repented their sins in preparation for God's final judgment. John the Baptist baptized Jesus at the relatively late age of 30, after which Jesus began to preach, teach, and perform miracles. He was both a healer and charismatic speaker.

Sacred Texts and Doctrine

The New Testament of the Bible, a collection of sacred texts originally written in Greek, contains Christianity's main precepts. The first four books are the Gospels; they document Jesus' life and contain accounts of his sermons. Twenty-one "Epistles," or letters, follow, most by Paul the Apostle, and the final chapter contains the Revelations of St. John, a prophetic vision of a new heaven and new earth after the "Apocalypse," the ultimate destruction of evil and triumph of good. The twenty-seven books of the New Testament were selected in the fourth century from various Christian writings circulating at the time.

Christ stressed faith, love, and charity as the three essential values. Most important are the beliefs that the world is an expression of God's love and that human beings are to mirror that love. Much of his moral message is contained in the Sermon on the Mount (Matthew 5 and Luke 6). Christ preached that the humble, meek, pure in heart, peaceful, merciful, and non-violent would be blessed and rewarded in heaven. He believed himself to be the saviour prophesied in the Old Testament, not a heretic, come to teach humanity to fulfill God's commandments and to believe (Matthew 5, 22).

> The word *Christ* comes from the Greek word *Christos* meaning "the anointed one" and is synonymous with *meshiach* or *messiah* in Hebrew. It indicates his status, not his name, which was Jesus of Nazareth.[43]

Christianity's formal doctrine was adopted in 325 C.E. when Church leaders were called together by the Roman Emperor Constantine. Constantine had converted to Christianity, and part of his agenda was political: he wanted to unify the Roman Empire under one faith with one set of teachings. Pagan rituals, symbols, and dates of festivals throughout the Empire were fused into the new state religion. For example, the weekly Christian holy day was originally the same as the Jewish Sabbath (Saturday), but was changed to coincide with the long-standing pagan veneration of the sun on Sunday[44], and the date of Easter was made to coincide with a pagan spring rite.

The Creed accepts[45]:

- The Holy Trinity. In God there are three divine persons: the Father, the Son, and The Holy Spirit who share equally the divine and timeless nature. The Trinity distinguishes Christians from Jews and Muslims.
- Jesus was conceived of the Holy Spirit and born of the Virgin Mary
- The Crucifixion and Resurrection of Christ for the salvation of mankind.
- Christ's ascension to heaven to sit at the right hand of God.
- The future return of Christ to judge the "living and the dead."

Christians believe that true repentance brings divine forgiveness allowing repentant sinners salvation and an afterlife in the spiritual realm of heaven. The concept of a physical hell of fire and torture for the unrepentant is still alive among fundamentalist denominations. Other denominations have softened the vision of hellfire and brimstone and describe hell as a mental torment.

Do you believe in heaven and hell? How would you describe them?

Christianity affirms the sanctity of life. How does this result in conflict for modern-day Christians with regard to abortion, capital punishment, and some forms of stem cell research?

Symbols, Practices, and Holy Days

Christianity is rich in symbols. The most famous symbol for Christ is the fish symbol, and although his earliest disciples were fishermen, there is another explanation. The Greek word for fish is *Ichthus,* and each letter points to a name or title[46]:

- I—Iesous (Jesus)
- Ch—Christos (Christ)
- Th—Theou (of God)
- U—(H)uios (Son)
- S—Soter (Saviour)

Christians engage in prayer and worship as a form of relationship with God. They practise, in one form or another, baptism and Holy Communion. Baptism symbolizes purification and rebirth in the Lord. The wine and bread of Communion represent the blood and body of Christ who is alleged to have said at the Last Supper, "This is my body" (bread) and "This is my blood" (wine), and as he passed it out, "Do this in remembrance of me."[47]

Easter, celebrating the resurrection of Christ, and Christmas, the birth of Christ, are two major holy days for Christians.

Divisions

Christianity held together as one universal "Catholic" Church for about 1000 years. A major schism, or division, appeared in the 11th century, dividing the Church into the Orthodox and Roman Catholic Churches. While similar, there are variations in ritual and doctrine. The Orthodox Church is further divided into Greek, Russian, and Coptic, and the Roman Catholic Church underwent a huge rent in the 16th century when Protestant and Anabaptist beliefs took hold. "Protestant" means not only to "protest" in the sense of "disagree," but also in the sense of "affirm" or openly proclaim a new faith. Protestants sought to interpret God's word for themselves as individuals, among other things. This key stance set the stage for further divisions within the Protestant branch. There are many Protestant denominations today, as well as a number of Anabaptist. Anabaptists, such as the Mennonites, disagree with infant baptism; baptism takes place when a person is old enough to choose Christ as his/her personal saviour. Differences in northwestern European cultures and Latin European cultures are partly due to the predominance of Catholicism in the south, and Protestantism in the north.[48]

Islam

There is no God but Allah, and Muhammad is His Prophet.

Islamic creed

Islam is the third great monotheistic faith. It was founded by Muhammad, a trader born in the Arabian Peninsula in about 570 C.E. One day, praying in the desert near Mecca, he experienced troubling visions of an angel who commanded him to "recite." He refused three times, but then, encouraged by his wife, he came to realize them as divine revelations he should communicate to his fellow Meccans. Muhammad saw himself as a prophet, the last of a line of prophets beginning with Adam through to Jesus, and messenger of God. Abraham's son Ishmael, brother of Isaac, is believed to be the father of the Arab people, and Muhammad's revelations were God's final message, recited to correct misinterpretations of His will.[49] Whenever the name of Mohammad (or any other prophet) is written or spoken, it must be followed by the words "peace be upon him." Muslims believe their God is the same God as the God of the Jews and Christians, and in the Virgin birth of Christ although they do not see Christ as divine.

The message given to Muhammad was that the purpose of humanity is to serve *Allah* (meaning "the deity," or God) and live a moral life. At the time of his revelations, pre-Islamic Arabians believed in many spirits and deities, in troublesome beings called *jinns*, and in evil spiritual forces. They lived in a period of social upheaval for which Islam provided a moral, spiritual, political, and economic guide.

The word *Islam* means "submission to God's will." The *Five Pillars of Faith* are the essence of Muslim belief and practice. They are[50]:

- Profession of the creed: belief in Allah as the only God, and Muhammad as his prophet: *La Allah ail-la Allah. Muhammad Rasool Allah!*[51]
- Ritual prayer five times a day facing Mecca.
- Almsgiving to the poor.
- Fasting from dawn to dusk during the holy month of Ramadan, a time of self-examination during which individuals ask forgiveness of man and God.
- Pilgrimage to the holy city of Mecca (*hajj*) at least once in a lifetime. The hajj involves a number of rituals that must be performed.

Muslims believe that God directs everything in a person's life; the phrase "God-willing" (*Inshah'Allah*) is often repeated by Muslims during the course of a day to reaffirm this belief. *Alhumdullilah,* meaning "God be praised," also peppers conversation.

Haram means "forbidden." Islam blocks all paths to wrongdoing. It forbids comparing anyone or anything to God, homosexuality, bestiality, sex outside of marriage, touching women (including shaking hands) who are not relatives, adultery, usury, eating of pork, touching of dogs' noses, ghosts, immodest dressing, drugs, and intoxicants. These things are believed to be unclean or immoral or to fog the mind. The Americans who mistreated prisoners in Abu Ghraib prison humiliated Iraqi Muslims by forcing them to do or simulate a number of things, particularly sexual, believed to be *haram*. So severe were these humiliations that suicide was an outcome considered by some molested prisoners.[52] Other forbidden things are murder, lying, and anything related to countering the Five Pillars.

Strict Muslims may not touch a woman who is not related to them.[53] This means that even shaking hands is inappropriate with colleagues, employers, or new acquaintances of the opposite sex. (In Iran, a man may put his hand on his heart to signal greeting without touching.) What is the appropriate response of non-Muslims to this rule in social situations? What is an interculturally competent response of a female nurse if a male Muslim patient expresses discomfort in being attended by a woman?

The Koran

Muslims' most sacred text is the *qur'an* (meaning "recitation"), or Koran. Muslims believe the Koran is the direct, literal word of God unmodified by Muhammad. It contains about 6000 verses arranged in 114 sections called *suras*.[54] It is taught orally, so that even illiterate Muslims and Muslims who do not speak Arabic can memorize and recite the words. The Koran contains rules for daily living, dietary rules, and a law code called *Shari'a*. Islam is a whole way of life: it incorporates economics, politics, and social organization into its practice.

Second to the Koran is the *Hadith* meaning "sayings" or "traditions." This is a body of work gathered by Muslim religious scholars containing Muhammad's sayings and information recorded about him. Its content is considered to be divinely inspired.

In most mosques, Friday sermons and prayers are led by *imams* (leaders). Any adult can become an imam (women may lead prayer for women only, although that tradition is currently being challenged by Muslim women in North America). An imam's role is similar to that of a pastor or priest in Christian churches or of a rabbi in Jewish synagogues.

Spread of Islam

The new religion spread quickly, and by the Middle Ages had spread to Spain and across the Middle East and North Africa. Muslim dynasties also ruled part of South Asia (the Taj Mahal was built by Shah Jehan in India). Today, Indonesia is the country with the greatest number of Muslims. Altogether, there are over 1.2 billion Muslims.

The Ka'aba

The Ka'aba is a stone building covered by a black silk cloth at the centre of the Grand Mosque in the Holy City of Mecca, and it is a symbol of divine presence. In pre-Islamic Arabia, Mecca was believed to be the home of a chief deity (called *al-ilah*, or *allah*).[55] A cubic-shaped structure had existed there for centuries as the focus of pilgrimage. Muhammad appropriated the symbol and associated it with Abraham and his son Ishmael, who, instead of Isaac, is believed by Muslims to be the son God commanded sacrificed. According to tradition, Abraham and Ishmael built a simple stone structure that contained a black stone, possibly meteoric, given to him by the angel Gabriel. It has been rebuilt many times, and the black stone is now set in silver in the east corner of

The Ka'aba is Islam's holiest shrine. Muslims face it when they pray and pilgrims to Mecca circle it in one of the rituals of the Fifth Pillar.

Source: CP Photo/Murat Atay/AA/ABACA

the Ka'aba about four feet above the ground. It is the focal point of the hajj and the rituals associated with it, such as circling the stone seven times and kissing it.[56]

Divisions

Islam is divided into two major sects: Sunni (from *sunnah*, meaning custom and law based on Muhammad's life) and Shia (from *shi'ah*, or "partisans" of Muhammad's son-in-law). Shias are the majority in Iraq and Iran, and Sunnis in other parts of the Middle East. Another sect, Sufi, is a mystical, contemplative branch of Islam. The puritanical Wahhabi interpretation dominates in Saudi Arabia; Osama bin Laden is a Wahhabi.

Festivals and Art

The two most important festivals in Islam are the *Eid Al-Fitr* and *Eid Al-Adha*. The *Eid Al-Fitr* is a feast marking the end of Ramadan. It cannot begin until the crescent moon has been sighted. The Eid Al-Adha is the feast of sacrifice marking Abraham's willingness to sacrifice his son Ishmael and is celebrated by the sacrifice of a sheep or goat.

Islamic art and architecture are much admired around the world. The Koran forbids the representation of living beings and, consequently, Islamic art has developed intricate designs and decorative patterns, often derived from Arabic script and the words of the Koran.

RELIGIOUS CULTURAL GROUPS

Some groups have based their cultural identity on their religious beliefs. Often, they have been persecuted and had to relocate as a group outside their lands of origin. In Canada, various Mennonite sects fit this description. For many Mennonites and members of other such groups, the religious worldview defines them; for others, cultural identity is more complex. What is the essence of being Mennonite? Is it ethnic, religious, and linguistic, based on family history and cultural traditions? Or is it simply religious?

Many Canadian Mennonites do not attend Mennonite churches, yet self-identify as Mennonite. They may accept the pacifism that is fundamental to Mennonite worldview, but feel Mennonite more because of family, language, and ethnic origins going back hundreds of years to Holland and Belgium, or Germany. Until the last twenty-five years, few Canadian Mennonites married outside their ethnic and religious group, and so the distinction between religious and ethnic Mennonite did not exist for the majority. Many Mennonites today, however, are converts from Asian, First Nations, and African ethnic groups, or products of mixed marriages between "ethnic" Mennonites and others. Their sense of belonging is based on faith alone, and not necessarily related to ethnicity.

The collective historical experience of persecution has also helped bind Mennonites, coupled with the biblical injunction to "be ye separate" from worldly influences.

What other groups in Canada define themselves on the basis of religion? Do their members share ethnic roots? If so, do they encourage endogamy (marriage with members with the same ethnic background) to maintain the group? What are their beliefs? Has collective experience solidified their bonds?

FUNDAMENTALISM

All religious traditions have fundamentalist forms. Fundamentalists believe they have the only correct interpretation of and practise the fundamental, original form of faith. They take sacred texts literally and do not alter their interpretations with changing times. Fundamentalists generally believe in some perfect past when their religion was practised in a pure form, and they long for a return to that mythical time. They see modernity as a threat to their beliefs, and attempt to hold the line against any change in practice or interpretation of their religion that impinges on its original expression.

Fundamentalists are not by definition violent. They may be intolerant towards the beliefs of others, but violence is a tactic adopted by only certain factions of fundamentalists.

SYNCRETISM

Syncretism is the blending of two religious traditions to create a new form that combines elements of both. For example, in Cuba the religious traditions of African slaves blended with Roman Catholicism and became a syncretized religion indigenous to Cuba called *santeria*. Santeria borrowed elements from both and is widely practised today. Similar syncretic religions are also common in Brazil and Haiti.

In Central and South America, the religious and healing traditions of Indian *shamans* blended with Roman Catholicism in another example of syncretism. Many people of indigenous descent practise a mix of Catholicism and their traditional forms of spirituality.

RELIGION'S ROLE IN CULTURE

Religion may underpin a culture's worldview, but does not define culture. There are many countries where Islam is the dominant religion, for example, and Islam may be at the core of key beliefs and practices of virtually all of them, but cultural differences exist among them that are not related to Islam. Saudi Arabian culture is not identical to Palestinian or Indonesian culture, and so on. There are many countries in which Christianity is the dominant religion, but Italian culture differs from British, and so on. Although the majority of Italians and the British share beliefs and values derived from Judeo-Christianity, a host of others is related to other facets of their culture such as their shared history and experience, class systems, and the evolution of institutions such as the family and others in their societies.

WORLDVIEW AND IDEOLOGY

Ideologies are theories about how economic, political, and social systems should work. They replace, compete with, or complement beliefs derived from religious traditions and other elements of culture. Below are a few of the major ideologies of today's world. Like religions, they have fundamentalist forms.

Capitalism preaches private ownership of *capital* ("wealth"), freedom of the marketplace, and economic competition. Its goal is the increase of profits. It believes all sectors of society profit from capitalism because, in theory, jobs are created by those willing and able to create wealth and compete in the business world. Capitalism accepts that a segment of society may always be marginalized or unemployed since competition for jobs must also take place among workers who, by competing for them, contribute to keeping wages advantageous to those who control capital. Capitalism marries well with individualism.[57]

Marx and Engels proposed *socialism.* Claiming that religion was "the opiate of the masses" and served the elites in maintaining a status quo of inequity, they proposed an economic and political ideology that was to replace religion and give workers control of the means of production and distribution. This would end capitalism and its inherent exploitation and oppression of the masses. "Workers of the world, unite, you have nothing to lose but your chains" became a popular socialist slogan.

Marx believed that socialist states would in time evolve into *communist* societies where all property was community owned, and social distinctions based on contribution to the economy would not be made. China still practises the political side of communism although it has embraced capitalism from an economic point of view. North Korea and Cuba are, at present, communist states both politically and economically.

Fascism encourages followers to submit to a combination of state control and religion,[58] while *Nazism* added the concept of racial superiority to fascism. Of concern in Germany is a resurgence of Nazism known as *neo-Nazism.* It targets immigrants and focuses on "Germany for Germans." Germans for them means ethnic Germans, or those with "German blood"; their Germany does not include Germans of other ethnicities who have citizenship.

Nationalism is a 19th century ideology concerned with borders, territory, and nation states based on the vague idea of national identities. Cultural nationalism is an ideology of cultural groups that want a recognized territory for their members and recognition of their culture as the basis for a nation state.

WORLDVIEW AND HISTORY

This section will take a very brief look at how experience informs the worldview of the nation states Mexico, Argentina, Russia, and France.

Mexico

The Mexican worldview derives from a number of historical experiences and centres on ambivalence over national identity. Mexico is wary of the United States, and uneasy about its cultural origins.

Octavio Paz, the great Mexican writer, described the Mexican identity as a collective inferiority complex caused by denial of its ethnic roots.[59] He believed most Mexicans suffer from a kind of schizophrenia in the denial of their origins, wanting to be neither Spanish (the conquerors) nor Indian (the conquered), although 60 percent of them carry the blood of both and 30 percent are of Indian origin only. Paz claimed that Mexicans are insecure and, for this reason, wear a "mask" to hide it. The cult of **machismo,** or manliness, is one such mask. Its displays of bravado, according to Paz, reflect a deep identity crisis.

This insecurity is enhanced by Mexico's proximity to the United States which conquered over one-third of Mexico's territory after a war in the mid 19th century. "Poor Mexico, so far from God, so close to the United States" is a well-known saying. Mexico seeks to be the economic equal of both the United States and Canada and joining NAFTA was to be a means of reaching this goal, although Mexico continues to suffer from high unemployment rates. Keeping the oil industry out of negotiations was a way of protecting Mexico's sovereignty and maintaining Mexican honour. Mexico took control of the industry from American ownership and control in the 1930s after a prolonged battle over the right to equal pay for Mexicans doing the same jobs as Americans.

Argentina

Argentina could be called a nation in search of an identity that its people, traumatized by historical events and geography, can be proud of. Argentina has always seen itself as a European culture (having killed off its Native population in 19th century wars). Yet so far from Europe and set on the continent of South America (seen by many as culturally inferior), it has had trouble maintaining this image of itself and seems to exist in denial of its geographical reality.

Many Argentines' view of the world is characterized by nostalgia. They are nostalgic for Europe and for a standard of living envied around the world in the early part of the 20th century. *Rich as an Argentine* was once a common expression in Europe and North America.[60]

Argentina lost its wealth after the 1950s. Internal political corruption, financial mismanagement, and the inability to compete in a globalized economy contributed to its economic decline. The national musical form, the *tango,* usually a sad lament about lost love and youth and good times, is a mirror image of the self-described national character. Argentines are among the world's greatest clients of psychotherapy, treated most typically for depression, and of cosmetic surgery in attempts to appear beautiful and young and to deny reality in yet another way.[61]

Events such as the Dirty War against communism in the 1970s and '80s (when up to 30 000 of its own citizens "disappeared" at the hands of the country's military leadership with the tacit support of the middle class), the loss of the Falkland Islands War in 1983, and the collapse of the economy in 2001, have all further contributed to Argentina's nostalgia for better times and loss of hope in the future. Argentines may yet overcome their malaise, however: workers are taking over unused factories and building democracy and employment from the bottom up, and at this writing, Argentina's economy is making gains.[62]

Russia

Much has been written about the "Russian soul" and the Russian capacity for suffering. The Russian soul is often seen as tortured, enslaved, and yet capable of rapture in its relationship with the land, "Mother Russia" (*Rodina* in Russian). History plays a major role in a worldview characterized by paranoia and fear of invasion, suffering, subservience to autocratic rule, and mystical attachment to the land.[63]

Russia is a vast country with borders largely unprotected by natural barriers. As it coalesced over a thousand years ago into a nation of peasants working the land for estate owners, invasions had already terrorized the largely Slav population. From the east had come the Mongols, from the west, the Poles, from the north, the Vikings. Russia's borders grew in attempts to provide space and protection for the heartland. Later, came Swedes and Turks. Napoleon, sweeping across the North European Plain, very nearly captured Moscow. Only winter destroyed his chances and his army. The German army in the First World War very nearly did the same; once again, winter intervened, but not before more than 20 million Russians had died. In the Second World War, Hitler's army came close once again, and once again Russia was saved by winter and the enormous sacrifices of the Russians, of whom 27 million died.

Meanwhile, Russian rule was autocratic and secretive from the beginning. Masses of serfs served the aristocracy and Czars, with neither freedom of movement nor participation in government. Later, under the communist dictatorship of the U.S.S.R., of which Russia was the leading republic, that same lack of freedom continued. The concept of individual freedom and civil liberties is new in Russia, an independent republic since 1991, and may not survive; the government under Putin is becoming ever more autocratic and secretive, and the standard of living of millions of Russians has fallen while powerful oligarchs control much of the economy and compete with the government for power and control. Freedom of speech is limited. Black luxury vehicles and armed bodyguards are common sights on the streets of Moscow and St. Petersburg. Meanwhile, poverty and deprivation describe the lives of many Russians.

Through much of their history, Russians maintained a mystical attachment to the land itself. Writers such as Leo Tolstoy made this a central theme of their work. Russia's future is uncertain, with little at present that might change a worldview informed by enormous suffering and inequity.

France

France is imbued with a sense of glory (*la gloire*) and pride in its culture. For much of the past millennium, France has seen itself as the height of European accomplishment. Its language was the language of courts across much of the continent and in England. In the nineteenth and twentieth centuries, it left its mark on parts of Africa and Southeast Asia through colonization.[64] It also prides itself on its contribution to the arts.

The term "Latin" America was coined by the French, who believed that French culture would serve as the model for the continent.[65] Indeed, French was the language of choice of the upper classes until almost the end of the 20th century, when it

The Millau Viaduct (bridge) is an engineering and artistic wonder and the highest bridge in the world. It echoes the design of the Pont du Gard, one of many aqueducts built by the Romans in France.

Source: CP Photo/AP Photo/Christophe Ena

began to be replaced by English. In Bariloche, Argentina, a fashionable ski resort in the Andes, a woman from Buenos Aires struck up a conversation with me a few years ago. We could have spoken Spanish, her first language, or English, mine, but when she realized I spoke French, she insisted we carry on in French although it was the mother tongue for neither of us. But it marked her as a cultivated woman.

The glory of French and France has somewhat faded. Its international influence has waned; its language is no longer the language of a world elite. It remains to be seen if France's worldview will evolve to fit a less prestigious role, or if France will find a way to sustain its view of itself as a superior nation, people, and culture. The French paradox is that while they look back nostalgically to an impressive past, they are at the same time moving towards creating a high-tech future.[66] They developed the TGV (train à grande vitesse) and go in for *grands projets* that assure ongoing respect. The most recent is the world's tallest bridge, the Millau Viaduct, a spectacular artistic, architectural, and engineering feat constructed over the Tarn River Gorge and opened in December 2004.

SUMMARY

A culture's worldview, or way of perceiving the world and the meaning of life, derives essentially from its history and its religious and ideological beliefs. In this chapter, we examined the key principles of the world's major religions to see how they have shaped the worldview of their followers, and we briefly looked at recent and current ideologies for their role in shaping worldview. Ironically, although similar key principles such as the need for compassion and brotherly love underlie all major religious traditions, religion has been the source of many bloody conflicts. Ideologies too have brought their followers to war with the followers of other ideologies. This human propensity to fight over ideas and beliefs indicates how powerful they are in human societies. The chapter concluded with an examination of history's role in shaping worldview. Some cultures have clung fiercely to history for a sense of identity and purpose, while others have realized that some elements of their history have had a negative effect on their sense of identity and purpose, and that they must change course for a renewal of hope in the future.

KEY TERMS

caste 157	karma 156	secularism 155
fundamentalism 173	machismo 175	spiritual tradition 155
Golden Rule 165	nirvana 156	syncretism 173
haram 169	religion 155	worldview 154
ideology 174	satori 161	

TOPICS FOR CRITICAL THINKING AND REFLECTION

1. (a) How should Canada and its public educational institutions deal with the traditional European Judeo-Christian celebrations? I asked two Canadian educators and got these opposing viewpoints. They might provide a starting point for your discussion:

   View A

   I always wonder why Canadians feel so guilty about their heritage. All around the world people are fighting to maintain theirs, and here we not only suppress ours, but allow, if not encourage, newcomers not of that background to celebrate their holidays. What is wrong with us?

   View B

   In a multicultural educational institution, it is inappropriate to celebrate religious holidays like Christmas. If we have a Christmas party, we should also have an Eid party for Muslim students. A Diwali for Hindu students. Or maybe a kind of generic party. And we should steer clear of Hallowe'en parties altogether. After all, ghosts are haram [forbidden] in Islam.

   (b) How do schools and colleges where you live deal with cultural and religious diversity?

2. Analyze the worldview reflected in such Canadian sitcoms as *Trailer Park Boys, Corner Gas,* and *Les Bougon?* What are its sources?

3. Research the worldview of the Aborigines of Australia, the Maoris of New Zealand, or of the indigenous people in another part of the world.

4. *Je me souviens* is the motto on Quebec licence plates. What does it say about how history has informed Quebec's worldview? How has religion contributed to it?

5. Canada's worldview is based on compromise and negotiation. How have history, religion, and geography contributed to its worldview?

Time Out for the Arab World: Tradition and Modernity Side by Side

The Arab world is a culture realm consisting of several distinct regions: North Africa, the Levant (both border the Mediterranean Sea), the Arabian Peninsula and Gulf Arab States, and the Fertile Crescent (Iraq). The dominant cultural groups in the region are culturally bound by ethnic Arab roots and by Islam.[1] Iran is not part of the Arab world although it is dominated by Islam.

Keys to Understanding the Arab World

Change

1. Western technology, health care systems, educational concepts, and political ideas have been adopted in varying degrees throughout the Arab world. Arabs are familiar with Westerners due to the long-established presence of foreign advisors and businesspeople, and many Arabs have been educated in the West and speak English and other European languages fluently. However, unemployment is high in many areas. In the Peninsula and Gulf regions, foreign workers from Pakistan and the Philippines do the majority of manual and domestic labour, while foreign experts hold many top technical positions. Gulf governments are in the process of educating their citizens to replace foreign expertise.

2. Quick change and enormous wealth have been disruptive to traditional Arab culture which is historically conservative, conformist, and unified despite the vastness of the region. Now, however, it is facing political, cultural, and social unrest. There is a "generation gap" in many families, while Islamic fundamentalism and modernization compete for adherents.[2]

3. Arab culture is highly patriarchal. The integration of women into the workforce and freedoms for women such as the right to drive, vote, or dress in Western styles vary greatly. In some countries, women have such freedoms and are active at all levels, while in conservative Saudi Arabia, few women work outside the home, and then just in female-only environments. Bahraini women can vote, drive, and run for elections, and Kuwaiti women are attempting to spearhead change. However, rising fundamentalism throughout the region, including the more moderate Emirates, is challenging gains made by women.[3]

Basic Values

1. Arab values revolve around dignity, honour, and reputation.[4] Family honour depends on its control of women, and patterns of behaviour have evolved to isolate them from situations where it might be at stake. Punishment can be severe for women who deviate from cultural norms. They may interact freely only with other women and close male relatives. Public display of intimacy between men and women even when married is forbidden.

   Hospitality and generosity to guests is also essential to reputation.[5] Offerings of sweet tea, coffee, and meals abound; hospitality includes pressing food on dinner guests until no food is left on the plate.[6]

   Face is important and Arabs strive always to create a good impression.

   Loyalty to family is paramount. Arab culture is essentially tribal, with family then clan loyalties prevailing.

2. Status is valued. Social class (royalty, middle class, or peasant) and family background determine status. Asking someone with status to undertake a manual task or something considered beneath him or her is considered demeaning. Manual labour is not generally respected.

3. Devotion to Islam is admired, and Muslims acknowledge that the will of God determines every aspect of their lives.

4. Arabs are proud of their culture and history. While Europe languished in the Dark Ages, Arab universities kept alive Western philosophy and contributed rich traditions in medicine and the arts.

Cultural Tips

1. Relationships are paramount and extend to business culture. The concept of friendship socially and in business includes the duty to help and do favours for friends to the extent possible.[7] Reciprocal favours, loyalty, and frequent visiting are expected. Relationships are so important that connections and intermediaries are often used to facilitate introductions. (See *wosta,* Chapter 8.)

2. Arabs will often answer "yes" to a request, but that is because etiquette demands a positive response, not because a commitment is being made. "Yes" indicates good will only, but whether something will happen or not is determined ultimately by God. Such fatalism can be frustrating to Westerners.

   Arabs are highly sensitive and take criticism as a personal insult. Emotion is a component of interactions, and objectivity in the examination of facts will not likely override a subjective reaction.[8] In negotiations, it is important that face and honour (see Chapter 8) be maintained for both sides irrespective of the outcome.

3. Neither time not privacy is of the essence. Arabs are polychronic (see Chapter 7) and comfortable doing several things at once—signing papers, greeting people, conversing. Interruptions are frequent in meetings, and meetings are easily cancelled.

4. Etiquette, dress, and good manners count: sit properly and never point the soles of your feet at anyone. Always shake hands when greeting someone, but if greeting a woman, leave the option to her to initiate. Take leave of everyone in a group, and stand when new guests arrive at a social gathering. Never use your left hand to eat, take food, or to touch anyone.

5. Arabs love language and, in particular, Arabic. Eloquence in the form of flowery speech, creative expression, and exaggeration is admired. Each region has its own colloquial Arabic, but everyone learns enough Classical Arabic to recite the Koran.

Common Expressions

Alhumdulillah	Thanks be to God (used frequently; may also be used to refuse more food)
Assalamu 'alaykum./ Wa 'alaykum assalam.	Peace be upon you./And upon you peace.
Insha'Allah	God willing
Ma'alesh	It doesn't matter./Never mind.

Source: Excerpt from Nydell, Margaret. *Understanding Arabs: A Guide for Westerners*. Yarmouth: Intercultural Press, 1987, p. 121.

Part III
Understanding Communication

Chapter 7
Understanding Communication

In this chapter we will explore:

- Essential communication theory
- Major elements of non-verbal communication, namely:
  - Silence
  - Paralanguage
  - Time
  - Space and distance
  - Touching
  - Smell
  - Appearance
  - Body Language

INTRODUCTION

Good communication skills are always important, but especially so in intercultural contexts. In addition to using them on the job, interculturally competent individuals know how to interact well in social contexts because, in many cultural environments, business and social contexts overlap more than they do in Canada.

In intercultural situations, three communication skills stand out as essential. Since, in unfamiliar settings, we cannot assume as much knowledge about the environment, the people in it, and their customs as we can in familiar settings, the abilities *to observe, to listen,* and *to learn from our observations* are paramount.

Listening and observing are active skills. Listen intently to what people say to you (and to what they do not say), and if you don't understand the meaning of their words or gestures or silences, ask them to explain and help you. In most instances, people will be happy to oblige. Observe how people behave in your host culture, and try to follow suit. This courtesy will often be enough to carry you through moments the meanings, symbols, and customs of which you do not understand at first.

Have you ever been in an intercultural situation in which you had no idea how to behave or what to do or say? How did you get through it?

COMMUNICATION: ESSENTIAL THEORY

Communication is the conveying or exchanging of meaningful messages. It has a number of characteristics.

Communication is first and foremost an ongoing *process.*[1] Think of it as a perpetual motion machine, a pendulum ceaselessly swinging back and forth. We spend much of our lives in the seemingly endless process of sending, receiving, deciphering, and returning messages, whether at home with friends and family, at work with colleagues, at leisure watching a movie, in private talking to God, or meditating. Even asleep, we dream in words and images that relay messages to us.

Communication is *dynamic.*[2] Once we have said or done something, we cannot "take it back." We have invited a reaction, which in turn, has engendered another, and so on, as ideas and feelings are explored and exchanged. Words, images, and actions have the power to provoke a response. That is why we use them.

Communication is a *system*.[3] It is made up of components that function in complex interplay like the parts of a machine. It operates according to rules. Dell Hymes devised a framework to explain all the elements of any communication act.[4] They include:

- *Context:* the time, place, and occasion of the communication. *So, how are you?* uttered by a dentist to a patient sitting in the dentist's chair will convey a different meaning and be said in a different way from the same phrase uttered by a lover in the context and location of the bedroom.
- *Purpose:* we communicate to inform, persuade, entertain, console, seduce, and so on.
- *Keys:* keys set the tone or mood of a speech act. A teasing or serious tone of voice, for example, is a cue to mood.
- *Players:* include the speakers, the relationship between them, their number.
- *Social rules and norms:* the context of the communication dictates the rules for it. Is it a formal occasion calling for a formal speech? Or a casual occasion allowing for a relaxed delivery? Is turn-taking allowed or does one speaker do all the talking? Is there a sequence of communication acts: for example, an introduction, a speech, a thank you?
- *Styles and genres of speech:* style includes choices such as slang, or formal or informal grammar. Genres include such things as face-to-face interaction, speeches, and monologues.

Communication operates in tandem with other systems that dictate rules governing relationships based on status, gender, age, social class, and personal relationship. However, "the largest system affecting communication is our culture, which is the context within which all of our interactions take place."[5]

Finally, communication is *symbolic*.[6] The five written symbols making up the word *table* evoke a mental image of what the symbols refer to—if we read English or French. They mean nothing if we don't recognize the symbols. Sound symbols also have meaning: they refer to concepts and to written symbols. Symbols are the bedrock of language and of all other means of communication. (Semiotics is a branch of linguistics that deals with the study of symbols, images, signs, and signifying systems [advertising codes, for example, or the colours of stop lights] and their meanings and functions in society.)[7]

Living and interacting within our own culture we tend to take for granted the complexities of communication and its interconnectedness to our culture. It is often only when we come into contact with a group of people using unfamiliar signs and symbols that we realize how complex communication is. The most obvious stumbling block, of course, is language. Language, however, is just that—the most obvious of the many symbolic systems operating within the context of communication and culture.

Hall believes that communication and culture are one and the same:

> As a means of handling the complex data with which culture confronts us, I have treated culture as communication. . . . The universe does not yield its secrets easily, and culture is no exception. Yet this insistence on culture as communication has its practical aspects. Most people's difficulties with each other can be traced to distortions in communication.[8]

Do any of you have a grandparent who speaks a language you do not understand? Are you able to communicate? Do you know how he or she feels about you? How so?

The Communication Model

Linguist Roman Jacobson devised a model of the communication process with reference to language (see Figure 7.1).

Figure 7.1 Jacobson's Model of Communication[9]

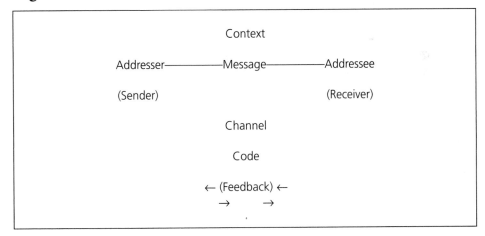

Source: Adapted from Hawkes, Terence. *Structuralism and Semiotics.* Berkeley and Los Angeles: University of California Press, 1997, p. 83; Jaworski, Adam & Nikolas Coupland, eds. *The Discourse Reader.* London and New York: Routledge, 1999.

An act of communication involves a ***message,*** a ***sender,*** and a ***receiver.*** The sender conveys a message to a receiver, encoding it by means of a language (**code**), in either its written or oral form using a ***channel,*** or medium of communication. The channel can be a face-to-face conversation, a telephone conversation, a letter, an email message, and so on. The message has a ***context*** or ***referent*** understood by both the sender and receiver; we don't send messages in a void—we know what we are talking about and why. The receiver ***decodes*** the message with the option of providing feedback to the sender. Feedback is implied in Jacobson's model: the addressee can become the addresser in response to the original addresser, who then becomes the addressee, and so they can take turns reversing roles. The response option is clarified by the ***feedback*** arrow in the diagram above. The communication process is complete and, conceivably, unending.

Meaning resides in the total act of communication and takes into account all parts of the model. Meaning is not absolute. It depends who the players are, the context, the code, the message, and the channel.[10] Meaning is created and negotiated by the players. It is elusive if they do not know and understand the variables in the act. For example, if someone shouts "you get it" while watching a hockey game in the living room and the phone rings in the bedroom, the listener in the kitchen has to be familiar with the context to understand the meaning.

Miscommunication occurs when something goes wrong in the encoding and/or decoding of a message. A sender may encode inaccurately, causing misunderstanding. Or a receiver may decode inaccurately. Lack of familiarity with the code, or background noise, hearing difficulties and, especially in intercultural communication, lack of contextual knowledge are examples of causes of errors in decoding.

Conversation overheard in a restaurant: What went wrong?

He: Are you a Torontonian?
She: No, I'm a Sagittarian. How about you?

Feedback is often essential for the accurate transmission of meaning. A simple request for clarification using ***metalanguage***—language used to talk about language—can prevent misunderstandings. "I don't follow you" or "what do you mean? are examples.

Extrapolating on Jacobson: Non-Verbal Communication

Communication involves more than just the linguistic code. Non-verbal codes of communication are equally important. They too are systemic, dynamic, culture bound, and symbol based, and part of the whole process of conveying meaningful messages.

Hall claimed that some non-verbal codes of communication are, like much of culture, hidden, but underpin cultural behaviour.[11] He is most associated with **proxemics,** the study of how space and distance communicate; **kinesics,** the study of how movement communicates; and with the study of attitudes towards time. In this chapter, we'll explore these and other non-verbal codes of communication (see Figure 7.2).

Style is perhaps the only uniquely personal thing we can add to any code—our choice of words, phrasing, and turn of phrase in the language code are uniquely ours—that personal something that makes us all individuals. Similarly, our choice of clothing, home décor, and cars is part of our style, even when we have the same cultural assumptions about these items as others.

Figure 7.2 Jacobson's Model and Hall's Non-Verbal Codes

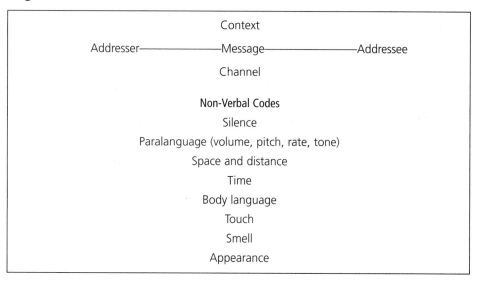

Source: Based on Hawkes, Terence. *Structuralism and Semiotics*. Berkeley and Los Angeles: University of California Press, 1977, p. 83.

Non-verbal codes support, nuance, or contradict the meaning of an orally encoded linguistic message. If, for example, a teacher hands back tests and says in a sarcastic tone, "Well, that was a great effort," and rolls her eyes for added effect, there is a good chance that everyone, if they have lived in Canada for some time, will understand the real message despite the words. A sarcastic tone of voice and rolled eyes have overridden the linguistic code. Words are believed to carry only 7 percent of the meaning of a message in face-to-face exchange, while tone of voice accounts for 38 percent, and facial expression 55 percent.[12]

Usually a number of codes interact to create meaning, making intercultural situations particularly complex. What does a certain eye movement mean in Korea when it accompanies an utterance? What does making a person wait signify in Mexico? Only by "putting it all together" is meaning accurately interpreted.

Misreading codes may be taken for racism in situations where the codes of disadvantaged cultural groups are misunderstood by members of an advantaged group who may wield power. They may react negatively to behaviours perceived to be disrespectful.[13] For example, in some cultures, such as Aboriginal and African-American, averting the eyes can be a sign of respect, while in others, such as dominant Canadian, it signifies the reverse. Misunderstanding due to communication behaviour is one reason why police forces in Canada and elsewhere now require intercultural training.

SILENCE

Jack Benny once had a popular radio show. His persona was that of a dreadful cheapskate. In one skit, he was held up by a thief.

"Your money or your life," demanded the thief.

The ensuing one-minute pause is said to be the longest moment of staged dead air on record. Americans and Canadians across the lands burst into laughter as the silence dragged on and they realized its meaning.

As the above vignette illustrates, "silence is an act of non-verbal communication that transmits many kinds of meaning dependent on cultural norms of interpretation. Our tendency to describe silence as an absence of speech reveals a particular cultural bias, implying that something is missing, but silence is a 'something' with purpose and significance."[14]

We are ambivalent about silence in interpersonal encounters in North America. Some expressions ("his silence spoke volumes") indicate an awareness that silence has meaning. Often, however, silence signifies emptiness. We speak of "dead air," implying that silence is a waste of time. "Don't they have anything to say to each other?" we may wonder about couples dining in silence. Silence may also signify hostility: "the silent treatment" is a sign of displeasure or punishment.

Silence may also have positive connotations. Depth of character can be attributed to quiet people ("still waters run deep"). We also speak of a man as being "the strong, silent type," or "a man of few words," which can have a negative or positive spin depending on the meaning shared by speaker and listener. The silence of the couple dining together may be a comfortable silence: they know and are "high context" with one another (see Chapter 5).[15] "Chattering like hens" implies silence is preferable to speech, but implicit is an insult to women.

Silence has a number of functions in North American culture. It can reveal status differences between people in role relationships such as the employer/employee relationship. A disproportion in the amount of talk often reveals an inequality in the relationship: the person of higher status tends to talk more and the person of lower status listens more.[16] Interruptions are considered rude on the part of the person of lower status. Some gender and discourse (talk) studies have revealed that men tend to dominate conversations and interrupt women more than women interrupt men, a phenomenon that has been interpreted to be illustrative of the power or status differential that still exists between men and women in North American culture.[17]

Silence, on the other hand, is expected in ceremonial or public situations. We are supposed to be quiet at the movies, for example, or during a wedding ceremony (except for crying), or during a lecture. Such is not the case, however, in West Africa at the movies. There, movie-goers may cheer and boo the screen action.

Silence is so significant that Malinowski identified a kind of speech that has the sole function of *filling* it that he called the **phatic code.** The phatic code serves to keep the channel of communication open with empty expressions when we have nothing of actual content—informative or emotional, for example—to transmit. We want only to transmit a feeling of togetherness and good will and to prolong the communication.[18] The repetition of *and* or *and a,* aimless gossip, banal chit chat, expressions like *Have a nice day* and *um* fall into this category. However, their banality, blandness, and pervasiveness—their perceived *emptiness*—annoy some people.

How do you feel about using and hearing expressions like *Have a nice day*?

Silence plays slightly different roles in other cultures, although the status differential seems to prevail.[19] Talkative and silent types are also present in all cultures despite cultural norms leaning towards one or the other.

In general, Eastern and Western views of silence differ. In Japan, silence indicates thoughtfulness, wisdom, or the desire to maintain social harmony. Where disagreement is present, it is better to remain silent than to speak in haste or in annoyance. "Dead air" in meetings is neither uncommon nor negative. It indicates that a person is taking time to reflect before speaking, or that the person is reluctant to disagree. Quiet people are perceived to be more credible than talkative people. The latter are perceived to be shallow, as illustrated by the proverb *Hollow drums make the most noise.*[20] Arab,[21] African, and Latin American cultures are comfortable with silence and people are often content just to be in each other's company.

In Aboriginal culture, silence also plays a different role than in dominant North American culture. While oratory is valued in some cultures, others, such as the Kaska of British Columbia and the Yukon, "did not value verbal fluency or use baby talk, and they used silence as a response to pain or frustration. Knowing how and when to keep silent was highly valued ... This has often been incorrectly interpreted by Euro Americans as reflective of a sense of dignity, or of lack of intelligence or emotion."[22]

Among the Ojibwe, older people are comfortable with long periods of silence. The younger generation may be less so due to increased contact with Euro-Canadian culture.[23] They are in transition, caught between two ways. Traditionally, it is customary to wait in silence before responding to a question or comment. The delay indicates that you are thinking and will respond after adequate thought, often either with a parable-like story or with a further delay because you wish to consult another person. Silence, after contact with Europeans and the residential school experience, also became the norm because to speak incorrectly, or to speak a native language, or give the wrong answer might precipitate punishment. The legacy of the residential schools remains embedded in First Nation communication norms and helps explain the relative silence of some First Nation students in class.

DEALING WITH SILENCE

Here is some advice if you find yourself in an intercultural meeting with people who are comfortable with silence and you are not:

- Take a deep breath and relax.
- Remind yourself that silence is not bad.
- Ask yourself what message is being conveyed through silence. Is it respect? Confusion? An indirect attempt to say no? Lack of comprehension due to language?
- Consider the options. Should you repeat your question? Or wait longer?
- Act on your analysis.

Source: Excerpt from Brislin, R.W. & T. Yoshida, *Intercultural Communication Training: An Introduction.* Thousand Oaks, CA: Sage Publications, Inc., 1994, pp. 112, 113.

Interrupting

Interrupting can be culture dependent: some cultures tolerate interruptions while others discourage them. Deborah Tannen calls interrupting "conversational overlapping." It can often signify high involvement.[24] Her studies indicate that New York City natives of Jewish background in conversation with speakers of different backgrounds are often perceived to be interrupting. All is relative, however. Mid-westerners tend to perceive themselves to be interrupted by easterners, while they become the interrupters in conversation with Athabaskan Indians who expect longer pauses between conversational turn-taking. The Finns, meanwhile, perceive other Scandinavians to be interrupters. The British respect turn-taking and frown on both overlapping and "everybody talking at once." Latins (French, Italians, Spanish, Quebecers) do not in general perceive overlapping to be rude, particularly during family and social get-togethers when it is quite common for everybody to be "talking at once."[25] Tannen's work also shows gender differences in overlapping.

PARALANGUAGE

Voice volume, pitch (stress, tone, intonation), rhythm, and rate of speech are elements of paralanguage that are both uniquely personal and also culturally determined.

Paralanguage reveals emotions in a way that mere words may fail to convey. Vocal cues like whining, whispering, shouting, and a choppy rhythm all send messages.

Stress on individual words in a sentence can influence meaning. Incredulity can be shown by emphasizing a different word each time the following sentence is uttered. How does changing the emphasis in the following question change its meaning?

You're driving to *Whitehorse*?
You're driving to Whitehorse?
You're *driving* to Whitehorse?

Intonation is the rising and falling of pitch. Rising and falling intonation does not alter the meaning of words, but carries messages of its own related to the function or meaning of an utterance. The intonation of English is predictable: the voice falls at the end of a statement and rises at the end of a yes/no question. Compare: *You are going to the store.* and *You are going to the store?* Beyond that predictability, we can use intonation, with tone and loudness, to convey meaning. Actors use intonation to great effect.

Tone and intonation together send messages in all cultures. The soft rising and falling exclamations of West African speakers for expressing surprise or pleasure or amusement have been maintained by Cubans of African (often Yoruban) or partly African descent. These gentle sound patterns are not typical of Cubans of Spanish descent who belonged to different speech communities, the norms of which were still evident in the 1980s and 1990s. The Cuban Revolution largely integrated the classes and eliminated systematic discrimination, but it takes a few generations to bring about sociolinguistic change.

Volume also speaks. Some cultures are generally soft-spoken, others less so. For Israelis, Italians, and Germans, a relatively loud voice indicates strong beliefs and projects authority and self-confidence.[26] American culture tends towards loudness. Americans in Ghana often asked the Canadians working there to speak up. "Why do you all speak so quietly?" was a common question. Ghanaians also tended to speak softly. Asian cultures are in general relatively soft spoken. A loud voice may be perceived as impolite, or aggressive or upset. To reveal any of these emotions might disrupt general well-being.[27]

In a study of mothers and children, dominant-culture American mothers interpreted as positive the aspects of their children's behaviour and speech that showed assertiveness, excitement, and interest. Navajo mothers, on the other hand, interpreted the same behaviour and speech as being negative, indicative of lack of discipline, lack of respect, lack of self-discipline, and discourteousness.[28]

Noises may be used to communicate messages. Gasps may indicate fear or shock. The Japanese often make small utterances called *aizuchi* such as *so* [so] or *e* [well . . . ; let me see] to indicate attentiveness;[29] while giggling may hide embarrassment or discomfort in Japan, Indonesia, and Malaysia.[30]

TIME

The study of time is known as *chronemics*. Kluckhohn, Kluckhohn, and Strodtbeck viewed time in terms of values, so definitive of a culture is its relationship with time.

Monochronic (M-Time) and Polychronic (P-Time) Classifications

Hall proposes a theory about how cultures function in time. He places them on a continuum, with monochronic (M-time) cultures at one end, and polychronic (P-time) cultures at the other[31] (see Figure 7.3).

Figure 7.3 M-Time and P-Time on a Continuum

M-Time——P-Time

In monochronic cultures, time is linear and blocked off into segments each of which is ideally filled with one activity. That activity is completed before the next one is begun. Life is an agenda. Every day and every hour is scheduled. People tick off what they have completed and attain the satisfaction of 'closure' after each tick. Meetings are segmented; appointments follow a pattern. "Time is . . . like a road or ribbon extending forward into the future and backward to the past. It is also tangible . . . saved, spent, wasted, lost, made up, accelerated, slowed down, crawling, and running out."[32]

Linear orderliness extends to lineups in M-time cultures. People wait their turn in North America and Northern Europe, but less so in other parts of Europe such as France where some body contact and jostling for position may take place. (In addition, body contact in Northern Europe and Canada is uncommon among strangers, making pushing and elbowing inappropriate for another reason.)

In a polychronic-oriented environment, time is elastic. People are comfortable doing many things at once. Loose ends are the norm. Things will get done in their own time: among Pueblo Indians, ceremonies and dances begin when the time is ripe, not sooner, even if that means midnight.[33] Polychronic cultures have a holistic, non-linear way of functioning in time.

North American and Northern European norms are monochronic, while Latin American, Middle Eastern, and Mediterranean cultures tend toward polychronism[34] as do Africans and South Asians. North Americans are often psychologically stressed when confronted with P-time systems where the iron hand of the clock does not rule.[35]

TIME IN CANADA

This sidebar, aimed at the parents of young children, appeared with an article "No more rise and whine" in a national newspaper. How does it socialize children to think of time?

To ease morning mayhem

Start the morning the night before to eliminate as many chores and decisions as possible.

Lay out clothes, sign permission slips and pack backpacks and some lunch items.

Decide whether baths and showers work best the night before.

Set your alarm clock a half-hour earlier than you'd ideally like and get out of bed before your children to strive for a less harried pace. If you oversleep, chaos is a certainty.

Put on your watch first thing so you can keep a close eye on the time.

Give your children their own alarm clocks and make them responsible for their own awakening each day.

Turn off the TV, computer and electronic games.[36]

Source: Excerpt from English, Kathy. "To ease morning mayhem." *The Globe and Mail,* Aug. 28, 2004, p. F6.

Life in the P-Time World

Life in the P-time world seems disorganized from an M-time perspective. Meetings, for example, do not seem focused from a North American perspective. People may wander in and out discussing matters not related to the one at hand, phone calls are taken, and there is a general air of many things happening at once. Meetings may last longer than "scheduled," or may not occur at all if something more important comes up and takes precedence. Business is often transacted in public while others wait. Everything is always being shifted around. P-time is the "chaos" dreaded in the above box.

According to Hall, social, business, and even sex lives are never ordered in P-time cultures.[37] Nor do P-time peoples place a high value on privacy. Latin Americans and Arabs are seldom alone.[38] They interact with more than one person at almost all times, and people alone are perceived to be lonely. Wishing to be among people, however, does not mean that interaction or conversation is always occurring. Latin Americans and Middle Easterners withdraw into silence in a group when they need to be "alone."[39]

In P-time cultures, people do not necessarily "wait their turn" in lineups. Whoever makes it to the front is served. I once tried to get to the reception at a large hotel in Moscow to register, for example. People pushed their way forward as clerks calmly served whoever managed to lurch into their presence.

That was mild compared to the pushing and shoving of the Middle East, parts of Africa, and parts of Asia such as China. I recall a desperate surge for the Syrian Embassy in Morocco when it opened one morning to dispense visas. The time period was limited, and the gate was inadequate for the surge, so people began climbing the fence. At one point, embassy staff began throwing visas out the windows. When I left Ghana, passengers rushed pell-mell for the plane even though we all had tickets and seats. And in Nigeria, we needed locals to get us through to the counter at the airport.

In China, a line-up quickly becomes a "wedge," and anyone who butts in will be served. A friend who frequents an Ontario casino claims to steer clear when a bus disgorges gamblers from a Chinese tour bus.

Time and Punctuality in Business

Punctuality is another culture-bound time-related difference. Generally speaking, punctual cultures include Japanese, Chinese, Korean, North American, and European, while less punctual cultures include Latin American, African, Middle Eastern, South Asian, and Aboriginal. Punctual cultures are more likely to be M-time, and non-punctual, P-time.

Punctuality is often related to power. In Latin America, a person kept waiting has less power than the person who imposes the wait. The longer you wait, the less power you have. Arriving late for a business appointment in Latin America indicates you have other important things to attend to, just as keeping someone waiting indicates you are not waiting, but also have important things to do. (This is also true of India.[40]) It may also indicate respect in showing that you don't expect someone important to see you on the dot. In the final analysis, since no one wants to be perceived to be idly waiting for someone else, punctuality is neither expected nor highly valued.

Punctuality can also relate to power in North America: the boss can keep you waiting, but you are unlikely to keep the boss waiting. Nonetheless, there is a genuine will to punctuality in North America because it relates to efficiency and efficiency to productivity: time, in short, is money.

In Arab culture, time and patience are necessary in order to do business.[41] Punctuality is not highly regarded, and, furthermore, to do business, you must be prepared to wait, to have coffee, not talk too much about business right away, ask about the "family" perhaps, (not the wife or wives), and generally learn to chat while they watch and assess you.[42]

West Africa is not highly industrialized, and life in adherence to the clock as it developed in the industrialized world of factories and time sheets never completely took hold.

There can be a double standard with regard to punctuality. For example, Latin Americans know that North Americans are clock bound and expect them to be on time. They may choose to operate according to their own rules, however.[43] A Latin American friend wanting a job with a Canadian company in Havana arrived late for his interview, then was infuriated when the Canadian kept him waiting. When I mentioned the inconsistency, he said, "Yes, but I am Latin and he is Canadian and he should have known better." Attempting to show power in a weak position, he was trumped.

Conversely, knowing the Canadian penchant for promptness, other Latin Americans choose to make the supreme effort to arrive on time.

Time and Punctuality in the Social Sphere

In Latin America, the Caribbean, India, and Africa, social time is particularly elastic . . . setting a time for a social visit is often done for form's sake. It is set, but the words signify little. West Africans, like Latin Americans, may agree to visit at, say three, but may arrive much later, or not at all. Sometimes, there is intent to follow through, but "the moment" intervenes. A person may be having a coffee with other friends, and having such a good time that he or she doesn't leave as intended and is consequently late for the next engagement, which doesn't necessarily have to be attended anyway.

Likewise, "I'll call you tomorrow," is not meant to be taken at face value. It just means "I might like to call you some day." Such a statement can just signify good will. God and fate willing, the person might do it. Or it may signify a kind and indirect rejection. It takes experience to decode such statements and be prepared for the actions they may or may not engender.

The Language of Time: Informal Time versus Formal Time

The terms informal and formal time are often used to describe how punctuality and time are valued. In African, Native Canadian, Native American, and Latin American cultures time is informal, while North American and Teutonic cultures operate formally, or by the clock.

Informal time cultures may use the language of formal time, as suggested above, but adhere to informal use of it. In West Africa and Latin America, people often joke about it to Westerners, as in, "See you at two o'clock, African time," or "We'll be there at six, Uruguayan time." Wink, wink. In India, "Indian Standard Time" is the joke.

At the train station in Bobo Dioulasso (in Burkina Faso, then Upper Volta), I once asked what time the train left for Ougadougou, the capital. "At two o'clock," said the clerk, "but don't get here before six." Ironically, in France, Burkina Faso's former colonial power, it is often said that you can set your times by the train. West African schools, however, modeled on the British or French systems, enforce clock time and keep to schedules.

Pace

North Americans tend to be in a hurry—fast tracking, fast food, fast wars (ideally), fast everything reflect a culture focused on what comes next. Other cultures "take their time," whether dining, doing business, doing business and dining, socializing, and establishing personal relationships. Even the pace of walking is often culturally influenced; in Africa, I learned to slow my walk but when I came back to Canada, I eventually speeded up again.

Although it takes time to establish a business relationship in China, social and business dinners are surprisingly quick. "Nothing ends faster than a Chinese meal," a Canadian working in China told me.

SPACE AND DISTANCE (PROXEMICS)

Proxemics refers to the study of space and distance, organized and used differently in different cultures. Hall identified three categories of proxemics[44]: fixed space (architecture and city layouts, for example); moveable space (such as seating and the arrangement of office furniture); and personal space (comfort zones of space between people). Each of these is largely culture bound.

Fixed and Moveable Space

Arrangements of space make symbolic statements about social groupings, social relationships, and cultural identities. Navajo homes face East. Latin American and Indian homes are often centred on an open courtyard around which rooms for sleeping, cooking, doing laundry, and bathing are organized. Family members gather—children to play and adults to talk and socialize—in the courtyard.[45] High walls may surround the Latin American home while the Arab ideal is to have enormous homes with few partitions. Arabs do not like to be alone, and envision the whole family together inside a protective shell, all intimately involved with and taking nourishment from one another.[46]

In Vietnam, furniture is arranged according to the age of family members and favourable directions. A southern exposure is the most preferred, followed by east, west, and north.

Feng shui is an ancient Chinese philosophy based on energy flow and living harmoniously in one's surroundings. How a home is positioned in its environment, where doors and windows are placed, and how furniture and objects are positioned can affect the fortunes of the people dwelling within.

Vastu, the ancient Indian philosophy that gave birth to feng shui, is also about creating healthy environments. For example, the northeast part of a room is supposed to induce calm and be free of large furniture, and natural materials and objects that relate personally to the dwellers are favoured.[47]

Office locations and seating arrangements within them communicate power or lack of it, or equality of work partners. In Canada in business or office settings, who gets to sit at the "head of the table" at a meeting? Who gets the office at the top of a building with a view? Who gets a cubicle and who gets an office? How are such placements determined? How is office space arranged in Japan? In homes at family dinners, who sits "at the head of the table," if anyone? How are classrooms organized (see box below)?

JAPANESE SCHOOLS

In Japanese primary classes, children sit in groups, around a circular table or at desks in groups of four facing each other. Often each group has a name—of a flower, or bird—and children in each group learn to function together for projects, sports, and other activities. When work is handed out, they wait until all members of the group are ready to begin: one child doesn't start ahead of the others. They talk about the assignment before getting started. In this way, the concept of the collective is reinforced in the primary school environment.[48]

Personal Space

Studies on animal territoriality triggered Hall's theories about space and how much space people leave between them in conversation. Hall views personal space as an extension of ourselves, and our spatial comfort zones as culturally determined[49] (see box on the next page).

Personal space for Middle Eastern cultures is much smaller than personal space for Canadians and many Europeans. Arabs come close in part to better read the eyes, so expressive and readable are they believed to be.[50] In conversation with close friends, Arabs may stand only six inches from each other's faces. On social occasions, they may also, however, sit on opposite sides of a room and talk across the room to each other.[51]

African, Middle Eastern, Southern European, and some Latin American cultures (Mexico, for example) also maintain smaller zones of personal space than do Northern European and Euro-American cultures. In general, cultures that favour individualism over collectivism (such as the United States, Canada, Great Britain, Germany, Australia, and Scandinavian countries) need greater personal space than do collective cultures. Those belonging to individualistic cultures are often perceived to be cold partly for this reason.

PERSONAL SPACE ZONES

Intimate zone: 0 to 18 inches [0–0.5 m], reserved for family and other intimate friends.

Personal zone: 18 inches to 4 feet [0.5–1.2 m], for private conversations with friends and keeping someone at arms' length.

Social zone: 4 to 10 feet [1.2–3 m], for acquaintances, colleagues, and strangers. Eye contact can be maintained but we are in the zone of impersonal transactions.

Public space: 10 feet [3 m] and over, is reserved for formal situations such as lecture halls.[52]

Source: Adapted from Hall, Edward T. *The Hidden Dimension*. N.Y.: Anchor Books, 1966, pp. 116–125.

Hall also observed that American space is very *closed*: on buses, trains, and in public spaces, Americans close in on themselves to discourage bodily contact and conversation with strangers.

TOUCHING (HAPTICS)

A recent study revealed that Parisian mothers touch their children much more than do American mothers. Another showed that Parisian teens at McDonald's touch each other more often than do American teens, who tend more to touch themselves by self-hugging, playing with their hair, and so on. They also found that French children are less aggressive on the playground than their American counterparts. Science suggests that this is not coincidental. Touch-deprived animals ". . . become aggressive, violent, even kill each other . . . In Romanian orphanages, children who weren't touched experienced stunted growth and all sorts of physical, cognitive and social problems."[53]

Touching is important to human development, and the amount of touching can be culture bound. France rates as a high-touch[54] or middle-touch culture,[55] and the U.S. as a low-touch culture (see Table 7.1, page 202).

In high-touch cultures, much non-sexual touching occurs: friends link arms or hold hands while walking, greet each other with a kiss or two on the cheek, stroke the hair or put an arm around each other's shoulders, and so on. Such gestures reflect warmth and good will and carry no sexual overtones. In Africa and the Middle East, men walk hand in hand with other men; women walk hand in hand with other women.

Table 7.1

Cultures and contact

DON'T TOUCH	MIDDLE GROUND	TOUCH
Japan	Australia	Latin American countries
United States	Estonia	Italy
Canada	France	Greece
England	China	Spain and Portugal
Scandinavia	Ireland	Some Asian countries
Other Northern European countries	India	Russia
	Middle Eastern countries	

Source: From Axtell, Roger. *Gestures: The Do's and Taboos of Body Language Around the World*, p. 40. © 1998 John Wiley & Sons. Reprinted with permission of John Wiley & Sons, Inc.

KISSING AND RUSSIAN POLITICIANS

Russian officials are trying to change the Russian custom of kissing among politicians. They believe the multiple kisses waste time and revolt people who watch. They aim to institute the handshake.[56]

Low-touch cultures (non-contact according to Hall) are uncomfortable with such body contact. Americans, Canadians, Germans, the English, and Scandinavians are not used to it, and may misinterpret such gestures as being sexual in nature. A handshake is the preferred greeting among men and women. "Hello" or "hi" is sufficient among friends. In these cultures, emotional restraint is valued and hands best kept to oneself. First Nations are also non-contact cultures.[57]

French-Canadian culture displays warmth through physical contact. A formal greeting between two people who don't know each other well is a handshake, but friends greet each other with a *bise*, or kiss on the cheek, whether same sex or opposite. Other Latin cultures do the same (*un beso*), both Mediterranean and Latin American.

And how do you know if you are considered an intimate enough friend for a greeting kiss? In Latin America, a man takes his cue from the woman: if a woman offers him her cheek, he responds with the *beso* (kiss). If you are a Canadian woman wondering whether to greet a Latin American man with a *beso*, a Latin man will wait until you give the signal, unless he decides to teach by example.

Eastern Europeans, Greeks, Jews, and Russians are also part of the "touching" and "kissing" world. Kisses may number more than two in these countries, and may include a hug.

HANDSHAKES AND GREETINGS

Canadians, Americans, and some Europeans tend to favour a firm grip, but Africans, Arabs, and other Europeans (the French, for example) favour a light, limp version of the handshake. In the Arab world, a verbal greeting is considered incomplete without accompanying haptic, kinesic, or proxemic behaviour such as a smile, a nod, a twinkle in the eye, or a hug. Too much distance between greeters can communicate negativity or even hostility.[58]

In Middle Eastern cultures, men greet men with a kiss or kisses (sometimes on the nose), but they do not kiss women. Arab males may shake hands with only female relatives and men and women may not touch each other in public at all.[59] In India, it is common to kiss the feet of someone to whom a person wishes to show respect. Otherwise, a common greeting is the *namaste* (clasping hands close to chest*)*, which does not involve touching another person.

In parts of Asia and Southeast Asia, particularly Thailand, it is inappropriate to touch children on the head, as the soul is believed to be located there.

Finally, on the subject of kissing, while mouth-to-mouth kissing is a sexual act in Western culture, it is not common in Asia. Most Asian cultures are not touching cultures; although in Japan, for example, girlfriends hold hands in a non-sexual expression of friendship.

In Muslim cultures, it is impolite to touch food or other people with the left hand as that is reserved for sanitary handling of body waste.

Gender differences exist both within and between cultures regarding touching. Some studies have shown than women use touch more than men in North America, while another study showed than women in Italy touch less and interact with greater distance than do Italian men and German women, while Italian men interact more closely than do men in North America and Germany.[60]

SMELL (OLFACTICS)

Aromas, scents, and odours communicate. Marcel Proust wrote volumes about his childhood memories just from getting a whiff of *madeleines* (a kind of cookie) as he walked down a Paris street one day.

Do certain smells conjure up places, people, or moments for you?

West Africans and Cubans are often put off by what they find to be the excessive body odour of Westerners. They feel Westerners don't shower often enough—once, or even twice a day is not always enough in the tropics. For people in these regions, the only excuse for body odour is lack of water or soap. Otherwise, a person should wash as often as it takes to stay fresh. Asians have traditionally found that Westerners smelled bad, partly due to meat and dairy consumption (a sour milk smell is noticed by Asians) and partly to the perception of Western inattention to hygiene.

What is clean and what smells bad are all relative. Arabs experience alienation when they move outside the olfactory zone of a friend or acquaintance. They like to feel the other's breath on their face.[61]

Perfume is highly appreciated in some cultures, such as Arab.

APPEARANCE

When you meet someone, what is the first thing you notice?

You likely picked some element of a person's appearance, perhaps their eyes, their body shape, their clothes. In Canada, as elsewhere, we make many assumptions about people based on appearance. We are attracted or not attracted to people on the basis of how they look and what they wear, and we draw conclusions about such things as their social class, age, intelligence, and ethnicity. Meanwhile, human beings have enhanced their appearance with makeup, face and body painting, and other adornments since time immemorial. While beauty, adornment, and dress are important to all cultures, concepts of beauty, the significance of hair, dress, and body adornments are culture bound.

Concepts of Beauty

Like other elements of culture, concepts of beauty evolve as cultures change. White skin was once highly valued among Euro Canadians and Europeans as an indication that a woman did not have to work in the fields. Now, a tan is desirable, but with our knowledge of the relationship between the sun and skin cancer, people are wary of tanning and are going to tanning salons for the "healthy" look now valued.

In many parts of the world, light skin is preferable to dark. In West Africa, my students felt happier if their skin was relatively light, partly because of the residual effect of British colonialism on self-esteem and identity (see Chapter 2). The diffusion of Western standards of beauty is apparent in other ways. In Korea and China plastic surgery to reshape eyelids and jaws, and even lengthen legs has become the fashion. In Mexico and Brazil where natural blondes are rare, advertising often features blondes because they represent a Euro-American ideal of beauty and cultural success. In Brazil, many women bleach their hair from black to blond, and in Thailand, Mexico, and elsewhere, skin lightening creams are popular.

Among Canadian men, not so long ago, body hair was assumed to be a natural sign of masculinity. Now young men have it removed or are self-conscious about it.

In China, the ideal of feminine beauty for centuries was a tiny foot, achieved by binding the foot and breaking it to form the ideal shape of a three-inch lotus.[62] Today, large eyes and pale skin are desirable.

Social and cultural factors also play a dominant role in the perception of body shapes. In Western societies, there is an inverse relationship between high social class and low body weight; in other words, high status members are more likely to meet the Western ideal of slender. The reverse is true in many African, Caribbean, and Middle Eastern cultures where "big is beautiful" because it correlates to assumptions about health and affluence. However, studies indicate that the longer immigrants from such regions have been in Western societies, the less obese they become and the more favourably they rate smaller female body shapes.[63]

What evidence is there in North American culture of extreme anxiety about body shape?

Dress

One of the case studies in Chapter 2 focused on dress and the messages it sends. In many parts of the world, such as Latin America, Asia, Africa, and much of Europe, it is important for both men and women to observe professional dress codes if they expect to be treated with respect.

Women in strict Muslim cultures must cover themselves. They are considered temptations that men cannot be expected to resist if their bodies or faces are glimpsed.

Women's hair is perceived to be so provocative that it too must be covered[64] (see photo).

Beachgoers at Jumeirah Beach Park in Dubai: how do the dress norms pictured here reflect the values of different cultural communities?

Source: © Lynsey Addario/CORBIS

Adornment

Jewellery, body art, and body shaping are all part of humanity's interest in appearance. Adornment is often an indicator of social status, wealth, or cultural affiliation. In Mali, rural women wear the family wealth in the form of enormous gold hoop earrings. In some Amazonian tribes, wooden lip rings are worn, while in West Africa, facial or body scarring used to indicate tribe membership, although the practice of scarring is dying out.

Tattoos are popular in North America at present. The origin of tattooing is controversial, with some believing it originated in Polynesia (tattoo comes from *tatu* meaning "to mark something" in Tahitian), while others believe it goes back to Egypt and the time of the Pharoahs. Tattooing has served various purposes over time from marking clan membership, to warding off illness, to calling forth the spirit of an image worn, such as that of a tiger.[65]

BODY LANGUAGE (KINESICS)

Cultural groups have different ways of walking, sitting, standing, reclining, and gesturing. According to Hall, whites do not move the way working class blacks do or the way Puerto Ricans or Mexicans or Pueblo or Navajo Indians or Chinese or Japanese people do.[66] The way we use our bodies is often unconscious. Tempo and rhythm contribute to the uniqueness of an individual walk, for example, but tempo and rhythm are also learned.

Body language, like language itself, is part of one's enculturation and socialization. Some cultures are more expressive both in body language and paralanguage than are others where self-restraint and emotional control are valued.

We send messages by means of our movements about our attitudes towards the person(s) with whom we are communicating (leaning towards the person indicates interest), our emotions (pacing or tapping our fingers indicates nervousness or impatience), and our wishes (gesturing for someone to come over). Usually body movements operate in tandem with verbal messages, and may support or contradict them.

Eye Contact and Gaze

How would you describe *bedroom eyes*? *Shifty eyes*? *Soulful eyes*? *Hard eyes*? What does a *thoughtful gaze* look like? Try to act them out. What other words describe eyes?

Dominant North American culture regards direct eye contact as a sign of trustworthiness and sincerity. In other cultures, such as African, Asian, and Native North American, to look someone directly in the eye is considered disrespectful (see box, *Culture and Eye Contact,* page 208). West African students are very attentive in class, but when spoken to individually, tend to avert their eyes as a sign of respect.

There are differences in eye contact between African-American and Euro-American culture. African Americans use more eye contact than whites when speaking, yet less when listening.[67] Latino children may also be socialized to avoid direct eye contact. This might affect their relations with a Euro-American teacher unaware of this cultural difference.[68]

Arabs engage in long direct eye contact with others as a sign of interest. The prolonged gaze can be disconcerting to people not accustomed to it. Eye contact is avoided, however, between men and women in Arab and Muslim cultures ("eye purdah") because it is considered erotically exciting.[69]

In Western culture direct eye contact is valued, but periodically broken by looking away and then resuming contact. The prolonged stare is part of the non-verbal code of the North American and Latin American homosexual communities.

CULTURE AND EYE CONTACT

Very direct eye contact: Middle Easterners; some Latin American groups; the French

Moderate eye contact: mainstream Americans; Northern Europeans; the British

Minimal eye contact: East Asians; Southeast Asians; East Indians; Native Americans.

Source: Excerpt from Chaney, Lillian H. & Jeannette S. Martin, *Intercultural Business Communication,* second edition. New Jersey: Prentice Hall, 2000, p. 111.

The eye can indicate emotional response. Pupil dilation indicates interest while contraction may reveal anger or disagreement or dislike. Arabs are particularly attentive to pupil response: "[S]ince people can't control the response of their eyes, which is a dead giveaway, many Arabs, like [the late] Yasser Arafat, wear dark glasses, even indoors."[70]

Gestures: Watch Your Moves!

While in Canada the "thumbs up" gesture is acceptable, in some cultures it has a negative connotation.

The amount and kinds of gesturing are both personal and culturally determined. Some cultures have a tendency to "speak with their hands" (Italian), while others make minimal use of body movement; the Japanese and Koreans, for instance, appear quite "still." Dominant Canadian culture does not make expansive use of gesturing—self-control and emotional restraint are highly valued as they are in Britain. Members of ethnic groups in Canada carry their own traditions depending on how close they are to the ways of their country of origin. Italian Canadians, for example, and other Mediterranean Canadians are often more physically expressive than the Anglo-Celtic norm.

Specific gestures are culturally learned. The hand gesture for "come here" in Canada is done with the palm turned upward and pulled towards the body. In West Africa, the "come here" gesture is done with the palm turned down and closed. It looks more to a Canadian like a signal to go away. The hitchhiking gesture in Canada is thumb turned up on an arm held up—a gesture that is rude in Australia.

The thumb and index finger formed into a circle is the "okay" sign in Canada and the U.S., but in Brazil, Germany, and Russia, it signifies the anus or vagina.[71] In Japan, it signifies money. In France, it signifies worthless, or zero.

The thumbs-up gesture is rude in Australia, Bangladesh, and Nigeria, where it means "up yours." The upraised middle finger is rude just about everywhere. The story goes that the Emperor Caligula in Rome would make his subordinates kiss that finger; as it was a phallic symbol, he was symbolically having them kiss his penis.[72] (In the Middle East, you hold out your hand, spread your fingers, and drop the middle one.)

In India, it is common to nod and bob the head, which to most Canadians signifies agreement. (Sometimes it looks as if the head is shaking, as in saying no.) In actual fact, all this means is "I hear you." Likewise, a nod of the head in Japan does not mean "yes."

Even the smile, a universal survival gesture, can be misunderstood. Russians do not smile on the streets, the French are put off by what they see as excessive smiling for no reason by Americans, and the Japanese do not smile under formal circumstances.

Posture

Posture is a category of kinesics. Slouching or draping yourself over a chair in Canada may indicate that you are relaxed. In class, it may indicate lack of interest; sitting upright and leaning slightly forward in class is generally assumed to indicate interest (however sincere). Sitting posture communicates everywhere—in Ghana, it is rude to sit with your legs crossed. In parts of East Asia and in the Middle East, it is rude to show the soles of your feet. In Canada, sitting with the legs crossed in the direction of the person you are sitting beside indicates attention or interest. Shifting legs to cross them away from the other person may indicate a change of emotion or discontinued interest.

The link between posture and cultural values can be illustrated by Japan, where hierarchy and formality are valued. When two Japanese bow in greeting or leave-taking, the person of lower status begins the bow, and bows more deeply than the person of higher status: for example, younger defers to older, female defers to male, student defers to teacher, seller defers to buyer.[73]

Body orientation when we are speaking to another person also communicates. Arabs face very directly the person to whom they are speaking; this, in conjunction with perceived "close talking" and intense eye contact contributes to the impression North Americans may have of aggressiveness.[74]

Facial Expressions

It has been estimated that the human face can display more than 250 000 different expressions.[75] Certain facial expressions and emotions are universal—the smile, the laugh, tears. What triggers them can be culturally determined. A smile, for example, in Canada can indicate encouragement, affection, or happiness. While it can transmit the same meanings in Japanese culture, it can also be used to mask a negative emotion or be used to avoid answering a question.[76]

There are gender differences in the function and frequency of smiling. Women in all cultures tend to smile more than men and for reasons for which men would not usually smile.

SUMMARY

Communication is a complex system involving a number of codes that operate according to rules and interact to create meaning. Non-verbal codes of communication often communicate more sincerely than verbal codes because we have less control over them than we do over what we say or write. Non-verbal codes are the "silent language"[77] and essence of the "water we swim in" that is our culture. They are often at the core of intercultural misunderstandings when neither side understands the meaning of the other's behaviour, and possibly not of its own either. This chapter examined non-verbal, culture-bound codes such as silence, paralanguage, time, space and distance, appearance, touching, and smell. Body language is also a complex culture-bound code. To be interculturally competent, people need to be especially aware that gestures may be similar across cultures, but may have very different meanings.

KEY TERMS

code 188	M-time 194	phatic code 191
haptics 201	olfactics 203	proxemics 189
kinesics 189	paralanguage 193	P-time 194

TOPICS FOR CRITICAL THINKING AND REFLECTION

1. How do you spend your leisure time? In organized activities? Hanging out with friends? A bit of both? To what degree do you share North America's obsession with making "good use" of time?

2. Here are the first two paragraphs of an article on fitness followed by other key points from the article. Do you agree with its basic premise about time? What does it tell you about our culture and its values?

   Do you think multitasking indicates a change towards polychronic time use in Canadian culture, or do you think it is popular because it is an extra-efficient form of monochronic time use?

TOTE THAT LAUNDRY, LIFT THAT BALE: FITTING IN FITNESS

By Barrie Shepley, former Olympic coach and president of Personal Best, a health consulting company

If pure athleticism is the first requirement for success in sport, time management skills are a close second. In my age group, marathon runners, mountain-bike racers and triathletes are often also senior managers in the companies they work in (or own).

They say if you want something done, give it to a busy person. That's because busy people know that they have to be organized to fit everything into their schedules. Creative scheduling and smart time management skills are necessary to fit 30 hours of modern life into the 24 we have available . . .

In my experience, people who exercise early in the morning are the most successful . . .

Try taking on two goals at the same time. An example: When you leave your children at their practices at the arena, pool or gymnasium, you can go for a run, power walk or visit a nearby fitness centre . . .

Multi-tasking is an important life skill . . .

Put an exercise mat and inexpensive resistance tubing in your living room so you can do three-minute "mini" workouts every time a commercial comes on television . . .

Plan your week's schedule (work, exercise, home chores, social time) on Sunday evening and do your best to keep to this plan. Put your exercises into your Day-Timer as a legitimate appointment you have with someone else . . .

Some restaurants will cook and package a full week of healthy meals that can be frozen and used all week . . .

Source: Excerpt from Shepley, Barrie. "Tote that laundry, lift that bale: fitting in fitness." *The Globe and Mail,* Sept. 21, 2004, A21.

---

3. Are you a monochronic or polychronic individual? Choose a day and keep notes about how you've passed the time.

4. When Canadians are ready to end a conversation, what changes in body movements signal their intention? Observe yourself and those with whom you come into contact for a few days and keep notes.

5. Tour your department and college/university to see how space is organized. Look into classrooms, offices of faculty, secretaries, and administrators, and public spaces, and try to determine what messages are being communicated by the organization of space, both fixed and moveable.

6. Here are some observations made by a family from Afghanistan that settled in Winnipeg in 2004.[78] They had spent 13 months in a refugee camp in Pakistan before coming to Canada. What do their observations say about their culture and its communication norms? About Canada's, as reflected in Winnipeg?

   • The children do not bring lunch to school, but rather wait until they go home to eat as a family. "We do not like to eat alone. We always feel we should share our food. We feel shy to eat on our own, quickly."

   • They wonder why members of the same sex do not walk arm in arm in the street, or hold hands as they do in Pakistan and Afghanistan.

   • They marvel at the sometimes sloppy clothes of Canadian teens—baggy jeans and baseball caps.

   • They are also surprised at how teens sit in school—slouched with their heads almost on their desks. "They do not stand up when the teacher enters the room, and never ask permission to go to the bathroom. They just leave the room."

   • They would like to meet more Canadians, "to see their houses, their dinners, their rooms. See how they live."

   • They find Canadians friendly, but reserved. Canadians do not have the same sense of communal living or hospitality as Afghans, who open their homes to strangers and treat guests like royalty.

Chapter 8
Cultures at Cross Purposes

In this chapter we will explore cultural differences related to:

- Communication styles
- Face
- Age and Gender
- Connections
- Honesty and fairness
- Friendship

Not all cultures are in agreement about what people may talk about to whom, let alone when and how to do it. This chapter is practical in nature and elaborates on some concepts touched on in previous chapters and introduces some new ones. It begins by exploring differences in styles of communication and goes on to discuss other concepts related to values and the behaviours they inspire.

Concepts of politeness vary across cultures. In some cultures, lining up in an orderly fashion is not the norm. What other variations in concepts of politeness have you encountered in your own experience?

COMMUNICATION STYLE

Direct and Indirect Communication

At the heart of communication style is the difference between direct and indirect methods of conveying information. This little story illustrates the concept:

> I once embarrassed a friend while living in Cuba for saying "no" too immediately to someone who had asked a favour I knew I could not possibly fulfill. I didn't like to refuse outright, but nor did I think it would be fair to give false hope. My friend was upset by my behaviour.
>
> "You never say you can't do something," he said. "That hurts a person's feelings. You say you will try, so they have hope, and then you just don't

mention it again. That way as time goes and you don't say anything, they will understand and accept it with less disappointment."

"What if they ask?" I countered.

"Then you say you tried and you were not successful. But they won't."

How would you have reacted in my situation? Were you surprised at my friend's reaction to my refusal?

If you would have answered as I did, you are likely a person who favours a direct style of communication. In Canada, a low-context culture, honesty is often believed to be "the best policy." In Cuba, however, it is impolite to refuse a request directly or to say "no" outright . . . it seems cruel. Cubans, like many peoples, like to soften their "no's."

Kofi Annan, Secretary General of the United Nations, once explained, "There are different cultures, ways of communicating. Americans are very direct, straightforward; other cultures are more subtle. You will never hear them say "no," the word "no." You must listen for *how* they say no. You must listen to what is *not* said—often what is not said is more important than what is said."[1]

Indirectness is often related to concepts of politeness and the avoidance of overt conflict valued in high-context cultures such as Arab, Latin American, African, and Asian.[2]

Relative directness is the cultural norm in North America where an articulate person who is unafraid to voice opinions is perceived to be trustworthy and credible. Germanic cultures also employ a particularly direct style of communication.[3] If speaking one's mind results in a disharmonious environment at times, then so be it— better "to have it out" than not have clarity. (Practitioners of both styles are found across cultures and degrees of directness vary with the situation.)

How then, can someone from a culture that values directness determine when someone from an indirect culture is actually saying *no*? The answer, if not the skill, is simple: it requires the reading of verbal and non-verbal clues.

Indirect cultures may imply or even say *yes,* but the agreed-upon issue may never happen. For example, if a person wishes to go somewhere, and it has been agreed that going is possible, but no date or time has been set, there is a good possibility that the trip won't take place. *Soon* or *we are waiting for approval* or *it will be better later* or other such evasions are ways of implying *no* without saying it.

An American negotiator described a discussion with a press officer for the Palestinian Liberation Organization named Nasser, whom he found to be likeable but evasive. Nasser once complained that Arafat had never said either "yes" or "no" to him when he asked him a direct question. "You would think he could do that much for his press officer!" The American sympathized. "Do you like Arafat?" he asked to which Nasser replied, "It's not a matter of liking or disliking. . . ." In three long talks, Nasser himself never once said "yes" or "no."[4]

From Korean Kwanghee Kim's point of view, Canadians can be quite rude in their directness. As she put it, "Oriental people try to think before speaking." She recounted an incident, not atypical in her experience here, where a Canadian student had said of another who was not present, "I hate so-and-so." Kwanghee was shocked. She said she would never say such a thing about another person although she might think it. She was taught not to express negative opinions about anything for fear of offending or hurting someone.

In Korea, the concept of **kibun** is of importance in understanding communication norms. *Kibun* refers to mood, feelings, and state of mind. A peaceful environment is necessary for the maintenance of kibun, which is easily disturbed, and the people with whom a person interacts are expected to maintain an environment conducive to its stability.[5]

Communication in Japan involves **omoi-yari,** or interpreting the unspoken meaning of exchanges.[6] Japanese negotiators involved in discussion regarding the resumption of Canadian beef imports, for example, were "polite and smile[d] but no way would they open the border back to Canadian beef," according to one of the negotiators.[7] In Japan, if a Japanese manager tells you that carrying out a request you have made " 'might be a little difficult,' he really means 'not in a million years.' "[8]

Ojibwe culture is based on non-interference.[9] If a person asks for advice, an answer is often conveyed thorough story-telling. A character might be drawn from the spirit world, for example, and a story told to make a person see the consequences of a course of action. In Ojibwe culture, a person cannot tell another what to do; people must make their own decisions.

Verbal Presentation

Differences in how people present themselves when speaking relate to culture-bound concepts of what impression of themselves they believe they should project. In some cultures, an air of assertiveness and control is desirable; in others, an air of tolerance and coolness is preferred. Verbal presentation also encompasses information expectations: people have culture-bound ideas not just of how, but of what they should say in order to project a desirable image.[10]

Speakers use a variety of stylistic speech devices to achieve their ends. Some cultures like flowery speech in the form of metaphors and poetic turns of phrase, exaggerated compliments and descriptions of their own abilities and accomplishments, and repetition of important points—all of which serve to aggrandize the speaker and listeners. Stylistic devices that minimize the attention focused on the speaker and the speaker's accomplishments include understatement, self-deprecation, demurring, and use of indirect communication to say "no."[11] Cultures that value empirical fact employ devices that clarify and focus on accurate information such as idioms like "dot the i's and cross the t's" and "get to the point" and "let's make sure we're reading from the same page."

Arab and Latin American cultures enjoy words and use them to impress. Wordplay, prescribed or ritual gallantries, exaggerations, double entendres, and rhetorical flourishes are common. Arabs use words for effect, and not just meaning.[12] They respect people who project their wealth, power, and influence, not people who understate or undervalue them. Strong words create strong images.

Nigerian and Ghanaian cultures also delight in wordplay, eloquence, and inventiveness.[13] West African cultures, although largely **literate,** are still relatively close to their **oral** roots. Oral patterns used by cultures with long oral histories are still much used in the talk and writing of members of these cultures today.[14] They include repetition and use of proverbs, metaphors, and formulaic sayings in addition to expressive body language and paralanguage. For example, if a chief has died, a person might say, "A mighty tree has fallen" rather than baldly relating the news.[15]

The delight in words has been carried through to African-American culture (their language accepted as a variation of English known as African-American Vernacular English)[16] and to Cuban culture. A Ghanaian chief giving welcome, a Cuban with country roots extemporizing a thank you, an African-American minister preaching, a Cairo merchant bargaining in the *souk* (market)—all illustrate a love of the sound and creative potential of language.

Great speakers like Winston Churchill and Martin Luther King naturally used forms of speech reminiscent of orality and humanity's early love of sound and voice. Search the Internet for the text of Martin Luther King's "I Have a Dream" speech delivered in 1963. Find examples of rhythm, parallel structure, repetition, and other devices that make the speech *sound* so compelling.

German, Irish, Turkish, Palestinian, Serbian, and Israeli speakers use **rhetorical forms** that project authority and control.[17] Voice volume and an emphatic style of speaking project the desired image. Cubans, although indirect when refusing or rejecting requests, present assertiveness in practical situations such as asking a friend to open a window, or close a door, for example. "Open the door" is preferred to a softened command like "Would you mind opening the door" or "Could you open the door."

Norwegian, Swedish, and some Asian cultures value the projection of patience, understanding, and empathy rather than dominance and control, while the English use understatement and euphemism to soften opinion and maintain emotional reserve.[18] Asian cultures, as we saw in Chapter 7, use silence as a device to project emotional control.

Formality and Informality

Cultures vary with regard to the degree of formality preferred—in speech, forms of address, and what is considered proper attire for a given occasion. North American norms tend towards greater informality than European, Asian, African, and Latin American norms. Canadians place somewhere between the more formal codes of Europe and the informal preferences of the United States.

Americans easily call each other by their first names upon making acquaintance, are not unduly concerned with formal dress when other cultures would consider it important, and do not go through elaborate greeting rituals. President George Bush has casually referred to Prime Minister Sharon of Israel as "Ariel," President Chirac of France as "Jacques," and Kofi Annan as "Kofi" during televised press conferences.

The American tendency to informality stems from the value it places on democracy and equality. Deference and formality are not appropriate between presumed equals. In Europe and most other parts of the world, social hierarchies are reinforced by formalities.

Titles and **honorifics** are important in Latin America, the Middle East, India, and parts of Europe such as Italy and Germany. Titles like professor and doctor or engineer should be used in both written and oral communication. Germans are particularly formal. They do not easily use first names. A man who is both a doctor and a professor is referred to as Herr (Mr.) Doktor Schmidt. Given Germany's relatively masculine orientation on Hofstede's continuum of masculine/feminine cultures, not surprisingly women are addressed by their husband's titles. Herr Doktor Schmidt's wife is not Frau (Mrs.) Schmidt, but rather Frau Herr Doktor Schmidt.[19]

In Australia, however, academic qualifications are downplayed in public. People are not respected just for having them.[20] In the Netherlands, titles may not be used in speaking, but are in writing. The Chinese, on the other hand, like titles. The Japanese also make use of honorifics in the form of suffixes added to words to signal a speaker recognizes the higher status of the listener.[21] *San* indicates respect, while *sensai* is used for respected professionals such as doctors.

Dress Formality

Business dress codes are very strict in many countries. In Latin America, a professional must look like a professional. That means wearing suits, having shoes polished, and for women, similarly professional dress. North American businesspeople who fly to warm Latin American countries to do business may dress casually because of the climate. This gives a very bad impression and is often decoded as lack of respect. North America is widely believed to have cheated Latin America in business over the past century or more; dressing casually is just another sign of disrespect.

Many cultures prefer more formal dress codes than do North Americans. Even casual attire worn outside the home is likely to be "dressier" in Europe than in North America. Italian women going shopping, for example, tend to dress well even if they are just going to the corner for bread.

BUSINESS CARDS

Bilingual business cards, with English on one side and the relevant country's language on the other are appropriate and expected in many parts of the world. In Japan, presentation is ceremonial. After the initial handshake or bow, the card is presented, Japanese side up so that it can be studied as a sign of respect. Cards presented to you should also be studied momentarily rather than popped into a pocket or wallet.[22] In the Middle East and parts of Asia and Southeast Asia, do not present the card with your left hand.

THE CONCEPT OF FACE

Before you read further, answer these questions[23]:

- What is the meaning of face?
- What is the meaning of face-giving?
- What is the meaning of face-losing?

The concept of face can be confusing. It is often associated with Asian cultures but, in reality, face is a universal phenomenon. It is comparable to reputation, the preservation of social standing and respect.[24] How we manage face—maintaining, saving, and respecting face—differs across cultures and involves the use of verbal and non-verbal messages.

Face in Japan has to do with the collective nature of the culture.[25] Anything that causes embarrassment, or centres someone out disturbs the delicate web of relationships. Everybody works together to preserve a harmonious façade.

Some anthropologists believe the Japanese are concerned with face in order to avoid shame, an external form of social control employed in some cultures.[26] Guilt, on the other hand, is an internal form of social control used by other cultures. Japanese children are taught not to bring shame on the family, or on themselves, or on whatever group they are a part of. To be laughed at is shameful. It is not common, for example, to make friendly jokes about a colleague at work. Irony and sarcasm are not used.

To bring shame on the group is so disturbing that a Japanese person will resign rather than challenge a criticism in a situation where a Canadian might consider it more honourable to fight than resign.[27] A Japanese student, for example, told me that if her father lost his job, the family would tell no one. They would move and make a new start.

From this point of view the concept of face is indeed an important facet of Japanese culture. However, the Japanese are not preoccupied with "saving" or "losing" face: they are preoccupied with maintaining group harmony and cohesion and have developed behaviours designed to achieve that end.[28] When they cover for one another, for example, if mistakes have been made, it is unlikely to be mentioned by anyone.

Being singled out in any way in Japan runs contrary to the maintenance of group face, as reflected in the proverb *the nail that sticks up is hammered down*. In more individualist Canadian culture, in contrast, standing out is not inherently shameful, unless for behaviour judged to be inappropriate. *The squeaky wheel gets the grease* illustrates the positive aspects of being seen or heard as an individual.

Other Asian and South Asian countries are also concerned with face. Bruce Macmillan, a marketing professor teaching in China, tells a story that indicates the sensitivity of the Chinese to saving face in a situation where he would not have thought it an issue. Teaching with an interpreter, he mentioned the word "junk food." The interpreter asked what it was, and Bruce, in order to continue, said, "I'll explain later." The interpreter said, "You must tell me now or I'll lose face." She felt she had to be able to translate everything to maintain the respect of the class. Once informed about junk food, the lecture predictably got derailed. His students then asked, "If you come from a developed country, why do you eat garbage?" This was difficult to answer partly because of the concept, partly because of Bruce's unhappy use of an idiomatic expression ("junk food") untranslatable in that context.

In West Africa, I used the audio-lingual method of teaching French as prescribed by the West African syllabus. Everyone in the first form responded well and recited back more or less correctly. At the end of each class, I would ask them in English, even though this was forbidden in audio-lingual methodology, "Did you understand today's lesson?" "Oh, yes, Miss" they would all respond.

When individual oral testing time came I was surprised to discover that, basically, in two months, no one had understood a thing. When classes reconvened, I confronted them, "But why didn't you tell me you didn't understand?" With embarrassment, they confided that if they had said they didn't understand, I would have thought they thought I was a bad teacher. They were saving face for me.

Mediterranean, Latin American, and Arab cultures are also sensitive to face although it is connected to the concept of personal honour and sensitivity to perceived slights, as well as to the avoidance of conflict.[29]

A study on feedback illustrates the concept of face in a multi-cultural engineering context. When feedback was put on a continuum, with unacceptable at one end, and acceptable at the other, some cultures were found to have a large neutral zone, others a large unacceptable zone, and others a large acceptable zone[30] (see Figure 8.1).

For example, a Mexican engineer was given some negative feedback by a Canadian manager in front of his colleagues. The Mexican resigned the next day, to the surprise of the Canadian who considered his feedback unworthy of such a response. The Mexican had a larger unacceptable zone than the Canadian, and a smaller neutral zone.

The neutral zone of Mexicans, Japanese, and Chinese is, on average, narrower than the neutral zone of Canadians and Americans according to this study. The French, however, demonstrated a large neutral zone, and often disregarded feedback considered negative and designed to elicit action by Canadians. It may take a Canadian manager several attempts before a French employee registers feedback as negative, at that point thinking it has come out of nowhere. According to Laroche, the French employee simply does not take offence easily.

On the other hand, the acceptable zone of Austrians was high in comparison to that of the Americans in the study. When an Austrian manager told his American employees that they had made a "totally unacceptable" presentation, they assumed they would be fired. The Austrian, employing the direct style of Germanic cultures, thought he had just emphasized the need to work on it.

Figure 8.1 Feedback Zones

| Unacceptable | ← Neutral Zone (varies) → | Acceptable |

Face Negotiation

Ting-Toomey collected data on concepts of face in relation to conflict styles and negotiation. Her research consisted of open-ended questionnaires and interviews with about 1500 students and colleagues and resulted in these conclusions:[31]

1. *Face-saving:* In response to the question "What is the meaning of face?" American students tended to equate face with saving their own face. Japanese students related it to maintaining honour, their own and the family or organization's.
2. *Face-giving:* Americans could not define this term, while Asians could. Face in Asia is mutual, a tango for two. In the West, it is dichotomous: we lose or save it.
3. *Face-losing:* For Americans this meant personal loss of self-esteem, while for Japanese and Koreans, it meant that group harmony had been disrupted.
4. *Recovery from face loss:* Americans and Canadians used humour as a strategy; failing that, they tried defensive or attack strategies, i.e., win-lose approaches. Asian cultures tried to maintain a win-win situation.
5. *Conflict:* American subjects tended to see conflict as a win-lose proposition aimed at saving face for themselves, while Asian subjects tended towards mutual-face preservation strategies.
6. *Shame:* Shame is common to collective cultures although its definition varies. If the Japanese disgrace their organization, they may also disgrace themselves and their family; for the Chinese, disgrace reflects upon family honour.

Covert Culture and Action Chains

YOU HAVE A PROBLEM . . .

Let's say your neighbour's tree hangs over your yard and swimming pool. It drops leaves and debris on your property all year round, but particularly in fall when you end up raking all their leaves and cleaning them out of your pool. You have decided you want your neighbour to trim the tree on your side of the fence. How will you handle the situation to achieve your ends? The tree might not survive the major cutting required, but you have had enough.

According to Hall, disputes are handled very differently in Northern European and North American culture from the way they are handled in some Latin American cultures.[32] The former employ "action chains" the steps of which have been internalized. Disputes start with non-verbal and body messages, which escalate to verbal hints or requests, then verbal confrontation, legal action, and finally force or physical action. Politeness and coolness are maintained as steps escalate. The paradigm is the same for household disputes, neighbours' quarrels, and management and labour disagreements.

Spanish-Americans studied in New Mexico had a "covert" style of handling disputes.[33] Social harmony and face are valued, and so confrontations are to be avoided, but they are also highly sensitive to criticism, with the added burden of pride and *machismo* among men[34] (see *Time Out for Latin America*). The combination makes them subject to emotional eruptions and has resulted in another system for dealing with disagreement. First there is brooding, since verbal confrontation is to be avoided, and the first show that something is wrong is often a display of force or drama.[35] Later, when emotions have subsided, the law emerges as an arbiter.

Working and living in Latin America suggested to this writer that Hall's theory is applicable to various other Latin American cultural groups as well. It is important in business and other negotiations with Latin Americans that North Americans understand that if this cultural pattern should occur, they should not become defensive as a response.

SOCIALLY ACCEPTABLE COMMENTS AND TOPICS OF CONVERSATION

Politeness and Political Correctness

Concepts of politeness are often culture bound.

In some cultures, it is impolite to comment on someone's appearance, or order them to do something; in others, it is not. Canadians in India recount being told bluntly and cheerfully they were "getting pretty fat." Personal comments about weight and appearance are not uncommon there. In some Latin American cultures, people may comment equally blithely on physical appearance. To Canadians, this is rude, unless we are complimenting, yet such comments are routinely made in other cultures without malice.

Likewise, it is common in China, India, the Arab world,[36] and parts of Latin America to ask about money: how much you earn, how much your possessions cost, and so on. You may also be asked your age, your weight, whether or not you colour your hair. People in Beijing felt quite comfortable asking Jan Wong which of her two sons she liked better—in front of them.[37]

Norms of political correctness, Canadian style, are not universal. Approving comments to women about their attractiveness are common in Latin America (*If you cook like you walk . . .* suggest Cuban males to passing attractive women, or *You are a goddess*) but not acceptable in Canada. That said, many Latin American women are tiring of voiced running commentary by men on the street and are working to effect change. Comments about age or ethnicity are also politically incorrect in Canada, but not elsewhere.

In many countries, political and religious topics are best avoided unless people are well acquainted, and even then they are not necessarily common topics of conversation. In France however, where intellect is valued, intellectual discussions about political and artistic topics are often enjoyed.

Canadians always feel safe talking about the weather and the weather forecast—a reliable topic of conversation and our own national phatic code (see Chapter 7). Talking about the weather serves as an impersonal ice breaker for people in line-ups or at parties or at the start of meetings, not to mention among friends. In tropical countries where the weather hardly changes from day to day, daily exchanges about the weather are understandably uncommon. The daily forecast in Ghana for about ten months of the year would have been: "high 95 degrees Fahrenheit or more, torrential downpour between one and two in the afternoon, lesser downpour between six and seven in the evening. Low of about 80 around midnight."

Disclosure

The term **disclosure** is used in cross-cultural jargon to refer to what kind of and how much personal information individuals tend to reveal about themselves. The French and the Germans, for example, disclose little of their personal life in business and in the workplace, while American and Canadian norms vary.[38] This may or may not be ethnicity related. An Icelandic Canadian told me only partly facetiously that Icelanders disclose nothing about anything, ever, even to members of their own families; my own Russian Mennonite relatives are much the same—or maybe it's a Manitoba thing: we both have roots there.

Non-disclosure for a Korean student who didn't hand in an important paper was preferable to giving excuses. When asked why, he remained silent. He later explained in another paper, without directly referring to this incident, that in Korea it is unacceptable to give excuses for failing to do something, no matter how good one's reason. In short, there are no reasons good enough to speak of if a person has failed an obligation. Better to say nothing.

In cultures where physically being alone is neither possible (due to crowded living conditions) nor culturally desired, people do not necessarily disclose much about their personal lives even to those with whom they live and interact closely. In Cuba, for example, where living conditions are crowded, government spies may be listening and few people want to be alone anyway, personal information is closely guarded and conversation kept to neutral topics or jokes. This serves a dual purpose: harmony is maintained in close quarters, and should anyone be questioned about another's activities, people "know nothing" because nothing has been explicitly disclosed.

In India, although people live in extended families, personal information is preserved by formality. Communication on the whole is very indirect and formal, within and outside family life. Saving face and dignity are important.[39]

Acceptable topics of disclosure change with generations. North American society is undergoing an explosion of disclosure, if "spill-your-guts" programs and reality shows are any indication. They mine the current vogue for disclosure and serve as a secular form of confession, not to mention a moment of media glory and attention for the disclosers.

Have you ever wanted to go on a reality TV program? What kinds of personal information would you be prepared or not be prepared to disclose publicly? What kinds of personal information are you comfortable or not comfortable disclosing to a close friend? Your parents? Your partner? A casual acquaintance? How do you decide what to disclose to whom?

Taboo Topics

Certain topics are considered inappropriate subjects of conversation.

Sex is a common non-starter, either for religious reasons or cultural traditions of reservation. Homosexuality and prostitution are generally taboo topics in China, India, and the Middle East for example. Observers claim that in China's larger cities, however, where various forms of sexuality have long been known about by many, and quietly explored and practised, it is becoming more common to discuss and acknowledge the formerly unspoken. After decades of revolutionary repression, the Chinese are openly curious about sex.[40]

In South Africa, Nelson Mandela broke a taboo in 2005 by admitting that his eldest son had died of AIDS, a subject not openly discussed in this nation of millions of sufferers. As President from 1994–1998, Mandela shied away from the topic because "as a Xhosa elder, he would not discuss issues of sexuality in a public forum."[41] Mandela broke the taboo to help bring dignity to those dying of AIDS.

Twenty-year-old Canadian Marlo Desjardins spent a year in Punjab and made good friends among Sikhs her age. She observed that sex is not talked about openly, but that there is a good deal of flirtatiousness between young men and women. Marlo speculated that, although talking about sex was taboo, and premarital sex forbidden, sexual interest was open, because both young men and women felt safe within the strict rules of their culture. They were free to flirt since to go beyond flirtation was so highly unlikely to happen. Marriages are often arranged among Sikhs, and virginity valued. Immigrants to Canada, however, sometimes experience generational conflict because the norms of the larger society are different from Sikh traditional norms (see Chapter 10).

Depression and mental illness are taboo topics in Japan, where a high suicide rate among young people is partly attributed to the fact that young people are discouraged from talking about their problems and partly to a cultural tendency to beautify death.[42]

TABOO IN CANADA

Money and personal finance are taboo topics for many Canadians. We clam up quickly when talk of salaries, credit-card debt, bank accounts, and investment portfolio values comes up. Only the rude ask how much you make or how much you owe. In this, Canada is similar to Britain and France, and unlike the United States and Sweden where people don't share our reticence. We're more introverted than Americans about money and most other things, and less driven by money.[43] Peter C. Newman, says that, "To ask rich Canadians how much money they have is like suggesting they describe their preferred sex position."[44]

Are you comfortable talking about your own or family's debt, what your parents earn or "are worth" . . . or do you even know?

Humour

Imagine that you are from a culture that does not practise irony or sarcasm.

A common greeting in Ghana when a person returns from a trip or an excursion is to say, "Good morning, So-and-so, you have returned." After her students had said this to her a few times, American Jean Mitchell saw a chance to crack a joke. She returned from a trip one day and answered a student's greeting with, "No, I'm still there." The student didn't laugh. Why not? Because she didn't see the joke.

Humour is one of the hardest things to grasp because humour varies greatly across cultures. Occasions where humour is considered suitable also vary. For example, in formal Germany, starting a speech with a joke to relax the audience and draw them in is not common.

AGE

North America is youth oriented, but many cultures highly respect the wisdom that is believed to come with age. Asian and African cultures fall into this category and when dealing with Westerners, may automatically assume that the oldest-looking person of a team or group is the person with the most authority. Even when informed otherwise, it may be hard for people from such cultures not to defer to or seek the opinion of the person who looks the oldest. White hair is an advantage in doing business in Asia, South Asia, and the Middle East.[45] The reverse is often true in the West, where people who have attained a top professional status are particularly admired if they have done so while still young.

THE ROLE OF WOMEN

It is often more difficult for women to adapt to a new culture than for men; many cultures are more strongly patriarchal than North America's is and women's lives are much more circumscribed than men's. Immigrants from strongly patriarchal cultures where women are expected or obliged to live secluded lives and whose primary purpose is to bear children may find it hard to adapt to a culture like Canada's where women are, in most respects, given equal freedoms, opportunities, and responsibilities.

It is a mistake, however, to assume that women in very patriarchal cultures such as Middle Eastern all crave Western freedoms. This is simply not the case. Some do, and work within their cultures for change, while others are content with the status quo and feel themselves to be valued and protected by the cultural patterns set by men.

In Latin America, depending on the degree of *machismo* (male dominance) prevalent in a particular country, women are expected to serve submissively in the home, but may have informal power within the family. The same is true in Spain and Italy; in public, women defer to husbands, but in private their opinion counts.

In rapidly evolving Spain, particularly in the south, however, women struggle for professional and personal equality despite new laws (including one obliging men to assist in housework) enacted to mixed reviews.[46] It is difficult, for example, for female nurses to get full-time jobs because nursing is a predominantly male occupation and full-time jobs are reserved for them. In addition, women in southern Spain are still expected to be at home at noon to prepare the noontime meal for the family.[47]

Similar scenes are common in Japan, India, and other parts of the world. Change is occurring, however, in both India and Japan. Many middle-class Indian women now work outside the home. In Japan, the percentage of single women has surpassed the percentage in other industrialized nations, and 43 percent of Japanese men in their early 30s are unmarried—double the 1980 rate. Why? Because Japanese women say they do not want to spend their lives cooking, cleaning, and deferring to traditional Japanese men.[48]

Women in parts of Europe and Latin America are used more flagrantly as promotional tools in marketing than in North America, and often appear scantily dressed, for example, at openings and in commercials. However, they have trouble making serious inroads in male-dominated bastions of business.

Canadian women working or living in Latin America, the Middle East, and parts of Asia and Europe often feel constricted by expectations there. They may be disoriented by the attention paid them in the streets, or the lack of attention, or inappropriate (from their point of view) attention paid them in professional contexts. Canadian women expect to be treated as professional equals, with their gender a non-issue, at least on the surface.

To achieve that respect, Canadian women working in male-dominated cultures need to be aware of how they communicate—in dress, language, speech, and body language.

Even women of high status and a certain age note the difficulties of relating to men as equals in many parts of the world. If a senior woman is accompanied by a man of lower professional status, counterparts in Asia and the Middle East may still look to the man for decisions and opinions, not to the woman.

It is uncommon to see women walking alone in the streets in the Gulf States. Western women may walk alone, but local Arab women generally go out accompanied. Filipinas, usually domestic employees, generally stay in or go out in groups. Western women are not likely to be bothered or harassed if they take the precautions of not meeting men's direct gazes (perceived to have a sexual connotation), dressing modestly, and going about their business with purpose. The ability to pass relatively unnoticed, however, has changed for both Western men and women in the light of 9/11 and its consequences around the world.

"Drinking with the guys" in Asia and South Asia, where women seldom drink, may also be misread as an invitation, while smoking may also indicate that a woman has "loose morals."

The Value of Women

In extremely patriarchal cultures, women are essentially property and their role is to produce children, males in particular, and if they are poor, to work.[49] In the Middle East and parts of Asia, women bear the responsibility of preserving family honour:

sexual transgressions dishonour the family and can result in consequences as severe as being shut away for life or even killed.[50]

In the Arab world, it is common to give money to nurses and doctors attending a woman in childbirth. If the woman gives birth to a boy, the gift is often larger.[51]

In Pakistan and India, most rural women have little control over their lives. Their purpose is to bear children, male children, partly because men are needed for the hard field work; they may be obliged to let infant daughters die, or to abort female fetuses if the sex of the child can be determined before birth. In India, the shortage of females is predicted to increase as many middle-class women abort female fetuses following ultrasounds. The practice is illegal, but doctors can be found to provide those services.

It is further predicted that the millions of men unable to find wives are a potential cause for serious social unrest. In China, where the urban one-child policy has resulted in a surplus of males and the fear that by 2020, there will be 40 million more men than women of marriageable age, the government has embarked on a program to encourage people to value girls equally. In the meantime, baby girls fill orphanages and are the source of adoption for many Canadian families. In 2003, 1108 came to Canada.[52]

If and when you have children, do you think you would have a preference for boys or girls? Why?

CONNECTIONS: FROM *PERSONALISMO* TO *GUANXI* TO *WOSTA*

Connections are invaluable for transactions of all kinds in many parts of the world from Africa to Latin America to Asia; and doing business in many cultures requires the establishment of trust between not just the companies or organizations involved, but also between the human beings doing the negotiating. To establish trust takes time and interest in the lives of counterparts.

Personalismo

In Latin America, the concept of trust is built upon a personal relationship known as *personalismo*.[53] It takes patience to build personal relationships—patience in the form of many meetings, often over lunch or dinner, and enquiries about the family, not to mention perhaps social outings. Businesspeople can't just fly in and expect to make a deal. In addition, it is best to have a mutual connection to introduce you to a potential business partner, or at least provide a letter of introduction. That way, your credibility has been vouched for. Otherwise, your phone call may never be answered or you may never get your foot in the door.

Given the importance of relationships, Latin Americans may not write things down; besides, the situation may change from day to day, and adaptability to changing circumstances is important in countries where the value of the currency may fluctuate. It is important to be able to deal with ambiguity and delay tactics when negotiating in Latin America.

In Latin America, passion and personality often prevail over fact and analysis when it comes to doing business, and North Americans fixated on fact may find themselves frustrated.[54]

Guanxi

China is another country where time is required to build trust. Continuity of contact is also important, and the same person or people should be used on visits to cement relationships. "Knowing who you are as a person," says China consultant Charles Craig, "is related to the need for continuity . . . you'll do what you say. They want the same person to come back, and if there is a change, a handover period is needed." Craig also notes that, while things are changing, "China is still a country where if you go to an art gallery, a painting considered outstanding will have been done in 1430 . . . in other words, time is long. . . ."

You need *guanxi* to be successful. The complicated system known as *guanxi* is difficult to translate. It connotes the interdependence between people, and can be synonymous with "connections" or "who you know" or "who is owed" depending on context.[55] If someone has *guanxi,* that person has some importance and connections and can likely make things happen. *Guanxi* relations are based on reciprocity, and are meant to be long-term and enduring. Western business relationships are predicated on law and legalities to a greater extent than are relationships based on *guanxi. Guanxi* relies rather on personal power and status.[56]

Wosta

Wosta is the Arab word meaning influence or intermediary. A person who has *wosta* can make things happen and can act as an intermediary. Personal contacts are more effective than following rules and regulations in the Arab world.[57]

CONCEPTS OF HONESTY

Behaviours are often misunderstood because of underlying value differences between cultures. Differing concepts of honesty are at the root of some miscommunications.

Truth and Lies

"People tell you what they think you want to hear." This is a familiar comment of Canadians posted in South Asia, East Asia, the Middle East, Latin America, and Africa, sometimes said in frustration, sometimes in amusement, sometimes verging on moral outrage.

It is important to understand that what one culture may call a lie is not a lie to another culture.

Lying is often related to concepts of politeness. In North America, we may "lie" on certain matters and consider it kindness or politeness. If someone asks how they look, we might automatically answer, "Oh, you look fine" even if we don't think so. In Canadian culture there is no firm line as to when we allow ourselves to say something that could be perceived to be unkind or negative, and when we don't in order to preserve feelings. The concept of "white lies" exists in Canada and means different things to different people, but also has culture-bound limitations not found in many other cultures.

In some parts of the world, "white lies" are appropriate in a great variety of contexts. What is perceived by Canadians to be obfuscation or lack of appropriate disclosure often occurs in situations where most Canadians would feel comfortable telling "the truth." Take the matter of giving directions.

I once crossed by car from the Brazilian side of the border to the Uruguayan in the twin cities of Santana do Livramento and Rivera. There were various customs and immigration formalities that had to take place at different checkpoints (one on either side of the border to get the car across, another on either side to get the passengers across—a total of four checkpoints). It was pouring rain and midnight, there were no signs, and we began asking passersby for directions once we got to Santana. Everyone was unfailingly polite and gave often detailed directions. Alas, they never led anywhere and we found the checkpoints by chance. Why did people give us directions when they had no idea? Because it would have made us unhappy to feel we didn't know where we were going, said my Uruguayan friends, adding that the passersby were "saving face" because they didn't know and felt they should have.

Hofstede quotes a comparative study done on England and Iran. In Iran, 20 percent of people in the street pointed a foreigner to a place that did not exist; in England, no one did. Hofstede concludes that "in some cultures, being polite is more important than supplying the objectively correct information."[58] Arabs too may give directions to be polite even if they do not know where a place is.[59]

In one study, researchers "explored the degree to which deception is perceived to be a socially acceptable form of communication."[60] They compared students from China and the United States and found that lies told for malicious or self-benefiting motives were considered to be less acceptable than lies told to benefit others. The cultural variable was found to be of slight significance: "As expected, Chinese respondents found lies to benefit others, affiliate, protect privacy, avoid conflict, manage impressions, and protect self as more acceptable than U.S. respondents did."[61]

They did not find that the U.S. respondents believed self-benefiting lies to be more acceptable than did Chinese respondents. Rather, there was a slightly higher acceptability for lies in general among the Chinese participants, suggesting, as have other studies, that ethical judgments tend to be more absolute in individualist cultures than in collective cultures.[62] Results may also indicate that people from China have a narrower definition of "lying," or that indirect communication is more highly valued than direct.[63]

Studies of this kind are interesting, but given the inaccuracy of translation of language and context meanings in cross-cultural research, it is difficult to draw valid conclusions from them. What does seem certain, however, is that the concepts of lying and politeness are often interrelated and culture bound.

Bribery and Gift-giving

What is the difference between a bribe and a gift?

Baksheesh (Arab world), *dash* (West Africa), *mordida* (Mexico), *pot-de vin* (France or Quebec) are all words with the loose English translation of *bribe* or *pot sweetener,* depending on context. Is it always wrong to sweeten the pot? Is a gift always a bribe? Is it always bad?

In countries like Canada, where rules count, little is negotiable in many situations. In other cultures, prices are not fixed in the markets, costs for services vary depending on how well one has been able to negotiate, and perks and gifts or assistance are traditionally offered to sweeten deals.

In India, offering a little something to sweeten a deal is not always seen as bribery. A person may need something that you can supply and offering it when negotiating is part of an age-old custom. It works partly because of the caste system (as a way to get things across caste and class lines), and partly because officials are often underpaid. A gift, in these circumstances, is seen as "just," because justice won't come officially.[64]

In Mexico, the *mordida* is widely accepted. A recent report indicated that over 22 percent of public services in Mexico City required bribes.[65] The Mexican government is eager to reduce what it sees as systemic corruption, but the *mordida* will be hard to challenge partly because of low wages in many fields and partly because of attitudes and custom.

Canadians abroad, however, are often all too eager to take advantage of perks they might get just for being foreign or for trying. San Miguel de Allende, Mexico is a retirement community for many Canadians and Americans who enjoy the weather, atmosphere, and low cost of living there. One woman there said she had learned a few words of Spanish before going "just to get by"—six words, to be exact. I kept wondering what six words would get a person by in any language, especially in San Miguel where a person can live in English anyway. I joked about this to former national editor of *La Reforma* newpaper, Leonarda Reyes. She just laughed. "Well, I know one," she said, "*descuento* [discount]. All the North Americans know that word."

Formal gift-giving practices in the business world also vary. In some countries, any gift can be perceived to be a potential bribe. Employees of many Canadian companies can no longer accept the traditional gift baskets or bottles of wine at Christmas in case they are seen to be bribes rather than expressions of corporate affection or gratitude. Such gifts have to be returned. One senior Ontario Hydro employee received an anonymous gift basket delivered to his home. He turned it in at the office and it was donated to a local charity—just in case. Such are the rules.[66]

However, gift-giving in Japan, for example, is common in social and business settings and follows established rituals. Your gift should be of roughly the same value as that of your Japanese counterpart, and it should always be wrapped. The Japanese usually do not open their gift in public; if they do, their reaction will be restrained and will not necessarily reflect how much they like it. Likewise, in India, gifts are not opened in the presence of the giver.[67]

In the Arab and Latin American worlds, gift-giving is also enjoyed. Take care, however, not to admire too much an object or article of clothing because your host may well offer it to you as a gift!

And remember that favours and gifts do not always come strings unattached. Reciprocity is often expected in many cultures, if not immediately, then at such a time when a return favour is needed. Canadians may feel flattered by attention and generosity, but need to keep this in mind.

CONCEPTS OF FAIRNESS

Differing realities and concepts of fairness also result in different behaviour patterns.

Service

While Hall equates lining up to M-time and milling about to P-time, jostling for attention may also have to do with justice. In many parts of the world, there is little expectation that justice will be served and people do what they must do to make justice happen: we passengers all had tickets when we ran for the plane in Accra, but too many of us may have had tickets (see Chapter 7). Justice, North American style, is not always served. When I went to buy tickets for Bamako, Mali on one occasion, the agent told me the plane was fully booked, but when I looked disappointed, he picked up a ruler, neatly put a line through two names and added mine and my companion's.

In North America, and Northern Europe, being served in the order of arrival and receiving what one has been promised are seen as fair; the fear that justice will not be done is minimal.

Domestic Help

Canadians working in India and the Middle East are often disturbed by the treatment of domestic help. It is common to have maids, cooks, and nannies, but from the Canadian perspective, they are often unkindly treated, ill-paid, rudely spoken to, and sometimes victims of sexual or physical abuse. While it may be difficult, an ethno-relative attitude is probably best adopted. Canadians who openly treat domestic help as "one of the family," and provide assistance or favours, report that when they leave the country, their former servants have become unhireable. It is feared that they no longer know their place. Discretion is important in dealing differently from local custom with hired help, and Canadians should also learn about the hierarchy that generally exists among household staff.

CONCEPTS OF FRIENDSHIP

The concept of friendship also varies. In North America, it plays out as enjoying the company of another person in social situations and possibly exchanging confidences with close friends. In many parts of the world, however, it also includes obligation. Friends, like extended family, are expected to help each other financially and physically, if necessary, and to give of their time when needed, no questions asked. North Americans sometimes find this more than they can handle, and Arabs and Latin Americans, for example, may feel let down by someone to whom they feel they have given and who has not adequately returned friendship.[68]

CULTURAL EXPECTATIONS

Foreigners are often not expected to know what to do or how to do something and allowances are often made, especially when host nationals sense goodwill. The Japanese believe their culture is highly complex, and tend to think Westerners cannot grasp its subtleties and therefore don't expect them to.[69] It is assumed, however, that basic customs like removing shoes inside homes are simple enough to grasp. In the Gulf States where it is also etiquette to take off your shoes when entering a home, you may not be expected to, however, because it is known that many Westerners do not.

SUMMARY

This chapter explored common causes of frustration among people living in environments where behaviours in everyday situations run counter to behaviours they are used to. Some cultures consider gifts bribery, while others see them as "part of doing business." Some cultures prefer to do business with friends; for others, a personal relationship is immaterial. In some cultures, people dress and behave formally, while in other cultures, informality is the norm. Women often have more trouble adapting to new environments because their value and role differ widely in different societies. In some parts of the world, elderly people find themselves respected for the wisdom that is believed to come with age in contrast to other parts of the world where the elderly are considered "past their prime."

Knowing what to expect in behaviour and conversation when we are in a new cultural environment can help reduce anxiety and annoyance over things big and small over which we have no control, nor should we.

KEY TERMS

action chain 222	*guanxi* 230	*personalismo* 229
communication style 214	honorific 218	rhetorical forms 217
covert culture 222	*kibun* 216	verbal presentation 216
disclosure 224	literate culture 217	*wosta* 230
face 219	*omoi-yari* 216	
face negotiation 222	oral culture 217	

TOPICS FOR CRITICAL THINKING AND REFLECTION

1. Have you ever been in a professional situation where you thought your gender or age worked against you? Discuss your experiences. Conversely, have you ever been in a situation where your age or gender worked for you?
2. Research shows that certain traits and personality types are more or less likely to result in the ability to communicate and make the most of an intercultural experience (see Table 8.1, page 236). How would you rate your suitability?

Table 8.1

Intercultural communications effectiveness

EFFECTIVENESS	INEFFECTIVENESS
High people, less task emphasis	High task, less people emphasis
Few self-statements	Many self-statements
Low ethnocentrism	High ethnocentrism
High tolerance for ambiguity	Low tolerance for ambiguity
High empathy, good listening	Low empathy, poor listening
High openness, low dogmatism	Low openness, high dogmatism
Cognitive complexity	Cognitive simplicity
Comfort with interpersonal relations, trust	Discomfort with interpersonal relations, mistrust
High personal control, low fatalism	Low personal control, high fatalism
High innovativeness	Low innovativeness
High self-esteem	Low self-esteem
Low communication apprehension	High communication apprehension
Positive conversational management skills	Low conversational management skills
Positive family communication	Negative family communication
Friendly, warm	Unfriendly, cold
Extroverted	Introverted
Rhetorical sensitivity	Lack of rhetorical sensitivity
High acculturation motivation	Low acculturation motivation
Familiarity with host culture	Unfamiliarity with host culture
Openness to strangers of host culture	Rigidity to host culture
Great amount of intercultural training	Low amount of intercultural training

A sense of humour is also important, to keep you from taking yourself too seriously![70]

Time Out for India:
Spirituality, Tradition, and Hi Tech

India, with a population of over one billion people, is the world's largest democracy. It is a land of contradictions and paradoxes. Its diversity—geographical, cultural, linguistic, and religious—is staggering: All the convergent influences of the world run through this society: "Hindu, Moslem, Christian, secular; Stalinist, liberal, Maoist, democratic socialist, Gandhian. There is not a thought that is being thought in the West or East that is not active in some Indian mind."[1] To this list might be added many more adjectives describing religious and political minorities and movements.

In India, the timeless and the modern, the First World and Third blend into a colourful tapestry laced with tradition, religious devotion, and, at times, conflict between communities such as Hindus and Muslims, or Sikhs and Hindus. Canada has identified India as one of the "emerging giants" with which it should seek closer ties and which should be part of an expanded G20 group of nations. Meanwhile, many Indians of different ethnic and religious backgrounds have immigrated to Canada to settle mostly in urban centres.

Modern India is known to the world for its high-tech industry. Based in Bangalore, it fueled the IT revolution around the world. India is also an outsourcing destination for multinationals, and the home of the world's largest film industry in Bollywood, on the outskirts of Mumbai.

Keys to Understanding Indian Culture

Change

1. While the caste system has been officially abolished, caste differences and social inequities remain. Minority Christians, Buddhists, and Muslims are outside the caste system, but majority Hindus are born into one of four castes. Two hundred million Indians are outside the caste system—not to be touched by caste members. They form the "untouchable" class and call themselves "Dalits," meaning "broken people" in Sanskrit.[2] Despite affirmative action programs, ancient attitudes die hard, and Dalits are discriminated against in many ways, particularly in rural villages. Even when they have achieved professional status, members of higher social classes in the workplace may behave as if superior. (Names reveal caste.) They might push ahead in line, for example, or expect that the person of lower class will fetch the tea at tea time. Caste and class are everywhere and caste politics are increasingly influential.[3]

2. Language is a complex, regional, and political matter in India. English, retained from two hundred years of British colonialism, is the badge of the social elite.

The middle and upper classes, numbering almost 250 million, speak and write English fluently, many having been educated in private schools. It is from their ranks that emerge the captains of industry and IT movers and shakers.

Most Indians speak some English, but accent and lack of fluency reveal origins outside the upper classes in this class-conscious nation. For this reason, a nationalist movement to replace English with Hindi has gained momentum. However, this is difficult, since English serves as a lingua franca in language-rich India. Hindi is not spoken, for example, in the Calcutta region where Bengali prevails. The nationalist movement is also pro-Hindu, cause for concern since secularism is enshrined in India's Constitution and India is home to many religious minorities who fear Hindu fundamentalism.

3. The Indian diaspora has resulted in large Indian communities in many parts of the world. Second and third generation children of immigrants are caught between traditional ways and the usually Western culture of the new country. Dating, marriage, dress, and individual freedoms are areas of cultural confusion and generational conflict. Arranged marriages are still common, however, and young people may go back to India to find a spouse. According to the *Sunday Times of India,* the phenomenon of diaspora has resulted in a set of acronyms and jokes that define the dilemmas. For example: How does a *desi* (native of India) recognize an ABCD (American Born Confused Desi)? Answer: He can't believe the Internet exists in India.[4]

Indian Values

1. Family is very important. Middle-class parents are involved in their children's education and pressure is intense on children to succeed. Education is linked to status, and professional degrees are preferred.

2. India is a hierarchical culture. Tradition is important and conformity is the rule. Subordinates hesitate to make decisions, preferring to leave decisions to the "boss." However, the concept of individualism is growing, perhaps because of the global spread of Western values.

3. The Indian work ethic is based to some degree on *karma*. Rewards are expected for work well done, but not demanded. If one does the work well, reward will sooner or later follow. According to Tito Mathson, an Indian entrepreneur living in Dubai, employers have been taking advantage of this for centuries.

4. Personal relationships are important in business.

5. Communication style is formal and indirect. Politeness is valued, and Indians are unlikely to baldly refuse a request. A "yes" may not mean "yes"; it may simply mean that a request has been heard, or that a person does not want to say "no."

6. Religion is central to Indian culture and, like westernization, a potential source of political and social tension. Depending on their family, class, caste, and regional origins, some of my more conservative Indian students were offended by *Monsoon Wedding* while others saw it as "realistic" in terms of the issues presented.

7. The role of women is full of contradictions. Rural India is still extremely patriarchal and the majority of women suffer poverty and discrimination. Educated, middle-class urban women are at the forefront of change, however, with power and professional careers. Nonetheless, the preference for giving birth to boys is still strong at all levels of society, with poor women sometimes obliged to kill a baby girl, and upper-class women choosing to abort after finding out the sex of a baby before birth.[5]

Cultural Tips

1. Personal questions are common, and questions about salary, weight, and other matters considered private by many Canadians are not impolite, but rather express interest. Privacy is not highly valued; people spending time alone are perceived to be lonely.

2. It is common for Indians to nod the head to indicate they have heard, or to indicate they are paying attention. Canadians often mistake this head bobble for agreement, or disagreement, as it can also look a bit like the head shake for "no" in Canada.

3. Greeting is commonly a *namaste* (hands with palms together in front of the chest). Another common practice is to touch the feet of someone to show respect; young people may touch the feet of elders, for example.

4. Rules are flexible and "bent" in more situations in India than in Canada. It might be called a culture of negotiation—more is negotiable in India than in Canada, and pot-sweeteners in deals are part of age-old custom.

5. Indians may respond emotionally in situations where Canadians do not expect an emotional response. When such responses occur, Canadians unused to them need not go on the defensive.

6. Face is important (see Chapter 8).

Chapter 9
Exploring Language

In this chapter we will explore:

- The origins and nature of language
- The Sapir-Whorf Hypothesis and its implications regarding:
  - The natural world and language
  - Worldview and language
  - Values and language
  - Cultural attitudes towards language
  - Thought patterns and cognitive styles
- Language families
- Language varieties
- Components of language

INTRODUCTION

Human beings alone of the animal world have both the physiological and intellectual capacities needed to produce complex language. The human brain and specialized physiology related to perception and language production are the result of hundreds of thousands of years of evolution.[1] Language is key to what makes us human.

No one really knows much about its origins—"how vocal cries about enemies, food and sex turned into language."[2] We can imagine bands of early modern humans (*homo sapiens*) on the African *veldt* or huddled in caves, terrified and puny, summoning all their faculties to survive the night. The ability to communicate through sound symbols, as well as body language, would have been invaluable.

Nor do we know when the gene(s) for language appeared. Some believe the process of evolution towards the ability to speak was very slow and began in Africa as long as 200 000 years ago; others believe there was a relatively sudden moment between 40 000 and 50 000 years ago in Europe which produced the branch of humans that began to create language.[3]

In theory, humans can understand, combine, and recombine their linguistic symbols into an infinity of acceptable utterances. We are limited only by our vocabulary (**lexicon** in linguistic terminology) and by what our imaginations and cognitive abilities can dream up. In theory, we could spend an entire lifetime using language and never say, write, or hear the same thing twice . . . such is the enormous flexibility and creative capacity of language.

In practice, it's unlikely anyone has ever managed such originality. Chomsky differentiated between **competence** and **performance** to illustrate the gap between what we can theoretically do with our internalized knowledge of language (competence), and what we actually produce in a given situation (performance).[4]

THE NATURE OF LANGUAGE

Whatever the origin of the capacity for language, languages themselves are in constant flux. Their lexicons, their word order (syntax), and word formation (morphology) are all subject to change.

Languages change for a number of reasons. They borrow words from other languages. They add and create new words in response to political, technological, geophysical, or social changes that require linguistic accommodation. For centuries, for example, the Inuit had no word for "twilight": in winter, the sun was always below the horizon, and in summer, always above. Global warming has necessitated the creation of a new word, as pale light now lingers in the southern sky when normally it would contain only stars.[5]

The English of Chaucer is not the English of England today let alone Canadian English; nor is Quebec French still the French of 16th century Picardy where many

Québécois originated. Languages that do not adapt to change tend to die out, while the more creative and adaptable languages survive best. English is a hodge-podge of German, French, Latin, Celtic, Persian, and Arabic, and a good many other sources and is flourishing as a language with international status. English has been worked on for centuries. Its huge lexicon (over 450 000 words in Webster's, and more could be included) has incorporated many regional and social variants—see *Language Varieties*, page 258.[6]

Japanese has incorporated many English words into its vocabulary: *pikunikku* (picnic), *sarariman* (salary man), and *sayonara hōmu ran* (home run) are a few examples. Many more have to do with sexual and sports topics. Their pronunciation has been altered to fit Japanese sound patterns.[7]

French has incorporated English words (*le parking, le hot dog, le weekend*) to such an extent that in Quebec it was feared that too many borrowings would result in the loss of the language or in some hybrid form of *franglais* (French and English). The Office de la langue française was created to protect Quebec French from such incursions. It proposes French terms for words borrowed from English such as *parc de stationnement* for "parking," *fin de semaine* for "weekend," and *arrêt* for "stop." France, too, is concerned about borrowings from English and much of the work of its Académie française, an organization founded in the 17th century to regulate French grammar and vocabulary, also involves inventing French words for English borrowings.

SLANG

Slang is a creative, fast-changing variety of language often created by young people. In Anglophone-Canadian slang at this writing, common words tend to have their meanings reversed: *wicked*, *sick*, and *retarded* mean *good*. Roger Federer, who won at Wimbledon in 2005, admitted his playing had been "really sick," meaning superb.

Ass is a popular suffix. It adds intensity, positive or negative, as in "That car is bad-ass!" and "His brother is a bad-ass." On its own, however, it means really bad, as in "that show was *ass*."

Crank, meaning drunk (from *crazy* and *drunk?*), is beginning to mean *excellent,* and *whack* has come to mean *strange*.

Current slang turns conventional meanings of common words upside down, an example of postmodern play with words. No meaning is fixed or clearly definable, and words contradict themselves.[8]

Have the meanings of the slang words above changed since this writing?

Language changes at the structural level as well. Structural change tends towards the reduction of grammatical forms and simplification in general. For example, English is reducing its dependence on case: how many people use *who* (nominative case) and *whom* (objective case) correctly? Which one do you think will die out? How many people use *I* (nominative case) and *me* (objective case) correctly? Sentences like "My mother went to the store with he and I" are becoming common and are indications of a simplifying trend in English.

All languages are integrated systems that linguists call **grammars.** All grammars have the same components. They have sound systems (phonologies), accepted word orders (syntaxes), and systematic ways of modifying words to fit their function or place in a sentence (morphologies), as in the English examples just mentioned. Since their words and sentences carry meaning they have a semantic system, or system of meaning.[9] The grammar of one language is not superior to that of another, merely different. We know that grammar evolved before writing—languages not yet or never written have grammars—and we know that illiterates understand and use the grammar of their language, however unconsciously they carry their knowledge. (For more detailed descriptions of the components of languages, see page 260.)

There is no such thing as a "primitive" or "simple" language, as once thought by Eurocentric scholars.[10] **Linguistic relativism,** like cultural relativism, recognizes that all languages are equal, capable of expressing whatever subtle and complex thoughts its speakers need to express, and capable of changing to adapt to new realities.

Have you ever been unable to find the words for what you are trying to say? Why do you think this happens?

LANGUAGE AND CULTURE: THE SAPIR-WHORF HYPOTHESIS

> . . . the 'real world' is to a large extent unconsciously built up on the language habits of the group. No two languages are ever sufficiently similar to be considered as representing the same social reality. The worlds in which different societies live are different worlds, not the same world with different labels attached. . . . We see and hear and otherwise experience very largely as we do because the language habits of our community predispose certain choices of interpretation.

Edward Sapir[11]

> *We cut nature up, organize it into concepts, and ascribe significances as we do largely because we are parties to an agreement to organize it in this way—an agreement that holds throughout our speech community and is codified in the patterns of our language. The agreement is, of course, an implicit and unstated one, but its terms are absolutely obligatory; we cannot talk at all except by subscribing to the organization and classification of data which the agreement decrees.*

Benjamin Whorf[12]

Many of our ideas about the relationship between language and culture come from Edward Sapir and his student Benjamin Lee Whorf. They worked with Native Americans in the American southwest in the 1920s and 30s and developed a hypothesis about the relationship between culture, thought, and language known as the Sapir-Whorf Hypothesis, or the Linguistic Relativity Hypothesis.

The Sapir-Whorf Hypothesis proposes that language shapes thought by serving as the screen through which we see and the means by which we construct reality. **Linguistic determinism,** a strong version of the hypothesis, holds that our thoughts, our perception of reality, and our worldview are determined by the language we speak. *Linguistic relativism,* favoured by Sapir and Whorf and more widely accepted, argues that this is only partly true: language influences how we interpret the world, but does not entirely determine it or we would be prisoners of the language we speak, incapable of learning other languages or adapting our own to encompass new concepts.

The theory's implications are far reaching. If the vocabulary of our language, its structures, and its classification systems are the means by which our worldview is shaped, then we can in general express and imagine only what our language permits us to express and imagine. We have the illusion of freedom in describing our world, but in reality, are limited by language.

Different cultures name, process, and categorize sensory stimuli (see Chapter 2) in different ways, and the languages they have created have come to both shape and reflect their perceptions of the natural world, their worldviews, their values, their attitudes towards language itself, and their thought patterns and cognitive styles.

According to Australian Aborigine creation myths, the world was sung into existence by the ancestors during a long-ago period called the Dreamtime. "Songlines" are the sacred paths that crisscross Australia and name the creeks and animals and rocks as they were dreamed into being. Aborigine creation songs are a musical map of a world and its inhabitants still sung by the elders of each region.[13] These timeless songs are clear expressions of the ancients' understanding of the power of the word and its relationship to the creation of reality.

Almost 7000 languages currently exist, although some barely. About 3000 of these are in the process of dying out.[14] Some scholars believe that the loss of unique worldviews represented by each language represents not only a loss of diversity, but a loss of cumulative human knowledge.[15] Others, Chomsky for one, are more sanguine. They take the Darwinian view that unless a language is adaptable, it cannot survive.[16] This is linguistic natural selection. English may some day die too, only to be reborn as some or several other languages just as Classical Latin died but evolved into the Romance languages. Cultural diversity is not lost, but rather evolves into new forms.

Which of the views above do you take on the demise of languages? Why?

The Natural World and Language

Language serves as a guide to how a culture perceives its physical reality and what importance it places on it (see box on Tiwi below).

The Inuit do not have a single word for "snow"; nor do they have a generic word for "bear" or "fish" or "people."[17] Inuktitut, their language, has many discrete (single) words for different types of snow (falling snow, snow on ground, hard snow, packed snow, soft snow, blowing snow), and has a single word for each of "black bear" (*atlak*) and "polar bear" (*nanuk*).

Bedouin Arabic has numerous words for camel and the Lapp language for reindeer.[18] Snow is important enough to the Inuit for them to have created discrete words to describe its properties, likewise camels for the Bedouin and reindeer for Lapps. English can distinguish between many kinds of snow, but requires circumlocution ("talking around") to do it: wet snow, blowing snow, dry snow, gusting snow.

Powdery snow is sometimes called "powder" in Canada, but may be a term still largely understood by skiers in the context of skiing. In general, it requires context for people to know when "powder" refers to snow, face powder, talc, or cocaine. The Inuit do not need context for their numerous words for snow. The words themselves carry the context.

Tiwi, an Australian Aboriginal language with many descriptive words, distinguishes "*arawunga*" ("early morning before dawn") from *tokwampari* ("early morning when birds sing"), and *yartijumurra* ("darkness before daylight") from *wujakari* ("first light before sunrise")."[19]

Why do you think the nuances of light are important in Tiwi culture?

Colour is often used as an example supportive of the Whorfian theory of how languages classify and compartmentalize differently and so affect views of reality.[20] The spectrum is a continuum of light waves of frequencies that increase from one end to the other. One "colour" merges into another without clear divisions, and cultures "draw the line" in different places. They identify colours that aren't identified by other cultures and count different numbers of colours in the spectrum. In other words, different cultures "see" the world in different colours and their language defines the colours they see. The Yanomamo of Brazil identify blue-green, yellow, and red, for example.[21]

Worldview and Language

Language also serves as a guide to a culture's perception of the world, or worldview (see Chapter 6).

Personal Agency versus Fatalism

A sense of fatalism is revealed in some languages. English and Indo-European languages, in general, describe human activities as if they derive from human will or capacity. "I see him" we say. The Inuit of Greenland, however, say rather, "He appears to me," indicative of a more fatalistic worldview where events happen without human control.[22]

In Spanish, when a person "drops" something, it is said to "fall from him/her." The English description of such an event implies responsibility and [lost] control on the part of the dropper: "I dropped the glass." In describing the same phenomenon, Spanish takes away personal responsibility: *se me cayo el vaso* ("the glass fell from me") suggests fatalism and passivity.[23]

Among Arabs, conversation is peppered with references to Allah like *Insha'Allah*—God willing—in many variations and *Alhumdulillah*—thanks be to God[24]—all reminders that God controls absolutely the destiny of all individuals. *Ma'alesh* is another word commonly use in the Arab world meaning "it doesn't matter" or "it's not important." It implies that only God's will is important.

Movement or Stillness

European languages emphasize nouns to a greater degree than do Amerindian languages. Western culture sees the world as primarily made up of things (nouns) that interact to create events. The Amerindian view is that the world is made up of events and processes that may temporarily take the appearance of being things. Amerindian languages rely more on verbs, therefore, to express a world of movement. Mi'kmaq, for example, suggests that "there are very few fixed and rigid objects in the Mi'kmaq worldview."[25] Many verb forms in Hopi require the speaker to observe various kinds of movement—flashing, waving, flaming, or vibrating movement, and so on.[26] Navajo also emphasizes movement. *One moves about newly* (is young), or *moves into clothing* (dresses), or *moves about here and there* (lives).[27]

_____

What do you think the linguistic emphasis on movement reveals about the Amerindian worldview?

_____

Time

Many languages, such as West African and many Asian, do not mark time by means of verb tenses (past, present, future). In English, the sentence "I walked to town yesterday" would be rendered in a West African language as "I walk to town [yesterday]." From the West African perspective, English is redundant. It marks the verb with a sound for past tense ("ed") and for good measure it adds *yesterday*. "I walk to town [yesterday]" is adequate for a speaker of Fante to know when the event occurred, either from the context of the exchange, or from other time indicators in the sentence or conversation. Marking time additionally with a verb tense is unnecessary; the word "yesterday" is also unnecessary if everyone knows the time being referred to anyway.

_____

What cultural pattern do you think the heavy linguistic emphasis on marking time in English, French, and other European languages might support?

_____

Whorf analyzed the Hopi language and concluded that it does not conceive of time as a dimension in that it can't be measured and divided into segments as in European thought. No law of nature, however, obliges us to view time the European way. Like the Mi'kmaq and Navajo, the Hopi see the world as a set of processes, not as measurable units along a continuum from past to future.[28]

Whorf concluded that modern Western physics (which relies on time as a dimension) would be incompatible with Hopi thought and worldview for this reason. However, since Hopi has its own system of time markers, the incompatibility between physics and Hopi thought was not insurmountable.[29] In essence, however, Whorf had observed the "domination of the structure of a language over 'reality.'"[30]

Number

Many languages do not mark plurality the way English does. For example, "I have two dogs" has two markers for plural: the number "two" and the "s" on "dog." French requires more agreement: *Voilà mes deux chiens* ("There are my two dogs") with a plural form of "my" (*mes*). In West African languages, and Mandarin and Vietnamese, for example, two or more markers are redundant. "Two dog" expresses the same reality with only one marker for plurality (the number "two"), suggesting perhaps the primacy of the collective category of "dog" over its individual members.

Values and Language

Language contributes to the maintenance of social cohesion by implicitly teaching values.[31]

Kinship

Kinship terms reflect the importance placed on different kinds of family ties. If your mother's male second cousin twice removed has a discrete word for his relationship to you, the extended family is likely of importance.

Japanese reflects a value placed on birth order. It has a number of words for "brother," with separate words making the following distinctions: "older brother," "younger brother," "my older brother," "my younger brother," "your older brother," "your younger brother."[32]

Swedish does not have discrete terms for "grandmother" or "grandfather," but specifies the side of the family the relationship is on. To do this, Swedish uses *far* for "father," and *mor* for "mother," resulting in these words: *mormor* (maternal grandmother); *farmor* (paternal grandmother); *morfar* (maternal grandfather); *farfar* (paternal grandfather). Interestingly, however, Swedish uses *moder* and *fader* for "mother" and "father" respectively.[33]

Russian kinship terms changed radically between 1860 when the serfs were freed and modern times. The importance of certain relationships was lost as the extended serf family broke apart, and generalized terms replaced single word terms. For example, *shurin* was the word for "wife's brother"; it is now *brat zheny*, "brother of wife."[34]

Taboo Words

Taboo words often provide clues as to beliefs and values. Saying taboo words out loud gives people a sense of freedom from society's restrictions. The German- and English-speaking worlds developed many swear words and euphemisms concerning bodily and sexual functions, suggesting the Protestant emphasis on the separation of spirit (good) and body (evil). Swear words related to religion are next in frequency.[35]

_____

What swear words do you or do people you know use most often? Do they relate to religion? Or to bodily functions? Or to something else?

In Roman Catholic countries, taboo words are often associated with religion. Saying sacred words in an unspiritual frame of mind in non-sacred settings is sacrilegious. Quebec's lively variations on *tabernac'* (*tabourette, tabernouche*), all forms of *tabernacle* ("tabernacle"), not to mention the creativity surrounding *calice* ("chalice") are indications of the strong hold the Catholic Church once had on the Quebec society, and the strong taboo against using religious terms sacrilegiously. In Norway, the strongest taboo words relate to the devil. Relaxation regarding the use and sanction of taboo words reflects changes in society, indicating that as social values change, so does language.[36]

> The Australian Aboriginal language, Mati Ke, forbids brothers and sisters to speak to each other after puberty. Only two speakers remain, Patrick and Agatha, a brother and sister, who may not even say each other's names.[37] And so their language must die out.

Insults often derive from taboos and sacred concepts. In Latin America, where the Virgin Mary is much revered and, by extension, mothers, insults that question the sexual virtue of a person's mother are the strongest. In Hindi, and English, extreme insults also involve mothers. In Japan, it is very cruel to call someone "stupid" if you are angry, although it can be playful in other contexts.

Egalitarianism or Hierarchy

English structure has evolved to reflect an egalitarian view of society. There is just one word for *you,* for example. In French, German, and Spanish, however, formality and social hierarchy are embedded in the language itself. In French and Spanish, *tu* is used among friends, family, and intimates, and the respectful *vous/usted* is used towards those whom you don't know well or who have superior status for one reason or another. You might also use *vous/usted* to show respect for a grandparent. In German, you choose between *du* and *sie* for the same reasons. In Quebec, the informal *tu* is used more readily than in France, suggesting that the democratic ideals of the new world influenced discourse norms in Quebec.

Japanese has numerous intricacies related to hierarchies of social relationship, and is more complex still, with separate vocabularies used to address superiors, peers, and subordinates. There are ten words for "you," depending on the relationship between the speakers.[38]

Gender Inequality

Gender inequality in the family is reflected in language in Japanese. Husbands generally address their wives by first names, or by either of these words meaning "you": *omae* and *kimi*. *Omae* is the word for "you" usually used by status superiors to those of lower status, and *kimi* is used for subordinates or intimates. If a wife, however, calls her husband by his first name, she adds the honorific *–san* to show respect. Or, she uses the word for "you" that is used by lower status to higher status people—*anata*.[39]

French also carries a bias towards men. For example, the words for "they" are *ils* (referring to boys or men or masculine-gendered words), and *elles* (referring to girls or women or feminine-gendered words). If there are ten girls in a group of children, and only one boy, "they" will be translated *ils* in deference to the lone boy. Spanish shows the same bias.

Individualism and Collectivism

The preeminence of the individual over the group is reflected in language (see box below). Two frequently used words in spoken English discourse are "I" and "you." It doesn't matter who the speakers are, whether there are differences in age, gender, social status, and so on. In Japanese, there are at least ten words for the English "I." Age, status, role, familiarity, and gender are all taken into account when choosing the appropriate pronoun. Other features of the language are also adjusted depending on who is speaking to whom. Some Japanese say they feel more individualistic when speaking English. Others enjoy being able to say 'yes' or 'no' outright when speaking English.[40]

"I" is always capitalized in English. In French, *je* ("I") is capitalized only at the beginning of a sentence, as are the Spanish *yo,* the Italian *io,* and the German *ich.* Which of these cultures is classified as the most individualist according to the classification systems we've looked at?

Try to spend 24 hours without using the words "I" or "me," or "in my opinion." Report next class on how you made out!

Japanese social norms also require apologies in more contexts than in Western cultures.[41] The Japanese are socialized not to infringe on others' rights, and they offer apologies for perceived intrusions and disturbances to others' well-being.

"Doing your own thing" is not translatable into Chinese.[42] The Chinese language has no equivalent for "personality" in the English sense. Personality in the Western sense implies an attribute of an individual separate and distinct from culture and society. The closest translations in Chinese are *jen* (or *ren*) which mean "person" as a "human constant," which includes not only the individual, but his or her intimate societal and cultural environment that makes his or her existence meaningful.[43]

Formality and Politeness

As we have seen in Chapter 8, Japanese culture stresses and makes use of honorifics to show politeness. Japanese includes words added to indicate respect for a person being addressed or referred to. For example, *ano hito* is a neutral reference meaning "that person"; *ano kato* is a reference indicating respect.[44] "Expressions incorporating negatives (along the lines of English "Wouldn't you like to . . .") are more polite than those without negatives; the longer the utterance the more polite it is felt to be; . . . you are more polite to strangers than acquaintances; your gender determines your use of honorifics. . . ."[45] These are just a few of the variables covering politeness in Japanese.

The French, Spanish, and German distinctions between the formal and informal forms of "you" are also linguistic expressions of the value placed on formality.

Language and Emotion

Language also reflects cultural norms of emotive expression. Euphemisms are often used to avoid emotional expression among the English,[46] and language is generally more subdued in England than in North America. Samovar and Porter contrast public signs such as "No dogs allowed" (U.S.) with "We regret that in the interest of hygiene, dogs are not allowed on the premises" (U.K.).[47]

Thought Patterns and Cognitive Styles

The Whorfian Hypothesis suggests that language structure influences thought and thought patterns. If people from different cultures perceive their environments differently, they will process (classify, sort, and categorize) information differently. In short, they will think differently. Different ways of thinking are known as **cognitive styles.**

Thought patterns developed by literate cultures for writing are different from those developed for speaking because writing means that more complex ideas can be expressed. The need to remember is lessened, obviating the need for repetition, and ideas can be set down, reread, and reworked as needed, making possible highly abstract and scientific thought.[48]

Linear and Non-Linear Language

English develops ideas in a linear way: A follows B follows C and so on. This way of thinking is related to Western concepts of time and logic (see Chapter 7). As in verb tenses, there is a definite past, present, and future time. A writer "gets to the point" in an almost mathematical progression related to time, or states it first, with "first things first," and then proves it "step by step" (see Table 9.1). In business negotiations and planning, as in essay writing, this direct, linear approach is unlike the patterns used in other languages and cultures.

Chinese and Japanese cultures traditionally develop ideas in a less linear, more indirect way.[50] South Asian culture is also non-linear. Non-linear peoples do not come directly to a point; they talk around ideas, move away, and then back, fluidly, as if avoiding the explicit statement of an end point and so-called conclusion. An inferred point is often more highly valued than an explicitly stated one.

Past, present, and future are intertwined and flow in and out of each other in many non-Western cultures, and so do ideas flowing from these general frames.

Table 9.1

Linear language[49]

–Keep to the straight and narrow.	–Set the record straight.	–Lay it one the line.
–Follow a line of thought.	–Keep someone in line.	–On the right track.
–Set someone straight.	–His days are numbered.	
–Don't beat around the bush.	–Try not to wander off track.	

 Can you think of another such expression?

Source: Adapted from Bonvillain, Nancy. *Language, Culture, and Communication,* 4th edition. New Jersey: Prentice Hall, 2003, pp. 64, 65.

Negotiations proceed intuitively, and so does the development of ideas in essays, which may appear "disorganized" to a teacher of English, but have their own internal, intuitive flow of logic. The concept of paragraph structure—one idea, one paragraph—and its inexorable flow of logical A to B to C patterning can be difficult for learners from less linear cultures.

Contrastive rhetoric studies the similarities and differences between languages in their use of written forms of language (texts) such as letters, essays, paragraphs, and reports. Each language and culture has its own conventions and structural patterns for these forms of writing, and contrastive rhetoric seeks not only to compare and contrast them, but also to analyze the possible differences in thought patterns that underlie the written organizational patterns.

Robert Kaplan identified differing cognitive patterns based on culture that he believed were reflected in their rhetorical structures. Logic, wrote Kaplan, is the basis of rhetoric, and logic derives from culture[51] (see Chapter 5). The patterns of rhetoric, then, he argued, cannot be universal. Good expository writing in English is coherent (linearly speaking), concise (including nothing extraneous or "irrelevant"), and peppered with concrete examples to support its hypotheses. Deductive and inductive reasoning are the bases for acceptable logical developments. Paragraph structure (and essay structure) can follow either of these strategies.

Kaplan analyzed some 700 student compositions and proposed rhetorical patterns underlying their writing (see Figure 9.1). He suggested that in **Arabic**, for example, paragraph development is "based on a series of parallel constructions, both positive and negative."[52] According to Kaplan, Arabic seemed to have the linguistic capacity for more complex forms of parallel structure than English.[53] **Chinese** and **Korean** patterns use an approach Kaplan characterized as marked by indirection: a paragraph develops by turning in ever-widening concentric circles around a central idea. **French** and **Spanish** students (from Latin America in his sample) often introduced material

Figure 9.1 Kaplan's diagrams of rhetorical patterns

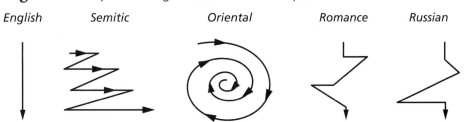

Source: Kaplan, Robert. "Cultural Patterns in Inter-cultural Education." *Language Learning*, 1996, 16, no. 1 and 2:15. Reprinted with permission of Blackwell Publishing.

apparently extraneous to the subject at hand. Kaplan concluded that "greater freedom to digress is available in French, or in Spanish, than in English."[54] His analysis of **Russian** writing led him to conclude that the development of a paragraph in Russian mirrors its sentence structure, which is vastly different from that of an English sentence. Other scholars aiming to test Kaplan's theory got mixed results. Like the Sapir-Whorf Hypothesis, it continues to inspire controversy and research although Kaplan holds to its basic premise.[55]

If writing and the printing press led to changes in thought patterns, do you think our increasingly visual culture is transforming our thought patterns and, by extension, the patterns we use in speaking and writing? If so, how? If not, why not?

Translation

The Whorfian Hypothesis acknowledges the complexity of translation. Many of us have had fun with menu translations (such as *roast peasant*), or been stumped when trying to convey the meaning of certain expressions that seem to be truly understandable only in their language of origin. French expressions such as *savoir-faire* and *laissez faire* are common examples used in English.

Gemütlichkeit sounds better in German. *Hacer sobre mesa* (Spanish) takes considerable circumlocution to render in English. It means sitting around after a meal, perhaps taking coffee and liqueurs, and generally relaxing with talk and a feeling of satisfaction and conviviality. And *amanecer?* In Spanish-speaking countries staying up until dawn is so enjoyed that there is a verb for it.

Single words or expressions are not the whole of translation. Translation is a holistic undertaking. There are different cultural contexts to be rendered. I once told a sandal-shod class in equatorial West Africa that they would have to "pull up their socks," then realized no one wore socks.

There are different stylistic, syntactical, and punctuation patterns which, if not followed, will alter meaning or mood. For example, in Spanish, commas are often used where English demands a period, or at least a semi-colon or colon. To put a period in an English translation in all instances where Spanish is content with a comma would render the English version choppy, and not convey at all the flow of the language and thought pattern. Most translators take artistic licence with English in literary cases of this type, and go for the comma—to better render the "feel" of the Spanish text.

Portuguese is similar to Spanish in this respect. The opening of José Saramago's *All the Names* is one sentence of more than a page, full of commas.[56]

True equivalencies may often not exist—how do you translate from a verb-dependent language to a noun-dependent one? Despite the challenges, however, translation occurs and we enjoy reading translated novels, plays, poems, and works of non-fiction. A skilled and sensitive translator can capture both the form and the spirit of a text.

http://www.engrish.com/faq.php is a website devoted to supposedly humorous translations of English in Japan. For example, at a closed wicket a sign reads: "You are available at the next window." Look up the website and decide if you think such humour is funny or offensive or both.

Interpretation

Interpretation is live translation. Accurate interpretation also requires cultural and contextual knowledge. For example, in health and healing situations involving Mohawk, Cree, and Ojibwe patients, interpreters need to be aware that health is believed to be in the hands of the Creator, and that apparent indecisiveness in responding to questions or outright lack of cooperation reflects this belief. Interpreters need to assist as well as translate in such situations.[57]

LANGUAGE FAMILIES

Many languages are related and related languages can be classified into groups called language families. Linguists speculate, nonetheless, about the possibility of a mother tongue for all languages and a time when all human beings spoke the same language. This idea is present in Genesis 11:1 of the Old Testament: "And the whole earth was of one language, and of one speech." Then the Babylonians decided to build a tower to heaven in order to reach God. God was displeased and said, ". . . let us go down, and there confound their language, that they may not understand one another's speech" (Genesis 11:7).[58] He dispersed and scattered the builders about the face of the earth. Ever after, the tower was called Babel, thought to be from the Hebrew word *balbail,* meaning *to confuse.*[59]

The biblical narrative about language diversity and dissemination may not be far from the truth. Geneticists theorize that the journey of humans from their origins in

Africa to Central Asia and from there to Europe and East Asia implies a single origin of both humanity and language. Spencer Wells, an Oxford geneticist, traced DNA samples and concluded that we are all children of the original African human family, forced by drought and famine to leave home about 60 000 years ago.[60] Archaeological finds indicate that the earliest anatomically modern specimen comes from Ethiopia and dates from about 100 000 years ago. Language may have developed from that time on. During the exodus from Africa, groups became separated and isolated from one another, which explains the evolution of different languages. In Europe, complex social systems, symbolic behaviour, and art date back to the Cro-Magnons of about 40 000 years ago, suggesting a time frame for the exodus from Africa. It is possible that collective memory was the basis for the biblical version of a time of one language and the exodus of human beings from Africa.

The Indo-European Language Family

The largest language family that contains the most number of speakers and is spread most widely throughout the world is the Indo-European family. It is divided into subgroups of Romance, Indic, Slavic, Germanic, Celtic, and Iranic languages. Romance languages, for example, derive from Latin and include French, Italian, Spanish, Portuguese, and Romanian.

Which related languages are part of the Slavic sub-family? The Celtic? The Indic?

English is a Germanic Indo-European language, the most widely disseminated and spoken language in the world today thanks in large part to the colonial spread of English with the British Empire. It was an English lawyer, Sir William Jones, a judge who went to India in 1783, who is responsible for putting together this part of the linguistic jigsaw puzzle.

Sir Jones learned Sanskrit and realized that it resembled Greek, Latin, and other languages with which he was familiar. For example, the English word *two* is *duo* in Latin, *dúo* in Greek, *deux* in French, and *dva* in Sanskrit. The English word *mother,* is *matka* in Polish, *meter* in Greek, *madre* in Spanish, *matar* in Avestan (spoken in Iran), and *mava* in Sinhalese (spoken in Sri Lanka).[61] From such observations of both isolated words and patterns of sounds, he came to the conclusion that all of these languages had sprung from the same source.[62]

Europe is a linguistic realm of mainly Indo-European languages (Finnish and Hungarian aside). Basque remains a mystery. Known as Euskara to its speakers, it is unrelated to Indo-European languages.[63] Modern genetic science backs up the linguistic lack of knowledge about Euskara: DNA patterning distinguishes the Basques from their neighbours and suggests they may have been the earliest people to settle in Europe.[64]

Other language families exist in other regions of the world.

Scripts

As you can see from Table 9.2 and the following photo, languages employ a variety of scripts, from pictographs, to alphabets, to syllabaries, to hybrids. There is essentially only one alphabet, devised by Semitic peoples about 1500 B.C.E. All alphabets today, including the English, derive from this original form.[65]

Table 9.2

The ten most spoken languages in the world[66]

POSITION	LANGUAGE	FAMILY	SCRIPT	SPEAKERS IN MILLIONS
1	Mandarin	Sino-Tibetan	Chinese	Close to 1 billion
2	English	Indo-European	Latin	337–377
3	Hindi	Indo-European	Devangari	364
4	Spanish	Indo-European	Latin	332 or more
5	Arabic (all forms)	Hamito-Semitic	Arabic	210
6	Bengali	Indo-European	Bengali	189 or more
7	Russian	Indo-European	Cyrillic	170
8	Portuguese	Indo-European	Latin	170
9	Japanese	Altaic	Kana (a mixture of Katakana and Hiragana)	126
10	German	Indo-European	Latin	98

Numbers of speakers vary according to sources. A range is given for this reason. *Speakers* in this table refers to those who speak the language as a *mother tongue*. English may be the international language of business, but it is not necessarily displacing languages of the heart—those spoken at home.[67]

Source: Adapted from Ladefoged, Peter. *Vowels and Consonants: An Introduction to the Sounds of Languages*. Mass.: Blackwell, 2001, p. 140.

"Peace" in seven languages and three scripts.

Source: CP Photo/St. John's *Telegram*—Gary Hebbard

LANGUAGE VARIETIES

Standards

Standardization is a term largely reserved for international or colonial languages. We talk of Standard English, Standard French, Standard Italian, and so on. Standardization is a concept hard to pin down.

A language or dialect is considered standard if it has been codified and has developed grammar books, spelling rules, dictionaries, and possibly a literature.[68] There are clear boundaries between it and other languages. It is accepted, by consensus or imposition, as the most prestigious variety of a language and is usually a variety spoken by an elite.

For many years, Standard English was accepted as the Oxford variety, or BBC English, with the proper accent known as RP (*received pronunciation*).[69] The RP accent was thought superior because of the remnants of glory attached to the British Empire. However, Canadian, American, and Australian accents are becoming increasingly popular among international English learners.

We now talk of a number of forms of Standard English, such as Standard Canadian, Standard Australian, Standard New Zealand, and Standard American English even though their exact forms and comprehensive descriptions have remained elusive.[70]

Likewise, it is largely agreed that West African English, in its educated form, has enough distinction to be called a standard variety, as does South Asian English in its educated form, although the educated elites of both India and West Africa continue to value and speak Standard British English with 'received pronunciation.'[71] In both West Africa and India, other languages compete with English as *linguae francae,* but enough people speak and use English for their forms to be recognized as standards.

Other forms of what is sometimes called "International" English exist. They have heavy doses of elements of pronunciation, syntax, and vocabulary tossed in from another important language in an environment where contact is strong between English and the other language and culture. In the Middle East, English is widely used and is imbued with the flavour of Arabic. Does it have validity as another Standard English? Opinions vary.

Dialects and Accents

It is also difficult to define the term *dialect,* but a dialect is a **language variety** that has not been elevated to a standard. Dialects come in two forms. One refers to a language variety spoken in a part of a language region. This is a regional dialect. Dialect can also refer to a language variety spoken by people of a particular social class. This is a sociolect. Dialects can be recognized by their vocabulary and syntax, and by the accent of their speakers.

Hybrids

Terms like *Spanglish* and *Chinglish* and *franglais* describe varieties where interference from a mother tongue colours the English spoken by linguistic communities living within a wider English-speaking community.

In Spanglish, elements of Spanish pepper the English of people whose mother tongue is Spanish. Spanglish can include code-switching (going back and forth between the two codes) and translating English expressions into Spanish even if the result is not idiomatic Standard Spanish. The Spanish expression for weekdays is *dias de trabajo (work days),* but contact with English has spawned *dias de semana (week days),* now widely used. Spanglish is so common in the U.S., where the largest ethnic minority is Hispanic, that Spanglish magazines exist.[72]

Purists frown on the mixing of codes in this way, but mixing exists wherever languages and cultures brush. Borrowings in the form of *calques* (direct translations, as in *dias de semana*) enrich languages. They do not change the structure of the language making the addition; rather, new words and expressions are simply incorporated into the vocabulary.

African American Vernacular English (AAVE) is a rich mix of African and English structures and sound patterns that have developed into a distinct and valid language. In West African languages, for example, there is no "th" sound; in AAVE the "th" sound is often rendered by the closest sound from a West African language, which is "d." For this reason, speakers of AAVE may say *dis* for "this" and *dat* for "that."

Pidgins and Creoles

A *pidgin* is a simple language of few words and structures that develops where speakers of different languages need to communicate. West African pidgin, for example, is a mix of English and African languages used by traders. It is no one's mother tongue. A *Creole* is a pidgin that develops and has been adopted as a mother tongue by members of a community. Jamaican Creole is a mix of English and African languages with some French.

Code-Switching

Do you know anybody who says half a sentence in one language and then pops in a word or two from another, then goes back to the first, and so on, without being aware of switching? If you do, you are familiar with the linguistic concept of code-switching. People who have learned a second language often do this, especially first generation immigrants. They are more comfortable in their mother tongue, but have become used to using their second language in everyday life. They forget, themselves, though, and go back and forth.

COMPONENTS OF LANGUAGE

Languages are made up of a number of components including phonetics (sounds), phonology (sound patterns), morphology (structure of words), syntax (sentence structure), and semantics (word meaning). Space does not permit depth in the following discussion, but here are a few points of general interest.

Phonetics

Different languages have different repertoires of sounds. For example, the French vowel *u* [y], as in *université* and *puce* (flea), is difficult for Anglophones to pronounce because no exact equivalent sound exists in English. Not only are they unlikely to hear it at first (the ear has to perceive the sound and is most likely to perceive an unfamiliar sound as a similar one that exists in English), but also they will have difficulty positioning the mouth, tongue, and lips in such a way as to make it.

Anglophones often feel embarrassed trying to pronounce the French [y], because the exaggerated pushing out of the lips required to make the sound connotes a kiss. They will likely at first pronounce the [y] as its similar English sound, the "u" in *university*. The French or uvular *r* sound, as in *roi* and *roué* and *virgule*, which requires producing the *r* at the back of the throat, is another stumbling block for Anglophones. (In Quebec, the *r* is often rolled and easier for Anglophones to produce.)

The pronunciation of the English interdental *th* sounds, as in *this* and *thought,* poses difficulty for speakers of languages that do not have these sounds in their repertoire. The lips must part for the tongue to be lodged between the front teeth for a moment. A friend of mine visited the Czech Republic with her husband of Czech origin. His old school friends found it fascinating to watch Irene speak English to him, and, when quizzed, admitted they found it highly erotic to watch her tongue come out between her teeth when she pronounced *th* sounds.

Czech speakers are likely to pronounce the aspirated *th* in English as *t,* as in *I tink* instead of *I think,* while French speakers, who don't have *th* sounds either, are likely to say *I sink* instead of *I think,* or *dis* or *zis book* rather than *this book* for the softer, voiced *th* sound. (Czech speakers do the same with the voiced *th* as in *this*). In both cases, speakers are using the closest sound in their mother tongue to render the hard-to-hear and hard-to-pronounce new sounds of English. Persian does not have the sound *w* as in the English *water.* A native Persian speaker is likely to say *I vent to Vinnipeg* instead of *I went to Winnipeg,* because the *v* sound is the closest equivalent to *w* that exists in Persian.

Sometimes the same letter will be pronounced differently in different languages. In German, a "w" is pronounced like a "v" in English, and a "v" is pronounced like an "f." The German car Volkswagen is pronounced *Fol–ks–vagon* in German (it means "people's wagon"); English speakers have given this German word English phonetic pronunciation.

In Canada most people are aware that in French the *h* is silent, or unaspirated (meaning that air is prevented from passing through the vocal tract). In speaking English, however, some French speakers put an aspirated *h* (as in the English *house*) with a strong release of air in front of vowels, a phonetic tic giving rise to this [bad] joke: What does the CH in the Montreal Forum stand for? (Answer: *Centre Hice.*)

Some letters or sounds are pronounced differently depending on where they are placed in a word. Pronounce the word "ton" and note how the "t" sounds. Now say "Martin." Did you pronounce the "t" in the same way?

Phonology

Phonology refers to the sound patterns of language—how we string together the phonemes (sounds) that make up our phonemic repertoire. Intonation, stress, pitch, and length of a sound are features of phonology. (See Chapter 7 for their role in paralanguage.)

Pitch

Pitch, in phonology as in music, refers to the note or *tone* of a sound. Humans can control or modulate level of pitch. They can also control *intonation,* the rising and falling of pitch they use in speaking.

While English speakers can control the pitch or tone of a word for effect, changing it does not change its meaning. In tonal languages, that is not the case. Tonal languages like Mandarin and Vietnamese employ tone to change the meaning of words; for this reason, they have a singsong sound to the English-attuned ear. *Ma* in Vietnamese can mean mother, horse, cemetery, ghost, or wheat, depending on the tone.[73] There are many tonal languages, from North and South American native languages, to African languages like Yoruba, to Asian. The number of tones varies, and they can include rising, falling, or level tones.

Stress

Say the following phrase twice, the first time with the main accent or stress on the first syllable of "novel," the second time with the main accent on the first syllable of "lovers": *novel lovers.*[74]

Stress joke: A Buddhist monk walks up to a bartender holding a cocktail shaker and says, "Make me one with everything."[75]

Stress refers to the degree of weight or respiratory emphasis placed on a syllable. Different languages have different rules for stress; many, like French, are consistent. It generally places the stress on the last syllable. English is inconsistent, despite supposed general rules. As in the example above, a change in the placement of the primary accent can alter the meaning of a word or phrase.

Length

Length refers to the duration of time given to the utterance of a vowel or consonant. In some languages, differences in length can change the meaning of words. In English, length is not particularly significant, although it can be used for effect, as in "Sooooooooo . . . what have you been up to?"

Morphology

Morphology deals with the structure and formation of words. Sentences are fluid—they come and go—and sounds are just sounds until combined to form meaning as words. The building blocks of sentences are words. Languages change and add or lose words over time, but they are always the foundation of language.

Words are made up of a number of elements, often a base form with endings or prefixes that affect meaning or function in a sentence. *Go* is a base form of a verb (the infinitive) modified with verb endings according to person and number: I go, she goes, they go, etc. *Dis* is a prefix, sometimes signifying *away from* (as in *disperse*), sometimes negating the root form of a word (*discontent/content*), and so on. Sometimes the root and affix forms are identifiable, although the root may not be a word without the affix. For example, we know that *couth* can be used, usually humorously, although we use mostly *uncouth*. But, what about *gruntled?*

In Spanish, the ending *ito* or *ita* is added to words or names as a sign of endearment or to denote something small: Eva Peron became known as Ev*ita*—Argentina's little mother. Julio becomes Jul*ito*.

The smallest unit that carries meaning in language is called a *morpheme.* Some morphemes are *free;* that is, they can stand alone as words with meaning (for example, house). Others are attached to another form, and are known as bound morphemes. The affixes mentioned above are examples of *bound morphemes.* They attach themselves to root forms of words, or stems.

Inflectional morphemes affect the grammatical function of a word. To add an 's to a word in English makes it possessive; adding *ed* to a verb usually makes it become a past tense. Inflectional morphemes never change a word's grammatical category: a verb is always a verb.

Inflection is a common phenomenon in languages. Many languages, like Japanese, Finnish, and Inuktitut, are highly inflected.[76]

English is highly inflected. West African languages, and Mandarin, do not have an inflected plural form for nouns as we saw above.

Syntax

> *Dog a tree cat in a barking the was at a.*

English speakers will recognize the above as English, but will reject the word order on the grounds that it does not form a logical sentence. In order to decide on the right order of words in a sentence, it is necessary to decide on the parts to be ordered. There is consensus on the parts of speech concerned: we speak of nouns, verbs, adverbs, conjunctions, and so on. We also speak of function components of a sentence, like subject, verb, phrase, and clause, to name a few.

Syntax is the component of grammar that deals with word order and the ordering of the components of a sentence. There are basic patterns used by most languages. They include the subject–verb–object pattern (SVO), as used by English and many other languages, and variations on this model, such as VSO (Irish Gaelic), SOV (Japanese).[77]

Chomsky sought to go beyond descriptive approaches to grammar. Equal parts philosopher, mathematician, and linguist, he searched for a universal grammar that could, like a mathematical theorem, describe and account for all possibilities of word order in language. His system involved the concept of underlying deep structures, which could generate all sentences, or surface structures according to a set of formal rules like theorems. "I will consider a language to be a set (infinite or finite) of sentences," he wrote.[78]

Two surface structures describing the same event could be *The dog chased the cat* and *The cat was chased by the dog.* Chomsky sought to formulate an equation representing the deep structure of the thought or event itself, the elements of which could, by formal rules, generate all surface versions of the idea to be described. His theory is called **generative,** or transformational **grammar** and is highly complex.[79]

Semantics

Larry MacDonald[80] wrote about his childhood perception of General Wolfe. It originated in his Grade Three class's lusty rendering of "The Maple Leaf Forever" in Saskatchewan. He and his friends greatly admired General Wolfe, all the more so because of Wolfe's disability. They would bellow with sympathy, "Wolfe the donkless hero came and planted firm, Britannia's rule, on Canada's fair domain." As an adult, MacDonald remembered his disappointment on hearing that Wolfe was not a donkless hero, rather just the ordinary dauntless garden variety. (This story has implications for phonetics also—the boys didn't hear "dauntless" because they didn't know the word; they did, however, create a meaning for "donkless.")

Semantics is the branch of linguistics that deals with the meaning of words—the conventional, dictionary description, or denotation of words "without reference to the speaker and communicative functions of sentences."[81] Words in a vacuum, you might say, although in reality, knowledge of philosophy and logic is necessary in this field, as it struggles with the nature of meaning itself. (A related field, *pragmatics,* deals with what a speaker might actually mean or intend to mean when using words, taking into account context, relationship between speakers, speaker's beliefs and attitudes, and other factors relevant to language in use.)

Sentences like *The window pattered on the rain* and *Wolfe the donkless hero came and planted firm Britannia's rule* strike us as odd not because of their syntax, which follows the pattern we expect in English (subject–verb–object, with adjectives preceding nouns), but because of their lack of meaning. They don't make sense.

Windows have a set of properties related to their meaning—one thing windows don't do is *patter*. Windows are inanimate objects, passive motionless objects, single not collective entities. Rain, too, is inanimate, but not motionless, and it is collective. It falls, drops, and can move in all sorts of ways windows can't. People and animals, however, can patter, so the defining feature that makes it possible for rain to patter is that it moves, not that it is inanimate or comes in groups of droplets. Semantics analyzes meaning in this way. Poets and rapsters play with meaning to move or jolt us into awareness of things we might not otherwise perceive.

Words like "the" and "a" are function words, and do not exist in all languages, such as Mandarin and West African languages.

The stress joke under "phonology" is also a semantics joke. Can you explain why?

SUMMARY

Language is the most complex of the symbolic codes of communication used by human beings. The origins of language are not known, although the evolutionary path of human beings veers away from that of other animals with the development of abstract thought possible only by means of complex language. The Sapir-Whorf Hypothesis suggests that language influences our perception of reality and our thought patterns and results in different cultural concepts of reality. Linguistic relativity recognizes that there is a relationship between language and culture, and that all languages are adaptable and capable of expressing what their users need to express. All languages are made up of the same essential components, and no one language is superior to any other. Languages are being lost at a great rate, however, as more powerful cultures absorb smaller ones, a cause for concern among some linguists, and not among others.

KEY TERMS

code-switch 260

cognitive style 252

competence 241

contrastive rhetoric 253

Creole 260

dialect 259

generative grammar 264

grammar 243

hybrid 259

Indo-European language
 family 256

language variety 259

TOPICS FOR CRITICAL THINKING AND REFLECTION

1. What languages, in addition to Hebrew, have been or are in the process of revival? Why is it so difficult to revive a language?
2. What phonetic and lexical differences exist between American and Canadian [Standard] English? Between regional Canadian forms of English?

Part IV
Understanding Intercultural Adaptation

Chapter 10

Understanding Intercultural Adaptation

In this chapter we will explore:

- Intercultural adaptation
- Models of the adaptation process
- Culture shock and re-entry stress
- Factors affecting cultural adaptation
- Identity change in acculturation
- Intercultural adaptation and conflict

Tina's Story

Tina is a student from the imaginary country of Manecha. She is in her first year at Concordia in Montreal. When she arrived three months ago, she was full of anticipation and excitement about coming to Canada. But now, with the weather turning cold and the days getting shorter, she is starting to feel lonely and depressed. Although she studied English at home, she finds that many people do not seem to understand her very well, and she is becoming shy about speaking in class and in the rare social situation in which she finds herself. Few Canadian students seem to know where Manecha even is, let alone anything about it, and even fewer seem to be interested. They appear cliquey to her, and so far she has not managed to make a close friend, nor has she managed to find other students from her country. There are large numbers of other international students who have formed cultural groups within the university and who get together regularly, but Manechans have not gotten organized.

Tina is from a small city, and finds Montreal enormous and intimidating. Getting around is complicated. She doesn't know very much French, although she had come to Montreal with the idea of learning it, and feels alienated on the streets of Montreal where so many people speak it. She thinks everyone looks very fashionable, and feels that she doesn't, although she considered herself fashionable at home. She doesn't have much money, and looks into restaurant windows and wanders through malls and stores imagining the happy lives of people she sees. She cooks Manechan food to remind her of home.

Tina wants to go home at Christmas, and feels guilty about wanting to. She is doing well academically, and knows that she is lucky to have this opportunity in Canada. Her family has sacrificed to make her dream come true, but now all she wants is to see her old friends and get her old life back. She often cries alone in her rented room.

What is Tina suffering from? What can she do to improve her life in Montreal?

INTERCULTURAL ADAPTATION

Intercultural adaptation, also called **acculturation,** refers to the process of becoming adapted to a cultural environment with different cultural patterns from the ones we are used to. It is a gradual process and often proceeds by stages. Tina is in one of those stages, as we will see.

There are degrees of adaptation. Bennett distinguishes between **adaptation** and **assimilation.** Assimilation is a "process of resocialization that seeks to replace one's original worldview with that of the host culture."[1] Assimilation, in other words, is substitutive. Adaptation, on the other hand, is the process whereby one's worldview is expanded to include behaviour and values derived from those of the host culture. It is additive rather than substitutive.[2] The assumed end of adaptation is to function in a new environment or to become a bicultural or multicultural person, while the assumed end of assimilation is to become a person who has adopted a new set of assumptions about life and a new set of behaviours. In the case of adaptation, transformation is selective of the cultural elements to be incorporated into the new identity.

What would you assume to be Tina's goal: adaptation or assimilation? Why?

Ting-Toomey distinguishes between the adaptive process of immigrants who embark on a long-term change process and the adaptive process of short-term sojourners in overseas environments. For her, the term *acculturation* applies to immigrants who integrate the values, norms, and symbols of the new culture and who must develop skills to meet its demands. She uses *adjustment* to apply to international students like Tina or individuals on short-term assignments known as *sojourners*.[3]

INTERCULTURAL ADAPTATION MODELS: SOJOURNERS

There are several models of the adaptation process that seek to identify the stages through which an individual passes in becoming adjusted to a new environment. The **U-curve hypothesis** was the first model and has been used as the basis for other models[4] (see Figure 10.1).

Sverre Lysgaard studied Norwegian Fulbright grant students in the United States, and developed the U-curve hypothesis based on their own reports of their experiences.[5] The U is a visual symbol mirroring the high, confident feeling experienced by travellers at the start of their adventure, followed by a low period in the new environment, and then a return to confidence and comfort. Lysgaard identified four phases in the acculturation process[6]:

- Phase 1 is a short period of *euphoria* where the excitement of travelling to a new land is the strongest emotion.
- Phase 2 is a period of *culture shock* (see page 272) when the person reacts negatively to living in the new environment. Reactions may include anxiety, hostility, depression, alienation, physical illness, or identity confusion. Tina, as you have probably guessed, is entering this stage.
- Phase 3 is the *acculturation* period. The person begins to function in the new social environment, become integrated, and gain confidence.
- Phase 4 is the *stable state of mind* phase, which may have three outcomes: 4a is a negative outcome where the person continues to feel alienated and discriminated

Figure 10.1 The U-curve hypothesis

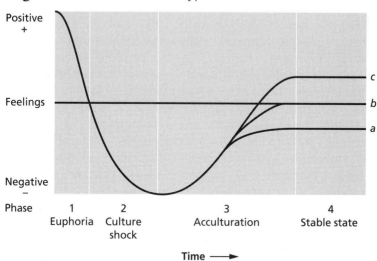

Source: From Hofstede, Geert. *Cultures and Organizations: Software of the Mind: Intercultural Cooperation and Its Importance for Survival*. New York: McGraw-Hill, 1997, p. 210. © Geert Hofstede BV, reprinted with permission.

against; 4b is a positive state where the person feels good and can be considered to be biculturally adapted; 4c refers to a "gone local" outcome where the person tries to behave and dress like people of the host culture. In Canada, where diversity is the norm and immigration the national experience, this kind of role-switching is not noteworthy. However, in culturally homogeneous environments, it may be inappropriate for visitors to appear to take on membership in the dominant culture. It can look as if they are putting the hosts into a classification they perceive to be lacking in complexity and easily "played" (see box, *On Going Local*, page 272).

The time taken to work through these stages varies with the individual. Some people remain a long time in one or another phase; others pass through relatively quickly, while others do not necessarily experience all phases.

The process of adaptation is tied to learning to communicate in a new environment.[7] It is stressful for this reason, but its reward is personal growth over time.

Many people who have spent years adapting to foreign environments often begin to long for home, however, realizing over time how deep culture is, and how difficult it is to fully acculturate. They become more, not less, aware of cultural and worldview differences between where they are and where they come from, and of a sense of identity formed elsewhere even when, as in many cases, they were once eager to leave and experience being "other."[8]

ON GOING LOCAL

For Canadians abroad, it can be insensitive to "go local." Diversity is not the norm everywhere, and unless we have spent many years acculturating to a new environment, we carry the marks of home with us for a long time—in our way of talking, walking, and interacting with others. It can be particularly insensitive, however, to presume to blend in if a visitor is from a wealthy, pluralistic, developed country like Canada and on assignment in a poor region of a developing country. Dr. Paul Farmer, an American doctor and philanthropist in Haiti, talks about appearance and "going native" in Third World countries. "The goofiness of radicals thinking they have to dress in Guatemalan peasant clothes. The poor don't want you to look like them. They want you to dress in a suit and go get them food and water."[9] While I don't agree that the poor necessarily want anyone to get them anything, I do think that we shouldn't jump into "playing them" as if it is a simple thing unless there are signs that we are welcome to enter their world in some way. Otherwise, this is a form of cultural appropriation that signals lack of respect: we are guests and they are hosts, not "locals."

CULTURE SHOCK

Adaptation models include a phase or stage of frustration, anxiety, and disorientation. *Culture shock* is the term popularly used to describe the stress of adapting to a new cultural environment. American anthropologist Kalervo Oberg coined it in a speech given to the Women's Club of Rio de Janeiro in 1954. In his speech, he underlined the relationship between the state of anxiety induced by immersion in a new cultural environment and the inability to communicate effectively in it.

Oberg spoke of "the anxiety that results from losing familiar signs and symbols of social intercourse. These signs or cues include the thousand and one ways in which we orient ourselves to the situations of daily life: when to shake hands and what to say when we meet people, when and how to give tips, how to give orders to servants. . . ."[10]

Signs and cues may be words, gestures, facial expression, customs, or norms acquired by everyone as they grow up without necessarily having conscious awareness of them. When we are transplanted to a new environment—the water in which others swim (see Chapter 3)—and we do not know the signs and cues.

Ting-Toomey sees culture shock as an emotional state involving a feeling of identity loss. Our sense of identity is shaken or strained with regard to values, status, profession, and circle of friends. We must make psychological adaptations to the new environment, which contributes to identity confusion and a sense of powerlessness from lack of control in unfamiliar contexts.[11]

Another way of looking at culture shock is to see it as a typical human response to transition, loss, or change and to recategorize it as *transition* shock, a subcategory of transition experiences such as those related to age, as we pass from one stage of life to another, or to disruptions like divorce or the death of a loved one.[12] Our adaptive processes are unable to meet the needs of the moment, and we are overwhelmed by the stimuli we have to take in. "Transition shock [is] a defensive response to the dissonance we feel when our worldview is assaulted," and an opportunity for personal growth as we expand our worldviews and life experiences.[13]

Culture shock generally refers to the disorientation we experience in moving to a foreign country. However, it can affect us in making transitions between cultural communities within national boundaries as well. Values, way of life, and often language differ, for example, across Canada's many regions, and moving from one to another within Canada, or from within the folds of one cultural group to another can cause culture shock. If we have always lived in a major Canadian city, we might well experience culture shock in moving to an isolated northern community in, say, Manitoba, where ice roads are used in winter, or to a west coast village in B.C. where the Alaska Marine Ferry service transports us from one town to the next. Moving to a Newfoundland outport might also lead to culture shock if we are from a Canadian urban environment, or from a prairie agricultural community.

First Nation Canadians often experience culture shock in moving from reserves into mainstream Canadian towns and cities to further their education or find work. Susan Aglukark, the singer who grew up in Arviat, NWT, population 1300, moved to Ottawa shortly after high school and suffered disorientation upon arrival. She missed her family and way of life despite the opportunities Ottawa afforded. Aglukark returns whenever possible to Arviat where the sights, sounds, people, and environment remain her inspiration and "home."[14]

James Bartelman, Ontario's first Aboriginal Lieutenant Governor, has worked to generate awareness of the transition difficulties experienced by First Nation individuals adapting to mainstream environments in Canada. Judge Harry S. LaForme, Robbie Robertson, Roberta Jamieson, and Cornelia Wieman are further examples of Aboriginal Canadians who have successfully managed intercultural adaptation to both serve their own communities and educate the wider society about Aboriginal cultural transition (see photos on the next page).

Symptoms of Culture Shock

People suffering from culture shock may stay hidden in their room, or experience extreme feelings of homesickness, anxiety, or fatigue, or take to drinking or compulsive eating.[15] They may believe they profoundly dislike the new country and all its inhabitants. Some people become withdrawn, others verbally or physically aggressive.[16]

Robbie Robertson: Internationally acclaimed composer, songwriter, guitarist, and singer.

Source: WENN/Landov

Roberta Jamieson: CEO of the National Aboriginal Achievement Foundation, Chief of Six Nations Band, first Canadian Aboriginal woman to earn a law degree and first woman Ontario Ombudsman.

Source: Courtesy of the National Aboriginal Achievement Foundation

Cornelia Wieman: Canada's first female Aboriginal psychiatrist.

Source: Courtesy of Dr. Cornelia Wieman, University of Toronto

Others exhibit "excessive concern over cleanliness and health; feelings of helplessness and withdrawal; irritability; fear of being cheated, robbed, or injured; a glazed stare; desire for home and old friends; and physiological stress reactions."[17] Some individuals approach a state of paranoia. All of these symptoms can lead to severe communication problems as the ability to cope degenerates due to mood swings and feelings of loneliness, tension, and isolation.

There also exists the shock of being visited. Anyone who lives in a popular tourist area will know that the hosts may also experience degrees of culture shock depending on the number of tourists, the duration of their stay, their comparative wealth, and the racial and ethnic prejudices of both the visitor and visited.[18]

Sources of Culture Shock

Culture shock can be triggered by many things. Consider the following bits of trivia on cleanliness that can contribute to a negative reaction to another culture:

- When Canadians take a bath, they soak, wash, and rinse in the same water. The Japanese use different water for each of these steps. How do you think the Japanese react to the Canadian bath custom[19]?

- In China, it is customary to spit and blow your nose onto the street, although authorities in Beijing are attempting to curb the habit. However, is it dirtier to spit and blow your nose on the street or to carry spit around with you in a Kleenex in your pocket[20]?
- In North American homes, a toilet is often located near the kitchen for convenience. Might this offend some people?
- West Africans and Latin Americans from tropical zones are often appalled at the body odour of Western co-operants unused to the heat of the tropics. Westerners seem to think one or two baths a day is sufficient on principle. Is it?

CULTURE SHOCK AND NORTH AMERICANS

Americans and Canadians working abroad, particularly women, often have negative reactions to sanitary and hygiene conditions and to the lack of modern conveniences.[21]

Americans further report culture shock from different attitudes towards women, non-verbal communication, clothing/business dress, family and marriage practices, housing, climate, and values and ethical standards,[22] as well as indirectness, formality and protocol, and a slow pace of life.[23]

They are also often frustrated by their inability to achieve results, while a common frustration among host nationals is that Americans "expect to accomplish more in the local environment than is reasonable."[24] The ability to fall short is important in coping with culture shock, since the North American value placed on achievement and success is not always mirrored in other cultures.[25]

Intercultural training is essential for people who set out to study or work in new cultural environments. Such things as "action plans" may not fit with a host culture's way of working, and ideas associated with being successful— such as what constitutes a successful meeting—may run counter to a host's ways of proceeding. A collaborative approach, for example, is not appropriate in cultures where power and authority are valued, such as in the Arab world.

In the workplace, Canadians are generally used to checks and balances that prevent workers from being fired at will and power blindly exercised by those who have it. Such checks and balances, in the form of committees, unions, or arbitration procedures, are not always present in other environments, and orientation programs need to explain realities of this nature.

Craig Storti makes a practical distinction between *country shock* and *culture shock*, both of which contribute to **acculturative stress**.[26]

Country shock (or what we might generically call ***environmental shock*** in order to include the concept of regional and intercultural moves within the same country) involves environmental adjustments required for such things as climate, doing without common things like food we may be used to, television programs that aren't available, books in our native language, or the availability of our favourite pastime, be it golf or dominoes or sitting around the pool with the neighbours. It also refers to the loss of familiar routines, such as going to the movies on Friday night or the mall on Saturday, or our grandmother's on Sunday. We miss not only the routine of going to grandma's, but grandma, too.

Other country/environmental-related stressors involve new transportation and communications systems. Newcomers from rural or developing regions may be terrified by the speed on some Canadian highways in highly populated areas, for example, while newcomers from developed countries and regions who go to developing areas may be frustrated by poor telephone and Internet service, bad roads, and the lack of other amenities.

Culture shock is the distress of adjusting to different values, beliefs, and attitudes related to living in a different cultural environment. These are the adjustments that affect us most deeply.[27] Different communication styles, non-verbal communication signals, attitudes to time, and language problems add to the disorientation we experience. We do not understand what is going on around us because we cannot decode the clues. "The natural order of things"[28] is not our idea of the natural order of things.

Frustrations with bureaucracy and "West African time" became irritants when I worked in Ghana, for example. I had to wait everywhere, for hours it seemed, often days, until the right person showed up to do what needed to be done. If I went to the post office in town to get a stamp, I might be told to come back the next day—the person who dispensed stamps could not come that day. Never mind that the stamps lay behind the wicket right beside the person I was speaking to . . . it was not his/her job to dispense stamps. That was someone else's job. Such was the natural order of things there. It was my responsibility to slow down and "go with the flow, not theirs to adapt to my ways."

Mild Culture Surprise

Expectations also affect people's reactions to a new culture. When newcomers expect things to be different and are psychologically prepared for difference, real trauma is less likely. Things are as expected: different. This is why orientation programs and previous travelling experience serve to mitigate transition stress.

Many international students in Canada experience mild surprise or discomfort rather than culture shock because they are psychologically prepared for cultural differences. Rajesh Rajan Singh, for example, arrived in Vancouver from India. He knew a few people already in Vancouver, but almost immediately got Canadian roommates also. Here is what initially surprised him[29]:

- How people said "hi" or "hey" to each other many times a day as they passed in the halls, even if they'd just seen each other two minutes before.

- How often people said "please" and "thank you," for example to the driver of a bus when getting off, or how often people said "excuse me" when passing in front of someone, say, at the mall in an aisle. Rajesh sometimes thought Canadians were "way too polite" although he appreciated the way people seem to be treated equally. He sometimes felt a misfit in situations where he was not used to saying please and thank you . . . if you are going to do a person a favour anyway, he found it unnerving to be so formal about it. "Among friends in India it is not necessary . . . you can ask people to do things straight out because you have gained that right through friendship. There's no need for "can you do me a really big favour . . .," and "please" and "thank you."
- How students got very drunk and made out in public at Canadian parties. He knew before arrival that such things were normal, but since they are a strong taboo in India, he nonetheless found it a bit strange.
- How politically correct and uncomfortable white Canadians often were in talking about racism or using the word in front of him. He had fun with the situation and let people know he was alright with the topic. Then they relaxed.
- How people talked behind others' backs about issues perceived to be negative. People do not mention that a person is fat to an overweight person, although they will talk about it when that person is not there; while in India "if a person is fat, he will be called 'fatso' by everyone . . . and even that person enjoys it."
- How direct Canadians are in saying outright that they don't want to do something. He liked this because it makes for fewer misunderstandings among people. In India, one always has to think about whether another person will feel bad, or whether "saying no" will create a rift.

Rajesh suffered little culture shock. Why is Tina's story different from his?

How do the communication codes discussed in Chapters 7, 8, and 9 relate to Tina's experience and Rajesh's observations? What elements of culture (Chapter 3) are relevant to their experience?

RE-ENTRY STRESS

Many graphs of the adaptation process include a final re-entry phase that characterizes the experience of sojourners when they return home after a stay in a foreign environment.[30] These models propose an extension to the U-curve of a second U making for a W-shaped model reflecting feelings and stages similar to those of the first U-curve.[31]

Re-entry shock is the trauma of readjusting to the old culture. It is a difficult time. Often, people in the home environment are uninterested in stories of the life away, and more significantly, the traveller has changed and doesn't exactly fit into the old patterns any more.[32]

People may feel disoriented by behaviours they didn't notice before. For a period on return, they live "half there" and "half here." They have learned to see in new ways. For example, the excessive use of packaging materials, the amount of garbage produced by a household, the speed of cars on the highways, the speed at which people walk all struck me when I came home to Canada from West Africa. It took me a while to stop stomping my feet (to scare away snakes) when I walked outside after dark. When I returned home from France after studying there, I couldn't get used to not automatically having wine with every meal. When I came home from Uruguay, I missed having dinner at 10 or 11 o'clock at night, and socializing wherever I went on business.

The disorientation usually passes. However, immersion in another culture may leave us forever changed because re-entry shock implies identity change—we must realign our new identity with a once familiar home environment and old identity.[33] We may have adopted new values and reorganized our worldviews. We may see power differences in a new light, or male and female roles, childrearing practices, social relationships, or treatment of animals, or feel estranged from old friends and colleagues. We are not quite the same person we were when we left home.

Re-entry shock for some people is more severe than the culture shock they experienced in the new environment, partly because they are less likely to expect it. Multinational companies often provide debriefing programs for their employees, their spouses, and children upon their return home to help them readjust to their old ways and lives.

LONG-TERM ADAPTATION MODELS: IMMIGRANTS AND REFUGEES

Everyone should have the experience of being an immigrant at least once.

Oscar Diaz[34]

The situation of immigrants and refugees is different from that of sojourners. Sojourners can go home. If they are overwhelmed by culture shock, they can cut short their stay or just "last" until the prescribed term is over. Immigrants and refugees seldom have that luxury. Adaptation is a must, and the potential for stress is particularly great if communities from the same ethnic, linguistic, or cultural background are not present to ease the way. Immigrants often have the additional stress of supporting families both in the new and home countries.

Berry Acculturation Model

Berry identified four patterns of psychological acculturation among immigrants, refugees, Aboriginals, ethnic groups, and sojourners in Canada,[35] and they correlated them with degrees of stress experienced by individuals in each of the patterns.

Integration: Newcomers maintain their old cultural identity while at the same time participating in the larger dominant culture. They are learning English (or French), working and socializing with Canadians, yet keeping social and language ties with other members of their home cultural community. Their level of acculturative stress is low.

Separation: Newcomers maintain their old cultural identity and avoid contact with the new one. Individuals (often women) fit this pattern if they stay at home and do not have the opportunity to learn the new language and interact with Canadians. They interact with only members of the same cultural community. Their level of acculturative stress is high.

Assimilation: Newcomers give up their old culture and adopt their new one. Children and teens often fit this pattern. They prefer to speak English/French, eat Canadian foods, and be with their Canadian friends. Their desire to assimilate causes them moderate stress.

Marginalization: Newcomers lose or reject their old culture but are not able to replace it by entering the new dominant culture. Individuals in this pattern do not value their ethnic roots, but do not feel part of the new culture and have not established friends. They feel caught between the old and the new, exhibit a high stress level, and are dysfunctional in both cultures.

According to this model, integration and assimilation are the least stressful modes of adaptation while marginalization is the most stressful.

Marginalization is such a significant stressor because an individual is rejected by both cultures. High school and post-secondary education counsellors need to be particularly sensitive to individuals suffering from marginalization and need to focus their assistance on the stresses it causes.

Have you experienced any of these patterns? Do you know individuals who fit them? Does your experience or theirs support the stress level attributed to each pattern?

FACTORS AFFECTING ADAPTATION

Adaptation revolves around the interplay between an individual and the new environment and its people. To adapt, the newcomer must learn to communicate and carve a place in the new environment, something that the environment can either facilitate or discourage both systemically and attitudinally.[36] In this section, we'll look at the skills, attributes, and personality factors that assist an individual as well as at the environmental factors that play a role in the adaptation process.

Factors related to the individual relate to psychological, social, and demographic factors.[37] They include:

- An adaptive personality. How outgoing, how flexible, how willing to make mistakes, how willing to learn, how hardworking is the person? Is the individual able to view different behaviours (role of women, differences in power distance) from an ethnorelative perspective?[38]
- A positive, confident personality.[39] Research has shown that individuals with realistic expectations and a positive attitude are more likely to adapt well than individuals with unrealistic expectations and apprehensive feelings.
- Cultural knowledge and sensitivity. Prior cultural experiences, language skills, awareness of problem-solving and decision-making styles as well as practical knowledge—how to hail a taxi, behave in a job interview—ease transition.[40]
- Motivation. How happy is the individual to be here? Is he or she sending pictures of themselves dressed in snowsuits home and saying "This is exactly what I imagined Canada to be!"
- Degree of independence. Independent individuals might do better in individual cultures while dependent people may thrive in collective environments.[41]
- Strong interpersonal skills such as stress management skills, communications skills, and the ability to establish meaningful relationships.[42]
- Demographic variables like age and education level also play a role in adaptation, with children adapting more easily than adults, and individuals with higher educations adapting more easily than people with lower.[43]

Factors related to the host environment can be divided into three categories and include:

Host Attitudes

- Receptivity.[44] How open to interaction is the host culture? Are newcomers viewed as intruders or welcomed? Oscar Diaz (quoted above), chose to return to Uruguay in 1983 after the dictatorship ended there. "I would rather be somebody at home, than nobody here," he said. His language difficulties kept him in jobs that did not meet his professional needs and working at several jobs did not give him time for language classes. And Canada in the 1970s and '80s was less welcoming to newcomers on the whole, according to Oscar and his family. When they returned to visit in 2002 and 2003, they found a new welcoming attitude. "People smile at you in the streets, offer to help you in the shops—Canadians seem to have changed."

- Conformity pressure. Is there pressure on newcomers to conform or is plurality valued? In monocultural societies like Japan, or in those stressing a "melting pot" of cultures like the United States, acculturation is usually one-directional: newcomers acculturate to the dominant culture.[45] In the United States, it is "unAmerican" not to. In Canada, with its multicultural "mosaic" policy, it is not "unCanadian" not to conform to the dominant culture immediately. People may live comfortably, or uncomfortably, in various stages of acculturation.

Host Infrastructure

- Availability of support services—social services, employment programs for immigrants, interpreters in hospital and medical clinics, language classes—facilitates acculturation.[46]
- Recognition of academic and professional qualifications and a clear process for accreditation.[47] Can newcomers find employment in their area of expertise? Research indicates that Canada's foreign-trained immigrants are better educated than native-born Canadians, but have a tougher time finding work in their fields; as a consequence, their incomes are falling behind.[48]
- Socio-economic realities. Host cultures appear to be more hospitable to newcomers when economic conditions are good and less hospitable during economic downturns.[49]

Communication and Culture

- Ethnic group strength. A strong ethnic community slows down the acculturation process in that newcomers can get things done within their own community, but also provides a social support system, comfort, shared experience, and assistance.[50] Going it alone is stressful.[51]
- Ethnic media. Access to local media in a familiar language can facilitate adaptation and ease stress.
- Cultural distance between the two cultures. Culture shock is often directly proportional to the degree of difference between the old and the new cultures.

VISIBLE MINORITIES AND THE CANADIAN WORKFORCE

Visible minorities in Canada often feel invisible when it comes to promotion opportunities says the Conference Board of Canada. Discrimination still exists, particularly against Canadians of African descent[52] and, despite the growing awareness of the benefits of a diverse workforce, potential employers often ignore resumes with foreign qualifications.[53] Certain strategies on the part of newcomers, such as marketing fluency in several languages and one or both of Canada's official languages, may help in overcoming the difficulty of rising through the ranks. "Doing things the Canadian way" is important, and can be encouraged through cross-cultural training by institutions and corporations and by seeking out mentors. There is growing interest in the corporate world to harness the talents of a diverse workforce, with BCE Inc., IBM Canada, and George Weston Ltd. contributing to Conference Board Research, along with the Canadian Auto Workers union and various public sector organizations.[54]

Immigrant Canadians of Note

Many Canadians who came to Canada as immigrants have become so well adapted to life here that they exemplify the best of it.

COPING WITH ACCULTURATIVE STRESS

People who experience symptoms of acculturative stress can take a few preventative steps before their symptoms become severe. They can:

- Force themselves to meet people. They can set an arbitrary goal, for example, talk to one new person a day. They should avoid mixing with only people of their own cultural background.
- Read and learn about their new culture; attend cultural events; look for the underlying values reflected in the behavioural patterns they observe.
- List positive things they have to say about the host country. The number may be surprising. They need to resist temptation to put down the host culture and rather find aspects with which they can identify positively and underemphasize aspects to which they react negatively.[55]
- Be conscious of the uniqueness of each person with whom they deal. Not everyone fits the norms of the host culture.[56]
- Develop a sense of humour and not take themselves too seriously.
- Be patient. More and more will become clear over time.
- Learn to live with ambiguity and expect things to be different.
- Learn to live with the paradoxes inherent in all cultures.[57]

Ujjal Dosanjh, Federal Minister of Health

Source: Courtesy of Minister of Health, Health Canada

Adrienne Clarkson, former Governor General of Canada

Source: CP Photo/Tom Hanson

IDENTITY CHANGE IN ACCULTURATION

The process of acculturation often results in personal change. Change may occur at surface levels—we may learn to kiss friends on the cheek when greeting them—and at deeper levels involving worldviews and values. Moving through the Berry Acculturation Model may take several generations in immigrant families. The length of time often depends on how strong their old culture is, how much desire individuals have to hold on to it, and how demanding the dominant culture is for acculturation. The euphoria of Greece's World Cup of Soccer win in 2004 among Greek Canadians spilling out into the streets of Montreal and Toronto was proof of the attachment to Greece among Greek Canadians. Often, the children and grandchildren of immigrants belong to dance, drama, or other cultural groups celebrating their ethnic origins, all the while being proud Canadians.

Newcomers or short-term sojourners may change to the degree necessary to function, but immigrants and especially their children and grandchildren are likely to adopt more and more of the dominant culture's values and beliefs as time goes on.[58] This can lead to assimilation in the long term, or hybrid identities, and to conflict and stress within the family in the short term. A finding of a study of 10 ethnic groups in Canada further revealed that heritage-language knowledge generally disappears after two generations.[59]

Canadian writers of different cultural origins treat the very Canadian theme of acculturation. Miriam Toews won the Governor General's Award for Fiction in 2004 for *A Complicated Kindness*.[60] It is about the identity issues of a young girl from the conservative Russian Mennonite town of East Village (Steinbach, Manitoba). Although the town has changed since its founding in 1874, it has held strongly to its Mennonite values. Young Nomi finds its moral and religious restrictions too much, its language (Low German, still spoken by many) archaic and embarrassing, and seeks to join the wider world of Canadian and American society.

While some immigrant communities remain attached for generations to their old cultures, other first, second, third, or fourth generation Canadians may have little or no such attachment. They may, in fact, not know the story of their family's immigration to Canada and identify solely with being Canadian. This is more likely in the case of Canadians whose origin is in the dominant culture—they assume their place in Canadian society quite naturally.[61] Few people ask how their names are spelled or what language they speak. One study revealed that 84 percent of Anglo-Celts called themselves solely "Canadian" (as opposed to some form of hyphenated ethnic Canadian or simply an ethnic label) as compared to 66 percent of other ethnics, and 17 percent of French Canadians.[62]

I remember my own experience of discovering I was "ethnic." My family had moved from Manitoba to Guelph, Ontario, a bastion of Anglo-Saxon culture at the time. As luck would have it, I stood first in class at Christmas. My teacher, Miss McColl, who had an English accent, announced that for the first time at Central Senior Public School, established in 1874 (the year my great-grandparents had come from Russia and lived in sod huts on the prairie), a German was first in class. I looked around, wondering who the German was. Miss McColl called upon the individual to stand up. No one did. She became annoyed and told me to get up. Until that moment, I had thought I was a fourth generation Canadian of Russian Mennonite origin.

Such things do not happen any more in Canadian schools, or are not supposed to, but the larger society still makes assumptions about people and their "Canadianness."

Have you ever had an experience similar to mine in which your ascribed identity did not match your avowed identity (see Chapter 2)?

Visible minorities may find it hard to shed their cultural and ethnic roots, not because they don't feel 100 percent assimilated, but rather because people remind them that they are "other." Questions like "Where are you from?" of Chinese or African Canadians whose families have been Canadian for generations serve to remind them of "otherness" when, in fact, their communication styles, attitudes, and values are Canadian mainstream.

One-third of adolescents in North America is of non Anglo-Celtic ethnic descent and many, particularly those of visible minority background, face questions of identity—stereotypes about their sexuality, social status, and manners may confuse them about how to think about themselves.[63] In addition, racial profiling issues raised by black and First Nation Canadians indicate that prejudice appears to be systemic in some Canadian institutions (see Chapter 2). Canadians who can most freely choose and "perform" their ethnic identity are those of Anglo-Celtic descent whose families arrived in Canada more than two generations ago.[64]

American-born Indians have an acronym for themselves: ABCD—"American Born Confused *Desi* ("natives").[65] They are raised in traditional environments, but in the larger society adopt Canadian, or American, or British norms. Their cultural identity is complex, and they are at a crossroads between old world values and new world temptations. A number of movies, such as the Canadian *Bollywood, Hollywood,* and the Indian *Monsoon Wedding* play on this theme with humour.

Canadians of Chinese descent sometimes refer to themselves as "bananas"—yellow on the outside, white on the inside—or CBCs, Canadian-born Chinese.[66] They are part of the dominant culture in terms of their behaviour, attitudes, and values, yet look Chinese. They may have little interest in Chinese culture. Like other ethnic minorities, visible or not, they can choose which elements of their culture of origin they wish to adopt and which elements of the dominant culture they espouse. However, the assumption by others that they are not Canadian is an example of Euro-Canadian or other ethnocentrism.

In pluralistic societies like Canada's, ideally, people are free to choose their primary cultural identity. It may be to their particular ethnic or religious group and encompass "the unique history, traditions, values, rituals, and symbols"[67] of that group. It may be to the national culture, or to a composite of both. In Quebec, the definition of national culture varies. It may mean Canada, but to Quebec nationalists, it refers to Quebec as a nation and culture. Other cultural identities across Canada may also add the variable of region. To Atlantic Canadians, primary allegiance may be to their region, or to Canada.

Cultural identity in Canada is complex and dynamic, fluid and shifting. Our allegiances and ethnic or cultural senses of identity shift and re-align themselves, often depending on the situation. A person who feels little national fervour over being Canadian at home may suddenly feel profoundly their Canadianness when living abroad.[68]

Citizens of the World

Some individuals have travelled the world, learned several languages, and consciously or unconsciously created a unique value system, worldview, and personal identity. They have selected what they like and need from many cultures and feel at home almost anywhere in the world, "committed to the basic unity of all human beings while at the same time recognizing, legitimizing, accepting, and appreciating the differences that exist between people of different cultures."[69] We call such people "citizens of the world," true international hybrids, at home, at ease, "fluent" almost everywhere. They are the embodiment of the *Peaceful Resolution* cultural scenario suggested in Chapter 1.

Pierre Trudeau, former Prime Minister of Canada, considered himself a citizen of the world. What justified his self-description? Can you think of other "citizens of the world"? To what degree would you consider yourself a "citizen of the world"?

On a modest level, many people in Canada live from an international perspective. They frequent ethnic restaurants as a matter of course, cook international cuisine at home, decorate their homes with items from around the world, appreciate world music and international films, and have a circle of friends from many different ethnic groups.

> There is for most people one language and one culture to which they revert when they need to say exactly what they mean, and be exactly who they are. It may be an adopted language and culture, but is so rarely. What is your language and cultural identity when you really need to be you?
>
> Some of you may be bicultural—bicultural individuals are people who function equally in two cultures and languages. They are often the children of parents of two different cultures and languages.

Third Culture Kids

Third Culture Kids (**TCK**s), also known as Trans-culture Kids, are children who spend their developmental years in a culture not their parents'.[70] They are the children of wanderers—military personnel, missionaries, diplomats, international managers, educators, and consultants. TCKs develop a unique culture and identity of their own, and often feel most at home with children from the same background. They often are marginal in all countries including their passport country. "Home" does not exist for them. Parents of TCKs often attempt to keep alive the idea of home for their children: they go home regularly, subscribe to magazines and newspapers from home, and keep separate the concepts of the transient here and now, and the permanent home. Sometimes, it is easier to move from place to place in order to keep the idea of home alive than to stay at one posting for many years, although children who do this often later "live on the road" too. Children who spend much of their life in a place not home, but just one such place, often have even more trouble relating to a home than the ones who go from place to place; they don't belong where they have spent much of their lives, but nor do they belong at home, with which they are unfamiliar.

INTERCULTURAL ADAPTATION AND CONFLICT

Cultures have different ways of dealing with and recognizing conflict.[71] The idea of studying conflict is, for starters, a Western one, in line with the European tradition of breaking things up into discrete units of study and analysis[72] (see Chapter 6). The Eastern holistic tradition, influenced by Confucianism, seeks to avoid conflict, not confront it.

LeBaron conducted research in Western Canada to learn how members of different cultures experienced conflict. One researcher returned with little data from her first interview with an elderly Chinese immigrant who claimed that he had experienced no conflicts since arriving in 1948. Efforts at using translations of words like *trouble* and *disagreement* yielded nothing either.

LeBaron and her colleagues realized that to admit conflict to strangers would be uncomfortable for this elderly Chinese gentleman, involving loss of face and pain. In addition, his cultural expectations, both gendered and generational, would lead him to expect deference and not questioning from the young Chinese-Canadian researcher.[73]

Whether or not he experienced conflict remained unknown, but he was able to communicate the concept of perceiving harmony rather than identifying conflict.

First Nation cultures too seek to avoid conflict, and traditions of healing circles and group conferencing are ways to bring about reconciliation and healing rather than punishment and retribution. In Manitoba, Saskatchewan, and other parts of Canada, Aboriginal family group conferencing is proving a successful way to deal with forms of conflict such as sexual abuse. Offenders, victims, family, and community members get together to talk about and share their feelings and perceptions in a holistic, caring way that stresses the connectedness of people and aims to find solutions that preserve that connectedness. The Western focus on facts, efficiency, time, and judgment is at odds with the Native approach to conflict resolution.[74]

Immigrants must make profound adaptations to life in Canada, very often the most difficult of which is the transition from a collective to an individualist culture. In collectivist cultures, the family is the most important unit, as is the importance of roles within it. Often conflicts arise within families over changing roles and degrees of acculturation of different members within the family. In collectivist cultures, disputes are often solved within the extended family, through intervention by respected family and community members. The concept of seeking outside help, be it legal or psychological, is not part of the culture.

Daily, newcomers go out into the wider Canadian world where the patterns may be different, then come home to another world. A father may try to remain authoritarian in the home, yet work at a job that has little status. He is subject to losing face at home or among the relatives. A mother may be isolated in the home, or conversely become the major breadwinner and strain family relationships by putting them into conflict with the norms of patriarchal communities. The husband may be suspicious of her if she meets men outside the home. The children may experience conflict as they acculturate to new values and challenge traditional patterns. In homes where fathers and sons have control over women, daughters may rebel against the lack of freedom they feel they have when they see how other women or girls their age are living. They may wish to date, or choose a marriage partner when traditionally marriages are arranged.[75]

According to research carried out in the Lower Mainland of B.C. among five different cultural groups, the "immigrant syndrome" affected all groups. They struggled with language, differences in roles and adaptations among family members, changes in socio-economic and employment status, changes in cultural values, and loss of identity based on national origin.[76]

The University of Victoria's Institute for Dispute Resolution undertook to increase awareness and understanding of the importance of the role of culture in conflict in terms of how conflicts are perceived, experienced, and resolved. The major emphasis of the project was ethnicity and other cultural factors relevant to immigration to Canada. Culture was defined broadly to include such factors as ethnicity, race, age, gender, socio-economic background, sexual orientation, and disability.

Some of its conclusions are as follows[77]:

- In conflict resolution processes, culture must be broadly defined as above, and take into account the diversity within cultural groups and the dynamic nature of culture.
- The same principles apply across cultures in conflict resolution. The need for caring, respect, and procedural fairness is universal. However, it has yet to be

determined what attributes and skills of interveners are universal and what are culture specific.

- Interveners must understand values, particularly those of collective and individualist cultures while being aware that all cultures have both individualist and collective features. When dealing with Latin Americans and Asians in the relatively individualist culture of Canada, these values must be recognized: the importance of family and respect for parents; the significance of spirituality and community values; the importance of roles in a stratified community or extended family; and the preference for insiders to resolve family or intergroup conflicts.
- Further research is needed on the cross-cultural meaning of face-saving and face-restoration (see Chapter 8) in relation to conflict resolution.
- Culture plays a role in determining what constitutes "a dispute" among individuals of different cultures.
- Issues of power, racism, and cultural discrimination are factors in many intercultural disputes.

The Institute for Dispute Resolution's project focused on five cultural groups in the Lower Mainland: Chinese, Latin American, Polish, South Asian, and Vietnamese. Interviews with individuals of these communities, representatives of selected community service institutions who were also members of the communities being researched ("key informants"), and representatives of eight institutions such as the Immigration and Refugee Board and Workers' Compensation Board, provided data on types of conflicts experienced and both traditional and transitional ways they are handled.

Family conflicts such as traditional generational and gender roles leading to loss of status for husbands/fathers were commonly identified by all groups. Younger respondents told of falling into the gap between traditional expectations of parents/elders and Canadian reality. These types of conflict were followed closely by conflicts between individuals and institutions such as police, government departments, and schools. Lack of cultural competence by police, educational workers, and other frontline service personnel caused stress and delay in the resolution of conflicts.

For example, key informants reported on the shame felt by a family if a teacher called home, the perception being that it is the school's duty to educate children and only in extreme cases involve the parents. In other cases, parents wish to have more influence and involvement in the school than expected.

Data gathered also showed that the use of mediation, or consensus-based dispute resolution programs in these conflicts, could be effective when individuals from outside the dominant culture were involved. Key informants believed that such programs should address the priorities of community members and reflect an understanding of and respect for values held by members of the communities.[78]

GENDER AND FAMILY CONFLICT

This example comes from *Conflict and Culture: Research in Five Communities in Vancouver, British Columbia* by Michelle LeBaron Duryea and J. Bruce Grundison:

> When conflicts occur, agencies and support services may be relied upon, but unsatisfying results are often reported. Individuals who adopt some Canadian values thus invite double jeopardy: they may find themselves without support from traditional networks, yet with inadequate services from dominant culture agencies. An example comes from the interview of a young South Asian woman who recently separated from her husband. She states that she was in an abusive relationship and that her family 'tried to change me to accept him the way he is.' Since she has left the relationship, she is now labeled as 'the bad one'. When she went to a transition house with her children, she found herself in a foreign environment. The food was always Canadian ("They don't like us making our own kind") . . . there was no counselor or worker who understood her situation. She states: "The police and the transition house people did help me, but they just did not understand my culture. They should know about our culture, and then they could help us better."[79]

Source: Reprinted with permission of the Institute for Dispute Resolution, University of Victoria.

Nonetheless, key informant participants suggested that the importation wholesale of traditional conflict resolution vehicles to Canada is unworkable because of changes in community structures in Canada, clashes with Canadian values, and the undesirability of replicating features like decision-making by male elders.

Ontario's 1991 Arbitration Act recognizing Muslim *sharia* law (along with other faith-based systems) in civil cases caused controversy in both the Muslim and wider Canadian communities because it was seen by its opponents to embody inherent conflicts with Canadian values and laws. Opponents of *sharia* claimed that Islamic law inherently discriminated against women, while supporters argued that the Arbitration Act protected them by stipulating that recourse to *sharia* be voluntary, and that its decisions fall within the bounds of Canadian law. In 2005, Premier McGuinty bowed to opponents and announced that his government would rescind the Arbitration Act and pass a law prohibiting all faith-based arbitration. Such a law will likely be challenged by proponents of faith-based arbitration using the Charter of Rights and Freedoms leaving the courts to decide the issue.

Culture-related conflict is inevitable in pluralistic societies like Canada's, but how we deal with it will define us as a culture and determine how our society will continue to evolve. In the wake of 9/11, 2001, not only Canadians, but much of the world is beginning to understand the need to interact with others armed with cultural knowledge and a spirit of respect and cooperation. Intercultural competence has never been so necessary.

By way of conclusion, then, this text will end with the words with which it began:

There has never been a time when civilization stood more in need of individuals who are genuinely culture conscious, who can see objectively the social behaviour of other peoples without fear and recrimination.

Ruth Benedict, 1935[80]

SUMMARY

People often pass through stages in adapting to new cultural environments. The U-curve hypothesis suggests four stages experienced by sojourners: euphoria, culture shock, acculturation, and emotional stability. Other models add a re-entry stage to account for the disorientation experienced by people when they return home. The Berry Acculturation Model describes an adaptation process particularly applicable to immigrants and relates the four patterns (integration, separation, assimilation, and marginalization) to the degree of stress they engender.

Identity change is a feature of adaptation as individuals absorb new behaviours and values. Intercultural adaptation is often at the core of generational, family, and societal conflict. Researchers are agreed that cultures have different ways of defining and dealing with conflict, and that knowledge of culture can help in dispute and conflict negotiation.

KEY TERMS

acculturation 269

acculturative stress 275

adaptation 269

assimilation 269

culture shock 272

intercultural adaptation 269

re-entry stress 277

TCK 286

U-curve hypothesis 270

TOPICS FOR CRITICAL THINKING AND REFLECTION

1. Your experiences: choose one of the two choices below, jot down your answers, and discuss them with your group or class.
   (a) If you are a newcomer to Canada, what contributed to any disorientation you may have felt. Divide your list into "country" and "culture" shock factors.
   (b) If you have experienced disorientation due to a move within Canada or a sojourn in another country, what factors related to "country" and "culture" shock fit your experience?

2. If you were to be transported to an isolated community in Canada's far north, what routines would you miss? What aspects of your visual and aural environment would you miss? Conversely, if you are from the north, what would you miss in the south?

3. Canada is often seen as a *mosaic* of cultures, while the United States is celebrated as a *melting pot*. Which approach do you think causes less stress for immigrants? Why? What are the advantages and disadvantages of each?

4. Bhutanese immigrant Bhim Subba and his family moved to Peterborough after originally settling in Toronto. They wanted to "experience Canadianness" and find role models to emulate in their quest to become Canadian. They appreciated the multiculturalism of Toronto, but found that too many people spoke languages other than English or French and kept to their own ethnic communities. In Peterborough, they feel they have found Canadianness and a national culture into which they can assimilate.[81]

   Do you agree with Mr. Subba that small, less ethnically diverse cities are the "real" Canada, not large multicultural, urban centres? Why or why not?

5. What are the arguments for and against faith-based arbitration in Canada? What were the specific arguments of those opposed to the implementation of *sharia* in Ontario? What were the arguments of those in favour?

6. **Case Study**
   A Canadian woman was posted to a strict Islamic country to work with a multinational company for a few months. She taught English to several of the employees and became romantically involved with one of them although liaisons with foreigners were forbidden. They got together in her apartment secretly, and attended local events together where she was publicly affectionate. Although advised to dress modestly, she took to wearing dresses more revealing than culturally accepted and refused to wear a head scarf. When time came to leave, she became distraught. Fortunately, the Canadian embassy became involved and an international incident was averted. Nonetheless, the behaviour on the part of both parties was dangerous on a number of levels. Why? Could this event have been avoided? If so, how? If not, why not?

Appendix I
Answers to In-Text Exercises

1. **Chapter 1:** National Poll, results for #1
    *   16% of males 18–30 said yes
    *   29% of males 31 and over said yes
    *   17% of females 18–30 said yes
    *   33% of females 31 and over said yes

    Source: Excerpt from Parkin, Andrew and Matthew Mendelsohn. *A New Canada: An Identity Shaped by Diversity*. The CRIC Papers (Canadian Opinion Research Archive). Montreal: Centre for Research and Information on Canada, Oct. 2003, p. 3.

2. **Chapter 2:** Case Studies: The French, the English, and the Canadian

    Cathy's Solution: She alternated French and English hikers and then showered last herself.

3. **Chapter 3:** Word Meanings across Cultures, results for #3

MARRIAGE MEANINGS	PERCENTAGE OF RESPONDENTS		
	U.S.A.	JAPAN	FRANCE
1. Love	30	16	28
2. Respect	27	12	10
3. Responsibilities	24	15	8
4. Understanding	23	18	20
5. Helping each other	22	11	14
6. Problem sharing	22	17	13
7. Trust	21	27	17
8. Mutual encouragement	21	8	13
9. Interpersonal sensitivity	17	5	19
10. Accepting mutual freedom	17	10	16
11. Maturity	17	1	1
12. Family	17	20	9
13. Marital fulfillment	16	6	18
14. Sex	14	11	22
15. Compromise	11	17	17

(Continued)

MARRIAGE MEANINGS	PERCENTAGE OF RESPONDENTS		
	U.S.A.	JAPAN	FRANCE
16. Passion	11	5	22
17. Children	13	16	7
18. United	9	6	15

FAMILY MEANINGS	PERCENTAGE OF RESPONDENTS	
	U.S.A.	KOREA
1. Children, brother, sister	19	25
2. Relatives	7	16
3. Happiness, fun	5	6
4. Family size, sex (gender)	0	5
5. Family support, livelihood	2	1
6. Activities, life	5	2
7. Togetherness, cooperation	6	3
8. Love, friendship	12	4
9. Home	11	6
10. Mother, father	30	29
11. Miscellaneous	3	3

Source: From Donald W. Klopf's "Word Meanings Across Cultures" in *Experiential Activities for Intercultural Learning*, Volume 1, H. Ned Seelye, ed. Yarmouth: Intercultural Press, Inc., 1996, pp. 127–128. Reprinted with permission of Intercultural Press.

4. **Chapter 4:** Table 4.1: Proud to be Canadian

Here are the national results of the poll on national identity from Table 4.1.

	VERY PROUD (8, 9, 10)	NEUTRAL (3–7)	NOT AT ALL PROUD (0–2)
The vastness and beauty of the land	88%	11%	1%
When the UN ranks Canada as the best country in the world in which to live	82%	15%	3%
When Canadian airports took in American planes that were diverted on Sept. 11, 2001	74%	20%	5%
The fact that people from different cultural groups in Canada get along and live in peace	70%	27%	3%

	VERY PROUD (8, 9, 10)	NEUTRAL (3–7)	NOT AT ALL PROUD (0–2)
Canada's participation in peacekeeping activities around the world	70%	25%	5%
Canada's politeness and civility	67%	29%	4%
Canada's scientific inventions, like the Canadarm	66%	30%	4%
Canadian Olympic hockey team victories	63%	27%	10%
The Charter of Rights and Freedoms	62%	31%	6%
Canada's participation in key battles of World Wars I and II	61%	31%	7%
Multiculturalism	54%	37%	8%
The success of Canadian musicians or actors or artists	53%	40%	7%
When Canada decided not to participate in the war on Iraq	49%	26%	25%
Canada's health care system	42%	47%	12%
Having two official languages, English and French	41%	38%	21%
The CBC	39%	49%	12%
Pierre Trudeau	37%	43%	18%
The Queen	27%	37%	36%

Source: From Parkin, Andrew, and Matthew Mendelsohn. *A New Canada: An Identity Shaped by Diversity*. The CRIC Papers (Canadian Opinion Research Archive). Montreal: Centre for Research and Information on Canada, Oct. 2003, p. 11. Reprinted with permission of the Centre for Research and Information on Canada (CRIC).

5. **Chapter 5:** results for #1

   According to Richard Nisbett, the social psychologist and interculturalist who created this test, odds are that that if you are a Westerner, you will think the chicken and the cow go together, following in the Greek tradition of putting objects into categories. Odds are that if you are an Easterner, you will pick the cow and the grass, following the Eastern tradition of seeing relationships. Nesbitt's experiments with Chinese and American students confirmed his hypothesis.

   Source: From Richard Nisbett, *The Geography of Thought: How Asians and Westerners Think Differently . . . and Why.* Toronto: Free Press, 2003, p. 141.

Appendix II
Suggested Film, Print, and Web Resources

Chapter 1

El Contrato—documentary about Mexican migrant farm workers in Leamington, Ontario. View this in the context of globalization and anti-globalization. Why does Canada not allow these migrants to apply for citizenship? Also appropriate for attitudes toward Mexican migrant workers in Canada (also Chapter 2).

Hotel Rwanda—for genocide (also Chapter 2—racism).

The Take—documentary about grassroots anti-globalization in Argentina (also for *Time Out for Latin America*).

Edward Said: On Orientalism—40-minute documentary (also Chapter 5).

Dying for Peace: Our Soldiers in Kabul—CBC *News in Review*, March, 2004: gives a 20-minute idea of what Canadian peacekeepers do and how international peacekeeping works.

The Constant Gardener—This movie covers themes such as colonialism, racism, and modern imperialism.

Chapter 2

Spanglish—for stereotyping of Mexican workers and dominant culture Americans.

Control Room—for perception (also *Time Out for the Arab World*).

Hidalgo—for stereotyping, also elements of Aboriginal culture such as circle symbolism (also Chapter 3).

Goodbye Lenin—for creation of parallel realities.

My Big Fat Greek Wedding—stereotyping of Greek Americans and WASPs.

A Fish Called Wanda—John Cleese spoof on American and British stereotypes of each other.

Chapter 3

Captain Corelli's Mandolin—illustrates Greek sense of *philotimo*. Novel also excellent.

Any **Stephen King** movie, for archetypes and archetypal symbols.

Kandahar—on Afghanistan, women in patriarchal culture.

Suggest to students that they watch the **Northern Games** broadcast on the Aboriginal Network and CBC at the relevant time of the year for a fascinating look at games devised by northern peoples to reflect skills needed in hunting.

Water—Deepa Mehta film rich in Hindu symbolism; can also be looked at from feminist perspective.

Chapter 4

What Border? The Americanization of Canada—CBC 5-part series on the relationship between Canada and the U.S. and changes since the 1960s.

Fahrenheit 9/11—Michael Moore on American culture.

Bowling for Columbine—Michael Moore on American culture.

Rick Mercer's *Talking to America*—TV series

Time Out for Latin America

Y tu mamá también ("And your mother too")—Mexico's classes

Motorcycle Diaries—Che Guevara's 1950s trip through South America

El crimen del padre Amaro (The Crime of Father Amaro)—Mexico and the Roman Catholic Church

Central Station and *City of God*—Brazil's gritty urban underworld.

Time Out for India

Monsoon Wedding—marriage in modern, First World India.

Bollywood, Hollywood—Indo-Canadian culture

Any **Bollywood** movie

Bend it Like Beckham—Indo-British culture

Water—See Chapter 3

Chapter 9

Talking Canadian, CBC—a lighthearted documentary on how Canadian English differs from American and English standards.

The Adventure of English, BBC—tale of the evolution of English and how it spread around the globe.

Recommended Reading

Chapter 6: *Life of Pi*

Recommended Websites

Program for Multicultural Health—Biweekly Multicultural Health Generalizations—Index by Culture—http://www.med.umich.edu/multicultural/ccp/culture.htm

Food First—"12 Myths About Hunger"—http://www.foodfirst.org/node/235

Settlement.org—http://www.settlement.org/index.asp

Cultural profiles of immigrant communities, Immigration and Citizenship Canada website. Type "cultural profiles" in the search box, then click on "Cultural Profiles—countries of the world"

Indian and Northern Affairs Canada—"Looking forward, looking back"—http://www.ainc-inac.gc.ca/ch/rcap/rpt/lk_e.html

Highlights from the Royal Commission on Aboriginal Peoples, 1997

Wideangle—http://www.pbs.org/wnet/wideangle/

Current information on various regions of the world.

Statistics Canada—http://www.statcan.ca

Statistics Canada contains information related to the most recent census, such as regional breakdowns of the population by ethnicity and other demographic statistics.

Notes and References

Chapter 1

1. Benedict, Ruth. *Patterns of Culture.* London: Routledge & Kegan Paul Ltd., 1935, p. 8.
2. Some scholars distinguish between inter-cultural and cross-cultural communication. "Intercultural" focuses on *interpersonal-interactive* nature of exchanges between different cultures, such as an intercultural communication exchange, an intercultural marriage, and so on. (*The American Heritage Dictionary of the English Language,* Fourth Edition, at www.bartleby.com/61/45/I01845000.html.) "Cross-cultural" is *comparative* in nature, as in the comparison and statistical analysis of patterns characteristic of groups as in a cross-cultural survey, or cross-cultural influences on an artist's work. (*The American Heritage Dictionary of the English Language,* Fourth ed., www.bartleby.com/61/22/C0762200.html). Other Sources: "Cross-Cultural Analysis," Judith L. Gillies, www.as.ua.edu/ant/Faculty/murphy/crosscut.htm, "The Use and Misuse of Questionnaires in Intercultural Training," John W. Bing, www.itapintl.com/useandmisuse.htm.
3. Hall, Edward T. *The Silent Language.* New York: Fawcett World Library, 1959.
4. Bennett, Milton J. *Basic Concepts of Intercultural Communication in Basic Concepts of Intercultural Communication: Selected Readings.* Milton J. Bennett, ed., Yarmouth, Maine: Intercultural Press, 1998, pp. 1–34.
5. Teevan, James J. and W.E. Hewitt, eds. *Sociology, A Canadian Focus,* 8th edition, Toronto: Prentice Hall, 2005.
6. Ting-Toomey, Stella. *Communicating Across Cultures.* New York: The Guilford Press, 1999.
7. LeBaron, Michelle. *Bridging Cultural Conflicts: A New Approach for a Changing World.* San Francisco: Jossey-Boss, 2003.
8. Trudeau, Pierre Elliott. Federal Multicultural Policy, Oct. 8, 1971 http://collections.ic.gc.ca/albertans/speeches/trudeau.html.
9. *2001 Census Dictionary–Internet Version,* Catalogue No. 92-378-XIE. www12.statcan.ca/english/census01; *Definitions of Concepts and Variables.* www.statcan.ca/english/concepts/definitions/ethnicity.htm; *Ethnic Identity and Race, Gypsies in Canada: The Promised Land?* News in Review resource guide online, Dec. 1997 www.tv.cbc.ca/newsinreview/dec97/gypsies/ethnic.html.
10. Ibid.
11. Teevan & Hewitt, op. cit.; Berry, John W., Uichol Kim & Pawel Boski. "Psychological Acculturation of Immigrants." In Kim and Gudykunst, eds., *Cross-Cultural Adaptation: Current Approaches.* Newbury Park, CA: Sage Publications, Inc, 1988, pp. 62–89.
12. *2001 Census Dictionary—Internet Version,* Catalogue No. 92-378-XIE. www12.statcan.ca/english/census01.
13. Adams, Michael. "My Canada doesn't include religiosity." *The Globe and Mail,* Jan. 10, 2005, A13.
14. Gauer, Stephen. "Losing our religion." *The Globe and Mail,* Feb. 19, 2005, F6.
15. Parkin, Andrew & Matthew Mendelsohn. *A New Canada: An Identity Shaped by Diversity, The CRIC Papers* (Canadian Opinion Research Archive). Montreal: Centre for Research and Information on Canada, Oct. 2003.
16. Statistics Canada www12.statcan.ca/english/census01/home/index.cfm.
17. Taibossigai, Lyndsay. *Ojibwe Culture,* paper submitted Dec. 14, 2004.
18. MacGregor, Roy. "Saskatchewan schools take on the province's two solitudes." *The Globe and Mail,* Dec. 30, 2004, A4.
19. Statistics Canada www12.statcan.ca/english/census01/home/index.cfm.
20. Ibid.
21. Teevan & Hewitt, op. cit.; "Canada's welcome mat." *The Globe and Mail,* May 31, 2004, A12.
22. Statistics Canada www12.statcan.ca/english/census01/home/index.cfm.
23. "Canada's welcome mat," op. cit.
24. Galloway, Gloria. "Black population growth dramatic, report shows." *The Globe and Mail,* Mar. 10, 2004.
25. Troper, Harold. *Immigrant City: The Making of Modern Toronto in a Passion for Identity: Canadian Studies for the 21st Century,* David

Taras and Beverly Rasporich, eds. Toronto: Nelson Thomson Learning, 2001, pp. 335–354.

26. Ibbitson, John. "Why Atlantic Canada remains white and poor." *The Globe and Mail*, Aug. 20, 2004, A4.

27. "Canada's welcome mat," op. cit.

28. Statistics Canada www12.statcan.ca/english/census01/home/index.cfm.

29. Barber, John. "And you thought our two solitudes were all about language." *The Globe and Mail*, August 21, 2004, M2.

30. Toughill, Kelly. "Maritimes lure rich immigrants." *The Globe and Mail*, Mar. 14, 2005, A1.

31. "Canada's welcome mat," op. cit.

32. Parkin & Mendelsohn, op. cit.

33. "Canada's welcome mat," op. cit.

34. Parkin and Mendelsohn, op. cit., p. 3.

35. Ibid.

36. "Canada's welcome mat," op. cit.; Parkin & Mendelsohn, op. cit.

37. Gray, Jeff. "When it comes to relationships, Canadians add race to the mix." *The Globe and Mail*, June 9, 2004, A14.

38. Ibid; Statistics Canada.

39. Parkin & Mendelsohn, op. cit., p. 5.

40. Ibid.

41. *On the Road: Vancouver*. CBC special aired Dec. 7, 2004.

42. Barnes, Rosemary. "Encouraging diversity key to success." *The Globe and Mail*, Sept. 11, 2004, B13.

43. Trompenaars, Fons & Charles Hampden-Turner. *Riding the Waves of Culture: Understanding Cultural Diversity in Global Business*, 2nd ed. N.Y.: McGraw-Hill, 1998.

44. Immen, Wallace. "Foreign interns get a leg up." *The Globe and Mail*, June 19, 2004, B10.

45. Galt, Virginia. "P&G leverages its cultural diversity." *The Globe and Mail*, Apr. 7, 2005, B1.

46. Ibid.

47. Ibid.

48. Ibid.

49. McLuhan, Marshall. *Understanding Media: The Extensions of Man*, 4th printing. New York: McGraw-Hill Book Company, 1966; Symes, Benjamin. *Marshall McLuhan's 'Global Village'*, accessed at www.aber.ac.uk/media/Students/bas9401.html, Oct. 21, 2004.

50. Dyer, Gwynne. *The Human Race Part IV: Escaping from History*. Montreal: Green Lion Productions, 1994.

51. McLuhan, Marshall. *The Gutenberg Galaxy*. London: Routledge & Kegan, 1962.

52. U.N. and Canadian Council for refugees stats cited in Médecins sans frontières fact sheet, 2004.

53. Hofstede, Geert. *Cultures and Organizations: Software of the Mind*. Toronto: McGraw-Hill, 1997, pp. 215–229.

54. "Ontario's Invisible Workforce," *Toronto Star*, Sept. 24, 2003, D1; "Visa facts," *The Globe and Mail*, Nov. 27, 2004, A4.

55. http://canadianeconomy.gc.ca/english/economy/globalization.html.

56. Wright, Ronald. "Modern societies, ancient errors." *The Globe and Mail*, Jan. 15, 2005, D3.

57. Pitts, Gordon. "Who will be the next Huntingdon?" *The Globe and Mail*, Jan. 8, 2005, B7.

58. Kluver, Randolph & Wayne Fu. "The Cultural Globalization Index," posted Feb. 2004, *Web Exclusive* www.foreignpolicy.com/story/cms.php?story_id=2494, accessed July 26, 2005.

59. Blackwell, Richard. "Canadians enjoy choice in TV, radio." *The Globe and Mail*, Dec. 15, 2004, B8.

60. *CBC News*, Sept. 8, 2004.

61. York, Geoffrey. "Trendy Chinese study Canada 101." *The Globe and Mail*, Jan. 20, 2005, A1.

62. FOCAL, 2004.

63. Fukuyama, Francis. *The End of History and the Last Man*. New York: Avon Books, 1992.

64. Hofstede, op. cit.

65. Nisbett, Richard E. *The Geography of Thought: How Asians and Westerners Think Differently . . . and Why*. Toronto: Free Press, 2003; Iyer, Pico. "Lhasa Vegas." *The Globe and Mail*, April 3, 2004, T1.

66. Nisbett, op. cit.

67. Brown, Ian, "Silk Cut." *The Globe and Mail*, October 23, 2004, L1.

68. Wong, Jan. "Will China join the culture club, or wield it?" *The Globe and Mail*, October 23, 2004, A3, A15.

69. Saunders, Doug. "All the world's a screen." *The Globe and Mail*, Oct. 17, 2000, A13.

70. Wong, op. cit.

71. Mehta, Suketu. "Bollywood Confidential." *The New York Times Magazine*, Nov. 14, 2004, Section 6, p. 60.

72. Hofstede, op. cit.; Saul, John Ralston. "The Collapse of Globalism: and the rebirth of nationalism." *Harper's Magazine*, March, 2004, online at www.findarticles.com/p/articles/mi_m1111/is_1846_308/ai_n6133966 retrieved Apr. 28, 2005.

73. Hofstede, op. cit., p. 12.

74. Teevan & Hewitt, op. cit.

75. Saul, op. cit.
76. Cited in Conversi, Daniele, ed., *Ethnonationalism in the Contemporary World: Walker Connor and the Study of Nationalism.* London: Routledge, 2004.
77. Huntington, Samuel P. "The Clash of Civilizations," *Foreign Affairs,* Summer, 1993, vol. 72, no. 3, 22–50; "The West Unique, Not Universal," *Foreign Affairs,* Nov.–Dec. 1996, Vol. 75, Issue 6, 28–47.
78. Goodwin, Jan. *Price of Honor: Muslim Women Lift the Veil of Silence on the Islamic World.* New York: Plume (the Penguin group), revised ed., 2003.
79. Said, Edward W. "Impossible Histories: Why the many Islams cannot be simplified," *Harper's Magazine,* July 2002, 69–74; "The Clash of Ignorance," *The Nation,* October 22, 2001, accessed at http://thenation.com/docprint/mhtml?i=20011022&s-said.
80. Said, op. cit.
81. Gee, Marcus. "Headlong into the future: seeking wealth, power and status." *The Globe and Mail,* October 23, 2004, A3, A8.
82. Salutin, Rick. "Welcome to Canada, Mr. Prez." *The Globe and Mail,* Nov. 26, 2004, A17.
83. Etzioni cited in Nisbett, op. cit.
84. Nisbett, op. cit.
85. Legrain, Philippe. *Cultural Globalization Is not Americanization. The Chronicle of Higher Education,* May 9, 2003, accessed Oct. 21, 2004 at http://chronicle.com/free/v49/i35/35b007001.htm.
86. *On the road,* op. cit.
87. Hall, Stuart. "What is this 'black' in black popular culture?" *Social Justice,* Spring–Summer, 1993, v. 20, n1-2, p. 104
88. Lyotard, Jean-François. *The Postmodern Condition: A Report on Knowledge.* Minneapolis: U. of Minn. Press, 1984
89. Rosenau, Pauline Marie. *Post-modernism and the Social Sciences: Insights, inroads, and intrusions.* Princeton: Princeton University Press, 1992
90. Lyotard, op. cit.
91. Hall, 1993, op. cit.
92. Steuck, Wendy. "Diamond firms fighting a bad rap." *The Globe and Mail,* July 8, B3.
93. Lyotard, Jean-François, op. cit.; Hall, op. cit.
94. Gwyn, Richard. *Nationalism without Walls: The Unbearable Lightness of Being Canadian.* Toronto: McClelland and Stewart, 1995, cited in Bumsted, Jack "Visions of Canada: A Brief History of Writing on the Canadian Character and the Canadian Identity" in *A Passion for Identity: Canadian Studies for the 21st Century,* 4th edition, Taras, David and Beverly Rasporich, eds. Scarborough: Nelson Thomson, 2001.
95. Morton, Desmond, "No magic to finding more soldiers." *The Globe and Mail,* Jan. 20, 2004, p. A17.
96. Teevan & Hewitt, op. cit; Saul, op. cit.
97. Parkin & Mendelsohn, op. cit.

Chapter 2
1. Benedict, Ruth. *Patterns of Culture.* London: Routledge & Kegan Paul Ltd., 1935, p. 2.
2. Ting-Toomey, Stella. *Communicating Across Cultures.* New York: The Guilford Press, 1999, p. 156. The filter metaphor in general is from Ting-Toomey.
3. Kohls, Robert L. *Survival Kit for Overseas Living: For Americans Planning to Live and Work Abroad.* Yarmouth, MA: Intercultural Press, Inc., 2001, pp. 86–87. This section on perception and optical illusions is taken directly from Kohls.
4. Robbins, Stephen P. & Nancy Langton. *Organizational Behaviour: Concepts, Controversies, Applications,* Toronto: Prentice Hall, 2003.
5. "Yes, I'm sure—That's the One!" *Newsletter of the Memory Disorders Project,* Rutgers University, Summer 2003. www.memorylossonline.com/eyewitness.htm; Willing, Richard. "Police lineups encourage wrong picks, experts say," *USA Today,* Nov. 25, 2002. www.usatoday.com/news/nation/200211-25-police-lineups-cover-usat_x.htm, accessed Apr. 27, 2005.
6. Benedict, op. cit.
7. Samovar, Larry A. & Richard E. Porter. *Communication Between Cultures,* fifth edition. Cal.: Wadsworth, 2004, p. 46.
8. *Rashomon,* Akira Kurosawa, 1950.
9. *Control Room,* Noujaim, Jehane, Magnolia Pictures, 2004.
10. Smith, Graeme. "For Japanese, the sun rises on unlikely St. Catherine's, [*sic*]" *The Globe and Mail,* Dec. 12, 2002, p. A3.
11. *Webster's New World Dictionary,* Second College Edition, N.Y.: Simon & Shuster, 1984.
12. Hall, Bradford 'J.' *Among Cultures: The Challenge of Communication.* Canada: Thomson Wadsworth, 2005.
13. Ibid, p. 199.
14. *In-depth: China,* CBC News Online. www.cbc.ca/printablestory.jsp, accessed July 30, 2003.
15. Ting-Toomey, 1999.
16. Wood, Michael. *Central America: The Burden of Time,* REMC Legacy Series, 1992.

17. Lederer, William J. & Eugene Burdick. *The Ugly American*. New York: Norton, 1958. (Note: the title of the classic was deliberately ironic. Americans portrayed were well-meaning, but inept and heavy-handed in Asia. The phrase has come to imply something else.)
18. Morley, Jefferson. *Michael Moore, Ugly American*. washingtonpost.com, July 13, 2004.
19. Parkin & Mendelsohn, op. cit.
20. Exercise based on Robert L. Kohls' *Survival Kit for Overseas Living*, 1996.
21. Smilie, Ian. "International Development Consultant," *CBC News*, Jan. 13, 2005 & other sources.
22. Little, Bruce. "Canada's latest report card has disappointing marks." *The Globe and Mail*, Oct. 4, 2003, p. B1.
23. Makin, Kirk. "Racism haunts Canada's first aboriginal appellate judge." *The Globe and Mail*, Nov. 23, 2004, A5.
24. Wright, Ronald. "Modern societies, ancient errors." *The Globe and Mail*, Jan. 15, 2005, D3.
25. Memmi, Albert. *Portrait du colonisé*. France: Gallimard, 1957.
26. hooks, bell. *Madonna: Plantation Mistress of Soul Sister in Black Looks: Race and Representation*, Boston: South End Press, 1992, pp. 157–164.
27. *Webster's*, op. cit.
28. Hall, Bradford 'J', op. cit., p. 198.
29. James, Carl E. & Adrienne Shadd. *Talking about Identity: Encounters in Race, Ethnicity, and Language*. Toronto: Between the Lines, 2001.
30. Ernest Becker, cited in Barna, LaRay M. *Stumbling Blocks in Intercultural Communication* in *Basic Concepts of Intercultural Communication: Selected Readings*, Milton J. Bennett, ed. Yarmouth, Maine: Intercultural Press, 1998, pp. 173–190.
31. Hall, Edward T. *Beyond Culture*. New York: Anchor Books, Doubleday, 1977.
32. Hale, John. *The Civilization of Europe in the Renaissance*. New York: Atheneum, MacMillan Publishing Company, 1994; Barna, op. cit.
33. Ting-Tooney, op. cit.
34. Davy, Paul. "Your Morning Smile." *The Globe and Mail*, March 27, 2004, p. 2.
35. Ting-Toomey, op. cit.
36. Storti, Craig. *Cross-Cultural Dialogues: 74 Brief Encounters with Cultural Differences*. Yarmouth: Intercultural Press, Inc., 1994.
37. Ibid.
38. Ting-Toomey, op. cit.

39. Galanti, Geri-Ann. *Caring for Patients from Different Cultures: Case Studies from American Hospitals*. Penn.: University of Pennsylvania Press, 1997, pp. 2–3.
40. Bennett, op. cit., p.196.
41. Hall, Edward T., op. cit., p.49.
42. Barna, op cit., p. 174.
43. Hall, Edward T., op. cit., pp. 49, 63.
44. Barna, op. cit.
45. Bennett, op. cit.
46. Barna, op. cit.
47. Ibid., p. 176.
48. Brislin, Richard. *Understanding Culture's Influence on Behavior*, 2nd ed. Fort Worth: Harcourt, 2000.
49. Hall, Bradford 'J', op. cit., p. 205.
50. Galloway, Gloria. "Ottawa rejects call to halt gay marriage." *The Globe and Mail*, Jan. 20, 2005, A1.
51. Clemenger, Bruce. "There is no evangelical conspiracy." *The Globe and Mail*, April 24, 2004, A25.
52. Memmi, op. cit.
53. Benedict, op. cit.
54. Saunders, Doug. "Libya offers migrants only disappointment." *The Globe and Mail*, Dec. 15, 2004, A21.
55. Wells, Spencer. *Journey of Man*. WNED. March 9, 2004, 8–11.
56. Ibid.
57. Kamiya, Gary. "Cablinasian like me: Tiger Woods' rejection of orthodox racial classifications point the way to a future where race will no longer define us," Salon, retrieved at www.salon.com/april97/tiger970430.html.
58. Adapted from "The Peopling of Canada, 1891–1921, 1946–1976," from *A Province of Immigrants: The Face of Prejudice & "The Ethnic Pecking Order."* The Applied History Research Group, The University of Calgary, © 1997, accessed at www.ucalgary.ca/applied_history/tutor/calgary/race.html May 9, 2005.
59. Troper, Harold. "Immigrant City: The Making of Modern Toronto," *A Passion for Identity: Canadian Studies for the 21st Century*, David Taras & Beverly Rasporich, eds., Toronto: Nelson Thomson, 2001, pp. 335–354.
60. Parkin, Andrew & Matthew Mendelsohn. *A New Canada: An Identity Shaped by Diversity*, The CRIC Papers (Canadian Opinion Research Archive). Montreal: Centre for Research and Information on Canada, Oct. 2003.

61. "Who was Neil Stonechild?" *CBC News Indepth, Aboriginal Canadians,* Oct. 26, 2004 www.cbc.ca/news/bacground/stonechild.

62. Rankin, Jim, Jennifer Quinn, Michelle Shephard, John Duncanson & Scott Simmie. "Singled out." *Toronto Star,* Oct. 19, 2002, A1.

63. Dallaire, Romeo, speaking at Conference "Navigating in the New World," hosted by Random House at University of Toronto, Nov. 6, 2004.

64. *Webster's,* op. cit.

65. Peritz, Ingrid. "Jews top hate list, crime analysis shows." *The Globe and Mail,* June 2, 2004, p. A12.

66. Storti, op. cit.

67. Ting-Toomey, op. cit.

68. Hall, Edward T., op. cit.

69. Bennett, op. cit., p. 31.

70. Hall, Bradford 'J', op. cit., p. 346.

71. Charles, Brian, Native Education Officer, Georgian College.

72. Kohls, 1996, op. cit.

73. Kohls, 1996, op. cit.; Kohls, 2001, op. cit.

74. Ibid.

75. *Y tu mamá también,* Alfonso Cuarón, 2001.

76. *Monsoon Wedding,* Mira Nair, 2001.

77. Gudykunst, William B., Stella Ting-Toomey, Sandra Sudweeks & Lea Stewart. *Building Bridges: Interpersonal Skills for a Changing World.* Toronto: Houghton Mifflin Co., 1995.

78. Ting-Toomey, op. cit., p. 16.

79. LeBaron, Michelle. *Bridging Cultural Conflicts: A New Approach for a Changing World.* San Francisco: Jossey:Bass, 2003.

80. Robbins and Langton, op. cit.

81. LeBaron, op. cit.

82. Bennett, op. cit.; Robbins and Langton, op. cit.

83. Rutka, Mari. "Should schools keep race stats? CON: Plan discriminates." *Toronto Star,* Nov. 17, 2004, B1.

84. Davis, Bruce. "Should schools keep race stats? PRO: Research needed." *Toronto Star,* Nov. 17, 2004, B1.

85. Kalinowski, Tess. "Muslim students can't skip gay ed." *Toronto Star,* Nov. 17, 2004, A1.

86. Peritz, Ingrid. "Human-rights body urged to take head-scarf stand." *The Globe and Mail,* Nov. 19, 2004, A10.

Time Out for China

1. This portrait is largely compiled from *The Globe and Mail*'s feature report on "China Rising," Oct. 23–30, 2004, including Barber, John. "Instant Modernity," *The Globe and Mail,* Oct. 23, 2004, R1; Barber, John. "Worlds apart," Oct. 23, 2004, M1; Dillon, Paul & Estanislao Oziewicz. "Diaspora form 'bamboo' supply chain," *The Globe and Mail,* Oct. 23, 2004, A16; Gee, Marcus. "Frogs, live sex and dead cats," *The Globe and Mail,* Oct. 23, 2004, R1; Gee, Marcus. "Saving China's endangered environment," *The Globe and Mail,* Oct. 23, 2004, A17; Grange, Michael. "Their tears are payment for a championship," *The Globe and Mail,* Oct. 23, 2004, S1; Mickleburgh, Rod. "Tibet: In the crosshairs and at a crossroads," *The Globe and Mail,* Oct. 23, 2004, A9; Pitts, Gordon. "Decade of revolution," *The Globe and Mail,* Oct. 23, 2004, E1; Pitts, Gordon. "Inco follows the money east," *The Globe and Mail,* Oct. 23, 2004, B2; Ticoll, David. "Is China next superpower? Entirely possible," *The Globe and Mail,* Oct. 28, 2004, B13; York, Geoffrey. "Looking Inward: Behind the boom: A struggle for identity and rumblings of revolt," *The Globe and Mail,* Oct. 23, 2004, A3; York, Geoffrey. "Low wages, cruel bosses, no rights," *The Globe and Mail,* Oct. 23, 2004, A6; York, Geoffrey. "Flexing its military muscle." *The Globe and Mail,* Oct. 23, 2004, A9; Wente, Margaret. "China Rising: all the bright, scary kids," *The Globe and Mail,* Oct. 30, 2004, A21; Wong, Jan. "Influences: Will China join the culture club or wield it?" *The Globe and Mail,* Oct. 23, 2004, A3; Wong, Jan. "In this Beijing family, ties still bind—comfortably," *The Globe and Mail,* Oct. 23, 2004, F3; Wong, Jan. "Dealing with the Dragon," *The Globe and Mail,* Oct. 23, 2004, B3.

Other sources include: CBC, Jan. 20, 21, 2005—two-part series; Hu, Wenshong and Cornelius Grove. *Encountering the Chinese: A Guide for Americans.* Yarmouth, Maine: Intercultural Press, Inc. 1991; Ma, Ringo. "Saying 'yes' for 'no' and 'no' for 'yes': A Chinese Rule." *Journal of Pragmatics* 25 (1996), pp. 257–266; Mcleod, Kagan. "The Arts of the Deal: If you wish to be a grand master of business in China, learn these basic techniques." *Canadian Business,* Nov. 8–21, 2004, tear sheet; Sabath, Ann Marie. *International Business Etiquette: Asia and the Pacific Rim.* N.J.: Career Press, 1999.

2. Young woman cited in Brown, Ian. "Shanghai surprise," *The Globe and Mail,* Oct. 23, 2004, F1.

3. Wong, Jan. *Jan Wong's China.* Toronto: Doubleday Canada, 2000.

4. Brown, 2004, op. cit.

5. Barber, John. "Wenzhou: capitalism unbound," *The Globe and Mail,* Oct. 23, 2004, A4.

6. Wong, 2000, op. cit., p. 287.

7. Wong, Jan. "Shanghai girls just wanna have fun," *The Globe and Mail,* Oct. 23, 2004, F2.

8. Brown, Ian. "Silk Cut." *The Globe and Mail,* Oct. 23, 2004, L1.

9. Wong, Jan. "Restaurant Rock 'n' Roll," *The Globe and Mail,* Oct. 23, 2004, L1.

10. Gee, Marcus. "Looking Outward: Headlong into the future: seeking wealth, power and status," *The Globe and Mail,* Oct. 23, 2004, A3; Wong, 2000, op. cit.

11. Chan, Wing-tsit. "The Orderly Realm of Chinese Sages, Great Religions of the World." National Geographic Society, 1971; Wong, Jan. "This numbers game is crazy for-8s." *The Globe and Mail,* Jan. 22, 2005, M1.

12. Wong, 2005, op. cit.

13. York, Geoffrey. "Nationalist fervour runs amok," *The Globe and Mail,* Oct. 25, 2004, A1.

14. Brown, "Shanghai Surprise," 2004, op. cit.

15. Bruce MacMillan, in conversation, May 14, 2002.

Chapter 3

1. Trompenaars, Fons & Charles Hampden-Turner. *Riding the Waves of Culture,* 2nd ed. New York: McGraw Hill, 1998, p. 20.

2. Benedict, Ruth. *Patterns of Culture.* London: Routledge & Kegan Paul Ltd., 1935; Ting-Toomey, Stella. *Communicating Across Cultures.* New York: The Guilford Press, 1999.

3. Hall, Stuart. "Introduction: Who Needs 'Identity'?" in *Questions of Cultural Identity,* Stuart Hall & Paul du Gay, eds. Thousand Oaks: Sage, 1996, pp. 1–15.

4. Hofstede, Geert. *Culture's Consequences: International Differences in Work-Related Values,* 4th Printing. Beverly Hills: Sage, 1988, pp. 13, 21; *Cultures and Organizations: Software of the Mind: Intercultural Cooperation and its Importance for Survival.* New York: McGraw-Hill, 1997, pp. 4–5.

5. Hofstede, 1997, op. cit., p. 4.

6. Bonvillain, Nancy. *Language, Culture, and Communication: The Meaning of Messages,* fourth edition. New Jersey: Prentice Hall, 2003, p. 2.

7. Teevan, James J. and W.E. Hewitt, eds. *Sociology, A Canadian Focus,* 8th edition, Toronto: Prentice Hall, 2005.

8. Ting-Toomey, 1999.

9. Trompenaars & Hampden-Turner, 1998; Hofstede, 1997.

10. Lee, Dorothy, *Cultural Factors in Dietary Choice, Freedom and Culture,* 2nd printing. Prospect Heights, Ill.: Waveland Press Inc., 1987.

11. Campbell, Murray. "Astérix promoting McBurgers in France." *The Globe and Mail,* Jan. 24, 2002, p. A3.

12. Teevan & Hewitt, 2005.

13. Skidmore, Thomas E. & Peter H. Smith, *Modern Latin America,* 3rd ed. New York: Oxford University Press, 1992.

14. Peters, James. *The Arab World Handbook: Arabian Peninsula Edition.* London: Stacey International, 2000.

15. Hall, Bradford 'J.' *Among Cultures: The Challenge of Communication.* Canada: Thomson Wadsworth, 2005.

16. Cohen, David, ed. *The Circle of Life: rituals from the human family album.* San Francisco: HarperSanFrancisco, 1991.

17. Ibid.

18. Ibid.

19. Taibossigai, Lyndsay. *Ojibwe Culture,* paper submitted Dec. 14, 2004.

20. Photo © Steven S. Miric/SuperStock.

21. Cohen, op. cit.

22. Harvey, John. "The traditions of mourning." *Toronto Star,* Jan. 21, 2005, E7.

23. Cohen, op. cit.

24. Hume, Mark. "B.C. natives fear tsunami, seek to move." *The Globe and Mail,* Jan. 26, 2005, A1.

25. Scholes, Robert. *Structuralism in Literature,* 9th printing. New Haven: Yale University, 1979, pp. 60–74 on Propp and Lévi-Strauss.

26. Hall, Bradford 'J.' 2005, op. cit., p. 75.

27. Bruce-Mitford, Miranda. *Signs and Symbols: Thousands of Signs and Symbols from Around the World.* New York: DK Publishing, Inc., 1996.

28. Geertz, Clifford. *The Interpretation of Cultures.* New York: Basic Books, 1973, pp. 4–5.

29. Bruce-Mitford, op. cit., 1996, p. 44.

30. Cohen, op. cit.

31. Bruce-Mitford, op. cit., pp. 8–11.

32. Ibid., p. 11.

33. Mickleburgh, Rod. "Stanley Cup bumped off Air Canada flight," *The Globe and Mail,* August 24, 2004, p. A1.

34. Hofstede, 1997, op. cit.

35. Bruce-Mitford, op. cit.

36. Boxer, Sarah. "Move afoot to detoxify ancient, once-benign swastika symbol." *The New York Times,* July 29, 2000. (http://seattlepi.nwsource.com/national/swas29.shtml),

accessed August 31, 2004; Renard, John. *The Handy Religion Answer Book.* Detroit: Visible Ink Press, 2002.

37. Wong, Jan. "This numbers game is crazy-for 8s." *The Globe and Mail,* Jan. 22, 2005, M1.

38. Blumer, Herbert. *Symbolic Interactionism: Perspective and Method.* Englewood Cliffs, NJ: Prentice-Hall, 1969.

39. Trompenaars & Hampden-Turner, op. cit., p. 6.

40. Teevan & Hewitt, op. cit.

41. Galanti, Geri-Ann. *Caring for Patients from Different Cultures: Case Studies from American Hospitals.* Penn.: University of Pennsylvania Press, 1997.

42. Kluckhohn, Florence Rockwood & Fred T. Strodtbeck. *Variations in Value Orientations.* Evanston, Illinois: Row, Peterson, and Company, 1961.

43. Trompenaars & Hampden-Turner, op. cit.

44. Hofstede, 1997, op. cit., pp. 8 & 17.

45. Singh, Rajesh Rajan. "Observations of Canadian Culture in Vancouver," 3rd year paper. Jan. 11, 2005.

46. Bues, Hans-Christian, in conversation, August 2004.

47. Hofstede, 1997, op. cit.

48. Keegan, Warren J. & F.H. Rolf Seringhaus. *Global Marketing Management,* 2nd Canadian edition. Scarborough: Prentice-Hall Canada, 1999.

49. Gudykunst, William B., Stella Ting-Toomey, Sandra Sudweeks & Lea Stewart. *Building Bridges: Interpersonal Skills for a Changing World.* Toronto: Houghton Mifflin Co., 1995.

50. Trompenaars & Hampden-Turner, op. cit.

51. Teevan & Hewitt, op. cit.

52. *Alive,* Frank Marshall, 1993.

53. Kluckhohn & Strodtbeck, op. cit.; Trompenaars & Hampden-Turner, op. cit.; Teevan & Hewitt, op. cit.

54. Murdock, George Peter. "The Common Denominator of Cultures." In *The Science of Man in the World Crisis.* Ralph Linton, ed. New York: Columbia University Press, 1945, p. 123.

55. Siemon-Netto, Uwe. "Hunger for God in the genes?" Oct. 20, 2004, www.wpherald.com, accessed Oct. 21, 2004.

56. Hofstede, 1997, op. cit., p. 5.

57. Teeven & Hewitt, op. cit.

58. Ibid.

59. Ibid.

60. *Webster's New World Dictionary,* Second College Edition, N.Y.: Simon & Shuster, 1984.

61. Summarized from: Kluckhohn, & Strodtbeck, op. cit.; Trompenaars & Hampden-Turner, op. cit., p. 24.

62. Dillon, Sam. "Smaller Families Bring Big Change in Mexico." *The New York Times,* June 8, 1999, reprinted in Goodwin, Paul Jr. *Latin America,* 9th edition, Guilford: Dushkin/McGraw-Hill, 2000, pp. 165–166; Galloway, Gloria. "Immigrant women opting for fewer children." *The Globe and Mail,* Dec. 23, 2003, A7.

63. Byrne, Eugene, cited in Kesterton, Michael. "Social Studies." *The Globe and Mail,* June 2, 2004, A22.

64. Benedict, op. cit.

65. Hall, Stuart. "Introduction: Who Needs 'Identity'?" in *Questions of Cultural Identity,* Hall, Stuart & Paul du Gay, eds., Thousand Oaks: Sage, 1996, pp. 1–15.

66. Ibid.

67. Bédard, Guy. "Québécitude: An Ambiguous Identity," in James, Carl E. & Adrienne Shadd, eds., *Talking about Identity: Encounters in Race, Ethnicity, and Language.* Toronto: Between the Lines, 2001, p. 28.

68. Hall, Stuart, op. cit.

69. Lee, Dorothy. *Cultural Factors in Dietary Choice, Freedom and Culture,* 2nd printing. Prospect Heights, Ill.: Waveland Press Inc., 1987, pp. 141–43.

70. Jordan, Terry G. & Lester Rowntree. *The Human Mosaic: A Thematic Introduction to Cultural Geography,* 4th ed. New York: Harper and Row, 1986.

71. Ibid.

72. Keegan & Seringhaus, op. cit.; Goodwin, 2000, op. cit.

73. Norris, Robert E. *World Regional Geography.* St. Paul, MN: West Publishing Company, 1990; Keegan & Seringhaus, op. cit.

74. Adapted from Norris, op. cit., p. 124.

75. Jordan & Rowntree, op. cit., p. 19.

76. Based on Donald W. Klopf's "Word Meanings Across Cultures," pp. 127, 128, in *Experiential Activities for Intercultural Learning,* Vol. 1, H. Ned Seelye, ed. Yarmouth: Intercultural Press, Inc., 1996.

77. Harvey, op. cit.

Chapter 4

1. Francis, Daniel. *National Dreams: Myth, Memory, and Canadian History.* Vancouver, BC: Arsenal Pulp Press, 1997.

2. *Great Canadian Quotes.* www.Canada4life.ca/quotes.php.

3. Hofstede, Geert. *Culture's Consequences: International Differences in Work-Related Values,* 4th Printing. Beverly Hills: Sage, 1988.

4. Troper, Harold. "Immigrant City: The Making of Modern Toronto," *A Passion for Identity: Canadian Studies for the 21st Century,* David Taras & Beverly Rasporich, eds., Toronto: Nelson Thomson, 2001.

5. Newman, Peter C. "The Secrets of My Success." *Report on Business,* November 2004, pp. 74–83.

6. Grabb, Edward & James Curtis cited in Ibbitson, John. "When two old friends kick back." *The Globe and Mail,* Nov. 26, 2004, A4.

7. Ibid.

8. Laghi, Brian, "Poll underlines differences between U.S., Canada." *The Globe and Mail,* Nov. 30, 2004, p. A6.

9. Hudson, Nicholas. "Hardly enlightening." *The Globe and Mail,* Jan. 11, 2003, p. A20; Walsh, Gerald. *A Global History, 1870 to the Present.* Toronto: McClelland and Stewart, 1975.

10. Walsh, op. cit.

11. Linder, Robert. "American Civil Religion and the New Religious Right." *Preservings,* No. 24, Dec. 2004, pp. 41–47.

12. Ibid.

13. Bush, George. Speech to the United Nations on Sept. 21, 2004. CBC *Newsworld.*

14. Freeman, Alan. "The freedom doctrine." *The Globe and Mail,* Jan. 21, 2005, A1.

15. Abrams, Jim. "U.S. bill would keep God in pledge." *The Globe and Mail,* Sept. 24, 2004, p. A14.

16. Galt, Virginia. "Canadians take dour view on jobs, bosses, angels." *The Globe and Mail,* Oct. 18, 2004, p. B1.

17. Shorto, Russell, "With God at Our Desks." *The New York Times Magazine,* Oct. 31, 2004, pp. 42–69; Solomon, Deborah. "The Science of Second-Guessing, Questions for Stephen Hawking." *The New York Times Magazine,* Dec. 12, 2004, Section 4, p. 31.

18. Shorto, op. cit.

19. Zernike, Kate. "Does Christmas Need to be Saved?" *The New York Times,* Dec. 19, 2004, p. 4-1.

20. Bumsted, Jack. "Visions of Canada: A Brief History of Writing on the Canadian Character and the Canadian Identity," in *A Passion for Identity: Canadian Studies for the 21st Century,* 4th ed., Taras, David & Beverly Rasporich, eds. Canada: Nelson Thomson, 2001.

21. MacArthur, John. "In God they trust" *The Globe and Mail,* Nov. 4, 2004, A27.

22. Linder, Robert. "American Civil Religion and the New Religious Right." *Preservings,* No. 24, December, 2004, pp. 41–47, p. 42.

23. Simpson, Jeffrey. "The South rises again, making Bush a winner." *The Globe and Mail,* Nov. 4, 2004, A27.

24. In Adams, Michael. *Fire and Ice: The United States, Canada and the Myth of Converging Values.* Toronto: Penguin Canada, 2003, p. 18.

25. Voronov, Maxim and Jefferson Singer. "The Myth of Individualism-Collectivism: A Critical Review." *The Journal of Social Psychology,* 2002, 142(4), pp. 461–480; Adams, op. cit.

26. Adams, op. cit.; Linder, op. cit.

27. Linder, op. cit.

28. *Fahrenheit 9/11,* Moore, Michael, 2004.

29. Adams, op. cit., p. 41.

30. Nesbitt, op. cit.; Samovar, Larry A. and Richard E. Porter. *Communication Between Cultures,* fifth edition. Cal.: Wadsworth, 2004.

31. Samovar & Porter, op. cit.

32. Galt, op. cit.

33. Bennett, Milton J. *Overcoming the Golden Rule in Basic Concepts of Intercultural Communication: Selected Readings,* Milton J. Bennett, ed. Yarmouth, Maine: Intercultural Press, 1998, pp. 191–214.

34. *American FactFinder,* U.S. Census Bureau, http://factfinder.census.gov/home, accessed June 14, 2005.

35. Huntington, Samuel. Interview with Steve Paikin on *Diplomatic Immunity,* TVO, aired Jan. 21, 2005 discussing his latest book: *Who are We? Challenges to America's National Identity.* New York: Simon and Schuster, 2004.

36. Ibid.

37. Fukuyama, Francis. *Identity crisis: Why we shouldn't worry about Mexican immigration.* The South Beach Diet on-line, posted June 4, 2004, accessed Jan. 23, 2005.

38. Malouf, David. *Person-2-Person,* TVO, 2004.

39. "Ethnic Identity Reinforces Attachment to Canada," Angus Reid, 1998 www.pch.gc.ca/progs/multi/evidence/series1_e.cfm?nav=2.

40. Ethnic Diversity Survey, www.statcan.ca/Daily/English/030929/d0300920a.htmm, Sept. 29, 2003.

41. Lipset, Seymour Martin. *Continental Divide: The Values and Institutions of the United States and Canada.* New York: Routledge, 1990;

Revolution and Counterrevolution: The United States and Canada in a Passion for Identity: An Introduction to Canadian Studies, Mandel, Eli & David Taras, eds. Agincourt: Methuen Publications, 1987, pp. 68–81.

42. Ramsay Cook in *Oh Canada, eh?* (1986) NFB documentary in which U.S. writer Tom Wolfe explores Canada's self-perceptions and attitudes.

43. Adams, op. cit.

44. Ibid., p. 103.

45. Adams, Michael. *Sex in the Snow: Canadian Social Values at the End of the Millennium.* Toronto: Viking, 1997.

46. Gregg, Allan, R. "Bumpy Ride." *Maclean's,* December 29, 2003, pp. 29–30.

47. Adams, Michael. Interview, *CBC News,* Dec, 1, 2004.

48. Axworthy, Lloyd at the "Navigating in the New World" Conference at the University of Toronto, Nov. 6, 2004.

49. In *Oh Canada, eh?,* 1986.

50. Ibid.

51. Lipset, 1990, op. cit.

52. Adams, 2003, op. cit.

53. Adams, 2004, op. cit.

54. Adams, 1997, op. cit.; Lipset, 1990, op. cit.

55. Berton in *Oh Canada, eh?* op. cit.; Adams, 1997, op. cit.

56. Newman in *Oh Canada, eh?* op. cit.

57. "Looking forward, looking back," Highlights from the Royal Commission on Aboriginal Peoples, 1997, available at www.ainc-inac.gc.ca.ch/rcap/rpt/lk_e.html.

58. *Oh Canada, eh?* op. cit.

59. Ibid.

60. Adams, 2003, op. cit.

61. *Great Canadian Quotes.* Canada4life.ca/quotes.php.

62. Ibid.

63. Adams, 1997, op. cit.

64. "Get Used To It: The Net Generation Knows More than Its Parents." *Financial Post* (*National Post*), Feb. 8, 2000, p. C10.

65. Morrison, Terri, Wayne A. Conaway & George A. Borden. *Kiss, Bow, or Shake Hands: How to Do Business in Sixty Countries.* Holbrook, Mass.: Adams Media Corporation, 1994.

66. Statistics Canada.

67. Bailey, Patrica. "Why Canuck TV sucks. . . . and Quebec shows thrive." *Winnipeg Free Press,* July 6, 2003, online, www.friends.ca/News/Friends_News/archives/articles07060302.asp; Yakabuski, Konrad. "Made in Quebec and cleaning up at the box office." *The Globe and Mail,* July 9, 2005, R8.

68. Anderssen, Erin & Anne McIlroy. "Quebec distinct in nursery too, poll finds." *The Globe and Mail,* Apr. 10, 2004, A1.

69. Smith, Graeme & Ingrid Peritz. "A runner's flash sparks cultural clash." *The Globe and Mail,* Aug. 24, 2001, A1.

70. Parkin & Mendelsohn, op. cit.

71. Cited in Boucher, Christian, *Canada–US Values: Distinct, Inevitably Carbon Copy, or Narcissism of Small Differences?* http://policyresearch.gc/page.asp?pagenm=v7n1_art_08.

72. *What border? The Americanization of Canada,* National Film Board, Part 1, 1997.

73. Ibid.

74. Welsh, Jennifer, *The Globe and Mail,* Nov. 12, 2004, p. A18.

75. Adams, 2003, op. cit.

76. Gregg, op. cit.

77. Adams, 1997, op. cit.

78. Adams, 2003, op. cit.; "Here, father doesn't know best." *The Globe and Mail,* July 4, 2001, p. A21.

79. Adams, 2001, op. cit.

80. Gillis, Charlie, "Just Say Yes." *Maclean's,* December 29, 2003, pp. 32–36.

81. Laghi, op. cit.

82. Newman, Peter C. 2005 interview with Steve Paikin, TVO, *Studio 2.*

83. Simpson, Jeffrey. "The South rises again, making Bush a winner." *The Globe and Mail,* Nov. 4, 2004, p. A27.

84. Robert Wolfe cited in Gillis, op. cit.

85. Den Tandt, Michael. "Cross-border amity eroding: poll." *The Globe and Mail,* May 9, 2005, A1.

86. Ibid.

87. Gregg, op. cit.

88. Walton, Dawn. "Stampede 101 no joke, U of C says." *The Globe and Mail,* July 6, 2004, A5.

89. Hurdle, Jon. "Evolution's dominance challenged in court." The Globe and Mail, Sept. 27, 2005, A13.

Time Out for Latin America

1. Goodwin, Paul Jr. *Latin America,* 9th edition, Guilford: Dushkin/McGraw-Hill, 2000.

2. Keegan, Warren J. & Mark C. Green. *Principles of Global Marketing.* New Jersey: Prentice Hall, 1997, p. 108.

3. Sabath, Ann Marie. *International Business Etiquette: Latin America.* N.J.: Career Press, 2000.

Chapter 5

1. Kipling, Rudyard. "The Ballad of East and West," from *the complete verse*. London: Kyle Cathie Limited, 1990, pp. 187–89.
2. Skidmore, Thomas E. & Peter H. Smith. *Modern Latin America*, 3rd edition. New York: Oxford University Press, 1992.
3. Hofstede, Geert. *Cultures and Organizations: Software of the Mind*. Toronto: McGraw-Hill, 1997.
4. Nesbitt, op. cit.
5. Ayers, Lou. *Altars of the World: The Eastern and Western Religions*. New York: Wellspring Media Inc., 2003.
6. Cited in Chan, Wing-tsit, "The Orderly Realm of Chinese Sages, Great Religions of the World." National Geographic Society, 1971, p. 128.
7. Hofstede, op. cit.
8. Nesbitt, op. cit.
9. Wong, Jan. *Jan Wong's China*. Toronto: Doubleday Canada, 2000.
10. Tung cited in Robbins, Stephen P. & Nancy Langton. *Organizational Behaviour: Concepts, Controversies, Applications*, Toronto: Prentice Hall, 2003.
11. Nesbitt, op. cit.
12. Condon, John C. *With Respect to the Japanese: A Guide for Americans*. Yarmouth, Maine: Intercultural Press, 1984.
13. Hofstede, op. cit.
14. Nesbitt, op. cit.; Hofstede, op. cit.
15. Hofstede, op. cit.
16. Nesbitt, op. cit.
17. Hofstede, op. cit.
18. Nesbitt, op. cit.
19. Hall, Edward T. *The Silent Language*. New York: Fawcett World Library, 1959.
20. Nesbitt, op. cit.
21. Trompenaars, Fons & Charles Hampden-Turner. *Riding the Waves of Culture*, 2nd ed. New York: McGraw Hill, 1998, p. 20.
22. Ibid.
23. Hall, Edward T., op. cit., p. 11.
24. Ibid.
25. Crenson, M. "Nobel Physics Prize Awarded." *The Globe and Mail*, Oct. 6, 2004, A2.
26. Hall, Edward T., op. cit., p. 86.
27. Ibid., p. 91.
28. Keegan, Warren J. & Mark C. Green. *Principles of Global Marketing*. New Jersey: Prentice Hall, 1997.
29. Hall, Edward T., op. cit.
30. Morrison, Terri, Wayne A. Conaway & George A. Borden. *Kiss, Bow, or Shake Hands: How to Do Business in Sixty Countries*. Holbrook, Mass.: Adams Media Corporation, 1994.
31. Hall, Edward T., op. cit.
32. Ibid.
33. Morrison et al., op. cit.
34. Hills, Michael D. "Kluckhohn and Strodtbeck's Values Orientation Theory," 2002, www.ac.wwu.edu/~culture/Hills.htm, accessed January 14, 2003.
35. Kluckhohn, Florence Rockwood & Fred T. Strodtbeck. *Variations in Value Orientations*. Evanston, Illinois: Row, Peterson, and Company, 1961.
36. Theroux, Paul. *Riding the Iron Rooster*. Cape Cod: Ivy Books, 1988, p. 79.
37. Samovar, Larry A. & Richard E. Porter. *Communication Between Cultures*, fifth edition. Cal.: Wadsworth, 2004.
38. Condon, op. cit., p. 58.
39. Goodwin, Paul B. Jr. *Global Studies: Latin America*, 10th ed. Iowa: McGraw-Hill/Dushkin, 2003.
40. *Bukra, Ma'alesh, and Insha'allah*, http://courses.liblodu.edu/engl/jbing/bukra.htm.
41. Samovar & Porter, op. cit.
42. Kohls, Robert L. *Survival Kit for Overseas Living*. Yarmouth, MA: Intercultural Press, Inc., 1996.
43. Nydell, Margaret. *Understanding Arabs: A Guide for Westerners*. Yarmouth: Intercultural Press, 1987; Peters, James. *The Arab World Handbook: Arabian Peninsula Edition*. London: Stacey International, 2000.
44. Goodwin, Paul, op. cit.
45. Ibid.
46. Samovar & Porter, op. cit.
47. Kluckhohn & Strodtbeck, op. cit., p. 12.
48. Chan, Wing-tsit, op. cit., p. 124.
49. Hofstede, Geert. *Culture's Consequences: International Differences in Work-Related Values*, 4th Printing. Beverly Hills: Sage, 1988, p. 25; Kluckhohn and Strodtbeck, op. cit., pp. 92–94.
50. Hofstede, 1997, op. cit.
51. Ibid.
52. Voronov, Maxim and Jefferson Singer. "The Myth of Individualism-Collectivism: A Critical Review." *The Journal of Social Psychology*, 2002, 142(4), pp. 461–480.
53. McSweeney, Brendan. "Hofstede's Model of National Cultural Differences and Their Consequences: A triumph of faith—A failure of analysis" (abridged), www.geert-hofstede.international.business.center.com/mcsweeney.shtml, accessed Oct. 30, 2004.

54. Rotondo Fernandez, Denise, Dawn S. Carlson, Lee P. Stepina, & Joel Nicholson. "Hofstede's Country Classification 25 Years Later," *Journal of Social Psychology,* 137(1), 1997, pp. 43–54.
55. Hofstede, 1997, op. cit., p. 107.
56. Trompenaars, Fons & Charles Hampden-Turner. *Building Cross-Cultural Competence.* New Haven and London: Yale University Press, 2000, p. 2.
57. Trompenaars & Hampden-Turner, 1998, op. cit., p. 27.
58. Trompenaars & Hampden-Turner, 2000, op. cit., p. 3.
59. Trompenaars, Fons. *Did the Pedestrian Die?* Oxford: U.K.: Capstone Publishing Ltd., 2003, p. 1.
60. Ibid.
61. Ibid., p. 3.
62. Trompenaars & Hampden-Turner, 2000, op. cit.
63. Ibid.
64. Ibid., p. 4.
65. Ibid., p. 73.
66. Ibid., p. 123.
67. Ibid.
68. Ibid., p. 145.
69. Ibid., p. 192.
70. Ibid., pp. 234–35.
71. Ibid., p. 238.
72. Trompenaars & Hampden-Turner, 1998, op. cit., p. 126.
73. Ibid., p. 296.
74. Morrison et al., op. cit.
75. Ibid., p. xii.
76. Trompenaars & Hampden-Turner, 2000, op. cit., p. 143.

Chapter 6

1. *Webster's New World Dictionary,* Second College Edition, N.Y.: Simon & Shuster, 1984.
2. Wood, Michael. *Central America, Legacy.* New York: Ambrose Video Publishing, 1991.
3. Epp, Marlene. *Women without Men: Mennonite Refugees of the Second World War.* Toronto: University of Toronto Press, 2002, p. 6.
4. Renard, John. *The Handy Religion Answer Book.* Detroit: Visible Ink Press, 2002.
5. Pollock, Robert. *The Everything World's Religions Book.* Mass.: Adams Media Corporation, 2002.
6. Martel, Yann. *Life of Pi.* Toronto: Vintage Canada, 2001, p. 53.
7. Chakravarty, Amiya. *Quest for the universal one. Great Religions of the World.* National Geographic Society, 1971, p. 53.
8. Martel, op. cit., p. 53.
9. Chakravarty, op. cit., p. 34.
10. Martel, op. cit., p. 53.
11. Ayers, Lou. *Altars of the World: The Eastern and Western Religions.* New York: Wellspring Media Inc., 2003.
12. Ibid.
13. Hemenway, Priya. *Hindu Gods: The Spirit of the Divine.* San Francisco: Chronicle Books, 2003.
14. Ayers, op. cit.
15. Bumiller, Elizabeth. *May You be the Mother of a Hundred Sons: A Journey Among the Women of India.* New Delhi: Penguin Books India (P), 1991.
16. Armstrong, Sally. "The untouchables." *Chatelaine,* July 2004, pp. 144–157.
17. Renard, op. cit.
18. Pollock, op. cit.
19. www.buddhaweb.org.
20. Ayers, op. cit.
21. Kipling, Rudyard. *Kim.* London: Penguin Classics, 2000.
22. Ayers, op. cit.
23. Renard, op. cit.
24. Ibid., pp. 342, 343.
25. Pollock, op. cit., p. 159.
26. Ayers, op. cit.
27. Ibid.
28. Ibid.
29. Ibid.
30. Pollock, op. cit.
31. Cited in ibid., p. 1.
32. Hofstede, Geert. *Cultures and Organizations: Software of the Mind.* Toronto: McGraw-Hill, 1997.
33. Pradhan, cited in Hofstede, op. cit., p. 159.
34. Pollock, op. cit.
35. *Holy Bible,* authorized King James Version. New York: The World Publishing Company, n.d.—all biblical references are from this version.
36. Pollock, op. cit.
37. Renard, op. cit., p. 77.
38. Pollock, op. cit.
39. Ibid.
40. Rasminsky, Anne. "Kosher knickers?" *The Globe and Mail,* Sept. 11, 2004, p. L8.
41. Harpur, Tom. *Big Ideas,* TVO, May 23, 2004.
42. From Ayers, op. cit.; Renard, op. cit.; Pollock, op. cit.
43. Pollock, op. cit., p. 11; young, john. *Teach Yourself: Christianity,* 2nd edition. Chicago: McGraw-Hill Ryerson, 2003, p. 121.
44. Brown, Dan. *The Da Vinci Code.* New York: Doubleday, 2003.

45. Renard, op. cit.; Pollock, op. cit.
46. young, op. cit., p. 121.
47. Ibid.
48. Trompenaars, Fons & Charles Hampden-Turner. *Riding the Waves of Culture: Understanding Cultural Diversity in Global Business,* 2nd ed. N.Y.: McGraw-Hill, 1998.
49. Renard, op. cit., p. 87.
50. Ibid.
51. Peters, James. *The Arab World Handbook: Arabian Peninsula Edition.* London: Stacey International, 2000.
52. Ragheida Hamade, Lebanese Canadian, second year nursing student, York University, March 28, 2005.
53. Lila, Muhammad Athar. "Let's not shake on it." *The Globe and Mail,* Mar. 2, 2005, A18.
54. Renard, op. cit.
55. Ibid.
56. www.saudinf.com/main/a832htm.
57. Tawney, R.H. *Religions and the Rise of Capitalism,* 12th printing. New York: Mentor, 1963.
58. Teevan, James J. and W.E. Hewitt, eds. *Sociology, A Canadian Focus,* 8th edition, Toronto: Prentice Hall, 2005.
59. Paz, Octavio. *The Labyrinth of Solitude.* New York: Grove Press, 1985.
60. Skidmore, Thomas E. & Peter H. Smith, *Modern Latin America,* 3rd ed. New York: Oxford University Press, 1992.
61. France, Miranda. *Bad Times in Buenos Aires.* G.B.: Phoenix, 1999.
62. Klein, Naomi & Avi Lewis, *The Take,* NFB, 2004; Rohter, Larry. "Economic Rally for Argentines Defies Forecasts." *New York Times,* Dec. 26, 2004, p. 1.
63. Ustinov, Peter. *My Russia.* Toronto: Little, Brown and Company, 1983; Tolstoy, Leo. *Childhood, Boyhood, Youth.* Middlesex: Penguin Classics, 1972 & *Anna Karenin.* Middlesex: Penguin Classics, 1973; Turgenev, Ivan. *On the Eve.* Middlesex: Penguin Classics, 1950; Rutherfurd, Edward. *Russka.* New York: Ballantine Books, 1991.
64. Zeldin, Theodore. *The French.* N.Y.: Kodansha Amer Inc., 1996.
65. Skidmore & Smith, op. cit.
66. Trompenaars, Fons. *Did the Pedestrian Die?* Oxford: U.K.: Capstone Publishing Ltd., 2003.

Time Out for the Arab World

1. Nydell, Margaret. *Understanding Arabs: A Guide for Westerners.* Yarmouth: Intercultural Press, 1987; Peters, James. *The Arab World Handbook: Arabian Peninsula Edition.* London: Stacey International, 2000.
2. Nydell, op. cit.
3. Goodwin, Jan. *Price of Honor: Muslim Women Lift the Veil of Silence on the Islamic World.* New York: Plume (the Penguin group), revised ed., 2003.
4. Nydell, op. cit.
5. Ibid.
6. Peters, op. cit.
7. Nydell, op. cit.
8. Ibid.

Chapter 7

1. Wood, Julia. *Gendered Lives: Communication, Gender and Culture,* second edition. California: Wadsworth Publishing, 1997, p. 36.
2. Ibid.
3. Ibid.
4. Hymes, Dell. *Foundations of Sociolinguistics: An Ethnographic Approach.* Penn.: Univ. of Pennsylvania Press, 1974, pp. 44–56; "Models of the Interaction of Language and Social Life" in *Directions in Sociolinguistics: The Ethnography of Communication,* Gumperz, J.J. and D. Hymes, eds. New York: Holt, Rinehart and Winston, 1972, pp. 35–71.
5. Wood, op. cit., p. 36.
6. Ibid.
7. See, for example, Barthes, Roland, "Eléments de sémiologie," *Communications,* 4, 1964, pp. 91–135.
8. Hall, Edward T. *The Silent Language.* New York: Fawcett World Library, 1959, p. 165.
9. Based on Hawkes, Terence. *Structuralism and Semiotics.* Berkeley and Los Angeles: University of California Press, 1977, p. 83; Jaworski, Adam & Nikolas Coupland, eds. *The Discourse Reader.* London and New York: Routledge, 1999. (Author added the feedback arrow.)
10. Jacobson cited in Hawkes, op. cit., 1977, p. 83.
11. Hall, 1959, op. cit.
12. Guffey, Mary Ellen, Kathleen Rhodes & Patricia Rogin. *Business Communication: Process and Product.* Toronto: ITP Nelson, 1999; Dodd, Carley H. *Dynamics of Intercultural Communication,* 5th edition. Boston: McGraw Hill, 1998.
13. Hall, Edward T. *Beyond Culture.* New York: Anchor Books, Doubleday, 1977, p. 74.
14. Bonvillain, Nancy. *Language, Culture, and Communication: The Meaning of Messages,* 4th edition. New Jersey: Prentice Hall, 2003, p. 42.

15. Ibid.; Wardhaugh, Ronald. *An Introduction to Sociolinguistics,* 4th edition. Mass.: Blackwell Publishers Inc., 2002.
16. Bonvillain, op. cit.
17. Wood, op. cit., p. 174.
18. Wardhaugh, op. cit.
19. Bonvillain, op. cit.
20. Condon, John C. *With Respect to the Japanese: A Guide for Americans.* Yarmouth, Maine: Intercultural Press, 1984.
21. Peters, James. *The Arab World Handbook: Arabian Peninsula Edition.* London: Stacey International, 2000.
22. Frank Darnell cited in Miller, Barbara D., Penny Van Esterik & John Van Esterik, *Cultural Anthropology,* Canadian edition. Toronto: Pearson, 2001, p. 350.
23. Brian Charles, Native Education Liaison Officer, Georgian College.
24. Tannen, Deborah. *You Just Don't Understand: Women and Men in Conversation.* New York: Ballantine Books, 1990.
25. Barzini, Luigi. *The Italians.* London: Penguin Books, 1991; Zelden, op. cit.; Manya Chadwick; Pierre Mineau; Lauro Palomba; Rosanna Difanfilo.
26. Samovar, Larry A. & Richard E. Porter. *Communication Between Cultures,* 5th edition. Cal.: Wadsworth, 2004.
27. Condon, op. cit.
28. Samovar & Porter, op. cit., pp. 51–52.
29. "Communication," *Japan Cultural Profile,* http://cp.settlement.org/english/japan/index/html.
30. Axtell, Roger, ed. *Do's and Taboos Around the World,* 3rd ed. New York: The Parker Pen Company, 1993.
31. Hall, 1977, op. cit.
32. Ibid., p. 19
33. Hall, 1959, op. cit.
34. Hall, 1977, op. cit.
35. Ibid., p. 17.
36. English, Kathy. "To ease morning mayhem." *The Globe and Mail,* Aug 28, 2004, F6.
37. Hall, 1977, op. cit., p. 18.
38. Ibid., p. 22.
39. Hall, Edward T. *The Hidden Dimension.* Garden City, New York: Doubleday, 1966.
40. According to conversation with Nisha Mathson & Genevieve Marian, students from New Delhi, April 17, 2001.
41. Peters, op. cit.
42. Friedman, Kenneth. "Learning the Arabs' Silent Language: Edward T. Hall interviewed by Kenneth Friedman." *Psychology Today,* August, 1979, pp. 45–54.
43. Morrison et al., op. cit.
44. Hall, 1959, 1966, op. cit.
45. Hall, 1959, op. cit.
46. Hall, 1966, op. cit.
47. Gray, Jeff. "Annexing an ancient philosophy." *The Globe and Mail,* Jan. 10, 2004, M4.
48. Condon, op. cit.
49. Hall, 1966, 1977, op. cit.
50. Friedman, op. cit.
51. Hall, 1966, op. cit.
52. Hall, 1959, 1966, op. cit.
53. Field, T. "Preschoolers in America are touched less and are more aggressive than preschoolers in France." *Early Child Development and Care,* 151, 1999, 11–17; Kesterton, Michael. "Social studies." *The Globe and Mail,* 2003, A22.
54. Field, op. cit.
55. Axtell, Roger, *Gestures: The Do's and Taboos of Body Language Around the World.* N.Y.: John Wiley & Sons, 1998.
56. Köhler, Nicholas. "Russian Politicians + Kissing = 'Revolting.'" *The National Post,* Nov. 1, 2004, A1.
57. In conversation with Noreen Lerch, Professor of Transcultural Nursing, University of Victoria, February 17, 2005.
58. Hussanain, Khalid S.A. "Saudi Mode of greeting rituals: Their implications for teaching and learning English." *IRAL: International Review of Applied Linguistics in Language Teaching,* Feb. 94, Vol. 32, Issue 1, pp. 68–78; Hall, 1977, op. cit.
59. Hussanain, op. cit.
60. Dodd, op. cit.
61. Hall, 1966, op. cit.; Hussanain, op. cit.
62. Yang, Yue-Qing. *Footbinding: Search for the Three Inch Golden Lotus.* East-West Film Enterprises, 2004.
63. Alibhai, N. and A. Furnham. "Cross-cultural differences in the perception of female body shapes." *Psychology of Medicine,* 1983, Nov. 13 (4): pp. 829–37; Furnham, A. and P. Baguma. "Cross-cultural differences in the evaluation of male and female body shapes." *International Journal of Eating Disorders,* 1994, Jan. 15 (1): pp. 81–89.
64. Seierstad, Asne. *The Bookseller of Kabul.* G.B.: Little, Brown, 2003.
65. *The History of Tattooing,* http://hobby.rin.ru/eng/articles/html/303.html.
66. Hall, 1977, op. cit., p. 75.
67. Samovar & Porter, op. cit.
68. Ibid.
69. Goodwin, Jan. *Price of Honor: Muslim Women Lift the Veil of Silence on the Islamic World.*

New York: Plume (the Penguin group), revised ed., 2003.

70. Hall, 1977, op. cit., pp. 47–48.
71. Axtell, op. cit.
72. Ibid.
73. Condon, op. cit.
74. Hall, 1966, op. cit.
75. Guffey et al., op. cit.
76. Samovar & Porter, op. cit.
77. Hall, 1959, op. cit.
78. Jiménez, Marina. "From Pakistan to the Prairies." *The Globe and Mail*, Sept. 25, 2004, F5.

Chapter 8

1. *Kofi Annan: Center of the Storm*, Grubin, David, and WNET New York, co-producers, aired WNED TV, Jan. 7, 2003.
2. Hofstede, Geert. *Culture's Consequences: International Differences in Work-Related Values*, 4th Printing. Beverly Hills: Sage, 1988, p. 27.
3. Laroche, Lionel. "Navigating Cultural Bumps in the Road." *Engineering Dimensions*, (Nov.–Dec., 2002), pp. 34–38.
4. Nydell, Margaret. *Understanding Arabs: A Guide for Westerners*. Yarmouth: Intercultural Press, 1987, p. 43.
5. Tung, Rosalie. "Personal Considerations vs. Western Logic." *Pacific Region Forum: Business negotiations with the Koreans: a Cross-cultural Perspective*, www.cic.sfu.ca/forum/tung.html, accessed June 10, 2004; Beller, Tanya, Michelle Pinker, Sheila Snapka, Denise Van Dusen. *Korean-American Health Care Beliefs and Practices*. www3.baylor.edu/~Charles_Kemp/Korean.htm.
6. *Communicating with the Japanese*. www.settlement.org/cp/english/japan/commun.html.
7. *CBC News*, Jan. 10, 2004.
8. Laroche, op. cit., p. 37.
9. In conversation with Brian Charles, Native Education Liaison Officer, May 15, 2001.
10. Dodd, Carley H. *Dynamics of Intercultural Communication*, 5th edition. Boston: McGraw Hill, 1998, p. 128.
11. Ibid.
12. Reynolds, Sara & Deborah Valentine. *Guide to Cross-Cultural Communication*. New Jersey: Prentice Hall, 2004.
13. Drohan, Madeleine. "Toronto the Good's name is mud in land that has fun with language." *The Globe and Mail*, September 16, 2000, A2.

14. Ong, Walter J. *Orality and Literacy: The Technologizing of the Word*. London and New York: Methuen, 1982.
15. Frances Mullen, Ghanaian-Canadian, Nov. 17, 2005; also see www.ghanaweb.com/GhanaHomePage/tribes/ashanti.html.
16. Ong, 1982, op. cit.
17. Dodd, op. cit.
18. Ibid.
19. Samovar, Larry A. & Richard E. Porter. *Communication Between Cultures*, 5th edition. Cal.: Wadsworth, 2004, p. 83; Morrison, Terri, Wayne A. Conaway & George A. Borden. *Kiss, Bow, or Shake Hands: How to Do Business in Sixty Countries*. Holbrook, Mass.: Adams Media Corporation, 1994.
20. Morrison et al., op. cit.
21. Hall, Edward T. *Beyond Culture*. New York: Anchor Books, Doubleday, 1977, p. 247.
22. Morrison et al., op. cit.
23. Matsu, Beverly & Stella Ting-Toomey. *Summary of "Cross-Cultural Face-Negotiation: An Analytical Overview,"* presented by Stella Ting-Toomey at the Pacific Region Forum, April 15, 1992, available on www.cic.sfu.ca/forum/ting-too.html.
24. Ibid., p. 3.
25. Condon, John C. *With Respect to the Japanese: A Guide for Americans*. Yarmouth, Maine: Intercultural Press, 1984.
26. Benedict, Ruth. *Patterns of Culture*. London: Routledge & Kegan Paul Ltd., 1935; Condon, op. cit.
27. In conversation with Asami Fukumoto, student from Japan, Nov. 7, 2004.
28. Condon, op. cit.
29. Nydell, op. cit.; Hall, 1977, op. cit.
30. Laroche, op. cit.
31. Author's adaptation from Matsu & Ting-Toomey, op. cit.
32. Hall, 1977, op. cit.
33. Ibid.
34. Ibid.; Paz, Octavio. *The Labyrinth of Solitude*. New York: Grove Press, 1985.
35. Hall, 1977, op. cit.
36. Nydell, op. cit.
37. Wong, Jan. *Jan Wong's China*. Toronto: Doubleday Canada, 2000.
38. Carhart, T.E. *The Piano Shop on the Left Bank: The hidden world of a Paris atelier*. London: Vintage, 2001; Morrison et al., op. cit.
39. In conversation with Genevieve Marian and Nisha Mathson, students from India, April 17, 2001, and with Noreen Lerch, adjunct professor of Nursing, University of Victoria, June 22, 2005.

40. Wong, op. cit.; Barber, John. "Frogs, live sex, and dead cats." *The Globe and Mail*, Oct. 23, 2004, p. R1.

41. Nolan, Stephanie. "Breaking a taboo, Mandela says AIDS killed son." *The Globe and Mail*, Jan. 7, 2005, A1.

42. York, Geoffrey. "Suicide websites leading to deadly connections in Japan." *The Globe and Mail*, Mar. 26, 2005, A12.

43. MacDonald, Gayle. "Show me the money." *The Globe and Mail*, April 24, 2004, F1.

44. Newman, Peter C. "The Secrets of My Success," *Report on Business*, November 2004, pp. 74–83, p. 77.

45. In conversation with Charles Craig, international liaison consultant, Georgian College, May 16, 2001.

46. Adler, Katya. *Housework looms for Spanish men*, BBC News, June 17, 2005, www.bbc.co.uk/2/hi/europe/4100140.stm.

47. In conversation with Irene Albornoz, nurse in Malaga, Spain, Feb. 27, 2002.

48. Kesterton, Michael. "Social Studies: Single in Japan." *The Globe and Mail*, Oct. 4, 2004, A20.

49. Bumiller, Elizabeth. *May You be the Mother of a Hundred Sons: A Journey Among the Women of India*. New Delhi: Penguin Books India (P), 1991; Goodwin, Jan. *Price of Honor: Muslim Women Lift the Veil of Silence on the Islamic World*. New York: Plume (the Penguin group), revised ed., 2003.

50. Goodwin, Jan., op. cit.

51. In conversation with Ragheida Hamade, Lebanese Canadian nursing student, York University, March 28, 2005.

52. Wente, Margaret. "China's boy trouble & connected by a thread." *The Globe and Mail*, Dec. 11, 2004, F5.

53. Goodwin, Paul B. Jr. *Global Studies: Latin America*, 10th ed. Iowa: McGraw-Hill/Dushkin, 2003.

54. Morrison et al., op. cit.

55. Wenzhong, Hu & Cornelius Grove. *Encountering the Chinese: A Guide for Americans*. Yarmouth: Intercultural Press, Inc., 1991.

56. Tung in Robbins, Stephen P. & Nancy Langton. *Organizational Behaviour: Concepts, Controversies, Applications*, Toronto: Prentice Hall, 2003.

57. Nydell, op. cit.; p. 25; Peters, op. cit.

58. Hofstede, 1988, op. cit., p. 27.

59. Nydell, op. cit.

60. Seiter, John S., J. Bruschke & Chunsheng Bai. "The Acceptability of Deception as a Function of Perceivers' Culture, Deceiver's Intention, and Deceiver-Deceived Relationship," *Western Journal of Communication*, 66(2) (Spring 2002), pp. 158–180 (p. 158).

61. Ibid., p. 173.

62. Trompenaars, Fons & Charles Hampden-Turner. *Riding the Waves of Culture: Understanding Cultural Diversity in Global Business*, 2nd ed. N.Y.: McGraw-Hill, 1998; Trompenaars, Fons. *Did the Pedestrian Die?* Oxford: U.K.: Capstone Publishing Ltd., 2003.

63. Seiter et al., op. cit.

64. In conversation with Genevieve Marian and Nisha Mathson, students from India, April 17, 2001; in written communication from New Delhi entrepreneur, Tito Mathson, received Nov. 18, 2002.

65. *Wide Angle*, PBS, "Corruption Chart: How Big is Mexico's Problem?" www.pbs.org/wnet/wideangle/shows/Mexico, accessed October 15, 2004.

66. In conversation with Tony Palma, engineer with Ontario Hydro, Niagara Falls, December 18, 2002.

67. Morrison et al., op. cit.

68. Peters, op. cit.

69. Condon, op. cit.

70. Kohls, Robert L. *Survival Kit for Overseas Living*. Yarmouth, MA: Intercultural Press, Inc., 1996; Kohls, Robert L., *Survival Kit for Overseas Living: For Americans planning to live and work abroad*. Yarmouth, MA: Intercultural Press, Inc., 2001.

Time Out for India

1. Thompson cited in Bradnock, Robert and Roma. *India Handbook*, 12th edition, frontispiece. Bath: Footprints Handbooks, Ltd., 2002.

2. Armstrong, Sally. "The untouchables." *Chatelaine*, July 2004, pp. 144–57.

3. In conversation with Nisha Mathson and Genevieve Marian, students from India, April 17, 2001; Tito Mathson (special thanks), New Delhi entrepreneur, written communication received Nov. 18, 2002; and in conversation with the following faculty members at the Canadian Institute for International Studies (CIIS) in Chandigarh, India: Bruce and Pat MacMillan (June 30, 2001), Dan Phillips (May 16, 2001), Nigel Ward-Paige (May 15, 2001), Heather White (May 21, 2001), and Geoff Dalton (May 15, 2001).

4. Rajghatta, Chidanand, "Identity Kit of an Acronym." *Sunday Times of India*, Oct. 6, 2002, p. 14.

5. Bumiller, Elizabeth. *May You be the Mother of a Hundred Sons: A Journey Among the Women of India.* New Delhi: Penguin Books India (P), 1991.

Chapter 9

1. O'Grady, William & John Archibald. *Contemporary Linguistic Analysis, An Introduction,* 4th edition. Toronto: Pearson Education, 2000.
2. Ladefoged, Peter. *Vowels and Consonants: An Introduction to the Sounds of Languages.* Mass.: Blackwell, 2001, p. 1.
3. Kesterton, Michael. "Social Studies." *The Globe and Mail,* March 10, 2003, A14; Ladefoged, op. cit.
4. Wardhaugh, Ronald. *An Introduction to Sociolinguistics,* 4th edition. Mass.: Blackwell Publishers Inc., 2002.
5. Smith, Graeme. "Global warming seen as ending long winter night in Canadian north." *The Globe and Mail,* Dec. 2, 2004, A17.
6. Ong, Walter J. *Orality and Literacy: The Technologizing of the Word.* London and New York: Methuen, 1982, p. 107.
7. Stanlaw, James. "English in Japanese Communicative Strategies" in *The Other Tongue: English Across Cultures,* Kachru, Braj. B., Ed. Urbana: University of Illinois Press, 1982.
8. Smith, Russell. "This big-ass column's retarded!" *The Globe and Mail,* Apr. 21, 2005, R1.
9. O'Grady & Archibald, op. cit.
10. Miller, Barbara D., Penny Van Esterik & John Van Esterik, *Cultural Anthropology,* Canadian edition. Toronto: Pearson, 2001.
11. Sapir, 1949, cited in Jaworski, Adam & Nikolas Coupland, eds. *The Discourse Reader.* London and New York: Routledge, 1999, p. 145; Hawkes, Terence. *Structuralism and Semiotics.* Berkeley and Los Angeles: University of California Press, 1977, p. 31; Wardhaugh, op. cit., p. 221.
12. Whorf, B. L. *Language, Thought, and Reality: Selected Writings of Benjamin Lee Whorf.* John B. Carroll, ed. Cambridge, MA: MIT Press, 1967 (1956), pp. 213–14.
13. Chatwin, Bruce. *The Songlines.* New York: Viking Penguin Inc., 1987.
14. Abley, Mark. *Spoken Here: Travels Among Threatened Languages.* Canada: Random House Canada, 2003; Shorris, Earl. "The Last Word," *Harper's Magazine,* August 2000, pp. 73–81.
15. Hymes cited in Wardhaugh, op. cit.; Hale, Kenneth http://web.mit.edu/newsoffice/nr/2001/hale.html.
16. Chomsky in Shorris, op. cit.; Wiwa, Ken. "Get beyond Babel." *The Globe and Mail,* June 22, 2001, A13.
17. Crucefix, Lanna. *Do the Inuit really have 200 words for "snow"?* Ask Us @ U of T www.newsandevents.utoronto.ca/bios/askus3.htm, n.d., accessed Nov. 13, 2004.
18. Trudgill, Peter. *Sociolinguistics: An Introduction.* England: Penguin Books, 1978.
19. Abley, op. cit., p. 28.
20. Wardhaugh, op. cit.
21. Tahar, R. *First Peoples: The Yanomamo of South America.* Minn.: Learner Publishers Co., 2002.
22. Leo-Spizser cited in Kaplan, Robert. "Cultural Patterns in Inter-cultural Education." *Language Learning* XVI Issue 142, 1966, pp. 1–20 (p. 3).
23. Goodwin, Paul B. Jr. *Global Studies: Latin America,* 10th ed. Iowa: McGraw-Hill/Dushkin, 2003.
24. Peters, James. *The Arab World Handbook: Arabian Peninsula Edition.* London: Stacey International, 2000.
25. Youngblood Henderson cited in Abley, op. cit., p. 51.
26. Todd, Jude. *The Hopi Environmental Ethos.* www.sacredland.org/resources/bibliography/todd.html, retrieved Sept. 19, 2005; Whorf, Benjamin. *Thought and Reality: Selected Writings of Benjamin Lee Whorf.* John B. Carroll, ed. Cambridge: The M.I.T. Press, 1956, pp. 55, 56.
27. Bonvillain, Nancy. *Language, Culture, and Communication: The Meaning of Messages,* 4th edition. New Jersey: Prentice Hall, 2003, p. 65; Cook, Mary Jane & Margaret Amy Sharp. "Problems of Navajo Speakers in Learning English." *Language Learning* XVI issue 142, 1966, pp. 21–33.
28. Wardhaugh, op. cit., p. 222.
29. Wardhaugh, op. cit., p. 223.
30. Hawkes, op. cit., p. 168.
31. Wardhaugh, op. cit.
32. Henning, Jeffrey. *Kinship Terms: Model Languages.* www.langmaker.com/ml0106b.htm, 1995, last updated Mar. 1996, accessed Nov. 14, 2004.
33. Ibid.
34. Trudgill, op. cit.
35. Ibid.
36. Ibid.
37. Abley, op. cit.

38. Condon, John C. *With Respect to the Japanese: A Guide for Americans.* Yarmouth, Maine: Intercultural Press, 1984.
39. Bonvillain citing Lee, op. cit., pp. 237–38.
40. Condon, op. cit.
41. Bonvillain, op. cit., p. 107.
42. Hofstede, Geert. *Cultures and Organizations: Software of the Mind.* Toronto: McGraw-Hill, 1997.
43. Francis Hsu, cited in Hofstede, 1997, op. cit., pp. 73, 74.
44. Bonvillain, op. cit.
45. Wardhaugh, op. cit., p. 279.
46. Trudgill, op. cit.
47. Samovar, Larry A. & Richard E. Porter. *Communication Between Cultures*, 5th edition. Cal.: Wadsworth, 2004, p. 147.
48. McLuhan, Marshall. *Understanding Media: The Extensions of Man*, 4th printing. New York: McGraw-Hill Book Company, 1966; Ong, op. cit., 1982.
49. Bonvillain, op. cit., pp. 64–65 (a few examples taken from Bonvillain, others added by author).
50. Kaplan, Robert. "Cultural Patterns in Inter-cultural Education." *Language Learning* XVI Issue 142, 1966, pp. 1–20; Hall, Edward T. *The Silent Language.* New York: Fawcett World Library, 1959; Hall, Edward T. *Beyond Culture.* New York: Anchor Books, Doubleday, 1977.
51. Kaplan, op. cit.
52. Ibid., pp. 6–7.
53. Kaplan, Robert. "A Further Note on Contrastive Rhetoric." *Communication Quarterly*, vol. 24, No. 2, Spring 1976.
54. Kaplan, 1966, op. cit., p. 12.
55. Kaplan, 1976, op. cit.
56. Saramago, José. *All the Names.* Orlando, Fl.: Harcourt, 2000.
57. Miller et al., op. cit.
58. *Holy Bible*, authorized King James Version. New York: The World Publishing Company, n.d.
59. Yule, George. *The Study of Language*, 2nd edition. Cambridge: University of Cambridge Press, 1996.
60. Wells, Spencer. *Journey of Man.* WNED. March 9, 2004, 8–11.
61. Jordan, Terry G. & Lester Rowntree. *The Human Mosaic: A Thematic Introduction to Cultural Geography*, 4th ed. New York: Harper and Row, 1986.
62. "In Search of the First Language," *NOVA*, WGBH: Boston, air date, March 18, 1997.
63. O'Grady & Archibald, op. cit.
64. Wells, op. cit.

65. Nakanishi, Akira. *Writing Systems of the World: alphabets, syllabaries, pictograms.* Vermont: Charles E. Tuttle Company, 1980.
66. Based on Ladefoged, op. cit., 2001, p. 140
67. Bragg, Melvyn. *The Adventure of English: The Biography of a Language.* London: Hodder & Stoughton, 2003.
68. Wardhaugh, op. cit.
69. Trudgill, op. cit.
70. O'Grady & Archibald, op. cit.
71. Kachru, B.B. "Teaching world Englishes" in Kachru, B., ed., The *Other Tongue.* Chicago: University of Ill. Press, 1992, pp. 356–365.
72. Johnson, Fern L. *Speaking Culturally: Language Diversity in the U.S.* Cal.: Sage, 2000.
73. Reuters, "A two-lobe language." *Toronto Star*, July 4, 2003; Thân, Thị Phú'ố'ng Thoa.
74. From Martin, Philippe, Experimental Phonetics class, University of Toronto, 1980.
75. Silverberg, David. "Your Morning Smile." *The Globe and Mail*, May 5, 2004, A2.
76. O'Grady and Archibald, op. cit.
77. Ibid.
78. Cited in Yule, op. cit.
79. Chomsky, Noam. *Syntactic Structures.* The Hague: Mouton, 1957; *Aspects of the Theories of Syntax.* Cambridge, Mass.: The M.I.T. Press, 1965; *Language and Mind*, New York: Harcourt Brace Jovanovich, Inc., 1968; Lyons, John. *Chomsky*, 6th impression. G.B.: Fontana/Collins, 1973.
80. MacDonald, Larry. "When Wolfe the donkless hero came, this was a far more fair domain." *The Globe and Mail*, May 13, 1997, A20.
81. Richards, Jack C., John Platt & Heidi Platt. *Longman Dictionary of Language Teaching & Applied Linguistics.* UK: Longman Group, 1996.

Chapter 10

1. Bennett, Milton J. "Basic Concepts of Intercultural Communication" in *Basic Concepts of Intercultural Communications: Selected readings.* Yarmouth: Intercultural Press, 1998, pp. 4–35 (p. 25).
2. Ibid.
3. Ting-Toomey, Stella. *Communicating Across Cultures.* New York: The Guilford Press, 1999.
4. Note: A number of other models exists, but space did not permit their inclusion. For information, readers are referred to: Gullahorn, J.T. & J. E. Gullahorn. "An extension of the U-curve hypothesis." *Journal of Social Issues*, 19, 33–47, 1963; Lewis, Tom J. & Robert E. Jungman, eds. *On Being Foreign: Culture Shock in Short Fiction.* Yarmouth, Maine:

Intercultural Press, Inc., 1986, pp. xvii–xxv; Kim, Y.Y. *Communication and cross-cultural adaptation: An integrative theory.* U.K.: Multilingual Matters, 1988; Kim, Y.Y. & B.D. Ruben, "Intercultural Transformation: A systems theory" in *Theories in Intercultural Communication,* Y.Y. Kim and W.B. Gudykunst, eds. Thousand Oaks, CA: Sage, 1988; Kohls, Robert L., *Survival Kit for Overseas Living: For Americans planning to live and work abroad.* Yarmouth, MA: Intercultural Press, Inc., 2001; Ting-Toomey, op. cit.

5. Lysgaard, S. "Adjustment in a foreign society: Norwegian Fulbright grantees visiting the United States." *International Social Sciences Bulletin,* 7, pp. 45–51, 1955.

6. Ibid.; summary also paraphrased from Hall, Edward T. *Beyond Culture.* New York: Anchor Books, Doubleday, 1977.

7. Kim, op. cit.; Kim & Ruben, op. cit.

8. Participant observation in Africa, Latin America, Canada, and Britain.

9. Kidder, Tracy. *Mountains Beyond Mountains: The quest of Dr. Paul Farmer, a man who would cure the world.* New York: Random House, 2003, p. 100.

10. Oberg, K. "Culture Shock: Adjustment to new cultural environments." *Practical Anthropology,* 7, 1960, pp. 177–182 (p. 177).

11. Ting-Toomey, op. cit., p. 245.

12. Bennett, Janet. "Transition Shock: Putting Culture Shock in Perspective," in *Basic Concepts of Intercultural Communications: Selected readings.* Bennett, Milton J., ed. Yarmouth: Intercultural Press, 1998, pp. 215–223.

13. Ibid., p. 222.

14. *Person-2-Person,* TVO, with Paula Todd, 2003.

15. Chaney, Lillian H. and Jeannette S. Martin, *Intercultural Business Communication,* second edition. New Jersey: Prentice Hall, 2000.

16. Kohls, Robert L. *Survival Kit for Overseas Living.* Yarmouth, MA: Intercultural Press, Inc., 1996; Kohls, 2001, op. cit.

17. Bennett, J., op. cit., p. 217.

18. Furnham, Adrian. *Culture Shock* in www.celestia.co.uk/wexas/p2_cultureshock.htm.

19. Kohls, op. cit., 1996.

20. Ibid.

21. Chaney & Martin, op. cit., p. 63.

22. Ibid.

23. Kohls, 1996, op. cit.

24. Ibid., p. 78.

25. Kohls, 2001, op. cit., pp. 110–11.

26. Storti, Craig. *Figuring Foreigners Out.* Yarmouth: Intercultural Press, Inc., 1999.

27. Oberg, op. cit.; Storti, op. cit.

28. Bonvillain, Nancy. *Language, Culture, and Communication: The Meaning of Messages,* 4th edition. New Jersey: Prentice Hall, 2003.

29. All of these points are from Rajesh Rajan Singh. *Observations of Canadian Culture in Vancouver,* 3rd year paper, Jan. 11, 2005.

30. See Lewis & Jungman, op. cit.; Gullahorn & Gullahorn, op. cit; Ting-Toomey, op. cit.

31. Ting-Toomey, op. cit.

32. Lewis & Jungman, op. cit.

33. Ting-Toomey, op. cit.

34. Uruguayan refugee/immigrant in Canada for 8 years—returned to Uruguay after dictatorship ended there.

35. Berry, John W., Uichol Kim & Pawel Boski. "Psychological Acculturation of Immigrants." In Kim and Gudykunst (eds), *Cross-Cultural Adaptation: Current Approaches.* Newbury Park, CA: Sage Publications, Inc, 1988, pp. 62–89.

36. Kim, cited in Hall, Bradford J. *Among Cultures: The Challenge of Communication,* 2nd edition. Canada: Thomson Wadsworth, 2005, pp. 283–287; Ting-Toomey, op. cit.

   Due to space limitations, this section on factors is simplified and summarized from the author's own experience as a sojourner and working with newcomers in combination with the two sources above. Readers are directed to them for complete descriptions of each of their models.

37. Summarized from Berry et al., op. cit.; Hall, Bradford, op. cit; Ting-Toomey, op. cit.

38. Kim, op. cit.; Ting-Toomey, op. cit.

39. Ting-Toomey, op. cit.

40. Kim, op. cit., Ting-Toomey, op. cit.

41. Ting-Toomey, op. cit.

42. Ibid.

43. Berry et al., op. cit; Kim, op. cit; Ting-Toomey, op. cit.

44. Ting-Toomey, op. cit.; Kim, op. cit.

45. Ting-Toomey, op. cit.

46. Ibid.

47. Ibid.

48. Keung, Nicholas. "Immigrants better trained, worse off." *Toronto Star,* Feb. 1, 2005, www.thestar.com (citing study by Jeffrey Ritz for Institute for Research on Public Policy).

49. Ting-Toomey, op. cit.

50. Kim, op. cit.; Ting-Toomey, op. cit.

51. Ting-Toomey, op. cit.

52. Foster, Cecil. *Where Race Does Not Matter: The New Spirit of Modernity.* Toronto: Penguin Canada, 2005.

53. Immen, Wallace. "Immigrants welcome, roadblocks ahead." *The Globe and Mail,* Feb. 18, 2004.

54. Galt, Virginia. "Visible minorities build a diverse work force." *The Globe and Mail,* Sept. 16, 2004, p. B9.

55. First three points from Kohls, 1996, 2001, op. cit.

56. Brislin & Yoshida, cited in Ting-Toomey, op. cit.

57. LeBaron, Michelle. *Bridging Cultural Conflicts: A New Approach for a Changing World.* San Francisco: Jossey-Bass, 2003.

58. Berry et al., op. cit.

59. Ibid.

60. Toews, Miriam. *A Complicated Kindness.* Toronto: Alfred A. Knopf, 2004.

61. Go back to your own essay (Chapter 2) on how important your ethnicity is to your identity—did you know the story of your family's immigration? Did you think of yourself as "ethnic"—why or why not?

62. Berry et al., op. cit.

63. Coon, Dennis. *Introduction to Psychology: Gateways to Mind and Behaviour.* Canada: Thomson Wadworth, 2004, p. 150.

64. Brym, Robert J., John Lie & Adie Nelson. *Sociology: Your Compass for a New World.* Toronto: Thomson Nelson, 2005, Note: "White" is used in this text, but author experience suggests "Anglo-Celtic" is more accurate.

65. Raj, Dhooleka, S. "The ABCD of American Desi." *Sunday Times of India,* Oct. 6, 2002, p. 14.

66. Leong, Melissa. "On bananas and other humans." *Toronto Star,* Sept. 2, 2003, p. D1.

67. Ting-Toomey, op. cit., p. 256.

68. LeBaron, op. cit.

69. Adler, Peter S. "Beyond Cultural Identity: Reflections on Multiculturalism," in *Basic Concepts of Intercultural Communications: Selected readings.* Bennett, Milton J., ed. Yarmouth: Intercultural Press, 1998, pp. 225–245 (p. 227).

70. Pollock, David & Ruth Van Reken. *Third Culture Kids: The Experience of Growing up among Worlds.* Yarmouth: Nicholas Brealey Publishing, 2001.

71. LeBaron Duryea, Michelle & J. Bruce Grundison. *Conflict and Culture: Research in Five Communities in Vancouver, British Columbia.* B.C.: University of Victoria Institute for Dispute Resolution, 1993.

72. Ibid.

73. Ibid.

74. Ibid.

75. Hofstede, Geert. *Cultures and Organizations: Software of the Mind.* Toronto: McGraw-Hill, 1997.

76. LeBaron Duryea & Grundison, op. cit.

77. Lund, Brishkai, Catherine Morris & Michelle LeBaron Duryea. *Conflict and Culture: Report of the Multiculturalism Dispute Resolution Project, Executive Summary.* B.C.: University of Victoria Institute for Dispute Resolution, 1994, p. 4.

78. LeBaron Duryea & Grundison, op. cit., p. xv.

79. Ibid., p. xxii.

80. Benedict, Ruth. *Patterns of Culture.* London: Routledge & Kegan Paul Ltd., 1935, p. 8.

81. Subba, Bhim. "Why I left Toronto to find Canada." *The Globe and Mail,* Sept. 18, 2004, M3.

Glossary

AAVE (African American Vernacular English): a variety of English spoken by some African Americans that incorporates linguistic features of West African languages.

acculturation: the psychological process of adaptation and accommodation to a new culture.

acculturative stress: the stress experienced by individuals in adapting to a new culture.

action chain: the internalized steps of disputes in Northern European and North American culture as described by Edward T. Hall.

adaptation: the process whereby one's worldview is expanded to include behaviour and values derived from the host culture.

adjustment: a term by Ting-Toomey used to describe the adaptive process of short-term sojourners in a new cultural environment who must adapt to be able to function in, but do not necessarily adopt values and behaviours of the new culture.

Age of Enlightenment: an 18th century European philosophical movement based on rationality and humanism that provided the framework for the American and French revolutions.

Age of Reason: the period of the 17th to 18th century in Europe stressing rationality over irrationality and superstition and beginning to divorce philosophy from theology.

ageism: bias against a person or group on the basis of age; can lead to acts of discrimination.

American Dream: the belief that through work and will power, any individual in the United States can achieve the ideals of success, prosperity, and happiness.

Anglo-Celtic: describes an individual of English, Scottish, Welsh, or Irish descent.

archetype: the original model on which subsequent models are patterned. In Jung's terminology, archetypes derive from humanity's collective unconscious of memories of the past and are recognizable in their current forms.

ascribed identity: the cultural identity assigned to us by others on the basis of appearance or other external factors.

assimilation: the resocialization of an individual, which replaces an original cultural identity with a new one and erases all traces of the original.

assumption of similarities: the misguided and naïve belief that "underneath" everyone has the same beliefs and views the world in the same way.

atman: the spiritual force within individuals that is part of the cosmic spiritual force called Brahman according to Hinduism.

autostereotyping: the assumption by a group of stereotypes held by others about them.

avowed identity: the cultural image or identity individuals use to categorize themselves.

Baksheesh: the Arabic word for pot-sweetener, tip, or bribe used to expedite a service or close a deal.

beliefs: what a person or group holds to be true.

Berry Acculturation Model: Berry's model identifies four patterns of psychological acculturation and the degree to which each results in acculturative stress. The four patterns are integration, separation, assimilation, and marginalization (see Chapter 10).

biculturalism: equal membership and comfort in two cultures.

bigotry: intolerance or ignorance of opinions and beliefs different from one's own.

bilingualism: equal fluency, written and oral, in two languages.

Brahman: the cosmic, infinite, creative, and spiritual force of the universe according to Hinduism.

Cablinasian: Tiger Woods' definition of his mixed cultural identity—Caucasian, black, Indian, and Asian.

calque: an expression introduced into a language literally translated from another language; e.g., Weltanschauung—worldview.

caste: Hindu hereditary class system defining social status. There are four castes: intellectual, warrior, mercantile, and laborer, and many sub-castes. A fifth group, the "untouchables," also developed.

circumlocution: talking around a word in order to explain it.

civil liberties: individual freedoms such as freedom of speech, freedom of assembly, freedom of religion, etc., which are the basic rights of citizens of democracies.

code: any system of symbols that communicates information; e.g., language, non-verbal communication, professional dress rules.

code-switch: a linguistic term meaning to change back and forth between two languages in the same communication act or series of acts.

cognitive style: thinking process or pattern of an individual or group.

collectivism: a cultural pattern in which people are considered to be interdependent and to have obligations to other members of the group, especially family, for its well-being and maintenance.

colonial period: the period during which European countries imposed their rule and elements of culture on other cultural groups throughout Latin America, Asia, and Africa, in particular. It began in the 15th century and ended in the second half of the 20th century when many African countries gained their independence.

communication: the process of transmitting information by means of symbolic codes such as language and codes based on non-verbal forms of communication.

communication style: way of communicating information, such as directly or indirectly, according to cultural and individual norms.

competence: a term coined by Chomsky to describe the internalized knowledge of an individual of his or her language.

Confucianism: a philosophy of life and system of ethics developed by Confucius about 500 B.C.E. based on mutual obligation, proper relationships, and social harmony.

continentalism: the idea that Canada should look to the United States as an economic partner due to shared geography and cultural origins.

contrastive rhetoric: the comparison of organizational patterns of writing practised by different cultures.

country shock: stress experienced by individuals in a new cultural environment based on physical adjustments to such things as climate, changes in routines, and new systems of transport and communication (Storti's term).

covert culture: a term coined by Edward T. Hall to describe cultures that do not employ action chains of escalating explicitness in disputes, but rather maintain a façade of harmony until driven to erupt emotionally or physically.

Creole: a mix of languages that has become the mother tongue of a group of speakers; e.g., Jamaican Creole (also known as patois) is a mix of English and West African languages with some French.

cross-cultural communication: used synonymously with intercultural communication in this text; can also refer specifically to comparison and statistical analysis of cultural patterns of different cultural groups based on surveys and other data.

cultural appropriation: taking over aspects of another culture as if they are one's own, either through literature, music, or other forms of expression.

cultural convergence: a theory of Francis Fukuyama's that predicts the global homogenization of cultures based on Western liberal democracy and capitalism.

cultural genocide: the destruction of a group of people and their culture by another group.

cultural globalization: the most visible form of globalization, the global spread of ideas, trends, fashion, media, cuisine, and other cultural elements. It can introduce new elements into traditional cultures and modify existing elements.

cultural model: a term coined by Bonvillain to describe culture as a construction of reality that is created, shared, and transmitted by members of a group.

cultural narrative: myths, legends, and folktales passed down by cultures to explain their origins and beliefs.

cultural nationalism: loyalty to a nation or ethnic group that does not have its own state, or loyalty to an ethnic group within a specific state or country; e.g., Quebec nationalism, Palestinian nationalism.

cultural patterns: patterns of thought and behaviour.

cultural relativism: the theory that cultures are "different but equal" and that people can understand another cultural group's behaviour by entering *its* frame of reference rather than evaluating it from their own perspective.

cultural universal: a pattern of behaviour common to all cultures.

culture: learned patterns of thought and behaviour shared and passed down by a group of people.

culture realm: regions where different cultural groups share a number of cultural patterns; can be defined on the basis of language, ethnicity, agricultural patterns, political patterns, religions, health and healing customs, and so on.

culture shock: stress and disorientation resulting from immersion in a new environment where cultural and communication patterns are unfamiliar.

cybernetics: the science of communication, control, and feedback to maintain order in society and individuals.

dash: the term used in West Africa for pot-sweetener or tip to conclude a deal.

dialect: a language variety that has not been elevated to a standard. There are regional dialects and sociolects, dialects spoken by particular social classes.

diffusion: contact between cultures that brings about cultural change.

disclosure: what kind of and how much personal information individuals reveal about themselves.

discrimination: negative treatment of individuals or groups based on prejudice or racism.

dominant culture: the culture of power or influence in a nation state, often the majority or founding culture.

economic globalization: the international mobility of goods, services, labour, technology, and capital, and the increasing connectivity and interdependence of the world's markets and businesses.

empirical: based on observation, experience, or experiment, not on theory or intuition.

empiricism: the view that knowledge comes from experience and observation of the world and the basis of the Western scientific method.

enculturation: the process of learning one's culture; also called socialization.

endogamy: marriage between people of the same tribal, ethnic, or cultural group.

ethics: belief in what is right or wrong and behaviour according to those beliefs; ethical behaviour is considered to be good, i.e., moral.

ethnic cleansing: the removal of an ethnic group from an area often by means of murder carried out by military forces; can be a euphemism for genocide.

ethnic group: a collectivity within a larger society united by emotional and cultural ties.

ethnicity: multidimensional term that describes the historical origins and cultural, religious, linguistic, and geographical environment from which a person or a person's ancestors have come.

ethnocentrism: the belief that one's own cultural group is superior to others and the evaluation of other groups according to the standards and behaviours of one's own group.

ethnonationalism: *see* cultural nationalism.

ethnorelativism: *see* cultural relativism.

Eurocentrism: the belief that European culture is superior to other cultures.

evangelical: relating to Christian churches that believe in personal conversion, faith based on the first four Gospels of the New Testament, and spreading the gospel or "good news."

face: reputation, the preservation of social standing and respect; positive self-image.

face negotiation: culture-bound concepts of face related to how face is defined and maintained based on research by Ting-Toomey.

First Nation: a term for first peoples of Canada including Indians, Inuit, and Métis.

First World: a term that originally (after World War II) referred to countries of the "free" or capitalist world as opposed to communist countries (Second World). It has come to mean today all developed countries.

Fourth World: less economically developed countries that have not benefited from economic globalization and whose economies are developing slowly. May also refer to indigenous cultures within nation states.

fundamentalism: belief in the literal interpretation of sacred texts and in a fundamental, original form of faith.

generative grammar: a linguistic term for the study of formal or "deep" syntactic structures that can "generate" various grammatically acceptable "surface" expressions of an idea.

genocide: deliberate destruction of an ethnic, cultural, or racial group.

global village: term coined by Marshall McLuhan to describe a world connected by modern mass communication reducing time and distance for the transmission of information to time and distance once limited to villages.

Golden Rule: an ethic shared by all major religions instructing followers to treat others as they would wish to be treated.

grammar: a linguistic term for the integrated system shared by all languages, which includes syntax, semantics, morphology, phonology, and phonetics.

guanxi: term in Chinese for a personal network of connections.

guilt culture: culture that relies on internal controls to induce and maintain appropriate behaviour.

halal: ritually fit in Islamic law.

haptics: a term for the study of touch.

haram: forbidden: refers to behaviours and practices forbidden by the Koran.

high context: term for cultures in which most of the information in a communicative act is conveyed implicitly through knowledge of the speakers, of conventions in a given context, and non-verbal clues.

holism: the idea that the whole is greater than the sum of its parts, i.e., that wholes are more important than the individuals or parts they are composed of; an Eastern value.

honorific: linguistic status indicators and expressions of respect; used widely in Japan.

hybrid: a composite resulting from the mix of more than one thing.

identity: the characteristics, beliefs, and values by which a person is defined by others (ascribed) or by him or herself (avowed).

ideology: a system of beliefs and ideas often shared by a group; according to Marx, a system of belief that supports the dominant position of the elites.

imperialism: the extension of power over a territory or people to control economic, cultural, and/or political activity.

individualism: a Western philosophy stressing the importance of the individual over the importance of the whole; contrast with collectivism and holism.

Indo-European: a linguistic term for the language family that includes Sanskrit (Indo), Persian, and most Northern Indian and European languages.

innovation: cultural change brought about by changes in technology.

intercultural adaptation: the process of becoming adapted to a cultural environment with different cultural patterns from the ones an individual is used to.

intercultural communication: a multidisciplinary field that focuses on the interaction between people from different cultural groups and how differences in culture affect that interaction.

intercultural competence: the ability to communicate effectively with people belonging to cultural groups different from one's own when culture, not age or gender or social class, is the main variable in the interaction.

intuition: instinctive knowing without a basis in rational thought processes or conscious reasoning.

karma: in Hinduism and Buddhism, the belief that actions of past lives determine one's form of reincarnation in the cycle of death and rebirth.

kibun: in Korea, mood, feelings, and state of mind. A peaceful communicative environment is necessary for the maintenance of *kibun*, which is easily disturbed.

kinesics: study of body movement.

kosher: ritually fit according to Jewish dietary laws.

language family: a group of related languages that stem from a common ancestor.

language variety: variations of language used by particular groups of people; includes sociolects, dialects, and idiolects (variety spoken by an individual).

lexicon: the collection of words in a language; vocabulary.

lineal: in a direct line of descent; lineality (noun)

linear: straight in relation to length and lines; linearity (noun)

linear language: language based on a way of thinking related to Western concepts of time and logic. A follows B follows C and so on. There is a definite past, present, and future time implicit or made explicit in the language.

lingua franca: Latin for "common language"—a language spoken by members of different linguistic groups to communicate with members of other linguistic groups within the same country or region; e.g., English in Nigeria and Ghana.

linguistic determinism: the idea that language determines thought; not widely accepted.

linguistic relativism: the idea that language influences thought, the main premise of the Sapir-Whorf Hypothesis.

linguistics: the science of language.

literate culture: a culture that has developed writing.

low context: refers to a culture that relies on words for the transmission of meaning in a communicative act.

machismo: the cult of male superiority in Latin American cultures.

Manifest Destiny: the belief that the United States had a God-given destiny to rule North America from coast to coast.

mantra: a sound or word used in meditation to help the mind focus on the spiritual.

marginalization: the sense of exclusion felt by members of minority cultures in the larger society.

matriarchy: a culture or society ruled by females.

miscegenation: interracial sexual relations or marriage.

monotheism: belief in one God.

moral relativism: belief that right and wrong are not absolute but are determined by culture or individuals.

mordida: "bribe" in Spanish; literally, "bite."

morphology: linguistic term for the structure and formation of words.

M-time (monochronic time): linear usage of time where individuals prefer to do one thing at a time, complete it, and move on to the next task or activity.

nation state: political term for a country; one nation or ethnic group is usually dominant and the basis of the 'nation' state.

nationalism: loyalty and emotional attachment to a nation or ethnic group within a nation state or to a nation state.

nirvana: in Buddhism, the highest spiritual state that can be attained in which an individual is released from suffering; in Hinduism, liberation from the cycle of birth and rebirth and state of complete peace.

non-linear language: language patterns not based on Western concepts of time and logic; they may be circular and intuitive in their organization.

norm: standard of behaviour considered appropriate based on rules of conduct and accepted practices within a culture.

North/South: terms used to describe levels of prosperity and development. North refers to developed countries, South to developing or less economically developed countries.

olfactics: the study of smell.

omoi-yari: in Japan, interpretation of the unspoken meaning of exchanges.

oral culture: a culture that has not developed writing.

Orientalism: term coined by Edward Said to describe the West's view of the East as childlike, subordinate, non-rational, superstitious; a view based on fantasy and lack of knowledge.

paralanguage: the use of rhythm, rate of speech, pitch, and volume to convey meaning.

participant observation: a form of cultural research in which the researcher learns the language of and lives with the community being studied.

patriarchy: society where males are dominant.

perception: the process of selecting, interpreting, and organizing sensory information in order to construct reality; feelings, attitudes, and images people have of different places, peoples, and environments due to factors that contribute to the selection and interpretation of sensory data.

perceptual filters: factors that influence perception such as culture, prejudice, assumption of similarities, and so on.

performance: Chomsky's term for language an individual is capable of producing.

performativity: postmodern term for legitimization of knowledge based on the criterion of how well it performs or achieves the desired results.

personal agency: idea that individuals have their own goals, aspirations, and will to achieve them.

personalismo: term describing the importance of personal relationships in doing business in Latin America.

phatic code: language and sounds used to keep the channel of communication open when individuals have nothing of actual content—informative or emotional, for example—to transmit, but rather want only to transmit a feeling of togetherness and good will and to prolong the communication.

phonetics: a branch of linguistics devoted to the production, transmission, and reception of speech sounds.

phonology: a branch of linguistics dealing with sound systems.

pidgin: a simple language of few words and structures that develops where speakers of different languages need to communicate; contains elements of more than one language.

pluralism: diversity of cultural identities within the context of a larger society (adj., pluralistic). Pluralism allows for common traditions from the larger society as well as the maintenance of specific cultural patterns.

polytheism: belief in more than one god.

post-colonialism: a cultural, political, and literary movement that focuses on the experience of colonized individuals, peoples, and nations, and on the consequences of colonialism.

postmodernism: an intellectual and artistic movement beginning in the latter half of the twentieth century that rejects absolutes and grand holistic ideologies, philosophies, and religions that provide systems of meaning for individuals. Rather, it deconstructs them, accepting that truth is relative, reality is fragmented, and personal identity is an unstable composite of various cultural possibilities.

pot-de-vin: French term for bribe or pot-sweetener.

prejudice: *pre-judging*—a negative perception of others without regard for facts or information.

Protestant work ethic: a teaching based on biblical scripture that stresses the moral value of work and its role in redemption for original sin. By extension, work results in prosperity for individuals and society.

proxemics: the study of space and distance.

P-time (polychronic time): use of time in a non-linear way, with many activities going on at the same time and a lack of concern for completing one before starting another.

Puritanism: a Protestant religious group founded in late 16th century England that followed the teachings of John Calvin and stressed strict rules of public and personal behaviour. The Puritans landed in New England in the 17th century and were influential in the religious development of the United States.

race: a designation for grouping human beings encompassing factors like skin and eye colour, hair characteristic, and stature. Abuse of the concept in the name of science has led anthropologists to now prefer the multidimensional term *ethnicity*.

racial profiling: a form of discrimination based on race where law enforcement officers, potential employers, and others take race into account in reacting to or dealing with visible minorities.

racism: the belief, unsubstantiated by science, that some "races" are superior to others in terms of intelligence or inherent moral character.

rationality: belief in the use of reason (as opposed to intuition or emotion) to obtain knowledge and truth.

re-entry stress: the trauma of readjusting to one's old culture after a period of time away during which new behaviours and ideas may have been adopted.

religion: belief system based on questions about the meaning of life, its origins, its purpose, and its nature.

rhetoric: the art of speaking or writing effectively by using culturally acceptable organizational patterns.

rhetorical forms (with reference to oral language): patterns of speech and stylistic devices used by speakers; (with reference to written language): organizational patterns and stylistic devices.

rule of law: the principle that every individual is treated equally before the law.

Russian Mennonites: Mennonites who emigrated as a group from Holland and Belgium to Poland, then to Russia in the 18th century, and then to Canada, mostly to Manitoba, in the 19th or 20th centuries, in each migration to escape persecution.

Sapir-Whorf Hypothesis: theory that language shapes thought and provides the means by which reality is both constructed and viewed.

satori: the experience of awakening or enlightenment in Zen Buddhism.

secularism: 1) the belief that religion should be excluded from civic affairs, government, and public education; 2) a belief system that denies the existence of a God or gods and uses human viewpoints as a basis for morality.

semantics: the study of meaning in language.

semiotics: the study of signs, symbols, and their systems, and how they function in society.

shame culture: a culture that uses external forms of social control, i.e., shames individuals into appropriate behaviours.

slang: a kind of sociolect that uses nonstandard meanings of words as well as creates words.

sojourner: an individual who spends a period of time in a cultural environment not his or her own.

sovereignty: military, political, and economic independence of a nation state.

spiritual tradition: a belief system, like a religion, based on questions about the meaning of life and its purpose. It may or may not, however, include the concept of a God or gods who must be worshipped and obeyed. Spiritual traditions, like religions, include a system of ethics to guide moral behaviour.

standard: a linguistic term largely reserved for international or colonial languages such as Standard English, Standard French, Standard Italian, and so on. A language is considered standard if it has been codified and has developed grammar books, spelling rules, dictionaries, and possibly a literature, and can be clearly distinguished from other languages.

stereotyping: a fixed and overgeneralized notion of a person or group of people held by an individual or group of other people that denies the uniqueness of individuals.

sub-culture: minority culture in a society. Canada's ethnic and religious groups are sub-cultures.

syllabary: a set of written signs or characters that represent syllables; e.g., Hiragana and Katakana.

symbol: a representation of something, often of a mystery beyond human comprehension, or of a wish or desire or of a belief. Language is also composed of symbols that represent sounds and words.

syncretism: the blending of two religions to create a new one.

syntax: the word order of a language.

taboo: a behaviour or word prohibited by a culture.

Taoism: a Chinese philosophical tradition stressing harmony with natural forces and belief in a universe in constant motion through the interplay of the principle of opposites, or yin and yang.

TCK (Third Culture Kid): a child who spends his/her developmental years in a culture not the parents'.

Third World: generally refers to poor or less economically developed, less modernized, and less industrialized nations of the world (originally referred to nation states aligned with neither the First [capitalist] World, nor the Second [communist] World).

transition shock: the trauma following experiences such as those related to age, as a person passes from one stage of life to another, or to disruptions like divorce or the death of a loved one.

U-curve hypothesis: the acculturation model developed by Sverre Lysgaard consisting of four stages: initial euphoria, culture shock, acculturation, and stable state of mind.

universal symbol: a symbol that transcends culture and is common to many, if not all, such as the Tree of Life, the moon, and the sun. According to Jung, they are part of the collective unconscious of humankind.

values: beliefs about what is important, what is good, what is fair, and what is right.

verbal presentation: culture-bound norms relating to how people present themselves when speaking, whether, for example, to display an air of assertiveness through language and paralanguage, or an air of gentleness and tolerance.

visible minority: non-white Canadian.

worldview: a personal philosophy of life and the universe that determines how people define reality and how they act, often shared with other members of the cultural group(s) with which they identify.

wosta: the Arab word for influence, connections, or intermediary.

yin/yang: Taoist words for the principle of the unity of opposites to form a whole. Yin is the moon, or passive, cold, feminine force; yang is the sun, or masculine, active, warm force.

Index